WITHDRAWN

PRISONS AND THE PROBLEM OF ORDER

CLARENDON STUDIES IN CRIMINOLOGY

Published under the auspices of the Institute of Criminology, University of Cambridge, the Mannheim Centre, London School of Economics, and the Centre for Criminological Research, University of Oxford.

GENERAL EDITOR: ROGER HOOD (University of Oxford)

EDITORS: ANTHONY BOTTOMS and TREVOR BENNETT
(University of Cambridge)

DAVID DOWNES and PAUL ROCK

(London School of Economics)

ANDREW SANDERS AND LUCIA ZEDNER
(University of Oxford)

Prisons and the Problem of Order

Richard Sparks, Anthony Bottoms, and Will Hay

CLARENDON PRESS · OXFORD
1996

Oxford University Press, Walton Street, Oxford OX2 6DP

Oxford New York Toronto
Delhi Bombay Calcutta Madras Karachi
Kuala Lumpur Singapore Hong Kong Tokyo
Nairobi Dar es Salaam Cape Town
Melbourne Auckland Madrid
and associated companies in
Berlin Ibadan

Oxford is a trade mark of Oxford University Press

Published in the United States
by Oxford University Press Inc., New York

British Library Cataloguing in Publication Data
Data available

Library of Congress Cataloging in Publication Data
Sparks, Richard F.
Prisons and the problem of order / Richard Sparks,
Anthony Bottoms, Will Hay.
p. cm.—(Clarendon studies in criminology)
1. HM Prison Long Lartin. 2. HM Prison Albany. 3. Prison
administration—Great Britain—Case studies. 4. Prisons—Great
Britain—Case studies. 5. Prisoners—Great Britain—Case studies.
I. Bottoms, A. E. II. Hay, Will. III. Title. IV. Series.
HV9646.S63 1996 365'941—dc20 96-1645
ISBN 0-19-825818-6

1 3 5 7 9 10 8 6 4 2

Set by Hope Services (Abingdon) Ltd.
Printed in Great Britain
on acid-free paper by
Biddles Ltd., Guildford and King's Lynn

General Editor's Introduction

Clarendon Studies in Criminology, the successor to *Cambridge Studies in Criminology*, which was founded by Leon Radzinowicz and J.W.C. Turner more than fifty years ago, aims to provide a forum for outstanding work in criminology, criminal justice, penology and the wider field of deviant behaviour. It is edited under the auspices of three criminological centres: the Cambridge Institute of Criminology, the Mannheim Centre for Criminology and Criminal Justice at the London School of Economics, and the Oxford Centre for Criminological Research.

Richard Sparks, Tony Bottoms and Will Hay's *Prisons and the Problem of Order* will undoubtedly be widely read for the significant contribution it makes to the understanding of how order is created, maintained, and sometimes fractured in maximum security prisons. It adds an important dimension to the contribution that the *Clarendon Series* has already made to the study of prison issues: through Jon Vagg's comparative analysis of accountability in European prison systems; Roy King and Kathleen McDermott's anatomy of prison conditions; Elaine Genders and Elaine Player's evaluation of Grendon's therapeutic regime; and Paul Rock's account of the attempt to transform the women's prison at Holloway.

The analysis rests upon a comparative study of two dispersal prisons, Albany and Long Lartin, carried out by the Cambridge Institute towards the end of the 1980's. Although these prisons have changed in several ways since then (Albany having left the dispersal system altogether), as have many aspects of prison policy and practice, the authors draw upon the wealth of data they collected, from interviews with both staff and inmates and from thousands of hours of patient observation, to explore and illustrate some of the abiding problems of creating an ordered environment amongst men in long-term captivity. Their comparison of prisons with different reputations, disciplinary profiles, histories of conflict, and styles of approach to handling disorder, provides the key to an understanding of prisons as complex institutions in which different ways of creating order emerge in response to different environments. At the heart of the empirical study is an analysis of the processes which lead to the breakdown of order and how this is reacted to by the authorities through transfers, segregation, and punishments. Special attention is paid to a Vulnerable Prisoners Unit and the vulnerability of prisoners within it.

The authors have reflected on the structures and processes they observed. In doing so they provide the most wide-ranging and up-to-date review available of the literature bearing upon the workings of the prison community. They also draw on wider sociological and political discourses concerned with the exercise of power and the legitimacy accorded to institutions and social processes. Their analysis not only clarifies some difficult theoretical issues relating to the nature of prison life, but contributes to the debate about how day-to-day order might best be secured in prisons: which, of course, is as much in the interest of long-term prisoners as it is of prison governors and their staff. In particular they highlight the tensions between 'situational' methods of control which rely on bolts, bars, security equipment and the control of individuals, and 'social' methods which seek to gain compliance from inmates based on an acceptance that authority is being employed in ways that are just and legitimate. The authors' discussion of the approach taken in recent reports on prison security, which they compare unfavourably to the broader social prescription laid down in the Woolf Report, shows how pertinent their research findings remain to current debates.

The editors welcome *Prisons and the Problem of Order* to the Series and are confident that it will join the "standard works" on prisons.

Roger Hood
Oxford, February 1996

Preface

FOR reasons that are variously too commonplace, too tedious or too embarrassing to discuss, this book has been a long time in preparation. As we explain in chapter 1, we do not believe that this has fundamentally reduced the relevance of our study either to policy debates or in terms of its contribution to theoretical understanding. In the end this will be for readers to judge.

Things change, however, and people move on. It is probably no bad thing for all concerned that when we refer in the text to staff members or prisoners at Albany or Long Lartin those individuals for the most part no longer occupy those positions. We do nevertheless want to thank them all (and their colleagues at Wakefield where we learned our craft), whether or not they clearly remember having been involved. We hope that they can at least recognize some of their concerns in what we have written. We know that for us the time we spent amongst them was an especially stimulating and personally challenging one. We cannot single out individuals, except to say that the Governors concerned—not least in allowing us to wander in such an unrestrained way around their prisons, but in many other ways too—were extraordinarily supportive. We would also like to thank the people within the Home Office who facilitated and encouraged the research, in particular John Ditchfield, Roy Walmsley, and Mark Williams.

For various forms of practical help we are especially indebted to Damaris Inie, Pam Paige, and Anne Musgrave. Amongst our academic colleagues we must particularly thank Alison Liebling, for many discussions and for commenting insightfully on drafts at short notice, and Jim Jacobs, who has greatly influenced our thinking.

The work recorded in this book has from start to finish been a fully collaborative undertaking. Almost all the data were collected and most of the writing was accomplished by two or all of us *together*. Richard Sparks has been voted first author because he has had the most continuous involvement, and has perhaps undertaken the lion's share of the work of actually preparing the text for publication. In every other respect we have made equal but distinct contributions (and the order of names of the second and third authors is simply alphabetical). Tony Bottoms devised the proposal, supervised the research, and has been centrally involved in the conceptual development of the project from first to last. Will Hay and Richard Sparks undertook the fieldwork and wrote the original report—out of which this book has grown—in every sense jointly, and Will took the lead role in updating several chapters. We have gained much from working together. One hears so many horror stories of collaborations gone awry. We at least end as firm friends.

Finally, we owe so much to and have made so many impositions upon those with whom we share households. Thank you, Elaine, Janet, Marion, Rosa, Sam, and Tom.

Richard Sparks
Tony Bottoms
Will Hay

September 1995

Contents

List of Figures

List of Tables

1
Introduction: the Research in Context

ONE of the central tasks of any prison administration is to maintain order within prisons. But achieving this goal is by no means unproblematic, and both the *means* used and the *conception of order* sought or imposed can vary significantly from one prison system to another, and even in different prisons within the same system.

One way of attempting order maintenance, extensively used in Britain, the United States, and other countries in the nineteenth century, is simply to try to keep prisoners completely separate from one another, so that they cannot foment disturbances (or at any rate, they can do so only with very great difficulty). But, as Gresham Sykes (1958) pointed out in his classic book on prison society (discussed fully in chapter 2, below) the nineteenth century experience of administering this kind of solitary confinement seemed to confirm empirically the truth of Kingsley Davis's (1949: 152) comment that 'the structure of the human personality is so much a product of social interaction that when this interaction ceases it tends to decay'. As a nineteenth century prison governor in New Jersey rather colourfully put it:

The choice between the congregate and solitary type of confinement . . . was fundamentally the problem as to whether vicious association is more to be deplored than mental and physical deterioration of the prisoners (quoted in Sykes, 1958: 7).

In the twentieth century, western societies have opted to allow prisoners at least a degree of shared association—partly for humanitarian and/or 'rights' reasons, and partly because of doubts about the efficacy of a solitary regime in meeting the prisons' stated aims, such as reducing recidivism. However, as soon as the authorities allow prisoners to congregate with one another, they will also tend to see the potential issue of what the New Jersey governor called 'vicious association' as being called into play. At their least orderly, prisons can produce major disturbances attracting national media attention over a prolonged period, as for example in Attica (1971) and Santa Fe (1980) in the United States; Hull (1976) and Manchester (1990) in England; or, bloodiest of all, at Sabaneta in Venezuela in 1994.

Major riots or disturbances in prison are fairly infrequent, but as every prison governor and prison officer knows, maintaining 'good order' on a day-to-day basis is a complex and multifaceted business; and whatever institutional order exists is the outcome of a continual process of 'working at' it. In that sense, it is certainly true to say that the maintenance of order is a *perennial problem* for prison administrators and staff—just as it is true that living under that order is the perennial problem of prisoners. On the other hand, there are times when the problem of order in prison acquires a very particular significance, and attracts special (and sometimes high-profile) policy responses: at such times, the problem ceases to be simply a mundane, perennial one for prison administrators and becomes a *special problem, often with significant political resonances*. At such times, it is by no means uncommon for politicians or officials to turn to prison researchers, presumably in the hope that some deeper understanding of the underlying issues can be generated.

This book is about the problem of order in prisons. It is not a book about prison riots, because we observed no riot, nor even a major disturbance (on riots see for example Adams, 1992). In that sense, this volume is centrally about what we have just described as the *perennial problem* of securing and maintaining order in prisons, rather than the *special problem* of the occasional complete or near-complete breakdown of order. On the other hand, the research on which this book is based was in fact commissioned by Home Office officials, in the context of a particular set of official anxieties (whose background we outline below) about the maintenance of order in high-security prisons in England and Wales.[1] For that rea-

---

[1] Within the United Kingdom, England and Wales constitute a distinct legal jurisdiction with a unified prison system. Scotland and Northern Ireland are each legally and (in their different ways) rather historically and culturally separate. This book reports research conducted within England and Wales. It so happens that all the maximum security 'dispersal' prisons in the prison system of England and Wales are on English soil; for this reason, and for brevity, we have adopted the convention of often referring to them as 'English' prisons.

son, in writing about *maintaining day-to-day order* in prisons, our thoughts have rarely been totally distant from *the special problem of high-profile disorder.*

We carried out our empirical fieldwork in two English maximum security prisons in 1988–9 (with an earlier extensive pilot period in a third such prison in 1987–8). We submitted a research report on our project to the Home Office (our research sponsors) in 1990,[2] but the present volume is being finalized some five years later. There are a number of prosaic but compelling reasons for this time gap (to do largely with our personal lives, though there have also been some administrative delays not of our making). More respectably, the intervening period has allowed us also to reflect theoretically on the problem of order in prisons, in the light of our empirical research experience, in a manner not unlike that recommended by the advocates of 'grounded theory' (Glaser and Strauss, 1967; see also Layder, 1993). We believe that the story we now have to tell has been substantially enriched by these theoretical reflections, which were present only in a very attenuated form in our 1990 research report.

The world, however, never stands still. The five years 1990–5 have scarcely been uneventful ones in English prison history with, among other things: (1) the Manchester riot of 1990, followed by the massive 1991 Woolf Report (Woolf, 1991); (2) legislation to allow the 'contracting out' of the running of prisons to private companies,[3] followed by the first group of such 'privatizations'; and (3), in 1995, the widespread introduction of so-called 'incentives-based regimes' in English prisons.[4] It might reasonably be asked whether, in such a changed context, research based on fieldwork conducted in the late 1980s has any real relevance.

[2] That report is: W. T. Hay et al. (1990) *Control Problems and the Long-Term Prisoner.* It contains little that is not present here in updated form, but, should any reader wish to consult it, copies are lodged (1) in the library of the Institute of Criminology, University of Cambridge and (2) in the Public Records Office, as part of the evidence of the present authors to the Woolf Inquiry.

[3] The relevant provisions are in Criminal Justice Act 1991, ss. 84–92. For detail on the background to these developments, see Windlesham (1993).

[4] We have highlighted the introduction of incentives-based regimes as of special importance in mid-1990s English prison policy, but we should emphasize also (see further below) that this development is closely linked, in official thinking, to other changes such as tighter security and more restrictive temporary release policies. The point remains, however, that the burden of our argument is not rendered obsolete by such policy changes; indeed, policy will most likely change again during the life-time of the book.

We are certain that it has, and for two reasons. The first reason is that, as explained above, the main focus of our study is on *the day-to-day maintenance of order in prisons*, and that remains as much an issue (as well as a puzzle) in 1995 as it was in 1988–9, despite the changed policy context. Secondly, however, in our view (as we shall explain more fully below), the underlying theoretical assumptions of different aspects of recent policy change have not always been identical: in particular, there is a distinct tension between the concept of *legitimacy* as a basis for order, as implicitly espoused in the Woolf Report, and the pervasive underlying *instrumental assumptions* of incentives-based regimes. Aspects of this tension, we believe, are illuminated by our research data, even though the precise administrative context within which we collected this data has now changed.

In the remainder of this introduction, we aim to accomplish two objectives. The first is to set out clearly and concisely the particular policy context in which our research was commissioned, as this constitutes a vital background for understanding the data in some of the chapters that follow. Secondly, we shall briefly indicate the main policy developments in English prisons since 1990, and try to expand upon the continuing relevance of our research findings (and our subsequent theoretical reflections) in the context of the mid-1990s.

The Research Project in Context

In England and Wales, maximum security prisons are known as 'dispersal prisons'. This somewhat strange name owes its origins to a celebrated official report of 1968 (the 'Radzinowicz Report') and to the particular policy debates of that period.

In the 1960s, there were several spectacular escapes from English prisons of nationally notorious prisoners, including some members of the gang that had perpetrated the celebrated 'Great Train Robbery'. All this came to a head in 1966 with the ridiculously easy escape of George Blake, serving sentences totalling 42 years for espionage offences, from Wormwood Scrubs Prison. Blake's flight precipitated an immediate and swiftly executed inquiry into prison security, led by Lord Mountbatten of Burma, formerly Viceroy of India (Mountbatten, 1966). Mountbatten concluded that there was no truly secure prison in England, and recommended a series of measures to remedy the situation, including the following:

Recommendations

1. Major improvements in physical security in selected prisons (stronger perimeter security; the introduction for the first time of television surveillance of key areas of the prison; the introduction of dog patrols; etc.).
2. The introduction of a new classification system, to be applied to all prisoners on the basis of their apparent security risk. This system would range from Category A ('prisoners whose escape would be highly dangerous to the public or police or to the security of the State') to Category D ('those who can reasonably be trusted to serve their sentences in open conditions').
3. The building of a new 'fortress' prison, to house all Category A prisoners, and situated on the Isle of Wight.

The first and second of the above recommendations were quickly accepted by the then Government, and subsequently implemented. The recommendation for a new 'fortress' prison (which inevitably came to be dubbed as the proposed 'English Alcatraz') proved to be much more controversial; and in the end it was not put into effect. The decisive blow to the 'fortress' proposal was delivered by a subcommittee of the then Advisory Council on the Penal System, chaired by the then Director of Cambridge University's Institute of Criminology, Professor (later Sir) Leon Radzinowicz (Advisory Council on the Penal System, 1968). In its report on *The Regime for Long-Term Prisoners in Conditions of Maximum Security*, the subcommittee expressed alarm at the potential difficulties of maintaining order within a single fortress prison housing—by definition—all those prisoners considered the most dangerous to the public.[5] As an alternative, therefore, the subcommittee recommended that Category A prisoners should be 'dispersed' in a dual sense: first, these maximum security prisoners would themselves be placed in 'three or four' prisons with a very high degree of security; and secondly, that the Category A prisoners, as a smallish minority of those held in each 'dispersal' prison, would be able to be 'absorbed into the general population of those prisons', consisting, in the main, of 'Category B' prisoners.

For the Radzinowicz subcommittee, there was a very real point in thus 'absorbing' Category A prisoners among lower security

---

[5] See, e.g., the Advisory Council's view (1968, para. 35) that: 'There is a danger that the atmosphere might . . . become repressive with the staff attitudes becoming affected by their anxieties about the attitudes and activities of a concentrated group of evil men who felt themselves finally rejected by society and who felt they had nothing to gain by co-operation and nothing to lose by revolt.'

prisoners. Unafraid to make explicit its moral commitments, the subcommittee argued that:

> If our society is concerned, as it is, and as it must be, with the worth of all individual men and women, and if it believes that in the last resort what men [sic] have in common is more important than their differences, then it cannot treat as less than human those . . . it finds necessary to send to prison . . . [Hence] we have tried always to bear in mind the need to preserve a prisoner's self-respect, to enable him to make choices in his day to day existence, and to give him access to a variety of mental and sensory stimuli that will help to combat the deadening effect of a long period of institutional life and the sameness of the environment.
>
> (Advisory Council, 1968: paras. 203–4)

Thus, while the Radzinowicz subcommittee fully concurred with Lord Mountbatten about the need for what it called 'an increase in the co-efficient of security in our closed prisons', especially those for long-terms, the subcommittee also wanted to 'develop a liberal regime for the humane and constructive treatment of long-term prisoners' (ibid.: para. 202). These two aims were not incompatible, the subcommittee argued: if effective security were concentrated especially *at the prison's perimeter*, then within the secure perimeter a constructive regime could be developed. Hence, the Radzinowicz subcommittee's blueprint for the new dispersal system was often encapsulated in the catch-phrase 'a liberal regime within a secure perimeter'.

It is worth pausing here to note that, beyond the specifics of the Mountbatten–Radzinowicz debate about 'concentration' or 'dispersal', there was a deeper underlying point. Mountbatten's overriding concern was with *security*, i.e. the avoidance of escapes, though other aspects of prison life were also considered. The Radzinowicz subcommittee's principal task was to advise the then government about the *regime* for those in maximum security prisons; hence this body was intrinsically more preoccupied than Mountbatten with the details of *day-to-day order* within prisons, including, as the subcommittee saw it, the need to 'preserve a prisoner's self-respect' in the daily routines. The Radzinowicz subcommittee's solution to the potential tension that it perceived between the needs of *security* and *good order* was to seek to optimize both by achieving very high security at the perimeter of the prison. In the longer term, however (as we show in the second half of this chapter), this security/order balance has proved by no means easy to deliver, and in the 1990s there has again been a return to a Mountbatten-like preoccupation with security—perhaps at the expense of other concerns.

After Radzinowicz, some external commentators continued to argue that 'concentration' would have been a better policy than 'dispersal' (see in particular King and Morgan, 1980: chapter 3). However, the official Prison Department view, from the late 1960s to the mid-1980s, was firmly in favour of the dispersal solution. A number of prisons were accordingly 'upgraded' in security terms, to meet with Lord Mountbatten's physical specifications for high-security prisons: and these 'upgraded' dispersal prisons included the two prisons which are the principal empirical focus of this book, namely Albany Prison, on the Isle of Wight, and Long Lartin Prison, in Worcestershire. Both of these were new prisons, first opened in the late 1960s or early 1970s; both were originally intended, at the planning stage, as Category C prisons, but both were rapidly converted into 'dispersals'.[6]

But the new 'dispersal system' certainly had its problems, amongst which were a number of major disturbances. By 1983, ten such serious incidents were publicly known to have taken place, two each in five of the then eight dispersal prisons.[7] In September 1983, therefore, the then Home Secretary asked for an 'acceleration' to the work already going on within the Prison Department on the issue of control in prisons, with special reference to 'the dispersal system's susceptibility to major breakdowns in control' (Home Office, 1984: 40). So was born the so-called Control Review Committee (CRC) whose 1984 report was to dominate the agenda on control problems in English prisons for the remainder of the decade. Indirectly, too, the CRC report was to lead to the commissioning of the research reported in this book.

In its own summary, the CRC emphasized three main features of it proposals (1984: chapter 7). They can be paraphrased as follows:

First, the committee reopened the concentration–dispersal debate. Agreeing with an earlier official committee (Home Office, 1979) that 'the argument for dispersal policy rests on the disadvantages

---

[6] For aspects of the early histories see King and Elliott (1977) (for Albany) and Dunbar (1974) (for Long Lartin).

[7] For a list, and brief descriptions of each incident, see Home Office, 1984, Annex D. Note also that the size of the dispersal system had, by the early 1980s, increased to eight, as against the 'three or four' envisaged by Radzinowicz.

hitherto seen in concentration rather than on any positive advantages in dispersal', the CRC argued that the 'technical advance'
made by so-called 'new-generation' architecture[8] seemed likely to
tip the balance of advantage towards concentration. If that were so
(and it would inevitably be a long-term strategy), 'it would then be
possible to plan for the end of the dispersal system in its present
style, which applies such a very high and expensive level of security
to so many prisoners and so many prisons' (Home Office, 1984:
40). Only 300–400 'very high security' places seemed necessary in
England, and, if new-generation architecture proved to have the
advantages ascribed to it, 'this number could be held in two small
prisons of the new kind' (ibid.: 8).

Secondly, and pending the resolution of these major questions,
the CRC sought to 'improve the basic structure' of the dispersal
system; this meant 'looking at the system as a whole' and trying to
ensure that it 'should run in accordance with an intelligible scheme'
(ibid.: 40–1). Particular issues that were thought to require development included sentence planning; a review of categorization procedures; and the development of a context where the prison system
would 'send the right signals' to prisoners (and not, to take an
example quoted by CRC, 'reward' bad behaviour in an unpopular
Isle of Wight dispersal prison by sending the prisoner to a more
accessible—and hence more favoured—mainland prison). CRC
sought to emphasize its message concerning the need to improve
the structures of the dispersal system by a somewhat damning aside
on that system:

There will inevitably be control problems if long-term prisoners are held in
a system that gives inconsistent messages about the course of their sentences or the consequences of their actions, and if prison managers' only

[8] In essence, 'new-generation architecture' consists of a set of smallish prison
units that *both* allow a high level of supervision *and* can be operated quite separately, whilst being sufficiently linked to permit easy access for staff from one to
another. See more generally Bottoms and Light (1987: introduction and ch. 5).

[9] The segregation unit (generally known in England as 'the block' or 'chokey'—in
Scotland as 'the digger') is a separate group of cells in which prisoners undergoing
punishment *or* those held apart from others in the interests of 'good order and discipline' *or* those kept separate 'for their own protection' may be held. Segregation
units in dispersal prisons are inevitably controversial (and sometimes physically conflictual) places, especially in view of these multiple uses. The idea that segregation
should have 'preventive' as well as punitive uses is deeply engrained in the history of
English prisons, and certainly attends the very birth of the dispersal system
(Advisory Council, 1968: para. 166). We return to some of these issues in ch. 8.

recourse in the face of disruption is to switch prisoners between normal location and the segregation unit,[9] and between one prison and another.[10]

(Home Office, 1984: 40)

Thirdly, and to complement these improved structures, CRC recommended a new system of small special units for long-termers 'designed to cater for those prisoners whose behaviour does not respond to the inbuilt incentives of a better structured system' (ibid.: 41).

In addition to these three main aspects of CRC's proposals, highlighted in its own summary, two other points from the report are worth emphasizing here:

Fourthly, while the CRC report paid little systematic attention to the daily regimes and routines of the dispersal prisons,[11] the committee was very clearly aware that, in its own words 'our package of specific proposals is only part of the story' (ibid: 6). In what has become a much-quoted paragraph, CRC emphasized what it saw as the crucial importance, for order maintenance, of day-to-day relationships in the wings, landings, workshops, and exercise yards of the dispersal prisons:

At the end of the day, nothing else that we can say will be as important as the general proposition that relations between staff and prisoners are at the heart of the whole prison system and that control and security flow from getting that relationship right. Prisons cannot be run by coercion; they depend on staff having a firm, confident and humane approach that enables them to maintain close contact with inmates without abrasive confrontation. This is the foundation on which we want to build.

(Home Office, 1984: 6)

Fifthly, CRC advocated the development of a research programme on prison control issues, since 'very little work seems to have been done on [such] issues in the UK, in contrast to the effort that has,

[10] Various kinds of transfer exist, including the 'simple' reallocation of a prisoner to another similar prison and, more controversially, the powers held by the Governor of a dispersal prison to impose a temporary transfer to a local prison at short notice and at his or her own discretion, under the terms of the relevant Circular Instruction (the somewhat notorious CI 10/74 at the time of our research, latterly CI 28/93). The events surrounding such transfers are amongst the most contentious of all aspects of long-term imprisonment. These too will be discussed in more detail in chapter 8.

[11] Though there is some discussion of regimes and programmes: Home Office, 1984: 27ff.

for example, been put into reconviction studies'. In order to 'assist the necessary change of emphasis' in this regard, the members of CRC further said that they would 'very much like to see eminent academics involved in both the compilation and the implementation of an integrated research programme' (ibid.: 36).

This is not the place for a full discussion of the CRC report (see generally Bottoms and Light, 1987), nor is it appropriate to discuss in detail here to what extent the committee's recommendations were implemented. It is sufficient, for present purposes, to note the following:

1. Little enthusiasm was evident in the higher echelons of the Prison Service for moves towards a 'concentration' policy based on 'new-generation architecture'; hence, the dispersal system has survived, albeit in a slightly different configuration following the Gartree escape of 1987.[12] (In the mid-1990s, however, 'concentration' policy has again become a live issue following some highly publicized escapes from dispersal prisons and a more general re-emphasis on security matters—see further below.)

2. Some moves to improve the 'structures of the system' were made, though not with complete success. Debates on these issues have now moved beyond the ambit of the dispersal system—for example, formal sentence planning has existed for all longer-term prisoners since the 1992 implementation of the Criminal Justice Act 1991, and issues such as 'earned privileges' and 'sending the right signals' are central to the incentives strategy applied to all prisons in 1995 (see further below).

3. A system of special units for prisoners presenting 'control problems' was developed, and three such units now exist. The numbers of prisoners recommended to the units by dispersal prison governors has, however, been lower than originally anticipated—an issue that we explore further in chapter 8, below.

[12] In 1987 two inmates were 'lifted' by helicopter from an exercise yard at Gartree (then a dispersal prison). This led to an upgrading of physical security at all dispersal prisons. The signs of this—especially the erection of wires over exercise yards and playing fields—were pervasive at the time of the fieldwork for the present study. It had already been decided, prior to this escape (and following CRC advice) to reduce the size of the dispersal system. After Gartree, the prisons that were to constitute the dispersal system were altered, and a distinction was introduced between those dispersals that could hold only 'standard risk' Category A prisoners and those able to house 'high risk' Category A prisoners (see *Prison Service News*, May 1989).

4. The Home Secretary established, in November 1984, a committee with a mixed membership of Prison Department officials, other relevant Home Office personnel, and three outside academics.[13] Known as the 'Research and Advisory Group on the Long-Term Prison System', this group was set up with twofold terms of reference: *first*, to act as 'a source of advice on the research needs arising from the report of the Control Review Committee'; and *secondly*, 'in particular to advise on the planning, co-ordination and evaluation of the proposed long-term prisoner units' (Home Office, 1987: 1).

We may concentrate here on the activities of the Research and Advisory Group ('RAG'). Much of the Group's energy was devoted to giving advice to Ministers on the development of an appropriate strategy for the special units, a matter that need not now detain us (see Home Office, 1987: sections 1, 2, and 4; Bottoms, 1991). The Group did also, however, spend time identifying research needs (ibid.: section 3 and Annex D), and recommending a research programme to the Home Office. This programme, as eventually implemented, had five separate elements,[14] as follows:

1. A literature survey on prison regimes in relation to control issues, carried out by John Ditchfield of the Home Office Research and Planning Unit (Ditchfield, 1990).

2. A research project on the development of 'an accurate and objective procedure' for the identification of control problem prisoners in dispersal prisons, carried out by members of the Prison Department's Adult Offender Psychology Unit (Home Office, 1987: Annex C; Williams and Longley, 1987).

3. A number of studies of the functioning of the new special units for prisoners presenting 'control problems', set up following CRC's general recommendations and RAG's more detailed advice (see Walmsley, 1991; Bottomley, et al., 1994).

---

[13] These included one of the present authors, Anthony Bottoms of the University of Cambridge, as well as Professor John Gunn, Institute of Psychiatry, University of London and Professor Roy King, University of Wales, Bangor.

[14] RAG's report (Home Office, 1987: Annex D) also lists among research projects recommended by the Group (1) a psychiatric profile of the prison population, carried out by the Institute of Psychiatry, University of London (see Gunn et al., 1991) and (2) a study of the therapeutic regime at Grendon Prison, carried out by Oxford University (see Genders and Player, 1995). In fact these studies had their origins elsewhere and were endorsed rather than initiated by RAG.

4. A short study of the special security units in the prison system,[15] carried out by Roy Walmsley of the Home Office Research
and Planning Unit (Walmsley, 1989). This study concentrated especially on those aspects of the special security units that seemed to
'provide useful pointers in connection with the establishment of the
special units for inmates presenting control problems' (Home
Office, 1987: 64).

5. A study entitled 'Control Problems and the Long-Term
Prisoner', carried out by the present authors at the Institute of
Criminology, University of Cambridge.

Our research, therefore, had its origins in a specific commission
from the Home Office, and was one element within a broader
planned programme of research. Given this context, it may be helpful to say a little more, *first* about the overall programme of
research, and how our particular study fitted into this programme;
and *secondly* about the terms of reference of our research project.

The research strategy recommended by RAG to the Home Office
essentially fell into three parts. The first was the commissioning of
Ditchfield's general literature review. The second was a thorough
programme of evaluation and monitoring of the new CRC special
units (within which may be included the study of the lessons to be
learned from the special security units). The third part of the
research strategy, unlike the first two parts, concentrated especially
on the *origins* of control problems, within the dispersal prisons
themselves. This part of the strategy itself had two dimensions. The
one, with an individualistic emphasis, set out to discover to what
extent one could reliably and validly identify particular prisoners
who appeared constantly to be 'misbehaving', 'causing trouble',
etc., and, if so, what were the characteristics of such prisoners.
Appropriately, this project was carried out by psychologists—
though it should be pointed out that, especially in later stages of
their work, these psychologists showed interest in some aspects of

[15] Special Security Units (SSUs) resemble 'special units' (as understood by CRC)
in that they separately house a small number of long-term prisoners (though SSUs
are more completely self-contained). Special Security Units have no particular penological aim beyond the 'normalized containment' (with extra surveillance and physical security) of prisoners reckoned to present exceptional risks should they escape.
They have tended to house, amongst others, a rather high proportion of 'terrorist'
prisoners. One of the reasons why the escape from Whitemoor Prison in September
1994 was treated as so publicly scandalous was that it took place from the supposed
impregnability of an SSU.

the environmental circumstances in which disorder occurred.[16] The other project that focused on the dispersal prisons themselves—our own research study—was, deliberately proposed by RAG to consider more fully the *social context* within which behaviour defined as 'control problem behaviour' arose, in its original milieu. The commissioning of this project, in addition to the more individualistic project carried out by the prison psychologists, reflected RAG's belief that:

Difficult prison behaviour is a function of many factors in addition to the prisoner's own character; these factors can include, on occasion, inappropriate prison regimes or mistaken handling of prisoners by staff. Except perhaps in the case of those prisoners whose behaviour is the product of mental disturbance or abnormality, all our experience suggests that most 'troublesome prisoners' present control problems only at particular times or in particular contexts.

(Home Office, 1987: 11)

In making this comment, RAG was of course drawing upon a growing number of studies, inside and outside the prison context, that have emphasized the extent to which behaviour can be influenced by its social and situational context.[17] Within prison studies, for example, this approach has led to a less reductively individualistic and more 'environmental' approach, to issues such as escapes and absconding (Clarke and Martin, 1971), suicide and attempted suicide (Liebling, 1992), and violence (Cooke, 1991; Bottoms, 1992).

The terms of reference of our research project, as formally set out by the Home Office, were:

To describe accurately and to explain the nature of control problems [in long-term prisons] and the conditions leading to their emergence, including an account of the circumstances under which prisoners are removed from normal location.

The first part of this brief was, clearly, a rather open-ended invitation to explore the emergence of defined 'control problems' within

[16] e.g., in later (unpublished) work, Williams and Longley analysed the locations of 'incidents'. They discovered that most of these (around 60%) took place in 'residential' areas of the dispersal prisons (landings and cell areas)—a finding which accords with our own information on the topic (see Table 7.2 in ch. 7).

[17] In the wider criminological field this has accompanied some retrenchment (including in 'official' or 'administrative' criminology) from old-style dispositional (offender-based) studies in favour of an emphasis on 'rational choice' theories and 'situational' crime prevention techniques (see e.g. Clarke and Mayhew, 1980).

the social context of dispersal prisons. To facilitate this exploration, it was decided to focus the study on two physically not dissimilar dispersal prisons, which nevertheless had rather contrasting
control histories, and different profiles on the available formal indicators of 'control problems'. The reasons for the choice of these
particular prisons, together with an account of some basic features
of the prisons, their populations, and their regimes, will be found
in chapter 3.

The second part of our research brief was somewhat different,
but complementary. RAG, and the Home Office more generally,
was interested in *the way in which control incidents were managed*
within dispersal prisons, once they had been formally identified.
There was a special interest in 'movements from normal location'—
that is, the deliberate and official movement of a prisoner away
from a normal cell block, either to the dispersal prison's segregation unit or by transfer to another (dispersal or other) prison, or by
transfer to a CRC special unit. A sociological study of official
responses to control incidents seemed to us—following Durkheim
and many others—to be a necessary counterpart to a sociological
study of the *emergence and definition*, within a specific social context, of defined 'social problems'; and we were, therefore, very willing to incorporate this additional dimension into the research.

Problems of penal order: the changing context

The field research that we undertook during 1988–9 at two dispersal prisons thus had its origins in the by then quite lengthy and
vexed history of the dispersal policy. We attempted both to discover new information on and insights into the problem of order as
this was practised and experienced in the daily life of two prisons,
and to place these findings in a properly sociological framework of
ideas. As we have already noted, since that time much has changed.
In order for our study to remain of fully contemporary interest we
think it is necessary not only to outline some of the major events
and policy developments of the intervening period, but also to consider the implications of our case-study in interpreting them. In this
sense at least, the lapse of time between the moment of our fieldwork and its eventual publication has proved positively beneficial,
as our sense of the theoretical scope of our study has developed
substantially.

In that we began from the issues that preoccupied long-term prison debates in the 1980s—concentration versus dispersal; the role of special units; 'getting the relationship right'; and so on— some of the terms in which we originally posed our questions have come to seem somewhat antique. They have been displaced, marginalized or overturned by transformations in policy and the tone of political debate. The two prisons themselves have changed (Albany has indeed ceased to be a dispersal), the dispersal system has changed its composition, and so on. But more profoundly, there have been changes of intellectual and political context, including those precipitated by some of the most drastic crises of penal order in modern British history. Our aim, therefore, in the remainder of this chapter, will be to outline how an empirical study of some years' vintage may help us to sharpen our conceptual awareness of the present.

1) Penal policy and the problem of order, 1990–5

a) The Woolf Report

Arguably the most drastic and publicly notorious event in the modern history of the prisons of England and Wales was the occupation and siege of Strangeways prison, Manchester, in April 1990 and the 'wave' of disturbances that rippled around the system over the following several weeks. The real significance of those events, however, came to be defined by the publication in the following February of Lord Justice Woolf's Report on them. With few exceptions (see Sim, 1994 for the most acute of these) commentators and pundits of various stripes queued up to heap praise on Woolf for his comprehensiveness, humanity, 'vision', and other virtues. We have argued elsewhere that the most significant features of Woolf's diagnosis of the causes and remedies of the disturbances lie in its conceptual framework rather than in any specific recommendation. Woolf identifies as the primary generative context of the troubles a widely shared sense of injustice amongst prisoners. He therefore organizes much of his discussion around the theme of 'justice in prisons', a term which for him encompasses the basic 'quality of life' for prisoners (adequate living quarters, food, and so on), various informal aspects of prison life (including the manner of prisoners' treatment at the hands of staff), and formal system features (especially the grievance and disciplinary systems).

Our inference from this (see Sparks and Bottoms, 1995)[18] is that, more clearly than anyone else, Woolf introduces into the lexicon of English official discourse a definite, though still implicit, recognition of the conditional nature of *legitimacy* in the maintenance of order in prisons (albeit that CRC and other statements of the 1980s might be taken as precursors).[19] Woolf accepts, that is to say, that the acquiescence or otherwise of prisoners to the kinds of authority claimed or exercised over them by officials is a variable matter. The ways in which such acquiescence or consent (or resistance) varies centre, in our analysis, on a complex matrix of interactions between prisoners' expectations of their captivity and, by necessary extension, whether they come to see the behaviour of their custodians as being justifiable, comprehensible, consistent, and fair or, alternatively, unwarranted, arbitrary, capricious, and overweening. We do not start from the assumption that Woolf *solves* the conundrum of legitimacy. We merely note that his account allows it to be raised as a pertinent issue. In chapter 2 and thereafter we develop our views on legitimacy in prisons in more detail. Suffice to say at the outset that in his influential report Woolf goes some distance towards acknowledging that prisons are complex institutions, subject to many of the same problems of morality and statecraft as arise in the governance of other settings of social life, albeit in special—and often specially acute—forms.[20] Much of the largely enthusiastic reception of Woolf's views amongst penal professions and reform groups viewed his intervention as decisively favouring a liberal conception of the prisoner as a bearer of rights (though not necessarily to the extent that those steeped in the human rights concerns of prison litigation might have wished to see). Additionally, the underlying view of the prisoner as a once-and-future-citizen chimed attractively for some with the 'just deserts' vocabulary that marked the formulation of the Criminal Justice Act 1991 (and especially the preceding White Paper (Home Office, 1990)).

A second strand in Woolf's liberalism was the introduction of a notion of 'contract' (or sometimes 'compact') to describe key aspects of the desired relationship between prisoner and system

[18] See also, for related responses, Cavadino and Dignan (1992); Player and Jenkins (1994); King and McDermott (1995).

[19] See the discussion of attempts to restate the aims or 'mission' of the penal system in Bottoms (1990).

[20] See in particular Woolf (chapters 10, 12, 14); see also Player and Jenkins (1994); King and McDermott (1995: 102–10).

(and indeed between different actors within the organization). Importantly, 'compacts' or 'contracts' for prisoners would, for Woolf, be *additional to* certain minimum entitlements which all prisoners would obtain under a formal (and legally enforceable) Code of Standards. Under such 'contracts' the prisoner would receive, in return for his or her promises as to behaviour and 'performance', certain undertakings regarding expected regime benefits, 'career' progress, and so on. In this way, Woolf argues, the 'contract' would 'underline both the prisoner's and the establishment's responsibilities in relation to the way an inmate serves his sentence' (para. 12.129). Woolf sees the contract as closely connected with sentence planning and proposes that, since the prisoner could 'receive progressively more under the contract as he progressed through his sentence' (para. 12.122), the contract provides a way of 'introducing greater incentives into the system' (*loc. cit.*). Woolf suggests that the benefits to prisoners of this device include that a failure on the system's side to deliver on a 'contract' might constitute a claim of maladministration or even grounds for judicial review.[21] Woolf believes that such innovations would clarify the prisoner's 'legitimate expectations' and that, overall, they would provide a means whereby 'standards throughout the service could be raised to acceptable levels by identifying the precise service to be delivered to prisoners' (para. 12.129).

Clearly Woolf regards the contract *both* as a device for raising 'standards' *and* as a compliance strategy for securing co-operative behaviour. Some commentators voiced objections to the language of contract from the outset. Sim, most notably, has argued consistently that the implications of mutuality and unforced agreement connoted by the term 'contract' assort ill with the asymmetries of power that inherently mark prison regimes, and that the advantages to the system of extracting promises of good behaviour from prisoners inevitably trump any putative benefits that prisoners may receive (Sim, 1992; 1994). Whether one fully accepts Sim's view or not (at least at the level of Woolf's *intentions*) it is plain that 'incentives'—interpreted primarily as levers for securing complaint

---

[21] Note that these would be *public law* remedies; Woolf did not envisage that the 'contracts' would be enforceable through the private law of contracts. Later official documents instruct Governors to prefer the term 'compact' to 'contract' to avoid language that might imply legal commitment; it is not clear whether this is thought to exclude public law as well as private law liability.

behaviour—have indeed latterly become a predominant feature of prison discourse (a point we develop further below).

A further strain in Woolf's account of the future of imprisonment is provided by an appeal to the notion of 'community'.[22] This term has played a recurrent part in the sociology of prison life at least since Clemmer's *The Prison Community* first appeared in 1940. In Woolf's usage (rather different from that of Clemmer or Sykes) the notion of 'community prisons' basically alludes to the desirability of a prisoner spending as much of his or her sentence as possible as close as possible to home (para. 11.56) and to the consequent enhancement of visits, family ties, home leave, and so on. To facilitate this, Woolf envisages the internal division of prisons into discrete 'multifunctional' units and/or the creation of 'clusters' of establishments within a region. He suggests that this will restore to the prisons some sense of service to or involvement with a locality, as well as avoiding some of the evident hardships and resentments that arise from prisoners being 'shipped' long distances from home. Whatever else might come of this proposal, it would have clear implications for the future (or otherwise) of the dispersal policy.

Finally, in this brief synopsis, Woolf pays considerable attention to the need for policy clarity and for the clear division of responsibilities—in particular those having to do with crisis or incident management—between Governors, Area Managers, central Prison Service managers, and Ministers. Although he insists that there need be 'no material change to the constitutional relationship between the Prison Service and Ministers' (para. 12.45), Woolf also calls for the Director-General to have 'the leadership and authority necessary to run the Service' (para. 12.43) and suggests that there has been a 'vacuum of visible leadership'. Woolf again uses the language of contracts to describe the desired relationship between the Director-General and Ministers. In his view, whilst elected politicians should continue to formulate policy, and be kept fully appraised of 'sensitive issues', they should nevertheless have a more 'hands-off' relationship with the Prison Service for everyday purposes. Meanwhile the Director-General should annually prepare an

---

[22] It has been widely noted elsewhere that 'community' is an especially charged rhetorical term, perhaps most particularly in relation to criminal justice. It is, as Stan Cohen (1985) and Raymond Williams (1976) have independently noted, a term that carries singularly few specific referents or commitments *and* almost no negative connotations. They are both thereby suggesting that it should be regarded with the gravest suspicion.

explicit statement of the 'tasks and objectives' of the Service, which would form the basis of a prospective 'compact' between himself and the Secretary of State. As we shall shortly see, it is the nature of this relationship (and of the model of management that should underlie it) that has come to dominate much policy-making activity and public discussion since Woolf.

b) Agency status and managerialism

In Woolf's vision, it would seem, everyone is contractually related to somebody else—the Home Secretary to the Director-General, the Director-General to Area Managers, Area Managers to Governors, Governors to prisoners. (The only relationship that never seriously arises is that of prisoners to one another, though this might plausibly be seen as of some significance to the problem of penal order.) Whilst he plainly favours clearer lines of responsibility and vertical accountability, Woolf insists that he does not want to get 'bogged down' in the question of whether the Prison Service should become an 'executive agency'.[23] Nevertheless, his position was widely interpreted as favouring such a move; and the development was unequivocally supported later in the same year by a second substantial report, this time specifically on such management issues, by Sir Raymond Lygo (Lygo, 1991).

The Prison Service became an 'executive agency' in 1993, with a brand-new Director-General, appointed from industry on a fixed-term contract including a substantial performance-related component. Amongst the more immediately visible signs of the new managerial style were a series of documents setting out the terms of the new dispensation.[24] One of the more important of these, the

---

[23] The concept of 'agency status' for governmental organizations has emerged rapidly in Britain since the mid-1980s, and is part of the managerialist approach outlined below. (An example is the handling of state benefits, now taken over by the Benefits Agency for the Department of Social Security.) Briefly, agency status creates quasi-autonomous bodies which, within a broad policy framework set by central government, are required to develop detailed 'operational' policies (and such other managerial devices as mission statements and business plans), which central government then sanctions and agrees to fund (or alternatively vetoes), all within strict cash limits. The agency is then held responsible for delivering the agreed services, within the cash limits set.

[24] See, e.g., the 1993 document We Are Now an Agency (which, perhaps wittily(?) recalls a remark of Mrs Thatcher's on becoming a grandparent), as well as successive versions of the Corporate Plan and Business Plan. On the new Prison Service management more generally see King and McDermott (1995: 47–57) and McLaughlin and Muncie (1994).

Corporate Plan, introduces a series of 'statements', adding to the existing 'statement of purpose' those on 'vision', 'goals', and 'values' (see Figure 1.1). Progress towards the realization of goals was to be monitored using measurable 'key performance indicators' (KPIs) covering escapes, assaults, crowding, sanitation, 'purposeful activity', time out of cell, visits, and costs.

These developments have many of the characteristics of what is now widely known—both in the criminal justice system and in other public sector activities—as 'managerialism' (see Pollitt, 1993; Clarke, et al., 1994; Bottoms, 1995). The role of central management focuses on setting clear objectives for the 'delivery' of a certain level of 'services', establishing monitoring systems for measuring these, and facilitating their implementation. There is an increased concern for uniformity of 'standards', but responsibility for implementing these (for example via control of budgets) may be devolved to lower levels of the organization (in the Prison Service this means to Governors in establishments). In principle these measures are supposed *both* to ensure the general raising of standards of 'economy, efficiency and effectiveness'[25] *and* to provide additional incentives, responsibilities, and opportunities for those lower down the organization. Managerialist initiatives are often represented by their advocates as providing the means towards the modernization of obsolete institutions and as promoting the more effective superintendence of complex processes.

The new managerialism evident in the Prison Service has not been without controversy. It is seen by its critics as eroding the traditional moral (including reformative) commitments of institutions in favour of an exclusive concern with *process* and measurement (and hence perhaps as a strategy for drawing the sting of their politically sensitive associations—a process of disenchantment of the kind long ago anticipated by Max Weber). One of the more visible aspects of the managerialization of prisons (not only in Britain but also in the United States and Australia) has been the privatization or 'contracting out' (that term again) of prison management.

---

[25] These terms, more commonly known simply as the 'three Es', became talismans of public sector management discourse during the 1980s. Such concerns have been a feature of Prison Service management for some time (see e.g. Train, 1985), but so far as we know they made their explicit entrée into the Prison Service in the document prepared by a firm of management consultants on *Prison Service Management Above Establishment Level*, which initiated the move from a regional structure (still in place at the time of our fieldwork) to one based around smaller 'areas'.

FIGURE 1.1.

PRISON SERVICE
STATEMENT OF PURPOSE, VISION, GOALS AND VALUES

Statement of Purpose

Her Majesty's Prison Service serves the public by keeping in custody those committed by the courts.

Our duty is to look after them with humanity and help them lead law-abiding and useful lives in custody and after release.

Vision

Our vision is to provide a service, through both directly managed and contracted prisons, of which the public can be proud and which will be regarded as a standard of excellence around the world.

Goals

Our principal goals are to:

• keep prisoners in custody

• maintain order, control, discipline and a safe environment

• provide decent conditions for prisoners and meet their needs, including health care

• provide positive regimes which help prisoners address their offending behaviour and allow them as full and responsible a life as possible.

• help prisoners prepare for their return to the community

• deliver prison services using the resources provided by Parliament with maximum efficiency.

In meeting these goals, we will co-operate closely with other criminal justice agencies and contribute to the effectiveness and development of the criminal justice system as a whole.

Values

In seeking to realise our vision and meet our goals, we will adhere to the following values:

• *Integrity* is fundamental to everything we do. We will meet our legal obligations, act with honesty and openness, and exercise effective stewardship of public money and assets.

• *Commitment* by our staff and to our staff. Staff are the most important asset of the Prison Service. They will be empowered to develop and use their skills and abilities to the full, while being held accountable for their performance. Teamwork will be encouraged. They will be treated with fairness, respect and openness. Their safety and well-being will be a prime concern.

• *Care* for prisoners. Prisoners will be treated with fairness, justice and respect as individuals. Their punishment is deprivation of liberty and they are entitled to certain recognised standards while in prison. They will be given reasons for decisions and, where possible, involved in discussions about matters affecting them. In working with prisoners, we will involve their families and others in the community as fully as possible.

• *Equality of opportunity*. We are committed to equality of opportunity and the elimination of discrimination on improper grounds.

• *Innovation and improvement* are essential to the success of the Service, requiring the acceptance of change and the delivery of continuing improvements in quality and efficiency.

Source: Prison Service Corporate Plan 1993–1996

Privatization 'goes with' managerialism in the sense that it construes the running of prisons as an identifiable set of tasks and competences whose success or otherwise can be measured, monitored, and costed. It distinguishes, that is to say, between the state's prerogative in the allocation of punishment and the contractor's obligations in the delivery of penal 'services' (on this see Sparks, 1994a; more generally see Ryan and Ward, 1989; Logan, 1990; Shichor, 1995). Privatization is an especially contentious aspect of criminal justice politics because it crystallizes a conflict of worldviews between a managerialist outlook concerned with utilities (the best prison is the one that most efficiently and correctly performs its allocated tasks) and one which emphasizes the moral and constitutional dilemmas of imprisonment (punishment is at best a necessary evil; it involves the exercise of power in imposing a painful deprivation and is hence a unique kind of *public* obligation). This is in no sense a book about prison privatization. It is, however, worth raising the question, to which we return very briefly in our conclusion, of whether privatization initiatives rest on an inadequate conception of the problem of penal order. One line of objection to privatization might well be that it misconstrues what, sociologically, prisons are and how they 'work'.

c) 'Prison works' and the new austerity

The years 1993–5 saw a number of troubling and controversial events in British prisons. There was a significant disturbance at Wymott Prison in Lancashire in September 1993 (on which the Chief Inspector of Prisons submitted a sharply critical report: HM Chief Inspector of Prisons, 1994). In 1994 there were further disturbances, perhaps most notably at Everthorpe Prison on Humberside, followed in January 1995 by the embarrassing cell suicide of alleged serial murderer Frederick West in Birmingham Prison. Most importantly of all, in September 1994 and January 1995 respectively, there were serious escapes from Whitemoor and Parkhurst dispersal prisons (the Whitemoor escape being from the prison's 'special security unit').

These events would have been newsworthy and controversial at any time. In the penal climate of 1993–5 they were especially so. Not only did they raise difficult questions about the division of responsibility between the Home Secretary and the Director General in the New Agency, but they also followed hard on the heels of a renewed and very deliberate politicization of penal affairs initiated by the Home Secretary himself. This prior stance—and the general tenor of retrenchment and increasing severity that went with it—seem to have conditioned the nature of the official response to the Whitemoor and Parkhurst incidents.

In his address to the 1993 Conservative Party Conference the Home Secretary, Michael Howard, took as a major theme the proposition that 'Prison Works', primarily on deterrent and incapacitative grounds. His remarks immediately followed the reversal (under the Criminal Justice Act 1993) of some of the sentencing provisions of the Criminal Justice Act 1991 that had generally been interpreted by penal reform groups as reductionist and diversionary (and by some sentencers as an excessive fetter on their discretion). Now the Home Secretary not only affirmed that he did not 'flinch' from the prospect that more people might go to prison, but announced the commissioning of six new private prisons. The Home Secretary further took the view that prisons should be 'decent but austere'—a phrase that also occurs in the Prison Service's *Corporate Plan*. These initiatives can be seen as signalling not merely a departure from an earlier commitment to limiting prison use (recalling that only a short time beforehand a rough consensus of informed opinion existed, of which both the drafters of the 1991 Act and Lord Woolf partook, that prisons could be 'an expensive way of making bad people worse': Home Office, 1990: 4) but also as portending a sharp retrenchment in terms of regimes and entitlements.

During 1992 (especially with the implementation of the 1991 Act on 1 October) the prison population in England and Wales had fallen appreciably. In the second half of 1993 it began to increase sharply, rising before that year's end by some sixteen per cent over its level twelve months earlier. These trends were sustained throughout 1994 (see *Home Office Statistical Bulletin 8/95*) and by early 1995 there were more than 51,000 prisoners in England and Wales (surpassing the previous record set in 1987) (*Independent*, 17 March 1995).

Another aspect of the renewed impetus towards penal severity was an increasing prioritization of the demands and sensibilities of 'public opinion' about the propriety of particular kinds of regimes and conditions in prisons. Buttressed by recurrent scandalized tabloid headlines, the Home Secretary capitalized on, and thereby sought to intensify, the punitive tone of public debate. In his 1993 Party Conference speech the Home Secretary said of the new private prisons 'Butlins won't be bidding for the contract'; and he was later reported as holding the view that 'prisoners enjoy a standard of comfort that taxpayers would find hard to understand' (*Observer*, 22 August 1994). Here the sensibilities of the taxpayers are assumed (perhaps plausibly) to demand more stringent conditions of confinement. Moreover, the Home Secretary repeatedly emphasized his view—thoroughly consistent with his views on deterrence—that 'privileges' in prisons must be *earned* by good behaviour rather than granted automatically.[26]

Whatever may have been the political strategy behind the 'Prison Works' initiative, its impact on the practice of imprisonment was substantial. Moreover, whilst the recurrence of overcrowding had the greatest effect on local and remand prisons, the main weight of the populist animus against 'cushy' prison regimes fell, partly in consequence of the publicity surrounding the Whitemoor and Parkhurst escapes, on the dispersal system and other relatively privileged long-term prisons such as Grendon ('JAIL PERVERTS LIVE IN LUXURY', *Sun*, 9 May 1994). These longer-term prisons were also particularly affected by a retrenchment of home leave policy, again following increased publicity and decreasing tolerance of any failure in temporary release arrangements. In such a climate, security issues naturally predominated, with (so far) no equivalent of the Radzinowicz Report to emphasize the problems of order (or the strain on family ties or employment prospects) that might arise from a dominant preoccupation with preventing escapes and home leave failures.

The emergent climate of influential opinion received further impetus in December 1994 with the presentation of Sir John Woodcock's report on the Whitemoor escapes (Woodcock, 1994). Woodcock saw a connection between failures of perimeter security and lapses of internal control (via the so-called 'conditioning' of staff by sophisticated prisoners). His diagnosis therefore demanded the reassertion of more stringently supervised and regulated regimes, and he insisted that power be wrested back for the staff (or as he put it that there must be 'a firm but fair regime where the

---

[26] In this as in other respects the Home Secretary's view stands in sharp opposition to Woolf's, given that the latter wanted to do away with the language of privileges altogether in favour of 'standards', entitlements, and expectations.

"dog" wags the "tail" ' (ibid.: 82)). Woodcock's favoured measures for the reimposition of control (ibid.: 87–95) included the more effective use of CCTV, more searching of prisoners (*and* of staff), better supervised visits, and the restriction of prisoners' possessions through the use of 'volumetric control' (meaning that they could have only such items as would fit into a designated space of a standard size).[27] The Home Secretary's prior views on privileges received Woodcock's imprimatur in that 'The underlying premise should be that all allowances or 'privileges' are to be earned by good behaviour and work performance, with sanctions for bad behaviour' (ibid.: 93).

In our view, the conjunction of a harder-edged political strategy on penal affairs in general, together with the character of reaction to the serious lapses of security at Whitemoor and Parkhurst in particular, facilitated the emergence of a revised version of the official discourse on penal order which, although formally compatible with some of Woolf's central concerns such as incentives and greater procedural explicitness, nevertheless signified a substantial shift of focus. Moreover, the re-emphasis on security issues, crucially affecting day-to-day prison life through its impact on matters such as searches and personal possessions, represented a final and decisive break with Radzinowicz's originating vision of the dispersal prison as having a 'liberal regime within a secure perimeter'.

d) 'Incentives', 'compacts', and compliance

Woolf's interpretation of the problem of order in prisons, whilst it also includes many managerial and operational issues, *centres* on the question of 'justice in prisons'. In somewhat similar vein, at around the same time, the Probation and Prison Services' document on a *National Framework for the Throughcare of Offenders* (1992) invokes a sense of involvement in 'good quality relationships' as being necessary to securing co-operation and motivated participation in programmes. In later documents the vocabulary is rather different. In the *Corporate Plan* of 1994, for example, traces of

---

[27] Woodcock's immediate recommendation was that the designated space should be 'the authorised cupboard, wardrobe and shelf space of a cell plus a maximum of two transit boxes'; though he thought that in time 'it may be possible to issue inmates with a large trunk' (p. 33). The impetus for volumetric control was provided by the fact that at Whitemoor the property of many prisoners was found to exceed allowances, and that both Semtex explosive and fuses and detonators were recovered from among prisoners' property.

some of these concerns seem to remain, but they are increasingly subordinated to other priorities. So, in the view of that document, the 'risk of a breakdown of order or loss of control is minimized' *inter alia* by 'providing active and purposeful regimes', 'fostering good staff–prisoner relationships', 'providing decent conditions', and, significantly, by 'operating systems which recognize and reward good behaviour' (p. 14). But the *prevention of disorder* is assigned to 'gathering, collating and assessing information', 'operating a discipline and adjudication system with effective sanctions', 'operating a system for dealing with disruptive prisoners', and 'providing a small number of special units with constructive regimes for violent and disruptive prisoners' (page 15).

The emphasis here falls on surveillance, intelligence, and the individualized control of problematic behaviour. Whereas in Woolf there is some sense that trouble in prisons can intelligibly result from shared grievances, here the problem of penal order has returned to its historically more common characterization—the failure adequately to control individual miscreants. An extension of these concerns comes in June 1995 with the circulation of an Instruction to Governors (IG 74/1995) on 'Incentives and Earned Privileges'. This document states that the systematic introduction of 'earnable and losable privileges' will encourage 'responsible behaviour', 'hard work', and 'progress through the system' and will serve to create 'a more disciplined, better controlled and safer environment' for prisoners and staff. The instruction requires establishments to introduce incentive systems with 'basic', 'standard', and 'enhanced' privilege levels, each reflecting the individual's 'pattern of behaviour' over a certain period of time. To qualify for privilege levels above the 'standard' (roughly equivalent to Woolf's 'threshold quality of life'), prisoners are required to demonstrate 'good and responsible' behaviour. The precise details of such incentives schemes are not our main concern here. What is at issue is the model of penal order which they presuppose (and by extension the kinds of motivation and response that they envisage in the prisoner) (see also Liebling and Bosworth, 1995). It is also noteworthy that, in line with the new concern with the punitive sensibilities attributed to public opinion, IG 74/1995 insists that all privileges must be 'acceptable to reasonable public opinion' and 'justifiable in the face of informed criticism' and '*Above all* . . . not bring the Prison Service into disrepute' (Annex A, para. 17, emphasis added).

2) The problem of order and the sociology of prisons

Different strategies for the maintenance of 'good order' adopted by administrators at particular times and places indicate different conceptions of prisons and prisoners; and these in turn connect with aspects of political discourse that have currency in the wider world (such as the aims of punishment, the language of rights, concepts of rationality or implicit psychologies of criminal behaviour, and so on). In our view, the incentives-based regimes envisaged in IG 74/1995 rather closely recall the assumptions of penological classicism, and in so doing show the imprint of neo-liberal political ideology.

Classicism is generally taken as having its origins in the rationalist philosophies of the eighteenth century. As a theory of punishment it takes shape (in somewhat distinct versions) in the writings of Cesare Beccaria (1764) and Jeremy Bentham (1789). What these authors, and their many successors, have in common is the premise that offenders, like other actors, rationally seek to maximize their own pleasure (or in later versions their 'utilities') and avoid pain. It follows that they are responsive to sanctions (hence deterrence is the focal concern of penological classicism) and incentives. These assumptions (admittedly in rather more sophisticated forms) have come to be regarded as axiomatic by many economists, though much less so by other social scientists.

As Beccaria would have demanded, the incentives system set out in IG 74/1995 takes care to insist that all procedures should 'conform to natural justice', not contravene legal rules, be openly and transparently operated, inform the prisoner of what is going on, be equitable on grounds of race, and so on. They must, in all these ways, be procedurally proper, and systematic in their operation. In this respect, like Beccaria's progressivism, they stand at some distance from the secrecies and discretions of the *ancien régime* and propose a distinctly more *modern* and more 'rational' position (and it would presumably be on such grounds that Prison Service managers might claim that they have not abandoned the Woolf agenda).

But just as classicism traditionally assumes far greater and more predictable effects of deterrent sentencing than empirical research has actually found, so it seems to us that the new 'classicism' of incentives-based prison regimes may be based on a number of questionable assumptions about prisons and prisoners. In particular, it assumes that the prisoner's compliance can be secured through an appeal to his or her individual rational self-interest. It proposes therefore, that, from the system's point of view, the best way of dealing with prisoners is on an individual footing. It takes the view that if the prisoner does not respond to being so incentivized then either he or she stands outside of rationality altogether (and is thus crazy) or else is accountable for their failures. The ball is thus very firmly placed in the prisoner's court. This view does not anticipate that prisoners will act in solidarity with one another, or for other than rational-utilitarian motives. It does not give much attention to the possibility that the incentives on offer may not be very meaningful to the prisoners (as would be Sykes's view, for example—see below, chapter 2) or, alternatively, that *any* formal regime feature may be less significant than other, less tangible, aspects of institutional climates and social relations. One question to be asked of incentives-based regimes, therefore, is how plausible is their implicit theory of order maintenance? Is it simply the case that whenever the ancient tension between 'security' and 'order' gets reiterated, security wins again? Or does the apparent new confidence that increased internal (i.e. not simply perimeter) surveillance, combined with individualized incentives, will allow the 'dog to wag the tail' drive out any acknowledgement that the 'problem of order' may be a distinct dimension of penal social relations?

One problem in this regard may be that the incentives-as-means-to-order view is neglectful (or at best has a very partial view) of the problem of legitimacy. For advocates of incentives-based regimes, legitimacy (to the extent that it is a relevant consideration at all) flows from consistency, procedural fairness, and, in a very current but overworked term, 'transparency'. But students of legitimacy, like David Beetham (1991), would argue that such rule-following is only one component of legitimate rule. The version of prison governance espoused in current rhetoric is perhaps, to borrow Tyler's (1990) vocabulary, excessively *instrumental*. In the time-honoured manner of official discourse it takes as already given what, sociologically, can never be assumed, namely the acceptance-as-legitimate of its own claim to justified authority.

Our suspicion that this and other currently influential stances on prison management frequently oversimplify what is at stake in the problem of order in prisons is in part what motivates us to reconsider in detail, as a prelude to the discussion of our empirical findings, some long-standing, but generally neglected, concerns of sociological writing on prison communities. As prisoners, prison officers, and governors know, prisons are in fact much more perplexing places, intellectually, practically, and morally, than is generally admitted. The remainder of the book is, accordingly, organized as follows:

In chapter two we examine some of the intellectual resources that are available for thinking through the problem of order in prisons. Some of these are rather specifically penological, because prisons are rather special places. But even those sociologists who take the *internal* ordering of the prison as their main focus—and here we isolate the contributions of Gresham Sykes (1958) and Thomas Mathiesen (1965) as having been of outstanding theoretical importance—draw upon assumptions about actors and institutions that have much wider reference. In general terms, our position throughout is that the problem of order in prisons is a special case of a generic issue, indeed perhaps *the* fundamental problem of social and political theory (Wrong, 1994). It follows, of course, that the most illuminating views on these wider questions may in origin have little to do with prisons. The challenge is to allow the sociology of prisons (with all the specificity and detail and peculiarity that those places have) and the larger concerns of social theory to inform one another creatively. We do not follow Foucault in seeing prisons as in some sense the emblematic institutions of modernity. We do, however, believe that one can learn something of importance about how other people and other institutions work by studying them, and vice versa. We have come to the view that the social theory of Anthony Giddens offers one avenue for thinking productively about these matters. We therefore take some care in chapter two to defend the proposition that the concerns of general social theory are very much germane to prison studies and to outline those aspects of Giddens's views that we have found helpful. What goes for the logic of enquiry goes also for the governance of institutions. By this we mean that we have also found it helpful to think about some aspects of penal order using concepts that derive from studies of order maintenance in quite other settings. Principal amongst these is the idea of *legitimacy*, and we draw on treatments of that term both in political theory (Beetham, 1991) and in empirical social psychology (Tyler, 1990) to demonstrate the point.

From here we move into our own case-study of two English dispersal prisons as they existed at the end of the 1980s. In chapter three we indicate some of the special features of each prison that made them uniquely interesting to compare. In comparing them we have before us, even within the same system at the same time, two 'models' (and there are many others)—two slightly different 'solutions' to the problem of penal order, two slightly different 'orders'. We think that such comparisons sharpen up our conceptual 'take' on prisons. They prompt us to ask what features of imprisonment are invariant and which, *per contra*, are changeable. In chapter three we also discuss some of the methodological decisions that we took and the definitions of terms that crop up throughout our study. Some of the more personal and biographical (but hence also *practical*) aspects of the research experience and how it was accomplished—and the ethical challenges thereby raised—are addressed in Appendix A.

Between chapters four and eight we report aspects of our case-study. We begin by discussing in chapters four and five respectively the views of staff and prisoners in each of the prisons from our interviews with them. In chapter six we consider the special perspectives of both staff and prisoners in the Vulnerable Prisoner Unit, as it then was, at Albany. In chapter seven we look in some detail at the narrative accounts of those involved in a certain number of 'control incidents' at each prison. Finally, in chapter eight, we consider relevant data about administrative 'movements from normal location' in the two prisons, together with the perspectives on such matters of some of those who were thus 'moved', and of those who had to decide to do the moving. The decision to segregate or compulsorily transfer a long-term maximum-security prisoner can be an especially fateful one for all concerned. With the exception of the death penalty, it stands at perhaps the furthest point of the repertoire of sanctions and compulsions available to a liberal democratic state outside time of war.

Our approach in this study has therefore been to begin by depicting something of the ordinary conditions of existence of each prison, through the institutional descriptions and staff and prisoner perspectives of chapters three, four, and five, as the context against which to understand the more exceptional moments detailed in chapters seven and eight. The latter incidents are of central importance, even though they directly affect only a relatively small number of prisoners. These moments of force tell us something about the limits of penal order. Understanding those limits is privotal both to the development of an adequate sociology of imprisonment in general and to developing an adequate accountability for its more draconian powers.

2

Social Order in Prisons: Theoretical Issues

The problem

What kind of social institution is a long-term prison? On what theoretical resources can we usefully draw if we wish to enquire into the enigmatic and perplexing nature of its interior life? Numerous sociological observers have been prompted to look into the forms of life conducted behind the walls. They have done so from a variety of intellectual and political standpoints and with uneven success. In this chapter we review some of the problems and possibilities posed by the tradition of sociological concern with the 'prison community' (Clemmer, 1940) and we attempt to distil from that body of work some strands that seem to us to be of especial value and interest for our purposes,[1] particularly in relation to 'the problem of order'.[2] In addition, however, we look somewhat beyond prison sociology as such. We also seek to situate the study

[1] We must make it clear that this chapter is not intended as any sort of comprehensive review of the social science literature on prisons. Hence, e.g., we say very little specifically about the voluminous literature on 'prisoner subcultures' (see Bowker, 1977; Thomas and Petersen, 1977), or about the important strands of work on 'coping' and 'adaptation' (on which see *inter alia* Toch, 1992; Zamble and Porporino, 1988). Neither, given our primary purposes, have we been able to devote much space to such important studies of individual prisons or prison systems as Glaser (1964) or King and Elliott (1977). The purpose of this chapter is the more limited one of selective review and theoretical development, to assist and illuminate the empirical analysis of later chapters.

[2] As indicated in ch. 1, that we are concerned with 'order' does not mean that we are primarily interested in the question of prison 'riots', though there is some tendency in existing scholarship to conflate these terms. This is understandable enough, but it can have limiting consequences—as if the question of penal 'order' were unproblematic *except when* it is subject to catastrophic breakdown. As insightful commentators show, 'riots' themselves may be most important for what they betray about the characteristics of prisons more generally: on this point see *inter alia* Adams (1992); Irwin (1980); Sim (1992, 1994); Thomas and Pooley (1980); Woolf (1991).

of prisons in relation to some larger concerns of recent social theory (in particular the work of Anthony Giddens) in the hope of extending and refreshing the tradition of prison studies and of contributing to the development of a contemporary activity of research and reflection about imprisonment. It may well be that the most illuminating perspectives on prisons actually originate elsewhere, in the study of other institutions, or in more general theoretical debates.

Much prison research begins (as we do) from a sense of the strangeness and particularity of prisons, perhaps especially long-term prisons.[3] They are, to begin with, inherently unknown and unfamiliar to many, and generally quite secretive, or at least sequestered. Prisons have some enigmatic and distinctive features, which can make them sources of various combinations of fascination and revulsion, puzzlement and horror. Often the prison researcher may feel like an explorer, reporting back to the outside world (often uncomprehending) about the doings of an alien and mysterious people (and some recent researchers have clearly identified themselves as anthropologists, for example Fleisher, 1989; cf. also the Morrises' comment that their research office—a converted cell in Pentonville Prison—was 'like the anthropologist's hut on the village street' (1963: 8)). But all this, while true enough in its way, does not mean that prisons are really wholly separate and apart, or incapable of being studied by analogy with other complex organizations and bureaucracies. Neither can we justify looking at imprisonment in ignorance of the impact upon it of ideological and economic transformations in the surrounding society.

Our interest in this chapter is directed towards some of the most general, enduring, and puzzling issues in prison studies. We are concerned with what is sometimes termed 'the problem of order', as it applies to prisons. Hence, we want to explore to what extent a stable and orderly form of life is achievable under conditions of

[3] This strangeness can be especially apparent in urban prisons, where in the space of 200 metres or so one can move from the everyday bustle of a busy shopping street to the enclosed world of a maximum security prison, with its elaborate security procedures and special languages. There—one is suddenly acutely conscious—one meets some prisoners who have not wandered casually down a shopping street for more than a decade. Wakefield prison, where the pilot work for our own research was done, is an example of such a prison, lying as it does close to the centre of a busy Yorkshire town and overlooked by the passengers standing on the platform of the nearby railway station.

confinement. What versions of social organization are possible? And what are their respective conditions of possibility? Are prisons inherently given to violent conflict, either between the keepers and the kept, or amongst the captives themselves? Or do they also incorporate countervailing impulses towards accommodation, co-operation, and sociability, so that the dialectic between the potentialities for order and disorder is more nuanced and intricate than at first appears? If some version of 'order' exists, what performances and strategies tend to support its reproduction? Alternatively, when that 'order' is interrupted or threatened, what mechanisms exist to rescue or repair it? What are the consequences for the captives of living under different possible kinds of 'order' in prisons, and what conditions are most likely to provoke resistance, refusal or rebellion?

We are acutely conscious that the concept of order as applied to penal institutions is fraught with difficulties, paradoxes, and contradictions'—even more than when applied to many other areas of social life. This is one reason why sociologists have repeatedly worried away at the issue of order in prisons, and have tried to formulate its distinctive features—or else have found themselves obliged to deny its possibility. It has long been recognized by informed observers (prisoners and prison staff as well as academics) that prisons are complicated social institutions, and that they inherently incorporate some basic antagonisms and conflicts. Hence many observers see problems of order in prisons as intrinsic. Roy King nicely puts this view:

there is no solution to the control problem in prisons, nor can there be. The control problem—of how to maintain 'good order and discipline'—is inherent and endemic. For as long as we have prisons—and an institution which has become so entrenched in our thinking shows no sign of becoming disestablished—then we will continue to hold prisoners against their will. At bottom that is what it is about.

(King, 1985: 187)

Such a conception leads some commentators to hold that, if some version of order does exist in prison, it must be produced mainly by coercion, fear, and visible or submerged forms of violence. For example, Scraton et al. (1991: 132) are scathing of 'the official quest for the prison Camelot of stability, tranquility and acquiescence'. On this view prisons (certainly as presently constituted) generate no genuine internal sense of order, merely an enforced compliance:

All forms of incarceration imply the use of force. Regardless of the out-ward appearance of compliance few people taken into custody would accept their loss of liberty so willingly if the full potential force of state coercion was not handcuffed to their wrists . . . The authority imposed by the prison is not a consensual authority. It is not derived in consultation and agreement, nor is it legitimated by any process of representation and accountability. The 'totality' of the institution, in terms of its political and professional autonomy, is underwritten by a degree of 'totality' in power relations which virtually strip the prisoner of civil rights . . . Life in most British prisons is an unrelenting imposition of authority.

(Scraton et al., 1991: 61–2)

We do not think that this is altogether an adequate way of stating the problem. We do not dissent from the plain truth that incarcer-ation implies force, at least in 'the last instance'. Prisons are domi-native institutions. In them people (predominantly men) are confined (sometimes for many years) generally against their will, in intimate daily contact with others whose company they have not chosen, under conditions they would not choose and can do little to change, attended by custodians who are formally empowered to regulate their daily lives at a minute level of detail. Under such cir-cumstances 'consensual authority' seems unlikely. On the other hand, we would also argue that an account that places its whole emphasis on the imposition of order by relentless force glosses over many important complexities of prison life and effaces some significant variations in the social organization of different prisons. One aspect of such difference (which we emphasize below) con-cerns the extent to which the staff of different prisons succeed or fail in legitimating their deployment of power and authority and the techniques and strategies which they deploy in seeking to secure such legitimacy (cf. Beetham, 1991; Sparks and Bottoms, 1995).

The obverse of the view that prisons are simply places in which inmates are cowed into submission sees them instead as sites of incessant violent turmoil populated by desperate individuals with 'nothing to lose'. This view poses 'the problem of order' in its orig-inal, stark form. It imagines that prisons are asocial and chaotic cauldrons, ungovernable except by force, in which Hobbes's (1651) vision of a 'war of each against all' has become real. Something close to this view seems at times to underpin the influential recent writings of DiIulio (1987), whose pessimism as to the possibility of power-sharing or democratization in prisons leads him to favour the adoption of a 'control model' of penal administration.

We think it has been convincingly argued that the conventional depiction of the Hobbesian problem of order has never provided an adequate basis for social analysis, nor played a central part in the development of sociological thought (Giddens, 1977: 225–6). Neither do we accept that we should begin from the assumption that prisoners are uniquely prone to descend into a 'state of nature'. Yet there are plenty of grounds in experience, whether in the explosive upheavals of Attica or Manchester, or in the more mundane conflicts and tensions explored in this study, for believing that problems of order and competitions for power are indeed chronic and endemic in the history of penal institutions, albeit in more complex and variable ways than our received ideas about prisons, prisoners, and their custodians often admit (see Adams, 1992).

The sociology of prison life must seek a more nuanced conception of problems of order in captivity than either of these stark alternatives. As Wrong notes, 'Like virtually all conceptualizations of social relations, order is a matter of degree' (1994: 9). One cannot but accept that prisons do generate important forms of conflict, at both collective and individual levels. Some of these are momentary and extremely violent, others are chronic and intractable. The history of prisons in Britain, the United States, and elsewhere also shows beyond doubt that such conflicts can sometimes reach catastrophic proportions (see New York State Special Commission on Attica, 1972; also Thomas and Pooley, 1980; Home Office, 1984, Annex D; Scraton et al., 1991). Yet we also know that other prisons have gone for years, even decades, without anything approaching such an event; and not necessarily (in apparent contradiction of Scraton et al.'s implication) just because they are more completely and efficiently coercive.[4] Indeed, just as prisons sometimes provoke

---

[4] Clearly there are some aspects of Scraton et al.'s important account of discipline and disorder in Scottish prisons with which we take issue, especially the more general claims they make which seem to us to pre-empt discussion of the problem of legitimacy—a point to which as will become apparent, we attach great significance. However, there are many substantive arguments and policy conclusions (especially their opposition to the individualization of 'trouble' in prison regimes) with which we are closely in agreement. Moreover, Scraton et al.'s allusions to the situation at the Barlinnie Special unit (1991: 16, 38) suggest a recognition of variation and alternative possibilities in the construction of penal order which is close to our own position. (On the Barlinnie Special Unit see Cooke, 1989; Bottomley et al., 1994.)

rebellions and riots, so do they also (and more often) generate their own peculiar yet 'ordinary' and 'mundane' form of life. To the extent that the social organization of the prison is *always* intellectually, morally, and practically problematic, the routinized reproduction of its everyday life (which constitutes the peculiar 'normality' of captive society) itself stands in need of explanation, at least as much as the incidence of any particular 'control problem' does. Indeed, the nature, level, and intensity of the 'control problems' that do emerge in different prisons at particular times can, in our view, usually only be properly understood in terms of pre-existing relationships, conflicts, and accommodations embedded in the routine practices of each institution. When we consider such matters with any seriousness or care, we may quickly find ourselves sharing Donald Cressey's sense of strangeness (1961: 2), and his view that the *explanandum* is how prisons 'go on' rather than why they 'explode':

One of the most amazing things about prisons is that they 'work' at all . . . Any on-going prison is made up of the coordinated actions of hundreds of people, some of whom hate and distrust each other, love each other, fight each other physically and psychologically, think of each other as stupid or mentally disturbed, 'manage' and 'control' each other, and vie with each other for favours, prestige and money. Often the personnel involved . . . are not sure whether they are the managers or the managed. Despite these conditions, however, the social system which is a prison does not degenerate into a chaotic mess of social relations which have no order and make no sense.

Pursuing this line of thought, some observers have gone so far as to claim that much of what goes on in confinement is 'not peculiar to the prison at all' (Irwin and Cressey, 1962). We would certainly accept that prisons bear certain strong analogies with other kinds of institution, and, moreover, that studying prisons calls upon the same conceptual and methodological resources and principles as are appropriate for thinking about social institutions and social reproduction more generally. Nevertheless, we would also argue that prisons pose a host of issues which are distinctive enough to call for special study.

With these matters in mind, we can now turn to a review of some of the attempts that sociologists have made to identify and conceptualize some central aspects of prison life.

Sociologies of imprisonment

Sykes on 'the society of captives'

Our starting point in this discussion is provided by the work of Gresham Sykes (1958), although earlier 'scriptural beginnings' (Cohen, 1988) would in principle be possible (for example Clemmer, 1940). We make this choice in part in recognition of Sykes's considerable influence on prison sociology (and indeed on prison administration) and because aspects of his work can still be regarded as contemporarily significant. But we also take his approach to embody a number of theoretical and empirical problems which have engendered much subsequent debate, which remain to some extent unresolved, and which are of central importance to the understanding of order in prisons.

In *The Society of Captives* Sykes presents a classic statement of the view that prisons generate unique patterns of relationships and activities. Sykes views 'the society of captives' as a 'system of action' (1958: 79), rather sharply bounded by the prison wall, and marked by its own conventions and codes of conduct.[5] For Sykes, the prison is a situation of relative deprivation and scarcity. Many of the ways in which prisoners characteristically act, and the roles that they adopt in relation to one another, can be understood primarily as responses to the special demands and deprivations which imprisonment imposes. According to Sykes, the main deprivations—his famous five 'pains of imprisonment'—are: the deprivation of liberty; the deprivation of goods and services; the deprivation of heterosexual relationships; the deprivation of autonomy; and the deprivation of personal security (ibid.: 65–78). These 'pains', it is said, account for many of the special features of captive society because much of what prisoners do arises from their attempts to adapt to or compensate for them. Prisoners necessarily encounter certain dilemmas, because their choices are limited and all the available options present problems. The possible 'adaptations' which prisoners can make lie on a polarity between 'individu-

---

[5] In our view this comment is correct notwithstanding Sykes's acknowledgement that that boundary is 'far more permeable than it appears' and hence that the penal institution is 'shaped by its [wider] social environment' and 'reacts to and is acted upon by the free community' (1958: 8). Our point would be that this recognition plays little subsequent part in Sykes's substantive argument. More central, for him, is the view that 'if the inmate community is shut in, the free community is shut out' (loc. cit.).

alistic' and 'collectivistic' outlooks (ibid.: 82–3), the latter of which, when achieved, generate inmate 'solidarity'.[6] In empirical reality, Sykes believes, captive society represents a compromise between these two theoretical extremes:

The population of prisoners does not exhibit a perfect solidarity yet neither is it a warring aggregate. Rather it is a mixture of both and the society of captives lies balanced in an uneasy compromise.

(Sykes, 1958: 83)

In the course of living together, Sykes continues, prisoners adopt distinct 'argot roles'.[7] Some of these are individualized and self-seeking (and hence 'alienative'). One at least is collectivist and solidary (and hence 'cohesive'). Sykes attaches a certain positive valuation to the latter, from the point of view of inmate society (compare for example his depictions of the 'real man' and the 'ball buster': 99–101).[8] He believes that the more the cohesive stances predominate, the more likely it is that the pains of imprisonment will be alleviated for the inmate population as a whole (ibid.: 107). The 'inmate code' which elevates the values of the 'real man' into a set of nostrums (do your own time, don't grass or 'squeal', show

[6] Writing on related themes a few years later Glaser reports data which he regards as contradicting Sykes's views. He suggests that in four out of five prisons studies most inmates (long-termers especially) registered a degree of ambivalence towards their fellow captives and 'wariness' about commitment to relationships with them (1964: 111). Most prisoners preferred at most some form of 'guarded friendship'. On Glaser's view there are many pressures towards 'voluntary isolation' which present obstacles to the development of inmate solidarity (1964: 98, 117–8). Whether this counts as much of a criticism of Sykes is dubious since it seems to rest on a conflation between 'friendship' and Sykes's less restricted notion of 'solidarity'. As Mathiesen (1965: 20f.) points out, following Etzioni, for there to be 'rank cohesion' (his term for solidarity) across a group of similarly situated individuals (as in a trade union) it is not even necessary that they all know each other, let alone be friends.

[7] 'Argot roles' are defined by Sykes as terms used in the special language of the society of captives to identify some 'distinctive social roles played by its members in response to the particular problems of imprisonment' (1958: 86).

[8] Sykes takes the behaviour of the 'ball buster' to be marked by 'blatant disobedience, physical and verbal assaults on the officials, the constant creation of disturbances'. 'Ball busters' 'continue to shout their defiance despite the ultimate hopelessness of their position'. Sykes comments that whereas one might expect this 'Promethean quality' to draw the admiration of other inmates, in fact the 'ball buster' is regarded with contempt as one who will sacrifice 'the well being of the inmate population as a whole for the sake of a childish, emotional outburst' (1958: 99–100). The 'real man' by contrast displays fortitude and manly self-restraint: 'Somewhat aloof, seldom complaining, he embodies the inmates' version of decorum' (1958: 102). Both the 'ball buster' and the 'real man' seek the retention of their personal autonomy, the first by relentless opposition, the second by stoical endurance.

reserved disdain for the guards) is itself a normative device which attempts (never in practice fully successfully) to promote solidarity (see Sykes and Messinger, 1960, for a more explicit account of this 'social system'). Under conditions of greater solidarity prisoners will, it is argued, feel less isolated, less oppressed by the staff, and less at risk from one another. Were it not for inmate solidarity and the normative force of the 'code', Sykes suggests, the 'Hobbesian problem' could become a reality in prisons:

as the population of prisoners moves in the direction of a warring aggregate the many problems of prison life become more acute. If a war of all against all is apt to make life 'solitary, poor, nasty, brutish, and short' for men with freedom, as Hobbes suggested, it would seem to be doubly true for men in custody. Even those who are most successful in exploiting their fellow prisoners will find it a dangerous and nerve-wracking game, for they cannot escape the company of their victims. And in so far as social rejection is a fundamental problem, a state of complete mutual alienation is worse than useless as a solution to the threats created by the inmate's status as an outcast.

(Sykes, 1958: 108)

In arguing thus, Sykes reaches what may at first sight seem a counter-intuitive conclusion, namely that solidarity among prisoners is beneficial to the stability of the institution, even though the values of the inmate code are not those of conformity. But whereas the 'ball buster' (see note 8) is often regarded as a fool who brings on the heat of official retaliation ('stricter surveillance, further restrictions, and the alienation of the guardians all flow from his useless . . . insurrection') (ibid.: 100), the values of the real man conversely suggest 'a system of shared, group-supported beliefs and values which will tend to *curb* forms of behaviour which . . . bring only retaliation' (ibid.: 108, emphasis added). Sykes holds that the custodians would therefore be ill-advised to seek to govern by strategies of divide and rule, or to fall prey to 'that excess of caution' (ibid.: 133) which seeks to prevent or punish every infraction of the formal rules. Given these stubborn realities, for Sykes any attempt to reform the prison which ignores its social system is 'as futile as the labours of Sisyphus' (ibid.: 134).

Sykes has a similarly ironic conception of the roles and powers of the custodians in their quest for order. He begins by enumerating the 'tasks' of the prison. He argues that the tasks of 'custody', 'internal order', and 'self-maintenance' predominate over those of 'punishment' and 'reform' because they bear upon the continued survival of the institution rather than merely its external legitimating principles. In pursuing these tasks, Sykes argues, prison officials ostensibly hold a 'grant of power without equal in contemporary society'. They:

have the right not only to issue and administer the orders and regulations which are to guide the life of the prisoner, but also the right to detain, try and punish any individual accused of disobedience—a merging of legislative, executive and judicial functions which has long been recognized as the earmark of complete domination.

(Sykes, 1958: 41)

Yet, although the prison is therefore inherently an 'authoritarian community' (ibid.: 133) the appearance of 'total power' (whilst real *in extremis*—tanks and guns can ring the prison, and 'in the event of an open battle victory inevitably lies with the guards' (1958: 81)) is in fact quite contrary to the actuality of the daily life of the prison. This is partly because staff are outnumbered by prisoners; partly because they cannot usually call upon an 'internalized obligation to obey' (ibid.: 48) yet are reliant on prisoners' co-operation for the performance of routine tasks; and partly because the staff in fact lack a very effective system of rewards and punishments (those that are meaningful from the point of view of the prisoner).[9] The apparent 'monolith' of total power is thus in certain respects 'cracked' (ibid.: 53). Hence:

Intrinsically inefficient as a method of making men carry out a complex task, diminished in effectiveness by the realities of the guard–inmate ratio, and always accompanied by the danger of touching off further violence, the use of force by the custodians has many limitations as a basis on which to found the routine operation of the prison.

(Sykes, 1958: 49–50)

[9] This point raises important issues about the vexed question of legitimacy in prisons, and the significance to them of what Giddens has termed the 'dialectic of control' (see our later discussion of these themes). For Sykes, prisons simply do not have 'that easily-won obedience which many organizations take for granted in the naïveté of their unrecognized strength' (1958: 47). This is not to say, however, that most prisoners overtly deny the legitimacy of their confinement—they do not; hence, Sykes claims, the study of the prison 'makes us realize that men need not be motivated to conform to a regime which they define as rightful' (ibid.: 48). On the many ambiguities of this issue see also Glaser (1964: 115); Scraton et al. (1991: 133).

In this sense, Sykes argues, the custodians, and more particularly the ordinary guard, may not feel in a very powerful position at all. Rather, given that the prison must accomplish complex tasks of self-maintenance and is much more than a simple 'container',[10] the guard encounters a series of pressures (the need to get routine jobs done, personal proximity with inmates, the 'claims of reciprocity' in human relationships) towards compromise and accommodation. Sykes rather tendentiously terms such compromises 'corruptions' (ibid.: 54). This pejorative implication is distracting and unnecessary, and most of the accommodations he has in mind are not 'corrupt' in the normal sense. He is simply describing a circumstance in which the guard is placed in the position of seeking some tolerable *modus vivendi* with prisoners whilst having limited resources of either reward or punishment at his disposal. 'Corruptions' result, Sykes believes, from 'structural defects in the prison's system of power' (ibid.: 61): it cannot function if it tries to enforce all those rules to which it claims adherence, while at the same time getting through the daily schedule of work and routines. Indeed, at times the custodians have difficulty in maintaining even a semblance of control (ibid.: 127). Perhaps the best they can usually hope for is to bargain with a dominant group of 'cohesively oriented' prisoners ('real men') who also have a strong interest in maintaining a quiet life.

Sykes is thus at pains to suggest that the real 'system of action' of the prison is quite distinct from its formal hierarchies. Staff have much less power than is pretended—prisoners somewhat more, at least when 'cohesively' oriented. Both the exercise of dominative authority and the use of force to underwrite it and compel compliance are, on a day-to-day basis, tempered by this reality. The lasting significance of Sykes's work lies in his recognition that the 'order' of the prison is in this sense a negotiated one, and that prisons in their 'normal' state are at some remove from the warlike chaos of public imagining. In any case naked force is not the modality of power most characteristic of them. Rather, amongst

[10] Sykes points out that 'if men in prison were locked forever in their cells, shut off from all intercourse with each other . . . the inmate population would be an aggregate rather than a social group, a mass of isolates rather than a society' (1958: 5). In fact however 'Humanitarian motives, combined with a growing doubt about the efficacy of solitude . . . [historically] led to a search for alternatives to isolation' (1958: 6). Once isolation is abandoned prison society comes into being, and the institution faces greater complexity in the effort constantly to reproduce itself.

Sykes's distinctive contributions is his focus on the prison *as a special kind of bureaucracy* (see Sykes's numerous approving references to Weber on bureaucracy in his chapter on prison staff), whose single greatest preoccupation is its *self-reproduction through the performance of routine tasks.*[11] Sykes indicates that such 'self-maintained' tends to predominate over any more substantive penological goals. This view anticipates a number of concerns which we go onto develop in what follows. These include the account which we outline (following Giddens) of the centrality of routine to the reproduction of social institutions generally (and to the definition and response to 'control problems' in prisons specifically) as well as the gradual infiltration into prisons of what have come to be known as 'managerialist' practices.

There are a number of possible objections to Sykes's views on both theoretical and substantive grounds. Subsequent commentators have done much to revise and qualify his claims on both the distributions of power within the prison and the relations between the prison and its surrounding environment:

1. It has been noted by numerous observers since Sykes (especially Jacobs, 1977; 1983) that his conception of the prison/society interface is vague and probably misleading and that this stems from Sykes's commitment to a strong form of teleological functionalism.[12] Sykes's continual emphasis on the prison as a system whose primary features—and their equilibrium-preserving tendency—are internally generated indicates this, notwithstanding his rather gestural remarks to the contrary (1958: 7–8). Most of the weakest

---

[11] See Sykes's 'Appendix B' on 'The routine of imprisonment', setting out detailed daily tasks of the guards hour by hour—an account which Sykes claims 'conveys the flavor of imprisonment as little else can' (1958: 137).

[12] In Merton's (1957) classic account functionalism has at its heart the study of 'those observed consequences [of social practices] which make for the adaptation or adjustment of a given system'. Critics argue this presupposes that one can identify real 'needs' of a social system, and go on to explain the continuity of social practices in terms of their survival value in fulfilling those needs. Objections to this line of argument include *inter alia* that it rests on a logical error (that an event can be explained by its outcome) and that it rests on an overextended analogy between social 'systems' and the self-regulation of biological organisms. Sykes comes closest to a full-blown version of this approach in his rather unsatisfactory remarks on the 'cyclical' character of prison riots (1958, ch. 6), but much of his general terminology (the prison as 'system of action', e.g.) owes a good deal to the functionalists' preoccupation with showing the interdependence of the elements of a 'system'. For a constructive critique of functionalism in general, see Giddens's essay 'Functionalism: *apres la lutte*' (in Giddens, 1977).

aspects of his case arise from this. Subsequent commentators, especially Irwin and Cressey (1962), Irwin (1970, 1980), and Jacobs (1977) have demonstrated a far greater responsiveness on the part of prison administrations, prison conditions, and prison populations themselves to surrounding economic, political, and intellectual circumstances than Sykes allows.

2. By extension, Sykes can be taken to task for a lack of adequate recognition of diversity in penal institutions—in his view all prisons are alike to some marked degree, they 'are apt to present a common social structure' (1958: xiii; see also Sykes and Messinger, 1960). However, subsequent studies in male institutions do not really support this (for example Street et al., 1966, on variation amongst juvenile institutions). Moreover, research on women's prisons (for example Giallombardo, 1966; Heffernan, 1972; Mandaraka-Sheppard, 1986; Carlen, 1983) suggest radically different dispositions of power and practices of control, in a way that compromises any claim to identify the 'essential' features of imprisonment as such. Sykes's analysis seems best attuned to something like the 'warehouse' conception of long-term prisons for adult men. Thus, Sykes's rather positive conception of the potentiality for solidarity within prison society probably derives from the particular circumstances under which it was elaborated, and lacks the general applicability which he would wish to claim for it. His views on this point have been challenged with particular force by Mathiesen (1965), whose position we outline below.

3. Sykes views the recurrence of crisis and 'equilibrium' in prisons as having a definite 'cyclical' aspect, moving repeatedly between order and disorder (1958: 110). On this view the transfer of powers inherent in a regime managed by 'corruptions' necessarily has a 'slippery slope' quality. And at some point pressure arises for that power to be snatched back. But the historical record of disturbances is not so neatly patterned. That history could equally, from an alternative theoretical perspective, suggest the fundamentally *contradictory* character of social relations in prison—generally submerged but giving rise to recurrent crises of control (Scraton et al., 1991; Adams, 1992). Still another view (perhaps closer to our own) regards the breakdown in order as contingent and non-necessary, and objects to the assumption of its periodic recurrence (cf. Giddens's (1984) distinction between contradiction and conflict). The latter position also attributes greater significance to the agency

of individual actors, and their changing consciousness of their predicaments, than is considered under Sykes's rather objectivist conception of the prison as a 'social system'. On the other hand, both Scraton et al.'s views and our own would include the suspicion that, in accentuating the central irony of the 'cracked' monolith of power, Sykes is led to *understate* the importance of force and compulsion in prisons, and hence also of resistance to them. Much of the analysis which we develop in later chapters is devoted to exploring the complexities of such moments of imposition and resistance.

Mathiesen and the 'defences of the weak'

One of the most insightful contrary positions to that of Sykes is that expounded by Thomas Mathiesen in *The Defences of the Weak* (1965). In our view this book has been unjustly neglected by most subsequent commentators. We take it to be just as theoretically significant as Sykes's more famous text. The reasons for its neglect are not entirely clear (though it is undeniably a dense book and no easy read). It may result in part from the dominance in academic discussion (and indeed in popular cultural depictions of prisons) of perspectives originating in the United States—the symbolic 'home' of long-term confinement in the industrialized world—whilst Mathiesen's book reports research conducted in Norway. It may also in part stem from Mathiesen's own later revision of his views in his more widely circulated text *The Politics of Abolition* (1974). However this may be, our exposition of Mathiesen's views here must be in some measure a work of recovery.

Mathiesen argues that prisons are far more 'disrupted' societies than Sykes imagines. Hence (1965: 122–36) prisoners experience a need for alternatives to the forms of peer solidarity which Sykes had claimed to identify. Prisoners, in consequence, are in a far weaker and more insidious predicament than they might be if the inmate code had much practical reality. A key point of difference on which much of this debate turns concerns the extent of prisoners' success in organizing to alleviate the deprivations of imprisonment. Sykes assumes that trading networks, cool rejection of the guards, and other constructive adaptations are (or at any rate, can be) sufficiently highly developed to compensate for a significant part of the sense of deprivation, thereby reducing the importance to prisoners of the formal reward and punishment systems of the prison.

Mathiesen, conversely, argues that prisoners are rather abjectly reliant on the distribution of 'benefits and burdens' by staff,[13] for staff control prisoners' access to a host of aspects of everyday life (food, possessions, contacts with family, etc.) which may seem almost trivial to the outside observer, but which can be immensely significant in conditions of captivity. Moreover, adds Mathiesen, living under staff power is itself one of the pains of imprisonment, not identified by Sykes. In Mathiesen's analysis inmates indeed largely lack the kinds of solidarity and peer support on which Sykes places so much emphasis. For Mathiesen, prison inmates are essentially 'lonely individuals' (ibid.: 12) for whom peer solidarity is a norm more honoured in the breach than the observance (ibid.: 122). Inmates are thus in a position of both psychological and material weakness, and their dependency leaves them in a situation analogous to that of a child unable to contest its parents' untrammelled power except by reference to a generalized expectation of fairness. The power of the guards is both very great and rather unstable because it melds both personal and bureaucratic elements. Thus, Mathiesen argues, the prison is characterized by a 'patriarchal' deployment of power, but one whose fairness inmates are apt to deny—hence *illegitimate patriarchalism* (ibid.: 100). Unpredictability in decision making by treatment experts and guards is simultaneously the token of their dominance and the source of its 'illegitimacy' (because it is seen as arbitrary and discretionary). Thus personal power is viewed by inmates as a failure of bureaucratic rationality, and vice versa.

The form taken by the inmates' denial of legitimacy, in its active guises, is what Mathiesen styles censoriousness'. Censoriousness means a form of complaint that the guards are failing in their duties of justice and efficiency (ibid.: 155), not observing rules and proprieties, not keeping promises, in short being unfair and falling down on the job. Deploying '*established* norms', inmates in effect use the 'pointed finger' to emphasize that staff are deviating from widely accepted principles (1965: 12). Censoriousness represents

[13] The easiest way of resolving this debate would be to argue that Sykes and Mathiesen have simply identified an empirical difference and that in Sykes's American long-term secure prison peer solidarity was real, whilst in Mathiesen's Scandinavian medium-security therapeutic prison is was not. Whilst this is not in itself at all implausible, it would be to underestimate the seriousness of the dispute between them. And in any case, even such a difference would compromise the theoretical generality which Sykes (1958) and Sykes and Messinger (1960) want to claim.

'criticism of those in power for not following, in their behaviour, principles that are established as correct within the social system in question' (ibid.: 23), whether these are strictly legal or moral and customary. Hence individuals can be censorious in differing ways and with differing degrees of conscious strategic intent, from the 'barrack-room lawyer' to the plaintive appeal to better nature:

> The individual inmate, standing alone, as the censor of staff, argues with the ruler of the basis of norms that the ruler also agrees with, trying to convince the ruler that he has not adhered correctly to these principles.
>
> (ibid.: 13)

For Mathiesen this is characteristic of people in weak positions because it presupposes that the complainer must accommodate more to the established norm of the institution than vice versa; hence the book's title of *The Defences of the Weak*. It is tactic which assumes 'a certain amount of consensus (however superficial) between ruler and ruled regarding basic norms and values' (ibid.: 13). Social subordinates who wish to have any purchase on the decisions of the more powerful seem required to accept (or at least pay lip-service to) the authority of already established rules. Such a position contrasts sharply with Sykes's views, for example when the latter asserts that in prisons 'the bond between the recognition of the legitimacy of control and the sense of duty has been torn apart' (1958: 47).

That censoriousness is born from weakness does not mean that it is necessarily an ineffective stance. *Tactically*, Mathiesen argues, it may place the prisoner in a rather strong position—in certain factual situations, it puts the guard or official in the wrong in respect of a norm whose legitimacy he is obliged to acknowledge. Equally, the prisoner may adopt a posture of identification with senior management, thereby 'going over the head' of the guard and seeking a 'vertical consensus' (1965: 84, 88). Moreover, Mathiesen argues, the 'illegitimate patriarchalism' which places the guard in the positions both of material provider and punisher imposes a set of expectations not all of which staff may be able to meet, at least not simultaneously. Thus, he suggests, the inmate can reliably 'put the guard in the wrong' by deploying competing norms of rule following and rule bending (ibid.: 84). In this respect the guards are in a rather different predicament from the one Sykes envisages. For Sykes the guards' accommodations with the captives stem from a lack of effective power and sanctions—the brute fact of being outnumbered, yet needing to get through a whole set of routine tasks. For Mathiesen, the guards retain many powers—as noted above, they control the 'distribution of benefits and burdens'. They may nevertheless find themselves in a form of 'double bind' when they seek to exercise their powers. A guard who insists on enforcing the letter of the rules can be censured by prisoners for being pettifogging and inflexible; one who operates in a discretionary way risks being accused of inconsistency and unfairness. The result is a 'disrupted society' all of whose members, including those close to the top, experience themselves as powerless and claim that the power really lies elsewhere (ibid.: 65).

In the face of such intractabilities, Mathiesen argues, the goals of the institution characteristically become reduced to the maintenance of 'smooth administration'. it is on this point that Sykes and Mathiesen are perhaps closest to agreement, though they differ as to the means and consequences of such administration. Whereas Sykes identifies the tasks of internal order and self-maintenance of the prison as engendering the need for 'corruptions', Mathiesen emphasizes instead the priority of bureaucratic formalism. Thus the prison seeks to defend its legitimacy by maintaining a 'smooth administration of benefits and burdens' and thereby to pre-empt censorious challenges. Of course any such smooth administration is in itself a demonstration of power. It presupposes the capacity to make the daily routine happen, to confer or withhold benefits and burdens (cf. our discussion below of Giddens on the 'smooth flow' of power). In this regard, notwithstanding the disrupted nature of prison society and its inherent problems of legitimation, the official power holders of the prison are, in Mathiesen's view, its *rulers* in a far more substantial sense than appears in Sykes's analysis (see Mathiesen's subsequent revision and extension of this argument in *The Politics of Abolition*).[14] Mathiesen's analysis thus also in some

[14] Mathiesen also published a transitional book (entitled *Across the Boundaries of Organizations*) in 1971. Here he argues that the *internally* 'disrupted' character of social relations apparent even among the prison's senior managers is evidence of the prison's 'weakness' in relation to its *external* environments. Thus the governor, chaplain, psychiatrist, and so on each have separate external commitments and obligations which impede their internal co-operation. For Mathiesen this is further evidence of the fact that the prison enjoys neither 'external bargaining power' nor 'internal solidarity'. His inference that this intrinsic 'vulnerability' encourages belief in the eventual possibility of the dissolution of the prison (1971: 137) helps to contextualize the adoption of the strategy of 'external critique' in *The Politics of Abolition*.

respects anticipates aspects of the subsequent trend towards 'managerialism'. That is, he suggests reasons why prison administrators might embrace highly 'bureaucratic-administrative' definitions of their activity (Kamenka and Tay, 1975) and processual evaluations of performance. It is possible that the kinds of administrative competence and consistency seen as associated with such a stance may act as a surrogate for other, and more elusive, sources of legitimation—a point we take up below in discussion of Jacobs's views.

None the less it remains arguable that Mathiesen's position is more similar to that of Sykes than at first appears. Mathiesen, too, was in 1965 working within a functionalist paradigm (1965: 16–17): for him censoriousness was thus seen as a 'functional alternative' to peer solidarity—it is the defensive reaction to which prisoners resort in the absence of a 'cohesive' stance. (Hence if the initial conditions outlined by Sykes were empirically satisfied, similar consequences might indeed follow.) Similarly, although Mathiesen is more concerned than Sykes with the social position of prisoners in wider societal terms as part of the explanation for their weakness, he too is principally interested in features of prison societies which are essentially internally generated rather than explicable in social-structural terms. This is one reason for his later, and in our view too emphatic, disavowal of *Defences of the Weak* in subsequent work (*Politics of Abolition, Part I*). Consequently, his analysis—which is presented in terms of grids of possible states of affairs and maps of 'horizontal' versus 'vertical' solidarities looks unduly formalistic. Like Sykes he is concerned to show how the social structure of the prison *constrains* action and he may be similarly vulnerable to the criticism of a lack of an account of agency in his theoretical scheme.

In this sense the debate between Sykes and Mathiesen perhaps posits a false choice between solidarity and censoriousness, when some fluid combination of each (plus some other alternatives) may equally be imaginable. It situates prisoners within a rather schematically 'mapped' and diagrammatic representation of the prison's internal order, thereby playing down the possibility of agency, and perhaps underemphasizing the issue of prisoners' (and staff's) understandings of and conscious responses to their predicaments. Yet while they share common limitations it is also possible that in a restricted sense Sykes and Mathiesen may both be right. Mathiesen is in the last resort correct to emphasize the disparity in power between prisoners and custodians and the problems which thereby attend any strategy of opposition by prisoners. Sykes, on the other hand, usefully draws attention to the compromises and negotiations implicit in everyday institutional management, and hence in the reproduction of routines.

Other work in the sociology of imprisonment has sought to settle accounts with these unresolved problems in divergent ways. If we accept for the sake of convenience that social research tends either to lay its emphasis on the immediacies of specific sites and contexts of interaction (and hence to invite the designation 'micro') *or* to fix its attention on larger patterns of social and cultural change and influence (loosely on a 'macro' level) we can trace two relatively distinct bodies of work relevant to the problems of institutional ordering in prisons. The first, from which we focus especially on the contributions of Goffman and of Cohen and Taylor, extends the interests of Mathiesen and Sykes with the particularities of prisons in terms of their interior organization and its impacts upon the lived experiences of those who inhabit and work within them. The second, which for present purposes principally includes the analyses of Irwin and Jacobs, emphasizes the impacts upon penal institutions of their surrounding social and intellectual environments. Having briefly outlined these two strands in modern prison studies we turn to some other sources in social theory, especially from Foucault and Giddens, in an attempt to mediate the micro/macro dichotomy (and the associated issue of the relationship between actin and structure in social analysis) and to seek a more satisfactory basis for further discussion.

Microsociology and prison life

Sykes's work clearly anticipates Goffman's (1961) formulation of the characteristics of 'total institutions'. For Goffman there are a range of social institutions (prisons, barracks, asylums, ships at sea, boarding schools) which have in common the tendency to encompass the whole of the lives of their inmates. They thereby also share a variety of features in common: hierarchy, routine, rituals of degradation and initiation, bureaucratic categorizations and segregation of their populations, and a complex interaction between formally acknowledged procedures and informally controlling social processes.

We will shortly encounter grounds (in the work of Irwin and Jacobs) for moderating the assertion of the 'total' character of such environments—the walls are inherently more permeable to external influences than they at first appear. This is not something that Goffman seeks to deny, even if he has in consequence been accused of a certain vagueness in his categorization of which institutions are properly regarded as 'total' (Jones and Fowles, 1984: 25). Nevertheless, Goffman reminds us, we cannot evade the issue of the particularity of their interior working. For example, interactions between inmates and custodians tend to be patterned in reiterative ways according to routine deployments of time which are more exacting than is usual outside. Total institutions involve 'batch living' based on allocation to relatively undifferentiated groups (prisoners, patients/guards, nurses) rather than on the kinds of individuated preferences and attentions which most of us seek and expect in other contexts. The successful allocation of individuals to batches requires processes of 'role stripping' and 'mortifications of self', often ritually enacted in induction procedures (haircuts, uniforms, numbers) and reproduced in daily practice. Total institutions thus commonly assert the authority to control the lives of their inmates at a level of intimate detail qualitatively greater than other contexts of living, and they generally reinforce that claim with a range of compulsions, rewards, and sanctions which is correspondingly extensive and detailed and which responds to infractions or improprieties regarded as too trivial for attention in the world outside. The primary aims of such measures are the reproduction of domination (cf. Mathiesen's 'smooth administration') through the generation of a subordinate 'inmate role' rather than any substantive 'therapeutic' objective properly so called.

The social relations of total institutions are thus marked by the differential powers and purposes of the participants—for the staff they are principally about sustaining the routine operation of the organization; for inmates they concern not only resources, perks, privileges, but the need to retain some degree of autonomy and sense of self, by subverting, circumventing or escaping momentarily the officially prescribed order of things. Goffman thus directs our attention not only towards the ritual, repetitive character of such interactions and their relation to competitions for power (cf. McDermott and King, 1988), but also towards the relationship between these matters and the issue of the maintenance (or otherwise) of the sense of self as such. Goffman regards an assault on the former self, especially where this is manifested in counter-assertions of individuality, as intrinsic to the character of the total institution.[15]

Cohen and Taylor (1981) extend these concerns to show that the career of a prisoner undergoing a long sentence (especially in very close confinement) is properly regarded as an *existential* problem. In so saying, they assert that there is a level of analysis beyond the Sykesian problematic of solidarity and prisonization. They compare the situation of the long-term prisoner to that of others in extreme, or disrupted, or isolated situations—migrants, disaster victims, lone explorers and sailors, and so on. Their concerns thus stand to one side of more conventional sociological accounts:

> We have tried to construct . . . a phenomenology of the security wing: how life there is given meaning, how one passes the time, how friends are made and lost, how one resigns oneself to the environment and how one resists it. We have, in other words, looked at quite commonplace matters such as time, work, friendship and self identity but looked at them in a world in which so much of the taken-for-granted elements in everyday life are problematic and even disturbing.
>
> (ibid.: 69)

Cohen and Taylor therefore focus on issues of friendship, relations with those outside, privacy, the management (or marking) of the passage of time, of strategies for sustaining meaning and identity, and of submerged or overt resistance to an intractable predicament.

Cohen and Taylor's analysis is of considerable importance—perhaps especially so given the subsequent consolidation of the trends they identify (1981: 205–6) towards the more frequent imposition of

---

[15] It must be borne in mind that Goffman is writing principally about psychiatric institutions and that (even leaving on one side the adequacy of his account of these) the application of the term total institution to other settings is an argument by analogy. It is at least arguable that the kinds of intimate personal control sought by such institutions are if anything more intensive than is usual in prisons, notwithstanding the deployments of medico-psychiatric power that also take place in prisons (cf. Carlen, 1986; Sim, 1990). The assumption that prisons too are seriously interested in such forms of knowledge and control is also one often attributed to Foucault. As we suggest below this view must be subject to some careful qualification. e.g. the invasiveness of psychiatric attention would seem to be rather highly differentiated by gender. To summarize crudely, a set of practices seems to have emerged which allows rather intense kinds of normalizing intervention for women in prison (Carlen, 1983; Dobash et al., 1986) whilst preferring a more 'warehousing' approach for many men.

very long sentences and the consequent gradual accretion of an ever larger population sequestered in the deepest reaches of modern penal systems (especially, amongst Western societies, in the United States and England and Wales).[16] Cohen and Taylor are writing close to the inception of the same strategy (the 'dispersal system') that this book considers in its mature form. Their pessimism as to that penal philosophy and form of administration, together with their requirement that the analysis of such situations be conducted reflexively in relation to its own political and methodological stand-points raise issues which a study such as this must confront (see chapter 9 and Appendix A below). Similarly, Cohen and Taylor's nuanced account of what prisoners say and feel, and their demonstration that prisoners do not passively *undergo* imprisonment but rather *live* it is theoretically crucial. In demonstrating that prisoners reflect upon their predicament and respond to it not automatically but strategically *Psychological Survival* returns to prison studies the issue of agency which an exclusive stress upon the systemic, organizational, and dominative features of penal institutions too readily occludes. Our acceptance of this emphasis is registered and developed in our adoption below of aspects of the social theory of Anthony Giddens.

On the other hand, it would be unwise to suppose that Cohen and Taylor's account is entirely adequate or unproblematic. There are several reasons why we cannot adopt it as a model. In the first place, the very specificity of the time and place in which the study was conducted (namely the 'particular enclave' (Cohen and Taylor, 1977) of Durham's high security wing, with its small number of somewhat notorious occupants, at the end of the 1960s) argues against its being very easily 'replicated' in any orthodox

---

[16] In England at least this results principally from changes in sentence lengths over the last decade or so, with an increasing proportion of those imprisoned receiving sentences of four years or over (Home Office, 1993: 52; Bottomley, 1994: 161–2). This is in part a product of the complex phenomenon of 'bifurcation' (Bottoms: 1977). Changes in parole policy for long-termers have also contributed to this trend. The 'mega-shift' in imprisonment rates in the United States since the late 1970s has been radically more abrupt, with a 188% increase in the number of prisoners in Federal and State prisons between 1980 and 1993 (US Department of Justice, 1994). In the United States much of this increase is attributable to the increased numbers and lengths of sentences imposed for burglary and, more particularly, drugs offences (see Zimring and Hawkins, 1994). These developments seem certain to be magnified by the 'truth in sentencing' and 'three strikes' movements (Moore, 1994; Davis, 1995).

methodological sense. As they put it 'We stumbled—by chance—upon an interesting group of human beings who were locked up in an exceptional environment' (1977: 68). We do not intend by this comment any routine arguments against ideographic methods (lack of reliability, lack of rigour, etc.), still less the kind of uncomprehending hostility which Cohen and Taylor received in some circles at the time (1977: 78–9). We simply acknowledge that the interest and insight of the study stems in part from its very rootedness in the particular situation it describes, many of whose features differ markedly from those of the more 'typical' conditions of our own study twenty years later. Secondly, the methodological constraints within which Cohen and Taylor worked (partly resulting from the terms of their original invitation into the prison as adult education tutors, partly externally imposed by a subsequent refusal of research access by the Home Office (Cohen and Taylor, 1977), and partly inherent in their theoretical preferences) are not ones that we would willingly reproduce. Cohen and Taylor's account derives from their analysis of conversation, semi-structured talk, and letters (that is, it is a study of prisoners' discourse) rather than from observation. For this reason Cohen and Taylor (notwithstanding their insightful discussion of time) had little access to the practical conduct of prison routines.

Moreover, whereas a central focus of our concern lies in issues of staff–prisoner *interaction* and the accomplishment of the prison's internal order, one result of their methodology is that the prison administration and staff appear only peripherally in Cohen and Taylor's account. Indeed, for all that they comment *en passant* that 'the prison officers are very much part of the prison community and we would have liked to know how they viewed the situation' (1981: 192) the effective result of their marginality in the account is to reduce the prison staff to the status of ciphers and to leave their activity more or less obscure (a feature of their work which also occurs in other radical prison sociology of the period, for example Fitzgerald, 1977). This means that *Psychological Survival* is not systematic sociology of imprisonment but rather (self-admittedly) a phenomenology of prisoners' experience of some of its consequences. Less indulgently, Cohen and Taylor's analysis may be interpreted as standing on the 'micro' side of the dualism of objectivism and subjectivism which has been so comprehensively criticized in recent philosophy of social science, most tellingly by

Giddens (1984), Bourdieu (1993), and others. There is relatively little developed sense of the 'outside', either here or indeed in
Goffman, either in the sense of its impact on the construction of
the penal complex of which Durham E-wing was a part,[17] or
indeed on the pre-prison careers of the men themselves. Cohen and
Taylor's brief remarks (1981: 177–8) on offence-type and personal
ideologies of coping with prison seem gestural and undeveloped
(and in any case are attributions to individuals rather than any
more careful survey of adaptations as suggested variously by Sykes
or Irwin). Indeed, as Cohen and Taylor subsequently say of themselves, it is as if they slipped 'into the game of classifying prisoners
into distinctive groups' (1977: 75)—a mania for typologies that has
been one of the more banal features of the 'prison community' tradition.

For these reasons Cohen and Taylor's analysis, in common with
all those discussed so far, suggests a rather interiorized and self-
contained (or to put it poshly, endogenous) view of social relations
in prison, their potentialities for order and disorder, and the origins
of styles and strategies of domination and control. Insightful as
such analyses have been (and we have reviewed only those which
seem to us especially important) they none the less beg some key
questions about the changing contours and conduct of imprisonment as such and its position in the surrounding society. We therefore now turn to some of those contributions which have sought to
supplement such views by placing the study of imprisonment more
securely within accounts of larger historical processes.

Macrosociology and penal change

The second important strand in prison studies has sought to specify
more clearly the influences on the prison from the surrounding society and the vulnerability of prisons to historical and political
change. These concerns are perhaps most evident in the work of
John Irwin (1970, 1980) and James Jacobs (1977, 1983). Irwin pos-
tulates a more various set of possible orientations towards imprisonment by prisoners than either Sykes or Mathiesen had envisaged,
and he connects these more directly with prisoners' previous

---

[17] There is some discussion of the penal policy context in Cohen and Taylor's
study study, but it is not central to their work, and sits uncomfortably with their
phenomenological preferences.

experiences and subcultural commitments. This is a development from Irwin's earliest published papers (Irwin and Cressey, 1962) which in turn are informed by his own experience as a prisoner. Irwin and Cressey argued influentially against the view (associated with Sykes and Messinger, 1960) that the 'inmate social system' in some sense sprang fully formed from the institutional experience of the captives, as a functional adaptation to the pains of imprisonment. They argued instead that many aspects of inmate culture and behaviour were 'not peculiar to the prison at all' but rather were 'imported' from without. (Unsurprisingly, the strongly stated initial opposition between the so-called 'prisonization' and 'importation' starting-points rapidly invited the discovery that some aspects of each were detectable, a finding that has been reiterated frequently ever since: see Thomas and Petersen, 1987.)

Irwin's subsequent work charts successive transformations in the character of prison life effected by demographic and other social changes in the relation between the prison and its surrounding society (Irwin, 1980). For both Irwin and Jacobs such influences are primarily organized around the politics of race in American society articulated with the prisoners' rights movement, the increased prominence of gang structures, and the increasingly explicit political orientations especially of Black prisoners (see for example Piven and Cloward, 1977; Carroll, 1974). In Irwin's view the reactive authoritarianism of prison administrators and politicians in response to such transformations (their failure for example to countenance and negotiate with relatively disciplined groups such as the Black Panthers) signalled a lost opportunity to harness the progressive potentiality of such movements (as Sykes would surely also have counselled)—and the increasingly unmanageable tensions between militantly oppositional inmates and entrenched administrative postures provides the context for understanding the violent upheavals of the early 1970s (see also Adams, 1992).

Jacobs's work tells a similar story in the historical development of a single institution. The successive eras in the history of Stateville Prison, Illinois, are marked by changing impacts upon the prison of prisoners' consciousness and commitments and by their interaction with successive managerial postures, themselves also linked to external political events. Thus, the long reign (1936–61) of the authoritarian Warden Ragen successfully suppressed many potential tensions. Ragen's Stateville was marked by his complete personal dominance (over staff as well as over prisoners), stringent supervision and internal control (including the draconian use of segregation where he saw fit), and a high degree of autonomy from other administrative, political or judicial agencies. Ragen's autocracy practised a form of 'total power' in which (contrary to Sykes's expectation) the 'cracks' were scarcely visible. Ragen claimed allegiance to a version of rehabilitation based not on any 'medical model' but rather on the implicit pedagogy of strict adherence to rules (Jacobs, 1977: 45–6). Ragen was a convinced adherent of the 'slippery slope' view of penal control: no compromise in his domination could be admitted for fear of unleashing further demands and the erosion of authority. After Ragen's eventual departure from public life, Stateville entered a more uncertain period. Jacobs shows that there was a transfer of power away from Ragen's successors as Warden and towards central correctional administrators committed to a modernizing 'rational bureaucratic' model of prison management. Whilst espousing a milder 'human relations' view of management the Wardens of the late 1960s and early 1970s never succeeded in securing the allegiance of the guards (many of whom hankered for a return to the certainties of the earlier era) nor in outlining a viable vision of the prison's future.

At the same time these transitional administrations confronted an increasingly complex and unmanageable series of demands. These included pressures from the staff (for the protection of their authority and indeed their physical safety); from central State-level administrators (for the imposition of uniform standards); from the courts (which—at first reluctantly—became more interventionist and more willing to recognize prisoners' rights in a changed politico-legal context); and ultimately from a prison population which was both increasingly politicized and increasingly internally divided. There was a marked increase throughout the later 1960s and early 1970s in overt conflicts, both between prisoners and guards and between increasingly large and highly organized 'supergangs' of prisoners, structured around ethnic identity and place of origin. Jacobs thus understands the troubles of the late 1960s and early 1970s as a crisis of legitimacy and authority engendered by the passing away of a repressive and increasingly anachronistic *ancien régime* (albeit one which in its own terms had long been very successful in exercising control, and hence which retained must support amongst an alienated and anxious guard force). In Jacobs's account the demise of that autocracy was inevitable—given changed conditions in the wider society—indeed, it was artificially delayed by Ragen's sheer longevity in office, and his personal power. Yet its departure left a void, into which rushed irreconcilable forces contending for influence over the prison's future. To paraphrase Matthew Arnold the prison was 'Caught between two worlds, one dead the other unable to be born'.

This period witnessed what Jacobs (1983) later termed the 'Balkanization' of convict society into mutually hostile cliques and factions (to which one might also add the increasing alienation between managers and guards). Jacobs argues that (at the end of his study) a degree of reconstruction is evident, associated with a 'scientific management' stance, committed—to borrow Mathiesen's terms—to the smooth administration of benefits and burdens. Thus the incoming Warden Brierton initiated numerous modernizing (and pronto-managerialist) developments involving regular consultation with individual prisoners, the rigorous logging of levels of regime provision, and so on. Such a stance defensively seeks a partial relegitimation of penal administration through a dispassionately bureaucratic style of management (and hence a claim to procedural fairness, rather than any more elevated commitment to substantive justice[18] or desert) and an element of 'consumerism' (see Bottoms, 1995; see also the discussion of Beetham and Tyler below).

This aspect of Jacobs's work deserves special emphasis, for Jacobs recognizes more clearly and presciently than any of the other studies reported here the gradual intrusion into prison administration of 'managerialist' concerns. In one respect this is simply an outcome of a much wider societal process of modernization which the prisons could not indefinitely resist. In another it is also an internal control strategy aimed at the recovery of power by the prison's rulers over its routine practices. The emphasis on systemic management thus has several objectives. It aims to secure prisoners' compliance through a combination of efficient service delivery, enhanced formal grievance procedures, and the rationalized use of sanctions and segregative control. It aims to protect the prison from controversy, scandal, and litigation through the strict observation of externally required 'standards'. Finally it aims to reassert control

[18] Note Jacobs's (1977: 210) comment that 'there is no assurance that the prisoners' own conception of substantive justice will not collide with the "formalism" and "cool matter of factness" of bureaucratic administration'.

over the guards by limiting their scope for discretion and insisting upon an increased level of formality and procedural correctness.

The particular benefits of the forms of analysis practised by Irwin and Jacobs seem to us to be as follows. First they make a stringent effort to situate the conditions prevailing in the prisons at any given moment in terms of their temporal and political co-ordinates—and to indicate the responsiveness of penal institutions to external conditions. This is expressed both at the level of successive versions of the 'keeper philosophy' (DiIulio, 1987) and of prisoners' political activity, especially during the ascendancy of the prisoners' rights movement in the 1960s and early 1970s.

Second, such a position is also sensitive to the unintended consequences of given policies. For example, under the 'liberal' regimes of the 'transitional' period in Stateville, not only did physical conditions in the prison deteriorate, but violence and antagonism between prisoners and guards increased and more prisoners were punished. Indeed, some of the measures taken to reassert control (such as the ill-fated Special Program Unit) were if anything more oppressive than the methods they replaced, and certainly incited massive resistance from prisoners.

Third, Jacobs attaches significant weight to the interaction between the prevailing managerial ideology of a prison and the culture and orientation of prison staffs. The 'guards' world' (Jacobs and Crotty, 1983), like the prisoners', is delimited by such conditions—and the power of the guards is defined by their capacity to enact or subvert managerial initiatives. This reminds us that both the high politics of penal policy and the informal practices of the custodians significantly affect the experience of imprisonment for inmates. But it also reminds us that the working conditions, morale, physical safety, readiness to embrace change or conversely to cling to familiar sources of security, union consciousness, and other aspects of the social position of the ordinary 'foot soldier' guard, are similarly variable and open to historical contingency. There is very little work in prison sociology that treats these questions at all seriously. Sykes, for example, begins by acknowledging the irony of the guard's predicament as one ostensibly possessed of powers which he is unable to exercise. But since he treats this predicament as insoluble, he rapidly moves on to what really interests him, namely the society *of* the captives. Such failure to extend the sociological imagination is widespread, and the literature which

encompasses the 'guard's world' is small indeed.[19] Yet this general
inadvertence is also an *analytic* failure. The very term 'total institution', for instance, conjures an imagery whose topic is not really
institutions but *confinement*. By easy extension it is possible for,
say, Cohen and Taylor to present the 'vulgar authoritarianism' that
they ascribe to prison officers as a given and not as being itself
worthy of especially close examination. This position is very different from the one which we seek to develop in this book. In our
estimation what the guards do, and the manner in which they do it,
is central to an understanding of 'what type of order' (Young, 1987:
99) the prison seeks to impose and its chances of 'success' in constructing it. Whilst we fully agree with Scraton et al. (1991) and
Sim (1994) that 'regressive', 'authoritarian', 'macho', and 'strident'
guard cultures exist and have deeply counter-productive and antagonistic effects, we cannot treat the existence of such subcultures as
self-explanatory or inevitable. Neither can prison sociology any
longer rest content with a depiction of the guards as merely shad-
owy figures, peripheral to the main action, who are just *there* as an
inertial and conservative influence. This is one reason why we go
on below to explore the relevance to prisons of concepts suggested
by Anthony Giddens. Without wishing to anticipate that discussion
too much, we take it to be intrinsic that the members of an organization (however unbalanced its power relations and however
unwillingly some of them are there) confront one another as actors
in a dynamic play of conflict, compromise, and mutual influence.
This is what Giddens terms the 'dialectic of control in social systems' (1984: 16). The variable contributions made by the guards—
and by more senior officials—under different regimes to the nature
of such dialectics is a central aspect of the topic under examination.

The underlying historical tendency which Jacobs claims to detect
suggests an increasing bureaucratization of penal practice—concerned with legality, central direction, and the limitation of individual governors' or wardens' power and discretion. This compromises
the adequacy of the Sykesian view of authoritarianism mitigated by
compromise. That is, it suggests that what Sykes presents as a general theory of imprisonment is actually of much more local applicability. Equally, however, it diverges quite sharply from Mathiesen's

---

[19] Contributions which do make some attempt to comprehend the 'guard's world'
include (for the USA) Carroll (1974), Jacobs and Crotty (1983), Fleisher (1989) and
(for the UK) Thomas (1972), Thomas (1994), and Marsh et al. (1985).

assumptions. Prisoners, acting in organized groups, can under certain circumstances have much more power than they do in the situation Mathiesen describes, and specific contests are capable of either violently oppositional or legalistic form. In either case, Jacobs forces attention to implicit differences between prisons in different times and places, thereby severely questioning the application of any general trans-historical analysis of 'the Prison' as such, on which functionalist accounts characteristically rely. Neither history (Garland, 1985; Harding et al., 1985) nor contemporary analysis (for example Barak-Glantz, 1981; DiIulio, 1987; King, 1991) can sustain the assumption that all prisons are basically alike.

However, whether the particular version of such a case that Jacobs presents is in fact sufficient and definitive is questionable. Jacobs relies heavily on Shils's 'theory of mass society' (1975). Shils envisions an emergent social consensus centring on a 'heightened sensitivity on the part of the elite to the dignity and humanity of the masses' (1977: 6) such that formerly peripheral social situations like prisons (where 'village Chieftains' like Ragen exercised untrammelled power) come much more to the attention of the 'core' social and political institutions. Jacobs depicts the struggle of the prisoners' rights movement for recognition and legitimacy as being part of this general process, and he is able to point to a corresponding judicial activism (1977: 7; 1983) in the Supreme Court under Chief Justice Warren and elsewhere in support of the thesis. Meanwhile, other social changes (especially the spread of television and other mass media) accentuate the ever greater permeability of the prison wall to external influences and confirm, in Jacobs's view, 'the movement of the prison's place in society from the periphery towards the center' (1977: 6). Nevertheless, one may doubt whether the narrative that Jacobs relates is in fact a demonstration of his espoused theory. In the first place it seems doubtful that one should now accept the optimistic implicit teleology of Shils's views either in penal affairs or in other spheres. More specifically, many of the same developments noted by Jacobs are open to quite divergent interpretations. For example, the professionalization of prison management and the associated development of specialist quasi-technical expertise are regarded by Garland (1990: 185) as signalling rather the insulation of penality from the public sphere than its integration into the social 'core'. Certainly, Garland and others would argue, prisons do seem to have become more and more subject to 'modernizing' influences, largely in the direction of increasing 'managerialism', which they have in common with other bureaucracies and criminal justice agencies (see also Peters, 1986; Bottoms, 1995). Some of these influences—the politics of rights; the imposition of externally derived operating standards; the development of systems of inspection and financial accountability—do seem to suggest openings in the prison's formerly impenetrable walls. In most Western societies the kind of autonomy and untrammelled power once exercised by a Warden Ragen would be unimaginable now. But such influences may be more attenuated in the still enclosed and sequestered world of the prison, or translated into distinct penal dialects and forms. And in any case their impacts on the prison as a system of social control may be ambiguous and difficult to anticipate. Hence the relation between prison problems, penal policy, and other social changes would seem rather more complex and uneven than Jacobs's theoretical apparatus (as distinct from his rich and subtle substantive account) allows. Many of the most basic questions involved in determining how change occurs in prisons, and how one would translate between the 'macro' level of social changes and their realization at the level of the lived reality of social relations in the everyday life of institutions seem unresolved. For these reasons a further activity of theoretical reflection remains necessary—a task to which our comments below are directed.

Our selective review of studies of 'captive society' suggests that the theoretical and substantive renewal of prison studies necessitates stepping outside the boundaries of penology as a field of study in order to achieve a more synthetic and interpretively powerful position. To speak about the problems of order and control in prisons today raises questions of power, of unintended consequences, of the impact of modern managerial techniques, and of the relationship between social structure and personal agency that prison studies have yet to confront adequately, but which are the very stuff of modern social theory.

Prisons and modern social theory

The problem of subjugation is not the same as the problem of ordering.

(Rabinow, 1984: 279)

We have chosen to organize this discussion in terms of a particular conceptual problem, namely the character of 'social order' in prisons. This further entails a number of subsidiary issues, including the different kinds of order that are observable or possible, the distributions of power on which each is predicated, and so forth. Our selective review of earlier work on these matters (even though it is selective in the sense of having referred only to those contributions which we regard as most fruitful for our purposes and from which we believe something of special importance can be learned) has left most of the key questions unresolved. That review suggests that studies of imprisonment, in common with other areas of social inquiry, tend to stand on one or other side of certain dualisms: functionalism (Sykes) versus conflict theories (Irwin), structure (Mathiesen, 1965) versus agency (Cohen and Taylor) as organizing principles; objectivity (Jacobs) versus empathy and naturalism (Cohen and Taylor) as modes of inquiry. At stake is the question of how one theorizes the problems of order, power, and change in penal institutions, and of whether one can indeed grasp them in such a way as to hold simultaneously in view both the minutiae of lived experience and everyday practice within prisons and their larger and more durable structural properties.

Foucault and the technologies of penal power

In the search for more powerful, synthetic theoretical approaches to the problem of order in prisons one cannot but consider (albeit briefly here) the influence of Michel Foucault whose work, as Garland notes (1990: 131) now constitutes a 'central reference point in the sociology of punishment'. This is not the place however for a full review of Foucault's theoretical position or historical scholarship, on both of which a large body of exposition and commentary already exists.[20] Rather, our concern must lie solely with the capacity of his theorization of power relations in prisons to illuminate or revise the questions at hand in the present project.

Foucault's interest in imprisonment centres upon the view that the construction of 'complete and austere institutions' is both emblematic of and instrumental in the diffusion of 'disciplinary' power in modern societies. The twin concepts of 'confinement' and

[20] See, *inter alia*, Dreyfus and Rabinow (1982), Cousins and Hussain (1984), Smart (1985), Garland (1990).

'panopticism' delimit, for Foucault, key aspects of strategies of power and control in modernity. Amongst the primary features of penal control which Foucault identifies are the design of buildings (factories and schools as well as prisons and asylums), the rigorous planning and surveillance of routinized and scheduled activity, and the deployment of the technical forms of expertise claimed by the 'human sciences' in the classification, examination, and correctional training of individuals.

On this view the internal ordering of prisons must be considered in terms of the 'micro-physics' of power operative in sustaining their regimes, timetables and strategies of work, discipline, education, segregative control, and so on. For Foucault, the prison from Bentham's time forward is one of the most complete realizations of a 'political anatomy of detail', subjecting its captives to uninterrupted surveillance and a panoply of disciplinary strategies of isolation, work, and other 'penitentiary techniques'. As Garland summarizes:

> The principles of surveillance, observation, and inspection and of disciplinary training, examination and normalization—together with the physical, architectural, and organizational forms in which they are embodied—are presented to us so clearly and in such detail that we can begin to understand the material practices upon which modern penal institutions depend.
>
> (Garland, 1990: 152)

Foucault's insistence on the detail of disciplinary technique is indeed a key feature of his contribution to the analysis of prisons and other institutions. For example, his concentration on timetables and routines is a matter whose importance we seek to elaborate in later chapters as a way of understanding the definition and institutional response to 'control incidents' in prisons. If, for Foucault, 'Power is articulated directly onto time; it assures its control and guarantees its use' (1979a: 160), any act or omission which disrupts the prison routine is axiomatically defined as troublesome. Foucault further remarks (ibid., 235–6) that:

> The prison has neither exterior nor gap; it cannot be interrupted, except when the task is totally completed; its action on the individual must be uninterrupted: an increasing discipline; . . . it gives almost total power over the prisoners; it has its internal mechanisms of repression and punishment: a despotic discipline.

Foucault's fascination for the detail of penal technique leads Garland to claim that 'Foucault addresses himself to the minutiae of penal practice and the intricacies of institutional life in a way which recalls—and goes beyond—the classic studies of prison life offered by Clemmer, Sykes, and Goffman.'

Whilst we fully acknowledge the insight and subtlety of Foucault's writing, however, we are not persuaded that this claim for Foucault's superior understanding of the internal ordering of prisons can be sustained, at least in the form his argument assumes in *Discipline and Punish*. There are several reasons for this.

First, as Garland himself notes (1990: 160), many readings of Foucault make a sweeping assumption about the general applicability of his contentions—an interpretation that his own vocabulary (for instance, when he speaks without qualification of 'the prison') at times encourages. Yet *Discipline and Punish* is ultimately concerned less with prisons as such than with 'the diffusion of disciplinary mechanisms *throughout the social body*' and especially during the first half of the nineteenth century. In fact Foucault is often very wary, in lectures and interviews, about being pressed into extending his analyses forward to the present. Moreover, apart from some remarks in interviews (see for example Gordon, 1980), there are very few references to (still less any sustained analysis of) late twentieth century prisons anywhere in Foucault's major published works (but see 1979a: 30).[21] This raises a number of problems of historical interpretation. For example Garland's own analysis in *Punishment and Welfare* (1985) of the 'uniformity' of Victorian penality in England somewhat compromises Foucault's insistence on scrutiny, *dressage*, and individualized normalization in *Discipline and Punish*. Similarly, subsequent developments towards professional bureaucratic management and aggregate processing (Feeley, 1979; Peters, 1986; Garland, 1990) suggest that contemporary prisons are not infrequently unconcerned with the prisoners' 'soul' in the way that Foucault is often taken to imply: it can be the case that Big Brother is ignoring you. One should treat this objection with some caution, of course. In Foucault's later work 'normalization' is clearly a less 'psychological' concept than it is sometimes read as being (or than it was in *Discipline and Punish*). Indeed, in the essay 'On Governmentality' (1979b) 'normalization' refers principally to the invention of population statistics, which enabled the depiction of individuals (as 'data') as things distributed

[21] This comment remains true notwithstanding Foucault's significant political activity in the *Groupe d'Information sur les Prisons*.

around a 'norm' (see also 1984: 266). In this vein, Foucault comes more often to use the terms 'government' and 'governmentality' in a way that anticipates and has much in common with the subsequent concern with 'managerialism' (see also Rabinow, 1984: 14–23; Smart, 1985: 127–32).

Secondly, Garland further acknowledges, in criticism of Foucault, that the latter's fascination with the image of the panopticon at times leads him to write as if the exercise of complete domination were a practical possibility. Thus Garland comments (1990: 160):

Foucault seems to assert that 'Benthamism' is, in fact, a deep description of the actual nature of modern punishment. Bentham's vision turns out to be a reflection of the very nature of things—we live in a thoroughly calculated, controlled, panoptic world—and Foucault's approach is to analyse social institutions in these terms.

In might be added that Foucault's methodological concentration on discourses recovered through textual traces is at some distance from an empirical sociology of social relations, oppositions, and competitions in the daily conduct of prison life. It is true that Foucault often points to the possibility of continual, dispersed oppositions to power. In one interview he comments that the 'plan' of a disciplinary institution and its real social relations are two different things: 'Fortunately for human imagination, things are a little more complicated than that' (1984: 255). This is also a theme of the late work on sexuality where he comments 'It is not that life has been totally integrated into techniques that govern and administer it; it constantly escapes them' (1984: 265). In general, therefore, he insists that he does not wish to present the operation of disciplinary power as complete and ineluctable; he does not wish to be read as assuming its 'success'. Rather he explains that he is concerned to analyze those movements in thought in which the *will towards* such complete administrative control first comes to the fore. So, for example (again in the essay on 'Governmentality' (1979b: 17)) Foucault explains that the early theorists of government were so preoccupied with 'ordering' in part precisely because they had 'discovered' something that resisted their will, namely the intrinsic and obstinate regularities of populations and economies. Yet his early substantive work on the prison more often suggests something closer to complete domination (*à la* Adorno's 'totally administered society'). If we take Foucault's later qualifications of his views with appropriate seriousness, it would seem that we should consider not so much the utter domination of the prison by state authority as the 'governmentalisation' of its operation (1979b: 20).

Thirdly, Giddens (1984: 154) criticizes Foucault's account of agency, both on the general level of theory and specifically amongst those undergoing (or, we would add, for that matter trying to impose) penal discipline. Foucault does state that power is always 'a way of acting upon an acting subject' (1982: 220). Yet, in Giddens's view, Foucault's presentation of the machine-like, depersonalized nature of disciplinary 'strategy' leads him 'into difficulties' in that:

Foucault's 'bodies' are not agents. Even the most rigorous form of discipline presumes that those subject to them are capable human agents, which is why they have to be 'educated', whereas machines are merely designed.

(Giddens, 1984: 154)

Giddens fully recognizes (and indeed elaborates in some detail) the importance of Foucault's concern with 'timing and spacing', but he goes on to compare Foucault's account of such matters unfavourably with Goffman's. This is partly a matter of the distinctiveness which Goffman attributes to the total institution. Where Foucault plays upon the continuity between penal institutions and other spheres of social life, Goffman is concerned to show how they 'also stand out in relief against those other contexts' (Giddens, 1984: 155) and for that reason pose special problems of transition, adjustment, 'civil death', and so on. But arguably also Foucault actually provides little theoretical *reason* (beyond his precautionary assertions) to anticipate resistance, subversion or innovation amongst the confined: 'Foucault's bodies do not have faces' (Giddens, 1984: 157). Giddens (ibid.: 156) suggests to the contrary that 'In carceral organizations the dialectic of control is still considerable' (a point which we explain and expand upon in some detail below). In brief, Giddens insists that the prisoners retain some means, however attenuated, of influencing the actions of their captors. Giddens argues that even in situations where 'that autonomy specifically characteristic of the human agent—the capacity to have acted otherwise' is severely limited, it is rarely negated entirely (1984: 156)—even if it is registered, as Goffman suggests, only in such 'secondary adjustments' as withdrawal into mute recalcitrance.[22]

[22] One might add that even in their respective critical commentaries on Foucault's views both Garland and Giddens themselves manage to minimize the scope for

In reality prisons quite commonly seethe and boil with human agency, passion, and conflict—in ways that are not infrequently magnified and rendered more intense precisely by the constraints and frustrations encountered there (cf. King and McDermott, 1990). Garland acknowledges (1990: 173) this when he comments that:

By studying more closely the nature of resistance, Foucault would have done something to balance his account of power . . . In particular he might have been led to describe the operation of power upon individuals as being less of an 'automatic' process and more a matter of micro-political conflict in which the individual subject may draw upon alternative sources of power and subjectivity to resist that imposed by the institution.

Amongst such 'alternative sources', as we will go on to show, are those which place in question, and call for further reflection upon, the *legitimacy* of the institution, its rules, and practices. The problem of legitimation may be one which at least implicitly underpins the concerns of prison sociology from Sykes onwards, though it is largely absent from Foucault's analysis. None the less its importance in interpreting variations in the nature of penal order and control requires careful elaboration (Sparks, 1994a; Sparks and Bottoms, 1995). We return to this question in some detail below.

At this point therefore we move from the exegesis of existing prison sociologies towards our own attempts to develop a contemporary perspective. We have learned something fundamental from each of the views that we have summarized thus far. From Sykes, for example, we retain the ironic recognition of a disparity between the formal and actual dispositions of power in prisons; and also the central importance to prisoners of the various 'pains of imprisonment', and their attempts to mitigate them. From Mathiesen we take the tortuous games of mutual influence in which the members of a 'disrupted society' can be ensnared, and the constraints and

agency in prisons. Thus e.g. Giddens comments that 'In prisons or asylums the "disciplining of bodies" comes close to describing what goes on' and suggests that the 'face work', the need 'to coax' subordinates, and 'strategies of control that have in some part to be elaborated by agents on the spot', are less relevant in prisons than in other forms of disciplinary supervision such as workplaces and schools (1984: 157). This seems to us to concede too much to Foucault, and to be based on a rather naive understanding of what does go on in prisons (in disregard of much of what Sykes and others had already shown). In this sense Garland's claim for Foucault's superior insight (as against Sykes or Goffman) is also quite wrong *if* by that one means (as is commonly meant) using *Discipline and Punish* as the basis for some sort of empirical sociology of social relations in institutions.

frustrations that follow; we note also the importance of prisoners'
appeals to established norms in a given society, especially with
regard to what is seen as 'fair'. From Irwin and Jacobs we draw
acknowledgement of the tense and shifting relations between the
prison and its surrounding environments, and the (often unintended, sometimes disastrous) impact upon the institutions's interior life of changing practices of management. From Cohen and
Taylor and from Goffman we retain a sharp sense of the ways in
which the unending routines of an encompassing institution can be
subverted for the sake of survival, and hence of the subtly active
nature of the problem of 'doing' time; and from Foucault we draw
the intricate operation of architecture, schedules, and forms of
expertise in the construction of penal power.

Yet we remain unconvinced that these eclectic sources 'add up'
to a coherent theoretical understanding of the 'ordering' of prisons,
still less of departures from or challenges to the imposed order.
Moreover the tensions written into the 'tradition' (between the
macro and the micro, determinism and voluntariness, structure and
agency) are too sharp readily to be reconciled. Our tasks in this
book involve us in theorizing observed aspects of order and disorder in prisons, and hence in exploring the connection between the
structural or systemic dimension of such problems and their contingent, local occurrence in specific times and places between real people. In pursuing that ambition we have found it necessary to step
outside the existing literature of imprisonment in order to bring it
into dialogue with the more general concerns of current social theory. For us this has meant, in particular, a number of tasks: first an
encounter with the social theory of Anthony Giddens; and second
the elaboration of two conceptual issues whose bearing on prison
life we think has not been made sufficiently clear, namely, the
problem of legitimacy and the problem of risk.[23]

Structuration theory and the prison

Why then have we found Giddens's 'theory of structuration' valuable in developing our views on order and disorder in prisons?
What has excited us about it, and what are its concrete implications

[23] As indicated in ch. 1, our thinking on these issues has developed considerably
since we embarked on this project. Relevant publications include Bottoms *et al.*,
1990; Hay and Sparks, 1992a, 1992b; Sparks and Bottoms, 1995.

for research? Before addressing these questions directly let us enter a few words of caution. We do not propose here to offer a full exposition of Giddens's views. This he has done himself in voluminous writings. We summarize aspects of his outlook to a specific purpose. Neither do we intend to embroil ourselves in the nuances of the increasingly large and intricate debate concerning the virtues and shortcomings of Giddens's project.[24] We do not feel it necessary to sign up for a camp or team, nor to insist that Giddens's 'correct views on everything' can simply be taken up and applied point by point to prisons, or indeed to any other sphere of social life. For all we know Giddens may never have set foot inside a prison, albeit that 'carceral institutions' occupy a position of some significance in his views and debates with his critics (not always in a way with which we are especially happy, as we go on to show). Nevertheless, we are convinced that aspects of his framework are 'good to think with' for those who have stepped behind the wall. In many respects the concepts which we principally take from Giddens are those which we have already identified as being important for our purposes but which our reading of his work enables us to render in more explicit and systematic fashion: order, structure, action, systems, routines, power, constraint, control.

Order (again)

It seems clear that whilst the problem of order has animated much sociological inquiry it has often been thought of in misleading and

[24] See e.g. the collections by Held and Thompson (1989) and Bryant and Jary (1991). For us as active researchers it is of secondary interest to seek to establish whether Giddens's views are wholly original, or to establish every point of similarity or difference with other authors to whom he has been compared. Giddens has himself on a number of occasions advocated very much the pragmatic use of his work which we intend to adopt, e.g. when he suggests that his ideas 'should be utilized only in a selective way in empirical work and should be seen more as a sensitizing device than as providing detailed guidelines for research procedure' (1989: 294); or again, 'In many more confined [sic] arenas of empirical research it is not especially helpful to drag in a large apparatus of abstract concepts. I like most those . . . in which concepts . . . are used in a sparing and critical fashion' (1991: 213). We would however strongly maintain our position against those who would argue that Giddens's views are not of much use in developing empirical work (e.g. Gregson, 1989). It is quite clearly Giddens's view that 'abstract issues of social theory do have a definite bearing upon concrete problems of social analysis' (1982: 212). In any case we will take issue with Gregson's view that 'it would be hard to convince anyone engaged in empirical research of the intrinsic value of [Giddens's] points' (1989: 240) simply by indicating their value to us.

confusing terms. On the one hand some writers assume that the possibility of the descent into the 'war of each against all' haunts all of social life. Sykes at times clearly seems to imagine that, in prisons, this is the alternative to the system-maintaining functions that he identifies. On the other hand, it has sometimes been held that for order to exist we must postulate some form of universal normative consensus (see Giddens's critical account of such views 1976: 95–8). In the prison context, such a view would naturally give rise to the assumption that we have already criticized earlier in this chapter, namely that no 'order' is imaginable in prison other than a spurious one imposed entirely by force and threat. Giddens proposes instead that if we are to retain the term 'order' we must limit its scope to a 'loose synonym for "pattern" or the antithesis of "chaos" ' (1976: 98). This does indeed seem a sensible starting-point, though it is not in itself very informative. In a similar vein, Peter Young in a valuable reflection upon the concept of social control as applied to imprisonment, modestly proposes that we consider 'order' as meaning 'that pattern of relationships that forms a whole' (1987: 106). 'Control', meanwhile, signifies those mechanisms that 'create and maintain this pattern' (*loc. cit.*). Thus:

Order can be achieved by a variety of different means of control and, similarly, the use of a specific means of control does not mechanically result in the maintenance of a particular type of order. Thus, although there is a necessary conceptual linkage between the two, the actual empirical or real-world relationship is various and contingent . . . This can lead to an exaggerated emphasis on the applied mechanics of social control, without any, or very little, attention being given to what control is for—what type of order one is seeking.[25]

(Young, 1987: 99)

The notion of 'order' plainly implies continuity and durability over time. As Giddens notes, order connotes 'reproduction'. In this sense the 'macro' dimensions of social institutions—their 'structural properties' (1984: 17), their systemic patterns, their 'fixity'—are logically

---

[25] This preoccupation with 'applied mechanics', usually in the form of a primary concern with controlling 'difficult' *individuals*, has historically been one of the features of official discourse on prisons that sociologists are most apt to criticize (for relevant discussions, see e.g. King and McDermott, 1990; Scraton et al., 1991; Sparks and Bottoms, 1995). One of the things that most interested us about the CRC Report (Home Office, 1984) and latterly about Woolf (1991) is that they seem in some measure to depart form this tendency, in a way that opens more receptively to other kinds of social enquiry.

dependent upon the coordination and reproduction of everyday conduct. It is not just that individuals' actions are 'caused' or brought about by institutions and powers. The reverse is also true: prison life, like routinized activities everywhere, only 'happens' because real-life, flesh-and-blood people make it happen. Giddens seeks to grasp this complex relationship in terms of what he calls the 'duality of structure', according to which 'the structural properties of social systems are both medium and outcome of the practices they recursively organize' (1984: 25). Giddens's reconstruction of social theory around this 'duality' stems from a profound dissatisfaction with the same 'dualisms' (structure and action; objectivism and subjectivism) which we have detected in the literature on prisons.

'Structures', in Giddens's terms are to be thought of not as 'things' but rather as a 'virtual order' consisting of 'rules and resources recursively implicated in the reproduction of social systems' (1984: 377).[26] In terms of the 'duality of structure' it is true *both* that 'structures are constituted through action' *and* that 'action is constituted structurally' (Giddens, 1976: 161). It is clear that 'structure' has a different sense here than in many usages—it does not refer to something 'imposed' ineluctably from without. Neither are 'structure' and 'system' at all the same thing. Whereas the notion of 'structure' as 'rules and resources' addresses itself to *how* the reproduction of social life is accomplished, the term 'system' refers to the 'patterning of social relations across time–space' that is the outcome of those 'reproduced practices' (see Giddens, 1984: 377; Bryant and Jary, 1991: 7). Hence 'the rules and resources drawn upon in the production and reproduction of social action are at the same time the means of system reproduction' (Giddens, 1984: 19). Hence also the proper domain of study of the social sciences is the investigation of 'social practices ordered across space and time' (Giddens, 1984: 2).

The key aspects of Giddens's views which we regard as importantly applicable in the study of prisons are, briefly, as follows:

[26] Some further aspects of this definition are worth elaborating. For the individual actor, 'structure exists only as memory traces, the organic basis of human knowledgeability, and as instantiated in action'. Yet precisely because individuals' knowledgeability about how to 'go on' in the world *is* intimately connected with the reproduction of social systems, so 'to study structures . . . is to study major aspects of the transformation/mediation relations which influence social and system integration' (Giddens 1984: 377).

1. Although the 'structural properties' of social institutions 'stretch away' across time and space and exceed any individual's capacity to transform them, they are not therefore fixed or static. Thus 'reproduction' neither signifies the 'consolidation of consensus' (1984: 24), nor implies that the institution which is 'reproduced' is unchanging. Instead reproduction is always itself open to investigation. A question of special interest concerns the 'circuits of reproduction' which permit the continuity of practices over time (as well as actions or events which break, interrupt or transform such circuits).

2. There is therefore no inherent separateness between the 'macro' dimensions of social analysis and the study of everyday life in particular contexts *because* the reproduction of institutionalized social practices is accomplished in and through the routine doings of knowledgeable human subjects. Even so, when certain practices are highly coordinated towards their own reproduction we may speak appropriately of 'institutions' and of 'organizations'. These are practices which 'bite deeply into space and time' and which enjoy a high degree of 'fixity' or 'systemness'. Prisons are institutions *par excellence* on this definition, as well as in more general uses of the term.

3. Most activity, although 'always and everywhere' the outcome of knowledgeable human agency, is not 'directly motivated'. It consists not of separate decisions but occurs within the 'flow' of everyday life; and, crucially, neither are all of its outcomes those which the agents intend, anticipate or desire. Rather most human activity belongs within the domain of 'practical consciousness' which 'consists of all the things that actors know tacitly about how to "go on" in the contexts of social life without being able to give them direct discursive expression' (1984: xxiii). Elsewhere we have used the example of the footballer who can score an extraordinary goal yet hardly be able to say how it was done as an illustration of this point. We did so in the context of an article suggesting that the complexity and refinement of what prison officers do often goes unremarked because there seems to be no vocabulary for talking about it (Hay and Sparks, 1991a).

4. Neither the knowledgeability of actors nor their freedom to act are unconstrained: they are preceded by 'unacknowledged conditions' and succeeded by an inherent inability to anticipate or control all the possible consequences of acting (not least because other

actors also act). This raises two further points that are central to Giddens's outlook. First there is the question of unintended consequences. Giddens is at pains to insist that his stress on agency should not detract from the recognition that social life is pervaded by the unintended outcomes of action, some of which indeed 'feed back' in regular ways into the reproduction of institutional practices. At least some such consequences are 'perverse' from the agent's point of view; they confound or contradict their intention (1984: 9–14). The most important sort of perverse consequences, for the present study, would be the possible unintended outcomes of particular control strategies in prisons. Is it possible for prison regimes (for example by over stringent enforcement of rules) to incite or provoke precisely the kinds of opposition or instability that they are most concerned to quell? (This question is also intrinsic to the discussion of the problem of legitimacy in prisons. We outline the relevance of this concept below.) The second key point raised by Giddens's discussion of agency and intention is that of constraint. Giddens does not accept a simple opposition between agency ad constraint. Even under severe physical and social constraints people remain agents, in Giddens's view. At the same time, even where obvious or extreme restrictions are lacking, agency is never in fact unconstrained. Giddens distinguishes three senses of constraint. 'Material constraint' alludes to the limits imposed on action by bodily capacities and by the material environment (and in prisons, of course, the material environment is precisely designed to constrain, both from the point of view of control and of departure). '(Negative) sanctions' (ranging from the threat of violence or even death to the expression of mild disapproval) derive from the use of power to achieve conformity or acquiescence. 'Structural constraint' refers to the way in which any situated actor confronts the structural properties of social systems as 'objective' or 'given': they cannot just be changed by an act of will (1984: 174–9; see also 1989: 258). Giddens summarizes his views on this point as follows:

The theory of structuration is not a series of generalizations about how far 'free action' is possible in respect of 'social constraint'. Rather it is an attempt to provide the conceptual means of analyzing the often delicate and subtle interlacings of reflexively organized action and institutional constraint.

(Giddens, 1991: 204)

In this study we will find ourselves in the presence of all three forms of constraint on many occasions. Prisons inevitably involve 'material constraint'; but one of the prisons we studied used it in a particularly deliberate way as a control strategy. Sanctions too are of the essence of most penal control strategies (albeit that they are often intimately enmeshed with 'perverse consequences'). Similarly, there can be few social settings in which 'structural constraints' are as evident or impinge so clearly on actors' awareness as in a prison. Nevertheless we take it as important that the nature and intensity of such constraints can vary markedly as between different prisons, with appreciable consequences for their habitability and the well-being of those concerned.

5. Giddens's concerns with the reproduction of social systems, *and* with everyday knowledgeability, suggest particularly close attention to the routine deployment of time. Routine is a key term in Giddens's outlook, and it has several applications. In the first place it is a basic and generic feature of human existence. The very idea of 'practices' and of 'day-to-day life' suggest a predictable, reiterative quality. In Giddens's view routinization is a precondition for the 'ontological security' of the actor and for his/her 'trust' in the reliability and durability of the life-world. We are, as it were, doomed to trust that the world is sufficiently predictable and solid for us to be able to act capably within it, to develop 'mutual knowledge', and so on. In the absence of such security the actor risks being 'swamped' by anxiety; and for a given individual or group the obverse of routine is the 'critical situation' in which the continuity of the social world is thrown into doubt. Giddens has however been criticized (for example by Urry, 1991: 168) for one-sidedly focusing on the reassuring and consoling aspects of routines rather than on their sometimes deadening tedium, and the many ways in which actors might seek to escape them. *Both* the centrality of routines *and* moments of resistance to them would seem to be especially important aspects of the prison situation (see further below).

But routinization is also a specific feature of *organizations*. For Giddens, the 'modern period is the era *par excellence* of organizations' (1987: 149). Organizations (offices, factories, schools, hospitals, prisons) direct the activities of their members via the precise control of time; their hierarchies are reflected and sustained in their 'zoning' of space; they monitor their own activities through surveillance considered both as the collation and storage of information (files, records, inventories, accounts) and through 'direct supervision' especially of subordinate members. Organizations use 'specifically designed locales' (1987: 157) to facilitate their continuous activity. Such buildings (of which prisons are an obvious instance, although not for Giddens, unlike Foucault, an archetypal one) are 'power containers: physical settings which through the interaction of setting and social conduct generate administrative power' (*loc. cit.*). Prisons are unusual amongst modern organizations in that whilst they share or even accentuate most of the focal features of organizations in general (bounded locales, timetables, zoned spaces, information storage, supervision) they remain not purely 'administrative'. Instead they continue to involve 'the direct control of the means of force' (1987: 164), though even there the significance of force is 'greatly reduced as compared to the extension of impersonally regulated procedures' (*loc. cit.*).

6. A modern organization, for Giddens, is a system whose main features are specifically designed to 'maximise control of system reproduction' (1987: 155): it is *there* in order to 'stretch' across time–space. In this particular sense 'The problem of order *is* the issue of time–space distanciation' (1987: 153; our emphasis). This inelegant term is therefore close to the heart of Giddens's concerns. It addresses the ways in which social systems 'bite into space and time' (1984: 171) and the 'mechanisms of societal integration' (ibid.: 181) on which their doing so relies. That is, Giddens tries to reconsider a question ('the problem of order') which is often posed in such a way as to sound unanswerably enigmatic ('How is society possible?') in more concrete terms. We can ask instead, just how do particular 'circuits of reproduction' (especially those features of organizations designed to coordinate the use of time and control the deployment of activity in space) actually operate? Giddens also introduces, though he does not develop it much, the notion of the 'sense of place', as a way of addressing, in some contexts, the complex of connections between the everyday activities of individuals, the larger trajectory of their biographies, and the special features of the locales in which they act. As he puts it:

The co-ordination of the daily paths of individuals within a given range of locales, plus what some researchers have called a 'sense of place', are concretized aspects of the duality of structure. The dialectic of 'daily path' and 'life path' is the way in which the continuity of the biography of the individual is expressed in, and also expresses, the continuity of institutional reproduction. A sense of place seems of major importance in the sustaining of ontological security precisely because it provides a psychological tie between the biography of the individual and the locales that are the settings of the time–space paths through which that individual moves.

(Giddens 1984, p. 367)

That is to say, sometimes particular locales are intimately bound up with the biography of individuals, their understandings of the world, and the reproduction of social life within that locale. All this is of course most likely to happen (1) when the 'locale' in question is fairly small, and bounded, and (2) when many of those spending time in the locale have been there (or been back and forth from there) for an extended period, so that they know intimately aspects of the history, traditions, and culture of the place, and significant events which, in the past, have helped to shape the way that social life is now lived there. Long-term prisons, of course, fulfil many of these conditions—indeed, as we shall see in the later chapters, some at least of the differences between Albany and Long Lartin derived from the ways in which life there was seen by their inhabitants as being imbued by their histories. They had significance *as places*; going there as a prisoner or working there as a member of staff meant somewhat different things in each case.

But as many social scientists have observed (including Giddens— see for example Giddens, 1990; Lash and Urry, 1987, 1994; Harvey 1989) in the modern world place is, generally speaking, of declining significance for individuals in terms of 'trust' and 'ontological security'. Instead, increasingly we try to organize the world using abstract categories which transcend place, since modern transport and communications technology enable people to interact with one another fairly easily across vast distances. Giddens expresses this as the radically increased time–space distanciation of the modern social world, i.e. the markedly increased 'stretching of social systems across time–space' (where 'social system' is defined as 'the patterning of social relations across time–space, understood as reproduced practices' (Giddens 1984: 377)). *Managerialism*, as we saw in chapter 1, is an increasingly important feature in understanding modern prisons; in the context of the present discussion, it is not hard to see that managerialism is intimately connected to the increased 'stretching' of social systems across time–space (see further below on various characteristics of modern managerialism).

That also means, however, that managerialism—with its reliance on abstract systems and categories—will typically not be too interested in the more 'dense' social relations, and the sensitivity to local historical traditions and past events, implied by the concept of 'a sense of place'. Paradoxically, modern long-term prisons are at the same time *both* bounded locales in which many participants have a strong 'sense of place', *and* important elements within a much more abstract, non-place-oriented national prison system. Both features are part of the way the modern dispersal prison 'bites into time and space', and both must—if we follow Giddens—be understood as part of the problem of order in long-term prisoners. (For a fuller discussion of some of these issues, in the context of 'environmental criminology' see Bottoms 1993; Bottoms and Wiles 1994).

7. Rather in the same way that Foucault speaks of the positive, productive aspects of power, Giddens remarks that power is *not just* a matter of one party imposing his/her will on another through force, sanction, and constraint. In its simplest definition power is 'the means of getting things done, very definitely enablement as well as constraint' (1984: 175) (cf. the centrality in recent political discourse of the term *empowerment* variously applied to parents, pupils, social work clients, victims of crime, prisoners). More generally, Giddens writes:

Power is the capacity to achieve outcomes; whether or not these are connected to purely sectional interests is not germane to its definition. Power is not, as such, an obstacle to freedom or emancipation but is their very medium—although it would be foolish . . . to ignore its constraining properties. The existence of power presumes structures of domination whereby power that 'flows smoothly' (and is, as it were 'unseen') operates. The development of force, or its threat, is thus not the type case of the use of power.

(Giddens, 1984: 257)

Prisoners naturally could be forgiven for emphasizing the constraining aspects of power, of which the severely reduced autonomy implicit in prison routines daily reminds them. Moreover it is in the use of force and the imposition of sanctions at moments of conflict that power becomes visible. Nevertheless, variations in the frequency and intensity of such impositions, by contrast with the 'smooth flow' of power under 'normal' circumstances are close to the heart of the concerns of prison sociology since Sykes. More particularly Giddens (1984: 16) comments:

Power within social systems that enjoy some continuity over time and space presumes regularized relations of autonomy and dependence between actors or collectivities in contexts of social interaction. But all forms of dependence offer some resources whereby those who are subordinate can influence the activities of their superiors. This is what I call the *dialectic of control* in social systems.

Although Giddens's references to the dialectic of control are in the main rather brief (see for example 1982: 199; 1984: 16; 1987: 162–5) it is clearly for him a key aspect of the theory of structuration. In like manner we consider that it is a notion which may be very fruitful to the social analysis of imprisonment. Giddens uses this concept to show, for example, why Weber's ideal type of a formally rational bureaucracy looks so little like what really goes on in bureaucratic organizations (1982: 204). Similarly he concludes his own examination of organizations and administrative power by indicating that their tendencies towards hierarchy and oligarchy are 'always accompanied by countervailing tendencies towards the recapture of power by those on the lower levels' (1987: 162). Likewise, we believe that real prisons are hardly ever very much like the ideal-typical 'carceral institution'. Much as E. P. Thompson (1968) depicted the class domination of early English industrial capitalism as having been 'warrened end to end' by the working class, so prisons are 'warrened' and rendered complex and unpredictable by the human agency of both captives and custodians. Let us then briefly flesh out our view of the application of Giddens's views to understanding prisons, returning to the idea of the dialectic of control shortly below.

Giddens 'on prisons'?

First, if the 'duality of structure' is, as we believe, an apt way of characterizing social action generally, this is not less true in prisons than elsewhere. In Giddens's terms action and structure entail one another. Structure is both the medium and outcome of practice. It consists of the 'rules and resources' drawn upon in the constitution of action. Giddens has been criticized on grounds of vagueness in this formulation, for example by John Thompson (1989). However, in our view the ambiguity of the term 'rule' can also be productive, at least in the prison context. It can mean both the formal rules governing institutional conduct (such as those in prisons which stipulate correct procedures and authorize the imposition of sanctions) and the mutual knowledges and expectancies that prisoners and staff have of one another. Both Sykes's 'system of action' and Mathiesen's account of 'censoriousness' can fruitfully be thought of in this way, as exploring the boundary between explicit and implicit kinds of rule following. Giddens comments that a large task of empirical work is to try to render an account of what the 'rules and resources' operative in any given circumstance might be. For instance in our study, examples of 'rules' in practice might include not just the 'Prison Rules' but also the various forms of local culture or tradition claimed by the members of staff of different institutions which they summarize as their 'ethos' or 'way' (terms of some importance in the comparative discussion in subsequent chapters), and which may issue in different uses of discretion. Conversely, prisoners sometimes legitimate their demands on staff by reference to what was done on another occasion, or the way things used to be round here, or what is allowed in another prison. Similarly 'resources' here might comprise (*inter alia*) both the kinds of recourse made to formally available powers and sanctions and the prestige of status of particular post holders ('authoritative resources') and the uses made of the physical plant, layout, and surveillance technologies of the prison itself ('allocative resources').

Second, all the practices, episodes, and events that we are concerned with in this book involve the study of agency in something close to Giddens's sense of the term. Giddens is concerned to show that human beings are almost always agents: they have knowledge of what they are doing, they exercise choice, and what they do can 'make a difference'. Indeed, Giddens uses prison illustrations to argue that even under the most extreme kinds of constraint persons remain agents (1981: 63; 1982: 198). John Thompson(1989) ripostes that there are circumstances in which the *feasible* options open to the individual reduce to one. He gives the example of an unemployed youth forced to go on a training scheme—Marx's 'dull compulsion' of economic relations. In that case, he argues, the relevance of the concept of agency dissolves (1989: 73). We accept, with Thompson, that there are many occasions when economic and political constraints operate with crushing force. Prisons are replete with examples of this. Giddens, in his determination to show the tenacity of human agency and to insist that persons are never mere dopes, dupes, victims, or 'bearers' of structures, seems tempted at times to understate such compulsions. Yet, with Giddens, we continue to see the question of agency in prisons, even under some fairly exceptional conditions, as relevant. We will provide many examples of circumstances in which people's choices are much more severely constrained than simply over whether to take a given job, however unattractive. These include cases involving long-term segregation and solitary confinement, physical restraint, and so on. The prisoners in such conditions see themselves and are seen by others in many ways—loosely as heroes, villains or fools[27]—but *never* (unless perhaps they are dismissed as entirely 'mad' and hence as the victim of an *inner* compulsion) as other than agents. Indeed, it is precisely the struggle to maintain a sense of personal agency in the face of overweening institutional constraint which motivates and sustains some of prisoners' most intractable contests with the system, long after they would seem to have 'lost'. Given that some prisoners will undertake a 'project' of obdurate resistance in the full knowledge that this will deliver an extended period of segregation, we are much less ready than Thompson appears to be to legislate over what represents a feasible course of action (see also Sparks, 1994b). It is our general view that the forms of knowledge-ability exercised both by prisoners and prison staff have too rarely been fully acknowledged in the research literature, perhaps to the detriment of both. Too often prison sociology has contented itself with producing anodyne typologies of 'adaptations' or 'argot roles' amongst prisoners (or conversely the pressures on staff to be a 'Good Joe') rather than exploring the implicit knowledgeability or rationality of their actions.

Third, Giddens's focus on the coordination of daily activity in terms of temporal and spatial organization, and especially on institutional reproduction via routinization, has special resonance in prisons (as Sykes, once again, noted with great acuity, though not in precisely these terms). Prisons, *par excellence* are 'bounded locales'. Moreover, the regionalization of activity within them is of the first importance. The organization of activity in its proper times and places (the movement of prisoners, the taking of meals, the locking up and counting of prisoners at night, the scheduling of times for visits, work, exercise, and so on) is of the essence of the definition of order and control as these are conceived of and

---

[27] This expression comes from O. Klapp (1956), 'Heroes, villains and fools as agents of social control'.

implemented by prison staff. Many infractions of prison discipline precisely arise when staff feel that the smooth running of the routine is in jeopardy, for example because prisoners are 'too slow' in going to work, or finishing showering, or leaving a television room. This is in part, clearly, a matter of compliance and the need felt by office holders to have their authority acknowledged; but it also reflects upon the importance to the organization of the routine as such. Whether prisoners too have an interest in the reproduction of the routine (either for the sake of 'ontological security' or more pragmatically for the reliable delivery of services they value, like food and visits) is a moot point. We suspect that very often they do, and hence co-operate more or less willingly in the running of routines (in this connection, see also the account offered by Bettelheim (1960)—and drawn on by Giddens (1984: 61–3)—of the extreme psychological consequences of the concentration camps, when all resources of ontological security were denied to their inmates, day-to-day events were extremely *unpredictable*, and 'the feeling of autonomy of action that individuals have in the ordinary routines of day-to-day life in orthodox social settings was almost completely destroyed' (Giddens 1984: 62)). Yet, in that the repetition of the routine is also the token of staff power, for a prisoner to interrupt it or depart from it, in however small a way, can be (as Goffman suggests) an assertion of selfhood and a small act of resistance (see also McDermott and King, 1988). As we have previously noted, Urry (1991: 168) takes issue with Giddens for his overemphasis on the psychological need for regularity and hence for presenting a depiction of social life which is 'too routinized, too boring'. Urry points by contrast to those many things which people may do precisely to escape from routines in search of excitement, distraction, change. Both these points would seem to have a special resonance in the prison context. On the one hand the prison is amongst the most visibly routinized of all social situations. Prisons, on the whole, certainly are boring even if the boredom may be sought in part by both staff *and prisoners* ('do your own time'). On the other hand Adams (1992) emphasizes the sheer hedonistic thrill reported by some prison rioters enjoying the ultimate carnivalesque break from prison routine.

As Sykes long ago saw very clearly, the institution needs to embed its routine if it is to reproduce itself in anything resembling an ordered way. Yet the routine is inherently fragile, because prisoners are agents who may refuse or resist as well as comply or co-operate. All this poses difficulties for prison staff. The fragility of the institutional order can also be unintentionally exacerbated by external influences—changes in shift patterns or staffing ratios, attempts to alter or restrict the regime, the presence or absence of sufficient work for prisoners, even a televised football match that runs into extra time and so goes beyond the point at which prisoners are usually 'banged up'. The 'face work' involved in negotiating even mundane features of the prison day without perpetual recourse to formal disciplinary measures can be intense (*pace* some passing comments of Giddens implying that this is less the case in prisons than in other situations (1984: 157)). These simple observations point to the fundamental importance of the 'dialectic of control' in prisons. The matter is of course highly variable. Some prison regimes come close to providing a limiting case of Giddens's argument. Such a one might be Marion Penitentiary in Illinois whose famously intensive styles of surveillance and 'situational' control (cf. Ward, 1987; Bottoms et al., 1990) approximate to total domination. But Marion is the 'end of the line' of the American Federal penal system, reserved for those prisoners regarded as too violent or recalcitrant to be accommodated elsewhere. It assumes that the prisoner does not recognize its legitimacy (see below).[28] Most prison systems incorporate some such deepest location (Sparks, 1994b). But these are also acknowledged to be in some degree exceptional: even within the system of 'total institutions' they 'stand out in relief' (see Giddens, *supra*). Different kinds of 'dialectic of control' suggest different models and possibilities of penal administration: indeed our own exploration of two contrasting English long-term prisons which provides the substantive core of this book can be seen as first and foremost a demonstration of exactly this point. At the opposite pole of penal possibility from Marion stands a prison such as the Barlinnie Special Unit in which

---

[28] The same might be said of early styles of penitentiary discipline, though this point is sometimes neglected. e.g. Foucault's famous treatment of Bentham's 'panopticon' emphasizes its efficiency as a means of exercising disciplinary power and achieving designated tasks. What Foucault does not bring out so clearly is that the necessity of constant surveillance is also motivated by terror of prisoners. Underlying panoptic systems of control is an assumed 'slippery slope', a view which envisages a direct line between the tiniest infraction of discipline and anarchy unleashed. The aim of such systems may indeed have been to 'grind out docile yet capable bodies', but not because prisoners were reckoned docile already (see Ignatieff, 1978; Radzinowicz and Hood, 1986; Adams, 1992).

(until its precipitate closure in 1994) there was a serious attempt formally to incorporate prisoners' participation in decision making (Field, 1989; Bottomley et al., 1994). We return in more detail to this range of penal possibilities in chapter 9.

Similarly, in that the notion of the dialectic of control refers to the means or resources whereby subordinate players in a power relation may influence those in more powerful positions, it encompasses a range of possible modes or dimensions of influencing. These range from outright shows of resistance or defiance to the 'censorious' use of formal channels of complaint and redress. Which of these is chosen by prisoners is likely to depend at least in part upon the prospect of obtaining some degree of success via the 'legitimate' avenues. Meanwhile, with few exceptions, prison managers prefer to avoid open confrontation, at least on a collective level. It presents many risks: to safety and to their own and the system's standing in public discourse. It may expose the relative paucity of their real resources of force and sanction. It may go against the grain of their vocational commitments. Crushing prisoners' resistance is not in itself an aim of the institution in the same way that ensuring the reliable reproduction of the regime is—one of Sykes's central and most enduring points. In each of these respects decision makers in prisons have powerful reasons for taking at least some account of the feelings and reactions of their captives. The existence of the dialectic of control explains why, contrary to the views of many who have opined on the subject, prisons cannot escape considerations of legitimacy.

Legitimacy[29]

Prison studies of both radical (Scraton et al., 1991) and conservative (DiIulio, 1987) casts have begun from an assumption of the non-legitimate nature of order in prisons.[30] This is apparent also, at

[29] The material in this subsection is abstracted from Sparks and Bottoms (1995) where a more extended discussion of the problem of legitimacy in prisons can be found.

[30] DiIulio's argument is admittedly a bit more complex than an outright rejection of legitimacy. Whilst he endorses a 'control model' of penal administration which asserts that 'those govern best who govern most' and disclaims ideas of prison power-sharing he also suggests that the achievement of higher levels of 'order, amenity and service' are likely to secure increased acquiescence from prisoners. That is, the prime legitimating principle is efficient service delivery and consistent application of known rules; anything more is on his view unrealistic. DiIulio calls this his

least in part, in Sykes and Mathiesen: the forms of accommodation and compromise which each identifies are precisely responses to a 'legitimacy deficit' (Beetham, 1991). We dissent to some degree from this consensus. In our analysis legitimation problems are inherent in the study of dialectics of control, though Giddens himself has been criticized for not sufficiently developing the distinction between 'the-taken-for-granted' and 'the-accepted-as-legitimate' (Gregory, 1989: 200; to which we might also add another concept, namely 'the-put-up-with-as-inevitable').

In *The Legitimation of Power* (1991) Beetham argues that all systems of power relations seek legitimation. The particular content of legitimating beliefs and principles is extremely historically and culturally variable but, Beetham contends, we can identify a common underlying structure which is very general (1991: 22). On Beetham's account that structure has three underlying dimensions or criteria in terms of which the legitimacy of any actually existing distribution of power and resources can be expressed and evaluated. Such criteria are almost never perfectly fulfilled, and each dimension of legitimacy has a corresponding form of non-legitimate power. Beetham expresses his scheme as shown in Figure 2.1.

Criteria of legitimacy	Corresponding form of non-legitimate power
1. Conformity to rules (legal validity)	Illegitimacy (breach of rules)
2. Justifiability of rules in terms of shared beliefs	Legitimacy deficit (discrepancy between rules and supporting shared beliefs, absence of shared beliefs)
3. Legitimation through expressed consent	Delegitimation (withdrawal of consent)
(*Source*: Beetham, 1991: 20)	

FIGURE 2.1. Beetham's dimensions of legitimacy

'governmental' perspective on prisons, but it also has much in common with what we elsewhere call 'managerialist' outlooks. DiIulio's views would seem to stand very close to the position actually adopted in England and Wales under the Prison Service Agency's *Corporate Plan*, with its focus on achieving and monitoring 'performance'.

The three dimensions shown in Figure 2.1 roughly correspond to the traditional preoccupations of three different academic specialisms which have considered issues of legitimacy: first, lawyers (has power been legally acquired, and it is being exercised within the law?); next, political philosophers (are the power relations at issue morally justifiably?); and finally, social scientists (what are the actual beliefs of subjects about issues of legitimacy in that particular society?) (Beetham, 1991: 4ff.). However, a central plank of Beetham's argument is that social scientists have been wrong to follow Max Weber (1968) in defining legitimacy as simply 'belief in legitimacy on the part of the relevant social agents' (Beetham, 1991: 6). To promote this view, Beetham argues, is to leave social science with no adequate means of explaining why subjects may acknowledge the legitimacy of the powerful in one social context, but not another (ibid.: 10). Beetham accordingly argues for an alternative formulation of the social-scientific view of legitimacy—'a given power relationship is not legitimate because people believe in its legitimacy, but because it can be *justified in terms of* their beliefs' (ibid.: 11). This may seem to introduce a rather fine distinction, but the alternative formulation is seen by Beetham as fundamental because it injects a crucial element of moral judgement into the definition. Additionally to this point, Beetham also suggests that the simple 'belief in legitimacy' view takes no account of those aspects of legitimacy that have little to do with beliefs at all, such as conformity to legal rules. Hence, the schema of legitimacy that he eventually proposes for social-scientific analysis (see above) deliberately includes all three of these different elements.

Beetham suggests that some currently influential views of power (especially those flowing from 'rational choice' models) ignore the fact that systems of social power inherently generate normative as well as prudential or self-interested elements (1991: 27). Thus, situations in which legitimacy is *not at all* necessary to the powerful will be very rare (Beetham considers slavery to be one such: whether prisons are too is a large part of the point at issue in this book). Ironically, of course, the modality of power which stands most in need of legitimation is not democratic discussion, which claims to be inherently self-legitimating, but force. For:

the form of power which is distinctive to [the political domain]—organized physical coercion—is one that both supremely stands in need of legitimation, yet is also uniquely able to breach all legitimacy. The legitimation of

the State's power is thus both specially urgent and fateful in its consequences.

(Beetham, 1991: 40)

Legitimacy and power are, on this view, two faces of the same
problem. The content and strength of legitimating beliefs radically
affects all parties in a system of power relations and only legitimate
social arrangements generate normative commitments towards compliance. Meanwhile, the need for legitimation constrains the actions
of the powerful since, as Giddens puts it, 'to speak of legitimacy in
the usual sense implies the existence of standards external to he
[*sic*] who claims it' (1977: 92). In our view many of the dimensions
of prison life which we detail, from the self-policing of staff conduct and informal on-the-spot negotiations to formal grievance procedures and law suits are unintelligible without reference to implicit
(albeit not necessarily consensually shared) conceptions of legitimacy amongst prisoners and staff, a point which recurred inces-
santly in our interviews with both.

To focus on the problem of legitimacy sensitizes the analysis to
variations in the nature of prison regimes and the manner of their
application. More especially it draws attention to the ways in
which prisoners experience these variations, to what they want or
expect from the prison and its staff, and to how the latter respond
to these demands. Amongst the dimensions of prison life which this
concern throws into sharp relief, we will argue, are questions of
consistency and discretion in the application of rules, and prisoners'
perceptions of the fairness or otherwise of disciplinary and grievance procedures. Moreover, we will suggest, the legitimacy of such
arrangements is generally integral to the success or otherwise of a
prison in sustaining order over time.

Tyler, in important work with a strong empirical element (1990;
see also Lind and Tyler, 1988) argues persuasively that legitimacy is
frequently a powerful factor in 'why people obey the law' and that
this in turn is intimately connected with the realization of shared
expectations and criteria of justice. Like Beetham, Tyler argues
against those positions which assume that when people observe
rules they do so mainly out of the fear of the consequences of
breaking them or because of some other estimation of their own
long-term utility. (Tyler regards such views, associated with a 'public choice' perspective, as being dominant amongst psychologists.)

Tyler argues that if this view were true then the regulation of social life would be a much simpler and more easily calculable matter than in fact it is—one would simply need simply need sufficiently powerful and certain forms of sanction (1990: 21). In reality, Tyler argues, 'the effectiveness of legal authorities ultimately depends on voluntary acceptance of their actions' (1990: 24) and hence on the existence of a 'diffuse' and durable disposition to accept their legitimacy (1990: 29). For Tyler, the key to securing compliance via the legitimate exercise of authority lies especially in people's experience of the fairness of procedures (1990: 63). People in Tyler's Chicago panel study who had had recent dealings with the police or courts expressed a strong interest in both distributive fairness and procedural propriety in evaluating how their case or complaint was dealt with. Indeed, Tyler's subjects evinced a greater concern for equality of treatment (1990: 73) and the *manner* of their treatment (1990: 88–9) than for the outcome of their own case *tout court* (though, in that empirical context, this was at least partly because of lack of knowledge of the outcomes in cases other than their own). On this view, people are more likely to accept an adverse outcome whilst retaining intact their prior view of the legitimacy of the system as such if they feel that their case has been dealt with in a procedurally correct way and that they have been accorded respect by those in authority (1990: 84). The situation may be subtly different in 'special populations' (see Tyler 1990: 153), of which prisons are clearly an example, where news travels specially fast and people know about one another's outcomes *as well as* about procedure and demeanour; in this case consistency of outcomes is *also* important. Legitimacy is more conditional, and caprice can jeopardize it fundamentally.

Tyler's account of subjects' encounters with persons in authority is especially interesting. In such encounters people review both the procedural correctness and the manner of their treatment as 'information about the group that the authority represents and to which the parties to the dispute or allocation belong' (1990: 175). Hence, every transaction with authority raises questions that extend 'far beyond those connected with the issue to be decided' (*loc. cit.*). Such issues include 'representation, neutrality, bias, honesty, quality of decision, and consistency' (*loc. cit.*) and more generally questions of esteem. In short, they reflect upon the nature of the power relations in question and the validity of claims to justified authority— that is, to legitimacy.

Writing from distinct disciplinary perspectives Beetham and Tyler have separately produced parallel and consonant analyses. According to Beetham, no governing authority can afford to disregard the problem of legitimation, no matter what manner of polity is in question.[31] If this is right, the received notion that prisons have always been autocratic in character and confront problems which are to some degree *sui generis* distracts attention from the fact that they are routinely beset by legitimation problems and that these are in key respects similar to those encountered in other settings. Tyler would broadly agree, but also draws attention to the ways in which legitimacy claims are placed in question in routine encounters and interactions, on both procedural and interpersonal levels. Perhaps therefore one can identify a number of facets of legitimacy relevant to the maintenance of order and the incidence of disorder in prisons. Amongst these one would certainly have to include the centrality of fair procedures and (within the 'special community' (Tyler, 1990: 154) of the prison: see above) consistent outcomes. A third component concerns the quality of behaviour of officials—regarded in some quite strong sense as *representing* the system (*loc. cit.*). Fourthly it is possible that the basic regime of the institution—its accommodation, services, and activities—may itself be regarded as illegitimate in failing to meet commonly expected standards (cf. Woolf 1991). Therefore one can envisage circumstances under which institutions meet some of these criteria but not others. A procedurally 'correct' and bureaucratically efficient regime might simply fail on grounds of impersonality and lack of humaneness (cf. Jacobs 1977), perhaps helping to explain why prison disorders can occur in brand new, uncrowded, well resourced facilities.

Legitimacy is by no means an easy concept to formulate, still less to study empirically in the contexts where it would most matter (O'Kane, 1993). The distinction pointed to by Gregory (1989) between the 'taken-for-granted' and the 'accepted-as-legitimate' is always a fine one. In prisons it is fiendish. It is, however, implicitly always at issue in the ways in which institutional struggles and negotiations take place in prisons, certainly in liberal democracies. It is also a multidimensional idea. On the one hand it is coolly explanatory: it simply locates points of contestation and conflict

[31] This claim has been sharply disputed. See the critical note on Beetham by O'Kane in *Political Studies* XLI, 3: 471–87, and Beetham's response in the same issue (488–92).

within power relations. On the other hand it has a normative 'face'. To claim to identify a legitimacy deficit is to argue for some substantial form of social change. It is difficult to see how any sociology which aspires to the status of critique can operate satisfactorily without a developed concept of legitimacy (see below, Appendix A).

Risk and responses to it[32]

In our view it is illuminating to think of prisons, as of other spheres of social life, as risk environments. The notion of risk is one that enjoys a growing centrality in social theory (Giddens, 1990; Douglas, 1986, 1992; Beck, 1992). In the work of authors such as these, it is an integral aspect of 'late modernity' that it engenders certain definite kinds of risk (most such discussions concentrate on the 'high consequence risks' of environmental disaster or nuclear war). This 'risk profile' is in large measure created by scientific knowledge and is managed, though never eliminated, by 'expert systems'. The awareness of such risks has ambivalent consequences for the 'adaptive reactions' of all of us in late modern societies (Giddens, 1990: 131–43). It is also clear that risk and its cognate terms (vulnerability, threat, anxiety, hazard, jeopardy, harm) have a special application within the fields of criminology and penology. The notion of risk can encompass both very personal experiences and actions (risk taking, risk avoidance, victimization, fear) and settled features of organizational behaviour (in this case, the prudential judgements of prison governors about threats to order in their prisons).

It is perhaps not too daring to say that various inflections of the problem of risk run throughout the history of prison studies, from Sykes's 'deprivation of security', through Irwin's and Jacobs's accounts of the gathering turmoil in American prisons in the 1960s and 1970s, to DiIulio's arguments in favour of the reassertion of firmer control. But there are numerous differing kinds of risk in question here. These range from the 'high-consequence risks' (Giddens, 1990: 131) of a major break-out or a New Mexico or Manchester riot to some of the most mundane features of prison life. Moreover, the latter arguably encompass not just the obvious

---

[32] This discussion of risk is a truncated version of material appearing originally in Hay and Sparks (1992a).

and visible issues of violence and victimization in prisons but also a whole variety of risks to health and well-being which imprisonment can magnify (the risks of suicide, HIV/AIDS transmission, risks of arbitrary or oppressive treatment, and so on).

If prison managers, like professional decision makers in other contexts, necessarily prioritize some of these risks rather than others, on what criteria are these judgements based, and with what intended or unintended outcomes? The real tension which Sykes identified between the 'excess of caution' which sought to minimize every possibility of the infraction of rules at the cost of the 'fearful loss of self-determination' of the inmate could be conceptualized as a prioritization of the occasional but 'high consequence' risk of riot or escape at the cost of accentuating the endemic risk of the reduction of quality of daily life. (The Radzinowicz Committee's notion of the dispersal prison as a 'liberal regime within a secure perimeter' (as discussed in chapter 1) was similarly an attempt to reconcile competing risk-laden demands.) Moreover, the unintended outcome of decisions that sacrifice a supportable quality of life to greater physical security or control might be precisely to stimulate frustration and opposition, and hence exacerbate the very challenges to order which one sought to avoid. This is what Sykes had in mind when he spoke of the prison governor as being in the unusual position of bringing about exactly the behaviour he sought to suppress (the one qualification being that the 'risk' literature shows this not to be unusual at all). Such dilemmas inherent attend prison management practices where these are thought of as involving the attempt to achieve institutional reproduction, custody, and self-maintenance in the face of potentially considerable legitimacy deficits.

In response to such intractabilities various options (all imperfect) are possible. Prison managers may place special emphasis on what we have elsewhere (Bottoms et al., 1990) characterized (following the terminology current in the crime prevention field) as situational measures, in which the physical design of the prison and the surveillance of activity within it are consciously utilized in order to minimize opportunities for trouble to develop. All prisons are highly situationally controlled when compared with most other contexts of living. But they vary in the extent to which such practices are refined and pursued. On the other hand, prison managers may conclude that the excessive use of situational controls frustrates other objectives which the prison sets itself, or simply that they are obtrusive and irritating to a degree which is delegitimating. In such a case they may place greater emphasis on specifically social attempts at stabilization, involving a consciously flexible and diplomatic manner of regulation by staff or indeed formal attempts at consultation and participation with prisoners.[33] These approaches are not mutually exclusive, and any real prison will generally encompass aspects of each. (Indeed it is worth noting that whilst we were, to the best of our knowledge, the first to apply the social/situational analogy expressly as an analytical device to prison regimes (Bottoms et al., 1990) some of the terminology of situational crime management was first developed by Cornish and Clarke (1975) in a study of residential institutions for boys.) These terms do, however, suggest a continuum along which actual or conceivably possible styles of control are ranged. Indeed the comparison at the heart of this study between two long-term prisons in operation in England during the 1980s provoked these reflections for us and will be theorized partly in these terms. To the extent that they are pursued consciously (albeit not necessarily in precisely this language) these dimensions of control strategies also intertwine with other aspects of modern managerialist practices and expertise. For example, the recent debates over prison architecture (especially with regard to 'New Generation' prison designs) owe much—though not always explicitly—to assumptions shared with the literature of situational crime prevention. The division of the prison into small units, open to constant surveillance, is a purposive attempt to manipulate the environment in order to reduce opportunities for trouble. On the other hand some versions of arguments for 'unit management' stress instead that smaller living units offer different settings for interaction, and perhaps scope for the explo-

---

[33] It is of course possible to seek to regulate prisons by other 'social' means'—ranging from token economies and behaviour modification techniques (and the current british preoccupation with incentives-based regimes steps in this direction, albeit relatively mildly) to the rule of terror. Many prisons around the world are indeed controlled by means of open or obscure violence; nor do we want to claim that British or North American prisons have ever been or are now free of them. The use of force and physical restraint remains part of the repertoire of penal technique, let alone all the other threats and promises to which prisoners may be subject. We have no intention of masking this where it arises in our study. But the analogy with the crime prevention field that we have immediately in mind here calls upon a particular and less openly coercive sense of 'the social'. For a fuller discussion of this concept, see ch. 9.

ration of novel and more co-operative kinds of social relationship (Cooke, 1989: Bottomley et al., 1994). To summarize, the loss of an already-fragile legitimacy is precisely one of the risks that prison managers confront. Increasing the intensity of situational controls (as a way of reducing other risks) may increase this risk. This is one reason why prisons are so often replete with perverse outcomes of control measures.

We will focus in particular on two dimensions of risk and risk judgement. The first concerns what happens when an individual is reckoned particularly troublesome or disruptive. What measures aimed at risk reduction come into play? How effectively do they work? Do they involve the imposition of subsidiary hardships? Do they court unintended, perverse outcomes either for the person concerned or more widely? The second problem arises when an individual is considered (or considers himself) to be particularly *at risk*, and many of the same considerations apply. What the two circumstances have in common are (1) the application of procedures of risk management by officials and (2) that these commonly involve the *movement* of the prisoner concerned away from the 'normal' range of prison locations and into some form of special handling. Historically this has almost always involved the segregation of particular prisoners either compulsorily under punishment or in the interests of 'good order and discipline' or at their own request on grounds of vulnerability. More recently it also encompasses the development of specialist units targeting the particular 'needs' of either the 'disruptive' or the 'vulnerable'. This recalls a number of issues raised above in discussion of Foucault and Giddens. It is inherently the case that the 'control' of the prison involves the regulation of its interior space. It is also more specifically true that the authorities' responses to certain kinds of risk principally consist in putting prisoners in especially highly controlled or protected spaces. Just what is going on in such cases, and the ways in which it is experienced and interpreted by the people affected, is one of the central topics of this book.

The question of risk also raises once more the issue of 'managerialism' in prisons. The gradual infiltration of risk management principles into prison administration is indicative of the curious and unevenly developed politics of imprisonment under conditions of 'late modernity'. Prisons in contemporary Western societies more and more seek to govern their fragile internal order in ways analogous to those of other complex organizations. They monitor their own activity. They commission research. They compile sophisticated databases on prisoners, incidents, budgets. Senior managers promulgate 'operating standards', publish 'mission statements', devise 'performance indicators', and monitor the implementation of these by their subordinates. Prison governors are as likely (indeed, probably *more* likely) to be sent on courses in business administration as in criminology. Bottoms (1995) distinguishes three dimensions of managerialism in contemporary criminal justice, each of which is registered in certain ways in prison administration. 'Systemic management' alludes to the monitoring and evaluation of internal processes, and the attempt to integrate such processes across a whole administrative system (see also Feeley and Simon, 1992; Peters, 1986). It is concerned to rationalize and regulate the daily operation of the system—what Foucault presciently called 'supervising the processes of the activity rather than its result' (1979a: 137). 'Actuarial management' refers in the prison context to the development of techniques for identifying various kinds of potentially troublesome, vulnerable or dangerous groups, individuals or situations (see for examples Williams and Longley, 1987; Gottfredson and Gottfredson, 1993; and for a critique Simon, 1988). 'Consumerist' management has to do with the ways in which organizations may respond to demands for proof of effective delivery of services and statutory entitlements, by asking their 'clients' how satisfied they are with certain things. In prisons this is evidenced most clearly in the production of prison surveys (Walmsley et al., 1992; Scottish Prison Service, 1992).

For the time being we raise these matters simply as relevant points of interest. The nature of the 'game' has changed; and some grasp of modern prison management postures seems integral to an understanding of what is going on, notably as regards the management of risk. How one responds to these developments, how they relate to the problem of penal order, and which of them one might welcome or oppose are questions that we postpone for the moment. It seems likely that managerialism in prisons, as in other spheres, is inherently an ambiguous phenomenon. It appears to its practitioners to offer powerful tools for modernizing archaic practices, rationalizing the use of resources, and informing action by ever better and more precise information. It also seems likely—to put it at its mildest—that to prisoners used to the antique and insanitary conditions and the capricious use of discretion and force characteristic of many penal systems, a dose of systemic/consumerist managerialism presents itself as no small improvement (an argument deployed to some advantage by proponents of prison privatization such as Logan (1990)). By the same token, convinced advocates of such modernizations are likely to view those who resist the trend as dinosaurs—unenlightened and reactionary people whose views of the prison are based on romanticism or superstition. It is also true that, for example, DiIulio's condemnation of Sykes-inspired experiments in prisoner participation are at their most trenchant on just these points. The conception of the 'prison community' as having its own arcane and mysterious chemistry has been, in DiIulio's view, disastrous (1987: 38–40). It gives rise to a situation reminiscent of some corrupt and backward outpost under Soviet communism—run as much by patronage and graft as by oppression, and by the exploitation of divisions amongst the oppressed themselves.

Yet doubts and questions abound. Is the view of the prison as merely another organization to be managed adequate? Or does it in the same breath misstate the real complexity of its social relations and obscure the deployment of its powers? Does it conflate smooth and consistent administration with justice? Are the personhood and claims to recognition as citizens of prisoners and guards overlooked in the drift towards the impersonal management of 'aggregate phenomena' (Peters, *loc. cit.*)? Does the anodyne processual language evade the issue of the intrinsically slender resources of legitimate authority on which the prison continues to depend, and fail to see that these are only protected (if at all) by an ethos of respect for persons? Is there an assumed technological solution to the problem of penal order in which architecture, electronic surveillance, and the actuarial prediction of behaviour are taken to have abolished the dialectic of control to a degree that is actually sociologically impossible? Some of these issues are raised concretely in our research. The discussion of managerialism in British prisons has emerged with great rapidity in recent years, at least partly in response to events—such as Lord Justice Woolf's report, successive internal reorganizations of the prison system, and the question of privatization—which postdate our own fieldwork (see chapter 1). But many of the issues are there in our evidence, at least in outline, as indeed are most of the other questions raised in this chapter. It is for us and our readers to interpret that evidence shrewdly enough to draw those questions forth.

Conclusion

In chapter 1 we have already outlined some of the ways in which these matters were registered in official discourse and policy in England and Wales over the last two decades or so. In the next chapter we go on to show how we operationalized the concepts of order, control, control problem, and the segregation and transfer of prisoners on control grounds in an attempt to make the issues researchable. In later chapters we discuss how such aspects of prison life are spoken about and experienced by the actors most directly involved—prison governors, prison officers, and prisoners—and sometimes during moments of extreme conflict. Our intent is at least twofold, namely (1) to illuminate the origins and immediate consequences of control problems in two rather different prisons and (2) to contextualize these within a more adequate understanding of the conditions of order and conflict in long-term prisons more generally.

In this preparatory discussion we have travelled no small theoretical distance. We have moved away from Sykes's version of the 'Hobbesian problem' and from Goffman's or Foucault's understanding of the total institution. We have attempted to supersede the 'dualism of structure and action' and to look instead towards the 'duality of structure'. Our core concerns are those of order, routines, critical situations, dialectics of control, power, legitimacy, and risk. We will look both at the 'normal' and the 'exceptional' happenings in two prisons and try to use each to inform our understanding of the other. What we will find there are people, acting with and against each other: the way they speak; the lives they lead.

3
Approaching the Research

In chapter 2 we considered some of the conceptual resources which we began to develop during our research study, and which we have since elaborated. Here we introduce the research study itself, including an outline of our research methods. It is a starting-point of most social inquiry that, as Giddens puts it, certain institutions (and prisons must surely be amongst them) 'endure beyond the lives of those individuals whose activities constitute them at any given moment' (1987: 145). In this spirit we have tried in this book both to convey some of the enduring features of long-term imprisonment and to capture something of the everyday, situated social world of the prisoners and staff who occupied particular prisons, at particular times. That is, we want to draw attention to some aspects of prisons that have rather general application; but at the same time we want to retain something of the sense of place and particularity that were so vividly apparent to us in the course of our work.

The task of this chapter is to introduce the two prisons in which we carried out our research, and to explain some of the decisions we made in going about it (our methods and our uses of certain terms). We offer some sense of the historical, geographical, and other factors that may be seen as having helped to produce the distinctive institutional identities of the two prisons. We also provide some statistical data about the prisons and their populations, by way of descriptive context. Additionally, we give some elaboration of how we applied certain important terms such as 'order', 'control', and 'control problem'. We have tried to use these terms in ways that make them researchable, and defensible in view of the sorts of conceptions of institutional orders that we outlined in chapter 2; accordingly, we have sought definitions that illuminate the contribution of routine practices to the reproduction of systemic patterns. Such concepts are intended to address recurrent characteristics of institutions and yet remain grounded in the everyday hurly-burly of prison life, as it is variously thought about and experienced by those who live and work within its walls. It is on this basis that we shall go on in later chapters to describe and account for the kind of order which each of the institutions that we studied sought to foster and maintain.

The Research Project: The General Framework

As explained in chapter 1, the terms of reference for the research project, as formally agreed with the research sponsors (the Home Office) were:

To describe accurately and to explain the nature of control problems [in long-term prisons] and the conditions leading to their emergence, including an account of the circumstances under which prisoners are removed from normal location.

As further indicated in chapter 1, the study was intended, within the overall research strategy recommended by RAG to the Home Office, to complement the more individualistic approach of concurrent research on control problems in long-term prisons carried out by the senior prison psychologists, Mark Williams and David Longley (see Williams and Longley, 1987).[1]

The original proposal for this research, as submitted to the research sponsors, argued that, as the central focus of the project would be on the way in which prison regimes might (unwittingly or otherwise) contribute to or help to prevent the emergence of 'con-

---

[1] Williams and Longley (1987) provide the best developed example to date in Britain of an approach to prison 'control problems' through an objective and accurate identification of 'the hypothetical minority of difficult and dangerous prisoners' within the dispersal system (pp. 281–2). They warrant their approach on two grounds: first the need 'to test the hypothesis that the smooth running of dispersal prisons is critically determined by the behaviour of a minority of difficult prisoners, and hence will be disproportionately improved by their selective removal'; and second, the requirement 'to explore the extent to which persistent offenders against discipline in dispersal prisons exhibit special treatment needs that might be met in environments outside those prisons' (1987: 282). One can readily agree that the first of these is a hypothesis that merits testing (though we would not ourselves assume an unprobematically affirmative result to any such test). Similarly, one can appreciate that the second arm of Williams and Longley's undertaking is intended to provide a certain kind of administratively useful information that might well strike prison managers as pragmatically helpful (even if many of them might still prefer to make judgements based on their own professional 'intuition'). Williams and Longley's research approaches are thus not antithetical to those of the present study, though clearly there is a difference of focus.

trol problems', it would be valuable to select for the main study two prisons with varying control histories and regimes.[2]

In fact, however, given that the research was about control problems in *dispersal* prisons, the choice of prisons was not large. At the time of the commencement of the research, some prisons were in the transitional stage of having only recently joined, or being about to leave, the dispersal system; while in two prisons there were other significant research projects in progress. As it turned out, therefore, only four dispersal prisons were realistic candidates for inclusion in the study, and of these only one (Albany) had experienced some of the major breakdowns of order that had led to the original creation of the Control Review Committee (see chapter 1; and see below for further details of Albany's control history). It seemed appropriate to us, therefore, that Albany should be one of the two prisons studied; and the Home Office agreed with this view.

The choice of the other prison for the study was not straightforward, and occasioned some debate with the Home Office. In the end, however, Long Lartin was selected. There were two major advantages to this choice: first, Long Lartin was one of only two dispersal prisons which, at the date of the fieldwork, had been running for fifteen years or more as a dispersal, yet without experiencing a major public breakdown of control;[3] and secondly, Long Lartin was known to operate probably the most 'liberal' regime within the dispersal system, whereas Albany (for reasons to be explained below) was at that time running the most 'restricted' regime. Hence, the two prisons not only had very different control histories, they also had, at the date of the fieldwork, probably the two most radically different regimes (the 'polar extremes' as they were sometimes called) within the dispersal system.

Published disciplinary data for the two prisons seemed to confirm that, at least *prima facie*, there were some marked differences

---

[2] One commentator on the research proposal within the Home Office suggested that it might be beneficial to study more than two prisons, to enhance the exploration of the interaction between 'regimes' and 'control problems'. We certainly would not disagree with this view in principle (as the discussion in chapter 9 should make very clear); however, inevitably resource constraints limited the scale of the study, and within the resources available we deemed it more sensible to opt for an in-depth study of two prisons, plus a comprehensive and meaningful pilot study (see later section on research methods).

[3] The other was Wakefield Prison, which was used for pilot work in the present study.

between the two prisons. Relevant data for 1987 and 1988 are given in Table 3.1.[4] From this table it is apparent that Albany punished more prisoners for more offences in both of the years considered; and that is so notwithstanding that the Albany data *include* prisoners in the Vulnerable Prisoner Unit (see further below), who, as will be seen later (see chapter 7), were arraigned much less often for disciplinary offences than were other Albany prisoners.

TABLE 3.1. Total numbers of disciplinary offences and prisoners punished, Albany and Long Lartin 1987 and 1988

| | Albany | | Long Lartin | |
	1987	1988	1987	1988
Average daily population (ADP)	300	316	401	410
No. of different prisoners punished	262	251	219	235
No. of prisoners punished as % of ADP	87.3	79.4	54.6	57.3
Total recorded disciplinary offences	723*	670	404	418
Offences per head of ADP	2.4	2.1	1.0	1.0

* The *Prison Statistics 1987* give the total number of disciplinary offences in Albany for that year as 733, but the specific categories of offences listed totally only 723. It is assumed that 723 is the correct figure.

Sources: *Prison Statistics England and Wales 1987*: *Statistics of Offences against Prison Discipline and Punishments England and Wales 1988*

Similar disciplinary data in respect of the two prisons (though for an earlier year) were presented in the original research proposal to the Home Office,[5] and it was argued in the proposal that the data perhaps strengthened the case for choosing these two particular

    [4] Given that the fieldwork period for Albany extended into 1989, it is relevant to note that the differences between the prisons shown in Table 3.1 extended also into the later year (prisoners punished as % of ADP: Albany 60%, Long Lartin 38%; offences per head of ADP: Albany 1.5%, Long Lartin 0.8%). As may be seen from these data, however, although the inter-prison differences were maintained, the offence rates in both prisons declined perceptibly in 1989. It is not clear why this was the case, not least since national data show that in male prisons and remand centres generally the 1989 disciplinary offence rate 'was a little higher than the 1988 level' (*Statistics of offences against prison discipline and punishments, England and Wales 1989*, p. 2).
    [5] The data presented were for 1984 (the latest data officially published at the time the proposal was first made). Offences per head of ADP in the two prisons were then: Albany 3.3, Long Lartin 1.6.

prisons. In respect of this point, however, a very valuable comment was made by an experienced prison psychologist, to the effect that, during the research fieldwork, care would need to be taken by the research team not to project any 'negative' image of Albany ('we have selected this as a prison with control problems'); as was correctly pointed out, such an attitude could be demoralizing to staff, and this in turn could lead to various 'contaminating' consequences for the research (reduced co-operation, etc.). Every effort was therefore made, during the fieldwork, not to present any such 'negative' image of Albany; and this approach proved to be fully justified because, as will be seen, in its final assessments the research project did not paint either prison as clearly 'better' than the other, though there were indeed significant differences between them.

Albany and Long Lartin: history and geography

Albany and Long Lartin were both constructed in the 1960s, as part of the building programme of new closed prisons that followed the White Paper *Penal Practice in a Changing Society* (Home Office, 1959). (Prior to these developments, no new closed prisons had been built in England for approximately half a century.) Both were built in architectural styles which deliberately moved away from the traditional English Victorian 'galleried' prison (as exemplified, for example, in Pentonville—see Morris and Morris, 1963), though in detail, their architectural plans are somewhat different (see Figures 3.1 and 3.2). At Albany, there are five adjacent cell-block wings (A–E), all opening out on to a single broad corridor, though each wing also has doors opening directly into a compound area, to facilitate access to workshops, etc. At Long Lartin, there are three main cell blocks, each containing two wings; these three cell blocks are at right angles to one another, and linked by a secure, enclosed one-storey corridor. Externally, like other modern high-security prisons Albany and Long Lartin present the passer-by with a somewhat blank appearance. They have smooth and featureless exterior walls, ceaselessly monitored by remote-controlled cameras and regular dog patrols; and, at night, they are brilliantly floodlit.

Neither Albany nor Long Lartin was built as a dispersal prison; rather, both were designed as 'Category C' prisons (i.e. closed, but of relatively low security). The decisions made to include them in the dispersal system, after that system was born following the

Radzinowicz Report (see chapter 1), obviously therefore entailed a substantial increase in security, especially perimeter security (this complex process is fully recounted, for Albany, in King and Elliott's (1977) important book on the prison). Albany was opened in 1967 and then became one of the first dispersal prisons in 1970; Long Lartin opened in 1971, and joined the dispersal system, following upgrading, in 1973. The first governors of both prisons (in their 'Category C' existence) were each well-known in the prison system for their strong emphasis on building relationships between staff and prisoners.

Like most new English prisons built since the Second World War, both Albany and Long Lartin are in somewhat remote locations. Albany, on the Isle of Wight, is one of three prisons standing close to one another in a dominant position on the hillside beside the road from Newport to Cowes. Long Lartin stands on the borders of the Cotswolds, in open countryside in the verdant Vale of Evesham. Clearly, though for different reasons, both these locations (but especially Albany's) make for some difficulties of access for prisoners' families and other visitors.[6]

As previously indicated, Long Lartin and Albany had experienced very different control histories during their first fifteen years as dispersal prisons. Long Lartin had avoided any major breakdown of order, but Albany emphatically had not. The two most notorious incidents at Albany were in 1972 and 1983 respectively; they were described as follows in the report of the Control Review Committee (Home Office, 1984, Annex D):

1972 Following an escape attempt on 16 August and the discovery of further escape material in the prison on 22 August, the Governor ordered a thorough search of the prison. While the search was in progress (i.e. from 25–28 August) all prisoners were confined to their cells. The prisoners became very restive at this lengthy period of confinement and on the nights of 26, 27, 28 and, to a lesser extent, 29 August they demonstrated by shouting, smashing cell windows and furniture and throwing lighted paper and clothing out of the

[6] Albany prisoners received a mean of 0.8 visits each per month during the first half of 1988 compared with the 1.5 visits per month that prisoners in Long Lartin received over the same period. This difference is partly attributable to population differences (Albany has a Vulnerable Prisoner Unit, and prisoners in such units receive fewer visits), but there is little doubt that the prison's island location also reduced the total number of visits, simply because of the difficulties of access for visitors.

windows. The fire brigade had to be called on each of the 4 nights to extinguish the number of small fires which resulted. There were no injuries to staff or inmates.

1983 Prior to the disturbance there were strikes in the mailbag workshop in response to changes in the work there. As a result the atmosphere throughout the prison became tense. On the evening of 19 May 4 prisoners broke away during outside exercise and climbed onto the workshop roofs: they remained there throughout the night. Staff attempted to end the exercise period but the majority of prisoners refused to go inside until the normal finishing time and showed support for the prisoners on the roof. The following morning (20 May), while the majority of prisoners were out on exercise, inmates in B Wing and later C Wing began smashing fittings. Staff were forced to withdraw from both wings and the prisoners blocked the staircases with debris. At about 12.40 pm MUFTI teams from HMP Parkhurst entered the two wings and regained control after about 35 minutes. The 4 prisoners on the workshop roof came down peacefully in the afternoon. Ten other prisoners who had gained access to the roof of the main cell block during the disturbance remained there; after negotiations 3 were brought down by hydraulic life on 22 May and the remaining 7 were brought down on 25 May. B and C Wings were extensively damaged and both remained out of action until the beginning of 1984. 19 staff and 17 prisoners were injured during the disturbance; the majority of injuries to prisoners were accidental and not sustained during encounters with staff.

A further, less publicly visible, incident occurred at Albany in 1985. On this occasion, as in 1983, control of a wing was again lost for a period. Even more seriously, during the incident some members of staff were trapped for a time on an upstairs landing. This incident, coming so soon after the 1983 incident, and involving a very obvious threat to staff safety, not unnaturally accentuated the anxieties of uniformed staff about their vulnerability. After the incident, staff were not slow to voice their feelings about what they saw as the inadequacies of Albany's architecture, and the inappropriateness of its then regime. As we shall see, this incident in particular led to the creation of the so-called 'restricted regime' that was in place at the time of our fieldwork.

Tradition and 'ethos'

At the time of our fieldwork, Long Lartin prided itself on the continuity of its traditions, going right back to its initial opening in

1971. As we have seen, it was opened as a 'Category C' establishment, and the initial regime had originally been planned with that
in mind. However, by the time the prison received its first prisoners
it was already known that it was to be upgraded to dispersal status; and the consequences of this were, as it turned out, twofold.
First, it was of course essential, as the first Deputy Governor put it,
to run the prison from the outset 'in such a way as to allow a
regime to develop' which would meet 'the needs of category "A"
and "B" prisoners' (Dunbar, 1971: 7). But secondly, it was decided
to retain as much as possible of the original regime planning
(geared to Category C inmates) as seemed compatible with the new
population to be received. In this connection, it is worth noting
that the design of the regime drew explicitly upon an interpretation
of research into the nature of prison communities, especially that
by Sykes (1958).[7] Long Lartin thus had as part of its rationale on
entering the dispersal system an attempt:

to give prisoners more responsibility, more variety, to mitigate what Sykes
has called 'the pains of imprisonment' and to neutralise the worst aspects
of the labelling processes involved in the allocation of a man to a prison
such as Long Lartin.

(Dunbar, 1971: 7)

Moreover, it was argued:

Choice, responsibility and self-respect only have any meaning to each of us
if we have some control over part of our environment; if we are involved
with others in the structuring of our lives. The regime is designed to help
men return to a free society by reproducing the challenges of free society
so far as this is possible, and providing advice and support in facing the
problems of release

(Dunbar, 1971: 8)

In their historical context these intentions were also bound up with
rehabilitative ideals. However, even in 1971 Dunbar already placed

---

[7] Dunbar noted that the regime as constructed owed much to research on the
social structure of prison communities which had, it was said, shown 'that the
inmate social system and the prisoners' acceptance of its norms and values are at
least in part a response to the experience of imprisonment. They are not merely
manifestations of a criminal culture outside the prison'. [This particular quotation—
used by Dunbar—is from para. 79 of the Radzinowicz Report (Advisory Council on
the Penal System 1968), commenting on a survey of research carried out for the
Advisory Council by the late namesake of one of the present authors, Dr Richard
Sparks].

the word 'treatment' in inverted commas and considered it as 'the sum of all the experiences a man will receive at Long Lartin'. As is well-known, the influence of such rehabilitative ideals has, since that date, receded further. Yet it is also apparent, as we shall see, that even at the time of our research—over 15 years after Dunbar's article—many people continued to value aspects of the Long Lartin regime to which rehabilitative ideals originally gave rise. The validity to their adherents of 'choice, responsibility and self-respect' as values within a prison regime may thus not depend entirely on the theoretical model in which these terms were originally couched. In 1987 the Governor of the day continued to argue that Long Lartin owed its twelve years of existence as a dispersal prison 'without a riot' to its 'good relationships, good foundations, good training and its innovation' (Jenkins, 1987: 273); and it was in terms of these historical continuities that advocates of Long Lartin defined and defended its success up to the time of our research. Such advocates very definitely included many of the uniformed staff, who often told us that they saw Long Lartin as 'the last Radzinowicz prison', the only dispersal to have held fast throughout to the founding principles of a 'liberal regime within a secure perimeter' (see chapter 1).

Albany's history was marked by much sharper discontinuities, by no means unconnected with its troubled control history (see above). The early history of the prison—including some discontinuities—has been fully detailed by King and Elliott (1977). For present purposes, the most relevant subsequent discontinuities arose from the major incidents of 1983 and 1985 (see above), and from the introduction of the Vulnerable Prisoner Unit to Albany in the mid-1980s. After the 1983 incident, the erection of a number of internal fences within the prison, creating a series of separate 'compounds' (see Figure 3.1), ended the previous policy of allowing a relative freedom of movement. The response to the 1985 incident was even more far-reaching. Many staff had by then become convinced that the pre-1985 regime had become untenable; and in the post-incident review, the local Prison Officers' Association lodged a heartfelt appeal for 'control, safety and supervision' as themes to be addressed in future regime planning, to meet the anxieties of staff. The Association's submission further asked for an assurance that staff would never again be 'overwhelmed as in the past'. Subsequently, a more controlled regime was instituted (see further below).

The advent of the Vulnerable Prisoner Unit had a different, and more external, origin. In the 1980s, an increasing number of prisoners were seeking protection from other prisoners (under Rule 43 of the Prison Rules), and these included some Category A prisoners. The available units for such 'own protection' prisoners were often cramped or otherwise inadequate, and not necessarily secure enough to hold Category A inmates. Prison Department headquarters decided that it needed a Vulnerable Prisoner Unit (VPU) within a dispersal prison, where such prisoners could be housed in decent conditions, and with appropriate security. Albany was selected as an appropriate location for this VPU, and by the time of our research fieldwork 'D' and 'E' wings had been selected as offering the most sensible accommodation for the unit (see Figure 3.1). A gate was therefore erected in the main corridor between 'C' and 'D' wings (see Figure 3.1), and care was taken that, so far as possible, prisoners from the 'VPU' and the 'main' wings never mixed. Thus, in effect, Albany had an important new feature: it was, to all intents and purposes, now two separate prisons within a single perimeter.

The most striking feature of Albany, at the time of our arrival there in 1988, was the regime which had been instituted in direct response to the deliberations of the review following the 1985 incident. This regime had a number of features which were somewhat distinctive among dispersal prisons at that time. Most notably, to restrict the number of prisoners in open circulation (and hence to reduce opportunities for creating disorder), only twelve prisoners per wing were allowed out of their cells at any one time during the daytime (when collecting meals, for example), while evening association (see Table 3.2, later in this chapter) was restricted to a maximum of two-thirds of the wing population per evening. This last restriction meant that prisoners, unless leaving the wing for classes or other special purposes, stayed in their cells one evening in three.[8] Without question, this 'restricted regime' helped to restore staff confidence, and by the late 1980s Albany staff were beginning to lay claim to a certain special 'ethos' (or 'way') of their own, in which they took some pride.

[8] This regime was applied to the VPU as well as to the main prison, notwithstanding that the VPU—by common agreement—posed little in the way of a threat to control. The main reason for applying the same regime throughout the prison was *consistency*: it was thought to be very important not to give the impression that some wings were more 'favoured' than others. See the fuller discussion in ch. 6.

We found that, in both prisons, the term 'ethos' was an important one for many prison officers when they wanted to allude to whatever it was that was special or particular about their prison as a place, and about their way of working in it as a code of conduct. We might follow Bourdieu in taking 'ethos' as meaning 'a systematic set of dispositions with an ethical dimension', that is to say revolving around 'a set of practical principles' (Bourdieu, 1993: 86). As Bourdieu has it, until one goes and asks people to talk about it specifically (which is an eccentric thing that sociologists do) an *ethos* is not usually articulated in the form of an *ethic* (this distinction recalls Giddens's contrast between practical and discursive consciousness: see chapter 2). As Bourdieu continues, proposing to assimilate the notion of 'ethos' to his own concept of *habitus*, 'because practical logic is turned towards practice it inevitably implements values'. It is 'a morality made flesh' (*loc. cit.*). 'Ethos' (and associated terms such as 'atmosphere' and 'tradition') is thus a complex word. Such notions evade unequivocal definition, because they are used by participants to summarize large domains of experience and self-identity. Their exact connection with the details of everyday practice can sometimes be difficult to trace; nevertheless, as general guides to action they can be immensely significant. What 'ethos' seems principally to convey in the context of a prison is a number of nostrums or injunctions about the best ways of dealing with prisoners—ways which in turn are held to encourage a certain 'atmosphere' or 'climate'. Discourse of this kind was very pervasive in both Long Lartin and Albany—though differing considerably in substantive content in the two prisons, as we shall see in subsequent chapters.

Regimes and Routines

'Ethos' and 'regime'—by which we mean an ensemble of routines, activities, and practices of regulation and supervision—are inextricably linked. Thus, operating a certain regime may tend to dispose staff towards certain styles of working, and hence encourage the development of a particular local occupational culture, and vice versa. For example, prisoners at Long Lartin had a relatively high degree of freedom of movement within the prison at certain times. Prisoners usually moved unescorted (though in a secure corridor) from wings to the gym or the library, or to make purchases at the prison shop. They were also allowed to visit each other in one another's wings provided that, when not in their own wing, they remained close to the wing entrance on the ground floor. They made their way to and from work and exercise under a lesser degree of visible staff supervision than at Albany (though in both cases they did so under the unblinking eye of CCTV cameras). These features of the regime were widely regarded by Long Lartin staff as playing a major, if not central, part in conditioning the atmosphere or ethos of the prison. Indeed, these matters were ones whose merits and demerits were a bone of contention among staff throughout the dispersal system. From the point of view of Long Lartin staff, such practices were clearly connected with a fairly explicitly stated 'soft-policing' model of regulation, in which a degree of manifest 'control' might be foregone in the pursuit of a more basic stability. As a grade IV governor put it:

There's a low level of policing on the wings. If you regard it as being like the policing of a place like St. Pauls in Bristol—it's certainly policed, but in a careful way. A bit like treading on eggshells, I suspect. We police the landings that way. The staff are there and they do patrol. But they don't actively seek out what's going on down there.

In this sense, rather than by intensive surveillance, staff at Long Lartin sought the maintenance of order through highly developed, informal channels of communication between staff and prisoners. Stress was thus placed on the avoidance of 'pettiness' (a word which we encountered many times in the discourse of both staff and prisoners) in the imposition of rules and regulations. The features of this outlook that were valued by prisoners included a commitment towards defusing troublesome situations by various mechanisms such as the use of tact, humour, and other interpersonal skills; and a recognition that prisoners needed a degree of privacy and personal autonomy.

Whereas Long Lartin's organizational concerns had much to do with the cultivation and implementation of what are generally thought of as *liberal* attitudes and beliefs, the regime at Albany seemed to us to be centred more on smooth and efficient administration and the belief that the best interests of the greatest number of prisoners were ultimately served by an even-handed firmness of approach. In general, staff at Albany felt that the measures introduced in 1985 had succeeded in stabilizing the previous volatility of the prison, and that the policies in place at the end of the 1980s were the correct ones for the future of Albany. It was thus envisaged that the regime would continue in the form that we witnessed for the foreseeable future (notwithstanding that Albany's function was to change with the post-Gartree restructuring of the dispersal system).

This is not to say that staff at Albany did not recognize the need for good staff–prisoner relations, only that their primary aim was to ensure that the 'right' kind of regime was in place. Only then could staff begin to think about relationships. As the Governor of Albany remarked:

My first briefing from a regional director was: 'Keep it clean, make sure it runs, give them clean clothes, clean bedding. Get them into a routine—there's some security in that. People can do their own thing within those routines and those limits. There is sufficient space for that. But if you don't provide the basics—food, canteen, gym, then you'll continually be running into crises' . . . Management supervision was saying 'Don't go overboard on the relationship bit, because if you haven't fed them, they'll kick you in the teeth'.

We do not wish to overdraw the contrasts between the outlooks of members of the staff of the two prisons. There are many points at which the comments made to us in interview were for all practical purposes indistinguishable, and there were certainly some individuals in each prison who felt 'misplaced' (i.e. who would have identified more readily with the culture of the other institution than their own). Nor for that matter do we want to suggest that Long Lartin did not have a structured regime. On the contrary, it did, and the relatively relaxed manner of its execution should not deflect attention from this fact. Indeed, as we can see from Table 3.2 which gives details of the timetables that were in place at Albany and Long Lartin during our fieldwork, Long Lartin's daily routine was different from that of Albany (and other long-term prisons) only in detail, though we do not wish to lessen the significance of this. Indeed, it is a point of some interest in interpreting the term 'ethos' (see above) that in some respects the actual 'regimes' of the two prisons differed somewhat less than staff's depiction of them might lead one to suppose.

We want now to convey something of the rhythms of life in these two prisons as these were recorded in their timetables and schedules of activity. It can be seen from data summarized in Table

TABLE 3.2. Daily timetables in Albany and Long Lartin

	Albany	Long Lartin
Unlock	07.45	07.45
Breakfast	08.15	08.15
Work/education/gym	09.00	08.40
Lunch	11.40	11.30
Lock-up	12.10	12.00
Unlock	13.30	13.40
Work/education/gym	14.15	14.00
Tea	16.40	16.30
Lock-up	17.15	17.00
Association	18.00	18.00
Lock-up	20.30	21.15
Hours out of cell (per day)	10 hours 40 minutes	10 hours 50 minutes

3.2 that, during 'run of the mill' days, prisoners at Long Lartin spent only a few minutes longer per day out of their cells than did their counterparts in Albany. However, it should be noted that Albany's policy of allowing only two-thirds of the prisoners out of their cells for evening association resulted, over time, in a drastically more marked disparity between the two sets of prisoners. Moreover, the bare data in Table 3.2 fail to reveal other important differences. Cell association, for example, was permitted at Long Lartin when prisoners were unlocked, but was not formally allowed at Albany. There was also a wider extent of choice in electing when and how often a prisoner could go to the gym, the laundry, the prison shop, and so forth at Long Lartin than at Albany.

Additionally, as Table 3.3 demonstrates, there were differences in the amount of time that prisoners were able to devote to particular regime activities. Both prisons planned fairly similar amounts of such activities (compare columns 1 and 3 of the table). Both failed to achieve the time that was allocated to prisoners for education

TABLE 3.3. Selected regime activities, Albany and Long Lartin, 1988 (Hours of regime activity planned and achieved per prisoner per week)

	Albany		Long Lartin	
	Planned	Achieved	Planned	Achieved
Gym	2.75	2.3	2.3	3.3
Education	20	17	21	18
Industries	23	22	27	19

and work-based activities. For education, both prisons failed to achieve the amount of hours set aside for education by three hours per week per prisoner. Long Lartin failed to meet its target for industrial activity by thirty per cent, compared with only a five per cent shortfall for Albany, though in making this comparison it should be noted that the original Long Lartin target had been higher. The greatest difference, however, occurred in the area of sports and associated provision ('gym'). Whereas Long Lartin exceeded the amount set aside for such activities by some forty per cent, Albany failed to realize the amount of time set aside for this activity by fifteen per cent; and the absolute level of 'gym' time achieved in Long Lartin was an hour more per prisoner per week. Two main points arise from these data. The first is again a reflection of Long Lartin's regime philosophy: priority was given to keeping the sports facilities open whenever possible, and, since 'gym' was popular with prisoners and they had greater freedom of movement at certain times (see above), a higher level of such activities was achieved than at Albany.[9] Secondly, the failure—in several instances—to meet planned regime targets is instructive. Staff and prisoners in both prisons repeatedly stressed the importance of *routines* in the prison (cf. also chapter 2), and prisoners placed particular importance on the delivery of regime features which they valued (amongst which gym certainly, and often education, featured prominently). A failure to meet institutional targets for some regime activities may thus be of importance in well beyond an administrative sense, and during our fieldwork we were repeatedly made aware of the frustrations that may occur when staff fail to deliver the full range of activities that prisoners associate with a sensible long-term prison regime. Indeed, as we shall go on to suggest in chapter 7, some 'control incidents' may result fairly directly from such frustrations.

Populations

Before proceeding further, it is quite important to introduce data on the populations of the two prisons. Obviously, the nature of the

---

[9] In fairness to the staff at Albany, it must be pointed out that they delivered three hours more industrial time per prisoner per week than did Long Lartin. Such an achievement would, however, be of lesser importance to most prisoners than the achievement of a high level of gym activity.

inmate population may have some effect on the life of a prison, and *inter alia* may have a bearing on the maintenance of order. Relevant data are presented in Table 3.4, with the population of Long Lartin shown as a whole, and the population of Albany divided into the two component parts of the 'main prison' (A, B, and C wings) and the VPU (D and E wings).

Not surprisingly given the reasons for its establishment (see above), Albany VPU housed a high proportion of sex offenders, and a relatively high proportion of Category A offenders. The population of the VPU tended to be older than either Albany main prison or Long Lartin, while the incidence of previous governors' reports, and violence against staff, tended to be less. Given this cluster of characteristics, one would not expect the Albany VPU population to pose much of a 'control problem' in the standard prison sense of that term, and this did indeed prove to be the case (see chapters 6 and 7).

Perhaps the principal interest of Table 3.4 lies in comparing the similarities and differences between the 'mainstream' population of Albany and their counterparts in Long Lartin. Mean ages for prisoners in Albany A, B, and C wings and Long Lartin were roughly comparable (31 compared with 34), though the proposition of people under 25 was significantly larger at Albany than at Long Lartin (31 per cent of the population compared with 14 per cent). Other notable differences between the two populations were that Albany contained, on its 'main' wings, proportionately more people serving determinate sentences of under eleven years (65 per cent compared with 46 per cent); fewer category A prisoners; more Afro-Caribbeans; and a strikingly higher proportion of people who had a previous conviction for a firearms offence (44 per cent compared with 9 per cent). However, some data of direct interest from a 'control' perspective, such as violence against staff, and GOAD[10] prior to arrival at the prison, showed no significant differences between the two prisons; and the numbers of Govenors' reports and total numbers of previous convictions were also broadly similar albeit slightly higher at Albany (p = <0.5). This is reassuring in terms of the main purposes of this research project (since, in an

---

[10] 'GOAD' = administratively placed in a prison segregation unit, under Rule 43 of the Prison Rules, because this has seemed appropriate 'for the maintenance of good order and discipline' in the prison. On the use of this provision in Albany and Long Lartin, see ch. 8.

ideal research design—though the methodological ideal was obviously not easily attainable in the particular circumstances of this research—one would study two prisons with identical prisoner populations, but radically different regimes and control problems). On the other hand, from the higher proportion of younger prisoners in Albany main prison, one would expect (from standard criminological knowledge: see for example some of the data in Gottfredson and Hirschi, 1990: chapter 6) that that prison would generate a somewhat higher assault rate than Long Lartin; and this expectation might be heightened in the present instance in view of the significantly higher proportion, in Albany, of prisoners who had been convicted of armed crime.

Research Methods

So far in this chapter, we have sketched our initial approach to the research, and described some important features of Albany and Long Lartin and their inmate populations. We must now explain briefly the research methods that we adopted.

Since the core of the study lay in understanding the social life of two prisons, and how this social life might have contributed to or prevented 'control problems', it was always obvious to us that the most important research resource available to us was *time*. It was essential to spend substantial periods of time in each prison, listening to staff, managers, and prisoners, and trying to understand the subtle dynamics of each prison's social life. We were fortunately able to convince our research sponsors that a lengthy fieldwork period in each prison was essential, and so two of us spent about five working months continuously at Long Lartin, and then again at Albany. (These fieldwork periods took place in Long Lartin from April to August 1988, and in Albany from November 1988 to March 1989.) All this was preceded by an almost equally lengthy 'pilot' experience at Wakefield Prison (another dispersal prison), going through processes of induction, observation, familiarization, and exploratory interviewing. Some might regard such a lengthy pilot period as a luxury, but for us it was a necessity, to ensure that we understood thoroughly what we would be doing before we set foot in the first of our two main comparison prisons.

If we were to give a label to our overall methodological approach, it would perhaps be that of a 'multistrategy approach'

TABLE 3.4. Characteristics of the inmate population at Albany (as at 1 January 1989) and Long Lartin (as at 31 July 1988)

| | | Albany | | | Long Lartin | |
| | A, B, and C wings | | Vulnerable Unit (D and E wings) | | | |
	No.	%	No.	%	No.	%
Population	227		146		415	
Age						
21–25	72	31	20	14	61	14
26–30	59	26	28	19	103	25
31–40	61	27	54	37	155	37
41+	35	15	44	30	96	23
Race*						
White	141	62	121	83	327	78
Afro-Caribbean	58	25	18	12	50	12
Other	28	12	7	5	40	10
Security category						
A	28	12	32	22	69	17
B	157	69	105	72	305	73
C or D	42	18	9	6	41	10
Current offence†						
Sex with violence	11	5	69	47	31	7
Other sex	4	2	37	25	20	5
Violence	79	35	51	35	189	46
Robbery	110	48	26	18	163	39
Drugs	38	16	4	3	70	17
Sentence length						
Under 5 years	15	7	19	13	2	0.5
5–10 years	133	58	79	54	190	46
11 years+	56	25	22	15	109	26
Life	23	10	26	18	114	27

GOAD this sentence up to arrival	56	25	11	8	105	25
Violence against staff this sentence up to arrival	19	8	6	4	40	10
Governors reports up to arrival						
0	69	30	78	53	140	34
1–3	55	24	45	31	129	31
4–9	50	22	10	7	59	14
10+	53	23	13	9	87	21
Previous convictions†						
Robbery	63	28	25	17	76	18
Violence	117	51	62	42	200	48
Sex	12	5	54	37	42	10
Drugs	38	16	11	8	46	11
Firearms Offences	101	44	18	12	39	9
No. of previous convictions						
0	32	14	27	18	67	16
1–4	38	17	36	24	114	27
5–9	77	34	38	28	110	27
10+	80	35	45	31	124	30

* For Long Lartin, data on this variable are given as at 31 May 1988, when the prison's population was 417.
† Prisoners convicted of more than one type of offence are shown under all relevant categories; hence percentages do not add to 100.

(see Layder, 1993: 108–9). Such a stance, Layder asserts, should be understood not as merely 'eclectic', nor as characterized by an 'anything goes' relativism, but rather as involving a form of 'disciplined flexibility'. In a similar spirit, we have tried to proceed systematically, but in full awareness that the setting itself imposed many kinds of pragmatic constraint. Thus, we have not ignored the necessity of gathering quantitative data, where quantification has seemed informative, though this was often based on records and documents that were frustratingly fragmentary and haphazard. However, the kernel of our study is provided by the qualitative reporting of observations, and of semi-structured interviews with staff and prisoners that were conducted in the process of our ethnographic fieldwork. Further details of these sources are provided in the succeeding paragraphs; for a fuller account of the practical and ethical aspects of the research see Appendix A.

(a) Qualitative data

At each prison we spent hundreds of hours observing what went on ('soaking and poking' as DiIulio (1987) describes his method) and talking informally to both staff and prisoners about day-to-day in the prison. We spent about six weeks doing this in each prison (often remaining in the prison until after evening 'bang up') *before* we conducted any formal interviews (see below). We visited many parts of the prisons. We spent most of our time 'on the wings', but we were also frequent visitors to segregation units, workshops, hospitals, classrooms, and (amongst places where prisoners did not go) offices, rest rooms, control rooms, board rooms, and so on. We were present at various meetings including the morning briefing conducted by the Governor, work allocation meetings, and meetings concerned with reviewing prisoners' career plans.

Two sets of semi-structured interviews were then conducted in each prison. The first we shall term 'general interviews'. Here we questioned staff (of all grades in proportion to their numbers) and prisoners (of different age, race, offence-type, sentence length, and security category) on many topics about the nature of their daily lives and their interactions with one another. These interviews (all tape-recorded) had a set list of topics to be covered, but there was no fixed order to the questions, and the way in which questions were to be phrased was not prescribed in advance. Thus, in many ways the interviews were rather like structured conversations. The interviews covered such issues as: what kind of relationships existed between staff and prisoners, and amongst prisoners themselves? What were the core values of staff? What skills and kinds of knowledge did staff need? Were they (in their own eyes or those of prisoners) equipped to deal with the sorts of problems they confronted? What did prisoners and staff think of the present regime? To what extent could each of the prisons lay claim to a particular 'ethos' or tradition and how might such intangible but important concepts be described and analysed? How did troublesome incidents occur? More tangibly, how frequently did they happen? How were they accorded priority? How were incidents dealt with, and what were the consequences (both intended and unintended) of the action taken? Perspectives gleaned from the 'general interviews' are primarily reported in chapters 4, 5, and 6.

The second set of interviews ('specific interviews') were more precisely focused and selectively sampled. We sought to contact all those prisoners and key staff named in the relevant files as having been involved in recorded incidents over a four month period in each prison (for further details, see chapter 7). This often entailed us visiting prisoners in other gaols (as far apart as Dartmoor and Durham) to which they had been moved, usually as one result of the incident. In specific interviews we sought people's views on what the background to the incident had been; what happened; how it was dealt with and the ramifications for the individuals concerned. In all cases we sought to make sense of the incident by collation and comparison of participants' varying accounts. That is, we were concerned to understand the existence of plural conflicts and to acknowledge the plurality of actors' accounts of them. Our primary purpose was to explore the links between contingent 'events' and underlying patterns of social relations in the two prisons; hence, we were not concerned to apportion blame or to privilege one narrative of events over others. The data from the specific interviews are discussed in detail in chapters 7 and 8.

Taking general and specific interviews together, we conducted at Long Lartin 25 taped interviews with staff and 44 with prisoners; the corresponding figures at Albany were 41 and 39 respectively. Interview numbers were higher (proportionate to the total size of the prison) in Albany than in Long Lartin, in order to ensure adequate coverage of the VPU as well as the 'main' prison. All formal interviews (general and specific) were fully transcribed, and formed a rich source of qualitative data which is freely drawn upon in the following chapters.

(b) *Quantitive sources*

In addition to statistical information on the populations of the two prisons (see above), we collected various statistical data which we believed might offer insights into problems of order and disorder. These included: the numbers and types of recorded 'incidents'; where and when such incidents occurred; figures for the number of alarm bells; the numbers of transfers of prisoners both within and between prisons; numbers of people in segregation and the length of time spent there. We had several purposes in collating these data: to offer the reader some sense of the scale and complexity of what is undertaken in the name of regulating and securing order in prisons; as a basis for illuminating comparisons between the two institutions; and as a context for understanding, and perhaps for confirming or otherwise, some of the claims made in interview by staff and prisoners.

Conceptual issues—defining and investigating 'order', 'control', and 'control problems'

'Control' is a term much used by prison staff and prisoners alike. The concept, however, is an enormously problematic one, for a range of reasons. It is a highly charged and emotive term. It signifies differential power relationships—those who control and those who are controlled. The vocabulary of 'control' is suffused with allegation and denial. At one level, 'control talk' (to borrow Cohen's (1985) phrase) in prisons is readily understood: at least everybody acknowledges that control happens. However, it has not always been apparent precisely what is meant by 'control' or 'control problems' in prisons. For example, the CRC report (Home Office, 1984: para. 43) acknowledges that its use of the term 'control problem' covers a range of phenomena incorporating 'disorderly behaviour', 'subversion', and 'mental disturbance', and stretching from persistent minor infractions to killings in prison.

Given this background, before conducting a study of 'control problems in dispersal prisons' it seemed to us important to pay some serious initial attention to conceptual analysis and clarification. As a starting-point for such analysis, we can note that each instance of defined 'control problem behaviour' emerges out of interactions between staff and prisoners. In this sense, the defining of behaviour as 'problematic' for staff or prisoners is *processual*, and possibly contested, rather than a simply discrete or isolated act (and that is true even if the act itself is apparently sudden and 'one-off': for there are still different ways of *responding to* such acts). The notion of a 'control problem' is thus by no means self-evident. Rather it suggests that staff make various decisions (at various stages of the process). These may be according to the rules, sanctions, and powers that are provided by the system, or by recourse to informal channels of power. The type and severity of the incident, the circumstances in which decisions are made, the precipitating events, the kind of institutional climate or 'ethos' that is sought within the prison, and the priorities of staff are thus not only inextricably linked, but *central* to what gets labelled as a problem situation. Bearing in mind these complexities, during our pilot period at Wakefield we decided to produce formal definitions of what we meant by the terms 'order', 'control', and 'control problem', as a guide to the subsequent ethnographic fieldwork. These definitions (which were subsequently slightly revised) are, in their final formulation, as follows:

Order: an orderly situation is any long-standing pattern of social relations (characterized by a minimum level of respect for persons) in which the expectations that participants have of one another are commonly met, though not necessarily without contestation. Order can also, in part, be defined negati· ely as the absence of violence, overt conflict or the imminent threat of the chaotic breakdown of social routines.

Control: the use of routines and of a variety of formal and informal practices—especially, but not only, sanctions—which assist in the maintenance of order, whether or not they are recognized as doing so.

Control Problem: a critical situation, event or sequence of events perceived by staff as sufficiently serious to warrant the imposition of a sanction or special administrative procedure in the interests of maintaining their own authority and the stability of the prison.

'Order' is thus a larger and more inclusive word than 'control'. Different forms of order are, of course, both theoretically and practically possible. We are adopting the term throughout to mean those patterns of relationships which together 'form a whole' and which are capable of being sustained over time without undue disruption or resort to exceptional measures (cf. Young, 1987). 'Order' alludes to the range of practices and activities which become routinized and embedded in the daily life of institutions. In this sense order is, paradoxically, both a mundane and an organic, dynamic concept.

Prison routines and activities are clearly observable. They revolve around fixed and repeated practices such as locking and unlocking, the serving of food, the provision of set periods for education, association, work, and so on. We reserve the term 'control' for the *strategies* that people utilize to maintain a regime that they consider orderly. By extension 'control measure' means the steps that are taken to re-establish authority when order is overtly threatened or disrupted.

If 'kinds of order' are somewhat variable and contingent, then it follows that certain types of 'control problems' will assume greater or lesser importance by virtue of their relation to the form of order that is sought within each prison. A central corollary of this is that problematic events or situations may be defined and acted upon differentially. They may happen more or less frequently and they may be regarded as more or less important in different contexts. Similarly, the range of control strategies that staff deem to be appropriate to secure the smooth running of the prison may also differ in quite marked ways. But for methodological purposes, and to aid the comparison between our two prisons, we decided upon the following working definition of a 'control problem', based on certain administrative categories:

1. disciplinary offences leading to a sanction—loss of earnings, loss of remission, segregation, and so on;

2. movements of prisoners within the prison on control grounds under Rule 43 GOAD (see note 10 to this chapter); movements between wings; or to special cells; or the hospital;

3. movements of prisoners between prisons under the provisions of Prison Department Circular Instructions, and other transfers on control grounds;

4. incidents deemed sufficiently serious to warrant notification to higher levels of management (beyond the establishment).

We have thus confined the definition of 'control problems' to events which were officially defined and acted on as such. We have adopted this approach for a number of reasons. In practical terms, we could not *assume* that an incident had taken place unless it had been formally defined as such and acted upon. There were occasions when it was common knowledge that 'incident-like events' had happened but not, for a variety of reasons, been acted upon by staff. We need not be too surprised at this. It has been a near commonplace of prison sociology since Sykes that the prison could scarcely function if each and every instance of rule breaking was acted upon with equal vigour. It can, of course, be argued that the pursuit of such lines of enquiry might have enabled us to comment in more (and much needed) detail on the existence of the 'dark figure' of control problems (we did pursue some data sources of this kind—see chapter 7—but not any that involved direct questioning of inmates or staff). But in considering this option, we decided that it could have been invidious to ask people to talk in detail about incidents that had not 'officially' taken place. Rather than inviting them to put their side of the story we would have placed them in the position of confirming or denying a rumour. Moreover, we were centrally interested in the *definition* and *handling* of threats to the maintenance of order. Hence we were concerned to establish the key points in the decision making processes about the use of particular control mechanisms. Our central theoretical concern was thus to look not only at the 'incident' itself, as if it were self-defining and apart from its surrounding milieu, but also to locate it in a chain of circumstances—both of antecedent events and of subsequent organizational responses, and, in turn, *their* further consequences.

Kinds of Control Problems

It is apparent that the term 'control problem' covers a diverse array of events. These include curious or one-off happenings that seem to defy prediction, and others that clearly have detectable patterns. It is equally clear that certain kinds of control problems assume greater or lesser importance by virtue of their relation to the prevailing routines and customs of the prison. In this sense, it may be neither the most frequent nor even the most apparently dramatic incident that is regarded as posing the greatest threat to the sway of the established order (see further discussion in chapter 7).

On the basis of our pilot work, we reached the view that endemic 'control problems' (as distinct from unique or momentary crises) might helpfully be classified under the following three main headings:

Interpersonal violence

Violence, either real or threatened, is perhaps self-evidently a control problem. Staff and prisoners alike often observe (recalling Sykes's 'deprivation of security') that it is for them an intrinsic feature of prison life that a violent incident may erupt without warning. However, 'violence' is a notoriously extensive and fuzzy term, covering events that range from life-threatening assaults to incidents that are not seen as particularly serious. Events tend to be defined as less serious where the violence is seen as a purely individual matter (the prisoner was under pressure) or an isolated and momentary event between prisoners (a fight between friends or a scuffle in a food queue). Violence comes to be regarded as a much more major problem where it is extreme, persistent or related to conflicts between particular groups of prisoners (for example, a campaign by 'straight' prisoners against 'nonces'; or competition for control of a drugs market)—especially when it contains the possibility of becoming concerted or escalating.

The Informal Economy

By 'informal economy' we mean gambling, money lending, the trading of goods, importation of drugs, manufacture of alcohol, and other *sub rosa* trading. In our study, both staff and prisoners affirmed that a certain level of these activities was endemic, and not necessarily always a matter of the most serious concern. A range of doubts and conflicts can exist over activities that, for some staff as well as many prisoners, provide some harmless consolation and diversion for prisoners, and may thereby contribute to the smooth running of the prison (Sykes, 1958; Kalinich, 1980). There is also a measure of agreement that major threats to order arise mainly as a result of indebtedness and extortion rather than from, say, drug taking *per se*.[11] That is, power and influence tend to be concentrated among certain groups of prisoners who may assert and protect their position by force. Problems posed for staff thus concern the management of a chronic problem and how to act without destabilizing an existing situation, or losing legitimacy—an issue to which we shall return.

[11] There are certain important exceptions. The physiological effects of prison 'hooch'—a potent but unsophisticated beverage—are sometimes one, either in terms of aggressiveness (or parasuicidal depression) or the straightforward danger of alcoholic poisoning. The health risks involved in needle sharing are another.

Protest, disobedience, and abuse

The withdrawal of co-operation by prisoners takes a variety of forms. These range from stubborn silence or verbal abuse to sophisticated litigation and 'censoriousness' (see chapter 2). The importance of these phenomena, which frequently appear trivial in isolation, is that they pose direct or implicit challenges to the legitimacy either of the administration of rules or of the rules themselves. There are many subtle tensions in this area. In many cases it is difficult for staff to enforce open-textured rules without losing face and appearing to act in a petty manner. Yet, at the same time, they see the challenge itself as demanding a response. Many such situations include a possibility of escalation and disruption of routine. Thus, a range of ostensibly minor, but frequent, events are revealing about the negotiation of power relationships within the prison, especially if the assertion of a rule represents a change from practices which have become customary.

Each of these problems, together with a number of others, is almost certain to be present in any long-term prison in some degree. However, the incidence, definition, and management of them as 'problems' is also likely to vary. There may, for example, be differences in population composition and hence in the existence of networks on which trading depends, or in the degree of antagonism between individuals or groups of prisoners. There may be differences in opportunity as a result of differing policies of searching, surveillance or arrangements for association between prisoners. There may be some differences in the seriousness with which a particular kind of behaviour is viewed and hence in the way it is policed or in the disciplinary consequences which follow from it—for example, over what would prompt the decision to move a prisoner from 'normal location'. Such differences are, we have argued, intrinsically linked to the 'kind of order' which the prison seeks and thus to the grounds on which it stakes its claim to legitimacy. In subsequent chapters, we explore these issues using illustrations and comparisons drawn from observation, interviews, and analysis of various aspects of the running of Albany and Long Lartin.

Disciplinary Offences: a further look

In discussing, earlier in this chapter, the original formulation of the research design, we noted that Albany had a higher overall recorded disciplinary offence rate (see Table 3.1). We can now return to this issue in a little more detail, as a background to our further explorations in later chapters.

Table 3.5 shows *types* of recorded disciplinary offences in the two prisons for 1987 and 1988. In classifying the data, we have grouped the original offence types (which are based on the relevant paragraphs of Rule 47 of the Prison Rules, i.e. the rule that defines prison disciplinary offences in England and Wales) so that they approximate to the broad kinds of control problem outlined in the previous section. When this is done, it will be seen that two interesting differences seem to emerge. First, Albany has a higher proportion of its disciplinary offences attributable to 'disobedience' and 'disrespect', and the rate of such offences is substantially higher than at Long Lartin (1.1 in Albany per head of prisoner population in 1988, compared with only 0.4 in the same year at Long Lartin). Secondly, 'trading' offences (including drugs) constitute a slightly higher proportion of Long Lartin's total offences in the two years combined (16.4% against 10.8%) although—given that Albany's overall offence rate was higher—the actual rate per prisoner for trading offences in Albany was slightly higher (0.49 as against 0.33). Much caution is needed in interpreting these data; it has been well known since the time of Sykes (1958) that staff enforce the many rules about prison life very selectively, and this strongly discretionary element in enforcement clearly means that, in examining a set of data of this kind, one may be looking at the end-product of staff decisions as much as (if not more than) at differences in the behaviour of prisoners in the two prisons. Nevertheless, the data do provide an interesting starting-point for the deeper exploration to be undertaken in subsequent chapters.

For completeness, Table 3.6 provides data on the punishments awarded in respect of the disciplinary offences shown in Table 3.5. The first point to note is that Albany awarded more punishments per offence than did Long Lartin (bottom row of table). Then, considering *types* of punishment, the major difference is that Albany used the penalty of 'forfeiture of privileges' freely, while Long Lartin used it very little.[12] Clearly, then, we begin to see here

[12] Another apparent difference is the lesser use of cellular confinement at Long Lartin. However, this information should be treated with great caution, because in practice at Long Lartin 'non-associated labour' and 'cellular confinement' meant the same thing, and, as will be seen from Table 3.6, the proportionate use of non-associated labour was greater at Long Lartin than at Albany.

TABLE 3.5. Types of disciplinary offence, Albany and Long Lartin 1987 and 1988

Type of offence	Albany 1987			1988			Long Lartin 1987			1988		
	No.	%	Rate*	No.	%	Rate*	No.	%	Rate*	No.	%	Rate*
Assaults	42	5.8	.14	19	2.8	.06	25	6.2	.06	19	4.5	.05
Damage	9	1.2	.03	29	4.3	.09	10	2.5	.03	14	3.3	.03
Drug offences	20	2.8	.06	33	4.9	.10	18	4.5	.05	22	5.3	.05
Unauthorised possession/ transaction of articles	36	5.0	.12	62	9.3	.20	44	10.9	.11	51	12.2	.12
Disobedience	243	33.6	.81	248	37.0	.78	114	28.2	.28	101	24.2	.25
Disrespect	169	23.4	.56	114	17.0	.36	66	16.3	.16	64	15.3	.16
Other offences (Rule 47 paras. 12, 16, 20, 21)	204	28.2	.68	165	24.7	.52	127	31.4	.32	147	35.2	.36
Total	723	100.0	2.41	670	100.0	2.12	404	100.0	1.01	418	100.0	1.02

* Rate = Rate of relevant offences per head of average daily population (ADP). (See Table 3.1 for ADP data for the two years).

Source: Based on data taken from *Prison Statistics England and Wales 1987*; *Statistics of Offences against Prison Discipline and Punishments England and Wales 1988*

TABLE 3.6. Punishments for disciplinary offences, Albany and Long Lartin 1987 and 1988

	Albany 1987		1988		Long Lartin 1987		1988	
Type of punishment	No.	%	No.	%	No.	%	No.	%
Cellular confinement	75	5.1	83	5.4	9	1.6	10	1.6
Forfeiture of privileges	319	21.7	280	18.2	12	2.1	4	0.6
Stoppage of earnings	404	27.5	428	27.8	173	30.7	227	36.7
Caution	28	1.9	36	2.3	21	3.7	30	4.9
Non-associated labour	307	20.9	274	17.8	166	29.5	171	27.7
Forfeiture of remission	336	22.9	439	28.5	182	32.3	176	28.5
Total punishments	1469	100.0	1540	100.0	563	100.0	618	100.0
Total offences	723		670		404		418	
Punishments per offence	2.0		2.3		1.4		1.5	

Source: *Prison Statistics England and Wales 1987; Statistics of Offences against Prison Discipline and Punishments England and Wales 1988*

differences in official responses to formally-defined incidents in the two prisons—a theme that we shall pursue in other contexts in chapter 8.

Some outstanding questions

In this chapter we have sketched some aspects of the histories of and circumstances in Albany and Long Lartin that have been seen as important in shaping their practices. It is apparent that we have not been able to address questions about 'ethos' and regimes without encountering a considerable array of analytic and explanatory problems. When talk of 'ethos' arose, members of staff at each prison at once presented an implicit prospectus in terms of which they accounted for, and justified, their activities. With this in mind, it is important to note the kinds of pride and confidence that staff at Long Lartin attached to their never having had a major disturbance on the scale experienced at other dispersal prisons (for example Hull, Gartree, Parkhurst or Albany). The consolidation of routines and practices over time, staff argued, tended to produce a sense of trust and security in the expectation of the continued existence of a particular tradition. Staff at Long Lartin thus saw the continuation of their principles and regime as in many ways self-generating. A similar faith in the continuity of a particular 'way' of doing things was observed during our pilot work at Wakefield, the other original dispersal prison never to have 'lost its roof'. This was in marked contrast to the situation at Albany, where the staff's 'trust' in the regime had to be constructed by other means. In this respect, staff at Albany lodged some strong claims for the beneficial effects of the reconstruction of the regime after 1985. One key claim made by staff was that their morale had significantly improved since the changes. They said they were more confident of their ability to cope with troublesome situations, and that fewer assaults were occurring. Albany staff also argued that the changes restricted the scope for illicit trading, with the knock-on effect that 'ordinary, decent' prisoners were able to lead more peaceful and predictable lives. It was also widely held that vulnerable prisoners were better protected.

Above all, staff at Albany insisted that the firmer modes of control introduced in the mid-1980s did not prevent the formation of good relationships between staff and prisoners, nor the promotion of services and opportunities, such as pre-release and other courses. In sum, there was a strong consensus among staff of all grades at Albany that the combination of controlled unlocking, close supervision, and the effective delivery of regime activities had radically transformed a volatile and unstable institution into a relatively stable and predictable one.

Some problems concerning the maintenance of order seem endemic to dispersal prisons. It should by now be becoming apparent that Albany and Long Lartin were encountering these problems in differing degrees, and had adopted divergent strategies in confronting them. Staff at Albany regarded themselves as facing the unique problems of: a young population with a high incidence of offences involving firearms; an adverse geographical location; the folklore memories of Albany's own history; and uncertainty following an abrupt change of direction. The concern amongst staff at Long Lartin, meanwhile, revolved around how to maintain the prison's 'ethos' in the face of a variety of internal and external pressures. One major threat to the good relations claimed by staff at Long Lartin involved the erection of internal fences and anti-aerial aids over all areas of the prison which occurred during the summer of 1988 as part of the official reaction to the Gartree helicopter escape of 1987. These measures occurred during our fieldwork at Long Lartin, and they did cause some disruption in the

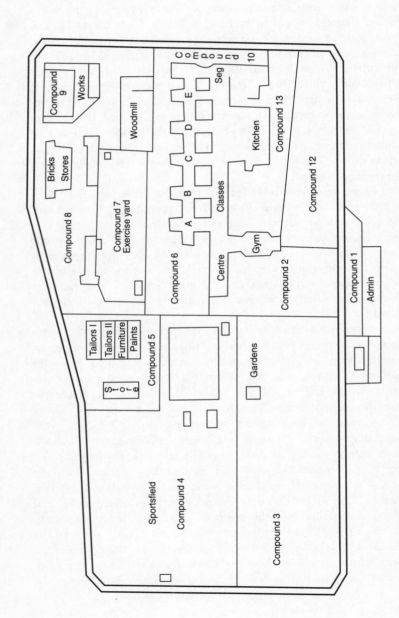

FIGURE 3.1. Outline plan of Albany Prison

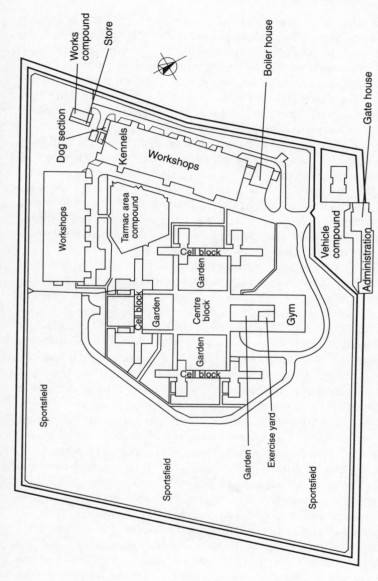

FIGURE 3.2. Outline plan of Long Lartin Prison

predictable daily flow of events (for example, outside recreation was severely curtailed). Many prisoners declared that they saw the erection of the internal fences (officially of course a 'security' measure) as the first step in imposing more stringent control at Long Lartin, and hence as the beginning of the end of the Long Lartin 'ethos'. For their part, staff at Long Lartin expressed the hope that they had enough 'credit in the bank' in their relations with prisoners to survive any conflict that might ensue.

Beyond these general questions lie some specific issues. Criticisms of Long Lartin had included allegations that it was inattentive to supervision even to the extent of allowing the development of 'no-go areas' for staff; that it had a tendency to allow free reign to 'gangsters'; and that it ran a policy of 'appeasement' of prisoners' whims and wishes. One point at issue, therefore, was whether this favoured potential 'predators' and, by extension, how the relative freedom of operation affected the lived of more vulnerable prisoners.

Albany, on the other hand, had to face the objection that their restriction of certain dispersal customs and practices was considerably at variance with the historical tenor of official thinking (let alone of more radical views) on the appropriate conditions of long-term imprisonment. To what extent did the additional complexities of timetabling and 'controlled unlocking' at Albany generate extra conflicts or antagonisms or lead to the punishment of infractions that would be disregarded elsewhere? Was it valid for Albany to justify its particular regime by reference to any 'special' or unique characteristic to its population, location, or other feature?

These large questions broach a number of moral dilemmas. Insofar as staff in both prisons were aware of criticisms that were levelled at them from elsewhere, they were anxious to rebut them. Staff at Long Lartin were at pains to differentiate between a 'relaxed' and a 'lax' regime. Albany staff, on the other hand, were concerned to insist that there was a difference between a regime that was controlled 'firmly' and one that was 'oppressive'. The differences and similarities which existed between Albany and Long Lartin thus provide a basis for empirical comparison and for broader reflection on the character of order in prison, and the range of control mechanisms by means of which the maintenance of order is pursued. In the next three chapters we consider further the world-views of staff and prisoners in the two prisons, and their orientations towards the penal environments they inhabited.

4

Social Relations: Staff Perspectives

THIS chapter discusses aspects of the viewpoints of prison staff in Albany and Long Lartin about 'control' and 'control problems'. It considers questions about governors' and prison officers' senses of their roles and tasks. How did people working in dispersal prisons view themselves and their jobs in relation to the institutions in which they worked? What views did they hold on appropriate ways of approaching and dealing with prisoners, and how did these vary? How did they think about problems involved in the enforcement of rules and the imposition of sanctions? What kinds of control strategies did they use? And where, in their view, did 'control problems' originate? (In chapter 5 we address many of the same issues from the prisoners' points of view.)

Throughout the research one of our aims was to find out about relations between people in everyday settings (ones which were, within the special environment of a long-term prison, ordinary). Our questions thus concerned how the various parties viewed one another and how they approached their dealings with each other. For example, we asked the Governor of each prison about the nature of the regimes that they inherited on their arrival and what they saw as their institution's present strengths and weaknesses. Similarly, we asked all prisoners and staff what they thought constituted 'a good prison officer', as a way of eliciting both the occupational values of uniformed staff and the expectations of prisoners. Our questions to officers also addressed matters of 'morale' and 'job satisfaction' and of how far members of staff felt at home in the corporate 'ethos' of the prison. Our questions to prisoners, meanwhile, were aimed at parallel aspects of *their* quality of life: at the kinds of pressures which prisoners experienced both from staff and in their relations with other prisoners, above and beyond the inherent 'pains of confinement'; at areas of particular contention between staff and prisoners, and the variations in these from place to place; at the kinds of feelings which are generated under different regimes and styles of control.

We also raised, with both staff and prisoners, the more overt senses of the terms 'control' and 'order', principally in relation to the enforcement of rules and the imposition of sanctions. Relevant issues included the kinds of choices and decisions involved in imposing rules and deciding how and when to take action; the boundaries of toleration; questions of style and tact in approaching potentially troublesome situations; and dilemmas encountered between consistency and discretion.

Going to a dispersal: expectations and realities

Many staff of all grades told us that they had contemplated their first arrival at a dispersal prison with some trepidation and misgivings. Dispersal prisons have a certain aura, given by the connotations of maximum security, the history of confrontation (see chapter 1), the notoriety of some of the prisoners who inhabit them. In consequence staff sometimes arrive expecting a certain level of violence:

I imagined a place obviously with a lot of security, and I imagined, falsely as it turned out, with a lot more problems, much more assaults on staff and so forth. Not unlike prisoners, staff have often heard alarming rumours and legends about characteristics of each prison. The truth is far different, especially as regards assaults . . . I expected almost to have daily problems here and the truth is far from it.

(Grade V, Long Lartin)[1]

---

[1] Since the staffing changes instituted in 1987–8 known as 'Fresh Start' the 'governor grades' and 'discipline staff' of the Prison Service have been termed 'unified grades'. The negotiations and controversies surrounding the implementation of 'Fresh Start' deserve detailed study in themselves. For present purposes it is sufficient to note that Grades I to V would still generally be referred to as 'governors' (and, in a reversal of what was originally proposed, not wear uniforms). The Governor-in-Charge of a dispersal prison would be a Grade I, though smaller or less sensitive institutions would be commanded by a person of less exalted rank. Grade V encompasses *both* the former 'Assistant Governor' role (commonly a youngish graduate) and the old 'Chief Officer' (commonly an older prison officer of great experience): it was thus, at least in the early days after 'Fresh Start', a somewhat ambiguous status. A Grade V would generally have responsibility, e.g., for one wing of a large prison. Grades VI to VIII are the (very much more numerous) uniformed members of staff—those who would call themselves prison officers rather than governors. These grades correspond to the positions of Principal Officer, Senior Officer, and Officer respectively. Whereas we use the terms Grade I to V to designate governors (with

This tone of surprise was typical for new arrivals at both Long Lartin and Albany. Such views, however, vary markedly with regard to past experience. In general, the reality of Long Lartin was presented as a relatively pleasant surprise, largely because the expectation for some had been so troubling. The transition to Long Lartin was particularly marked for those coming from lengthy experience elsewhere, especially in the more rigidly structured pattern of life of local prisons. Such people typically talked of the transition as being 'huge'. As one senior officer remarked 'it needs a mental adjustment of attitude and expectations'. It has been known for this period of adjustment to take many months. Some such startling experiences figure in this senior officer's personal account:

how to deal with people and how things were done, compared with Dorchester,[2] where there was an expected routine and inmates knew what to do and had to toe the line. At that time my concept of order was to have a clear landing and people who were supposed to be behind locked doors were behind them. I controlled those on the landing and those going to visits. I'd got the power of the key. I found here you haven't got a key at all, even at lock-up. You've got to use your personality to get everybody behind their doors at locking time, ready for the electric lock to go. The first day I was here I almost caused a riot at unlock by throwing doors open and shouting 'come on'.

For the new recruit (or New Entrant Prison Officer, universally known as a 'NEPO') meanwhile, the experience of arriving at a dispersal prison may represent a fearsome prospect, but one whose worst expectations may be quite rapidly overturned by experience. Thus, one new entrant of four months' standing thought Long Lartin was going to be:

a darn sight rougher than I found it to be. I was told it was—like—gangsters, and that it was going to be pretty rough and there was no communication between the officers and the rest of them. Whether I was being led on by the training staff at the College, I don't know, but it seems a lot more friendly, and sociable, than I was expecting it to be.

For staff coming to Albany, meanwhile, there was an expectation of a tough prison, but also a perception that times had changed.

the partial exception of '*the* Governor') we prefer Principal Officer (PO), Senior Officer (SO) and Officer for uniformed staff because these were the terms used *exclusively* by our interviewees to describe themselves.

2 A small local prison in Dorset.

Coming to the 'new' Albany, from the point of view of the new entrant, was often not so daunting as they believed the 'old' one to have been:

The stories at the College about Albany before the trouble was that it was a bad boys' nick. Since then I've been told that it's probably the tightest run of the dispersals and that morale between officers working here is very good. I've found this to be true. I knew that there would be a very secure perimeter and fairly relaxed regime inside, so I was prepared for that. I'm surprised how relaxed it is after Bristol, and that inmates aren't banged up all day long.

These perceptions indicate some of the 'myths and legends' about the nature of dispersal prisons which circulate throughout prison circles in England and Wales. Preconceptions are overturned by extended confrontation with the daily reality of each prison. Yet, ironically, in the course of that very process of assimilation, people may come to hold the 'myths and legends' about *other* prisons even more strongly. One can begin to see how it comes about that prisons become differentiated from one another. For many, becoming a 'Long Lartin officer' and an 'Albany officer' were somewhat different experiences, and led them to form different views. This bears on the theoretical problem of how it is that institutions sustain their own identity over time, in this instance precisely by providing their initially disparate staff members with a corporate ethos or identity in terms of which they can define their roles and commitments.

Managerial perspectives: governing, leading, coping

As we indicated in chapter 1, the recent period has been an eventful one in the prisons of England and Wales. Those who work in those institutions have been called upon to accept change in their working practices at a rate unprecedented for a system not hitherto widely noted for its dynamism. The changes concerned include new attendance and remuneration systems for prison officers; the switch from regional to area management and successive redistributions of tasks and functions within Prison Service Headquarters; the aftermaths of the 1990 disturbances and the Woolf report; the rapid acceleration towards the privatization of prisons, and the market testing of many posts and units; Agency status. As in other public sector bodies, new terminologies that were previously hallmarks primarily of commercial organizations have come to the fore— terms such as 'value for money', 'auditing', 'economy, efficiency, and effectiveness', 'performance indicators', are increasingly prominent aspects of present-day prison discourse, in public-sector as well as private prisons. The full history of prison management in Britain in recent times remains as yet unwritten (though see on various aspects King and McDermott, 1995; McLaughlin and Muncie, 1994; Adler and Longhurst, 1994; Finkelstein, 1993).

It seems apparent, however, that what governing prisons means and involves will also have changed significantly. The kinds of shift identified by Jacobs (1977; see chapter 2) from local 'Chieftain' to principal post holder would seem to have continued. Prison governors are subject to more, and more explicit, external direction; and they are vertically accountable within their organization to a much greater degree now than their counterparts in earlier generations. Policies, priorities, and resources are determined from the centre and filtered through area management. Yet governors still have to contend with exigencies which they inherit in specific prisons, and are routinely required to make decisions that can be fateful for the smooth running of the prison and for individual prisoners or staff members (cf. Train, 1985: 178–9). They are managers of complex organizations (like Chief Executives of local authorities) but they are also figureheads; and they remain vested with considerable quasi-judicial powers.

There may be many occasions when the various roles of the contemporary prison manager conflict—or at least create dissonance for the incumbent—and it is by no means clear that the twin definitions as functionary and figurehead can always be reconciled (in Giddens's (1990) terminology there is a tension between the 'place based' and non-place based' structures and systems in which they are involved). Incoming governors, for example, quickly become conscious that their freedom of action is not unconstrained, and that neither the tenor of the wider Prison Service organization nor the 'character' of the particular prison can be changed by fiat or declaration. Institutions may have no continuing existence independent of the consciousness and activity of their members, but that consciousness includes memories, folklores, identities, and enmities that have great resilience. One of the constraints that governors are under is often precisely the anxiety of uniformed staff that an incoming governor may want to change fundamental features of practice which, in their eyes, have 'worked' and which are central to their culture. Thus, for example, the Governor of Albany remembered that on his arrival he rapidly concluded that the anxieties of staff in the wake of the troubles of 1983 and 1985 would permit some innovations, but not others:

Looking around I saw fear and anxiety in people's eyes and real twitchiness and I thought 'I must start from where we are, and make something of what they've got and what they think they believe in, and then build upon that' . . . They were shell-shocked and they were physically fearful . . .

In a parallel vein, but in a dissimilar situation, the Governor of Long Lartin thought it necessary, from the outset of his term in office, to review or alter elements of the 'tradition' which seemed to him to have become merely habitual or 'appeasing', without at the same time disrupting the basis of institutional stability:

Many of them knew that in many areas things were totally unacceptable. I felt that the main element there when I came was fear. Fear of individual cons. collectively, fear of a riot, fear of losing the roof. And I remember after four or five months being able to say 'Well let's have a fucking riot' . . . Now I've brought in elements of control and searching where I'm saying, 'No, I'm sorry, you can be liberal and permissive, in certain areas, but then you come to a point where you don't accept that.'

Prisons have historically been rather hierarchical organizations, with the lion's share of power and decision vested at the top. Yet such power is not untrammelled, and governors are routinely in negotiation with others—uniformed staff, central administrators, prisoners, Boards of Visitors, and so on. It is often argued that traditionally in English prisons the relationship between governors and uniformed staff has been the most frequently conflictual of these. Certainly it could be held that resistance to organizational initiatives by uniformed staff (based upon their rather deep-seated distrust of those responsible for managing the service) has been a central feature of the Prison Service, as the history of poor industrial relations over the last several decades amply demonstrates (see Stern, 1987: 78–83). The firm of management consultants whose report helped to usher in the staffing changes known as Fresh Start in the late 1980s was of the opinion that:

The relationship between the operational and policy roles of the Service is unsatisfactory. Those staff concerned with policy and those concerned with operations view each other with a lack of comprehension and some suspi-cion. The consequence is that policy formulation is insufficiently well informed by a close knowledge of what actually happens in establishments while those responsible for the delivery of the policy at local level do not feel sufficient ownership of it.

(PA Consultants, 1989: 49)

Such sentiments were clearly very much in evidence during our study. This position also potentially moves beyond the common-place view of prison officers as a body of people who, at every opportunity, set themselves against the liberal and progressive pol-icy changes proposed by those responsible for managing the service, at both national and local level. Prison officers are often less reac-tionary, and prison governors and administrators less progressive than that neat caricature supposes.

In light of all this, it is scarcely surprising that the governors with whom we spoke (both formally in interviews and in numerous informal conversations) tended to speak of prison management in terms of 'balancing' or walking tightropes. Their imagery was con-cerned with reconciling competing priorities and concerns in the face of different kinds of constraint. What is acceptable to staff? Should the prison have a sense of mission and a philosophy of imprisonment and if so what should this be? What aims and objec-tives should be pursued, and what provision should be made for achieving them? What style of decision making is most appropriate for this prison at this time? These are some of the vexed questions which management routinely have to face. Clearly answers to them are complex and often elusive. Moreover, as Governors bring to the post their own individuals biographies, personal attributes, values, and commitments, they may well take up different positions in rela-tion to the problems that are raised by each of these questions, although it is perfectly apparent from the increasing managerialism of English prison administration (and as the views of Jacobs and others cited in chapter 2 might lead us to suppose) the scope for the exercise of charismatic individualism is rather smaller than it once was.

At the heart of these questions lie two fundamental problems. The first revolves around the extent to which individual prisons within the dispersal system should be managed (as far as is possi-ble) along broadly uniform lines and the degree of latitude that individual governors should be given to shape prison regimes in their own image. The second problem is not solely confined to prison management but would seem to be of central significance to the management of organizations more generally. It is this. What degree of control is it necessary to exert within an organization in order to ensure efficient functioning and how is this best brought about? In beginning to answer this question, Pugh (1990: x) suggests:

that two sides of a continuing debate may be usefully distinguished. On the one hand there are those who may be called the 'organisers' who maintain that more control and better control is necessary for efficiency. They point to the advantage of specialisation and clear job definitions, standard routines and clear lines of authority. On the other there are those who, in this context, may be called the 'behaviouralists' who maintain that the continuing attempt to increase control over behaviour is self-defeating, and that the inevitable rigidity in functioning, apathy in performance, and counter-control through informal relationships, means that increased efficiency does not necessarily occur with increased control.

This raises the question of the extent to which governors seek to stamp a particular form of management upon a prison or exert a charismatic influence upon the running of the institution, and the extent to which other staff either accede to or resist the various implications of this influence. From our own observations governors have certain dispositions towards a particular approach stemming from a blend of individual style and strongly held beliefs about how a prison should be organized and run. Each of the Governors in Long Lartin and Albany adopted a high-profile approach within the prison in that they were frequently seen by both staff and prisoners to be taking an active interest in the day-to-day running of the prison. However, the personal style of the two individuals could not be more different. One Governor sought to exert an influence upon the prison by, for example, 'leading from the front' in managerial meetings, visiting prisoners in their cells, carving out individual relationships and understandings with prisoners. The other preferred to adopt a strategy based upon attention to fine detail and consultation and greater devolution of decision making.

Two issues thus arise. To what degree does an individual Governor's style of leadership and his/her projection of a certain set of values command respect from staff? What part, in turn, does this play in the formulation of an 'ethos' or 'culture' of the prison and, by extension, what are the consequences for the quality of life of prisoners? Second, given the strong importance which prisoners traditionally attach to being able to contact the 'number one Governor' when they have a grievance, how the governor is perceived by prisoners is an issue of some significance. At the same time much of the drift of recent policy has been towards systematizing measures and a degree of uniformity. The monitoring of regimes and the delivery of 'Key Performance Indicators'; the demands made on Governors to institute incentives-based regimes: these and other measures suggest a transfer of influence from individual Governors to central decision makers. And there are many decisively influential issues (like staff–prisoner ratios) over which Governors may exercise very little control.

We now go on to discuss how some of the resulting dilemmas and decisions were experienced by the management teams in each of the two prisons, before turning to how these relate to some of the values and standpoints held by uniformed staff.

Long Lartin

Members of the Long Lartin management team suggested that the focus of their dilemmas lay in supporting friendliness, closeness, and flexibility in staff–prisoner relations, whilst at the same time resisting any degeneration into 'appeasement'. As one Grade IV governor pointed out:

A prisoner can cause us trouble because of our regime very easily. There is a low level of policing on the wings. The staff are there and they do patrol, but they don't actively seek out what is obviously going on, therefore it is relatively easy for misbehaviour to occur.

He nevertheless refuted the allegation that this inevitably leads to a slippage or drift into 'appeasement':

Our way is very carefully preserved because we tend to get flak from other dispersals who think that we're buying our peace. Until eighteen months ago we were the tightest adherents to the privilege system. We don't ever go easy on hooch or drugs. It is actively pursued. The regular charges that we do very little in terms of security are completely untrue.

In similar terms, a Grade V stated that:

Other people in the Prison Service probably say it's an appeasement type regime. I would deny that. I think it's less petty than some . . . I think coming here, in this grade, you almost come expecting to be reasonable, expecting to soak up a lot of aggression and so forth. But you have to learn that you can bite back sometimes . . . I argue strongly that we don't appease, I must say.

Prison managers at Long Lartin thus represent themselves both as supporting the 'tradition' of the prison, while, at the same time, distancing themselves somewhat from aspects of it. This is exemplified by the Governor of Long Lartin who asserted that when he came to the prison:

There were quite serious incidents which were being dealt with on the old boy network, and indeed at times, not even any official action being taken, because 'we work it out here. Even though I hit you on the head with a fucking hammer—it's not really important is it because we're all in prison—and you only had five stitches rather than twenty-five.' I felt staff would have been perfectly happy to continue in the way it was, because it was 'working' and it threw up less dangers and less confrontational situations for them . . . So I made it plain that everything was going to alter, and we would start to at least pull in gently the areas of concern whilst trying to maintain what.I accepted, even at that time, was a core or ethos which was well worth maintaining, and which I felt was there and bore no relevance to the bad practices.

Albany

Meanwhile managers at Albany stressed the need to balance the requirements of order, predictability, routine, and consistency against the avoidance of excessively or unduly 'repressive' measures. Moreover, Albany governor-grades were keen to argue that there was no internal inconsistency between maintaining a rigorous regime and the ability to enhance the quality of life for prisoners by providing worthwhile and constructive activities within it. They supported these arguments by reference to what they perceived of practice in other prisons, in particular those regarded as having a liberal regime. In terms of the first of these points a Grade IV commented:

A properly organized regime is not one which should be seen as oppressive, but one which is constructive. A laissez-faire one where prison officers just stand back and occupy space is not constructive. It may look as though it is completely open, but the undercurrents are actually destructive.

And in relation to the second, he continued:

While we are more repressive now as far as the regime goes, we are more and more encouraging them to get active. We've expanded the programmes on education. We've done a lot of work in the last two years in getting people into the prison. We had the Royal Shakespeare Theatre Company.

(Grade IV)

For his part, the Governor of the prison acknowledged that in many ways the regime at Albany was more restrictive than at other dispersals. At the same time, he pointed to the positive things that had, in his view, been achieved since its introduction. Thus in answering the question 'What would you say are the strengths of Albany's regime, and how should we evaluate its success?' he replied, firstly:

Prisoners continue to say, compared with what they knew before, that you can collect your food, and you can be sure of getting it to your cell and eating your own food.

Secondly:

Staff who've got the motivation and capacity to get involved with prisoners are able to do so, because there are enough things around to give them confidence to risk themselves in relationships with prisoners. It was manifestly clear to me when I came here that very few people felt they could talk to prisoners without either colleagues feeling they were compromised, or that they would be compromised. It was all negative if you were involved with prisoners.

Thirdly:

The level of stability has increased dramatically. If you look at the number of incidents—assaults on staff, alarm bells in the wings have gone down . . . there's much more tolerance. Although there are still a lot of reports here for abuse and challenge to authority it's much more absorbed than ever it was.

Moreover, the Governor saw the present regime as being one which not only needed to be retained, but which was capable of further development:

Some days I think I've got no vision at all. Other days I pick up things, I just move from where we are, and can see that there have been some good things recently. There is positive talk . . . 'Let's give them some worthwhile experience'. Good quality work for prison officers can only be good for human relations in Albany between staff and prisoners. The Education Department have done a lot in the last year with the range of activities, the range of classes, and the people coming in . . . the arts and crafts has actually taken some *very very* difficult men who've had a very long history of bad behaviour. Some human beings popped into this situation in good strategic positions with a bit of vision and discipline to them can actually give good opportunities which allow people to change their spots, or a little bit.

Managers of both prisons were well aware of the distinctions between their two institutions in terms of their regimes and methods of supervision, and they were conscious that their assertion of the validity of the arrangements and practices of their own institution could also be taken to imply criticisms of others. Similarly, they were alive to the sense in which each of their respective institutions may have looked unorthodox from the point of view of any central Prison Service requirement of consistency or uniformity. One way of fending off these implications was to insist not only that different prisons confront different problems, arising from their histories or the composition of their populations, but also that some benefits may result for the system as a whole from a diversity of regimes between the establishments which compose it:

The dispersal system probably needs a Long Lartin and an Albany, and it needs them to differ from one another as an incentive to prisoners to get around the system and find somewhere a bit better.

(Albany Grade IV)

Likewise, the Governor at Long Lartin saw a great deal of benefit in having a diversity of regimes, particularly in retaining the 'flexibility' to move prisoners strategically as and when this was required either in career terms or on control grounds. He asserts that this view was fairly widespread among other dispersal Governors:

They are all in favour of me doing the sorts of things that I would like to do because they see Long Lartin historically as being the place where people can move on to. Blokes who've maybe been a pain in the arse, for maybe seven, eight or nine years in Albany, finally say, 'OK I've got eight or eighteen to do, I've had enough. I'm burnt out. Send me to Long Lartin.'

Albany's Governor adopted a similar outlook. There was, he declared:

some mileage for us because I say to the Governor of Long Lartin regularly, 'I'm not pressing for you to do things exactly the same as me because there's a benefit of you having some differences. I can put up the idea to the prisoners that you're the top of the ladder. You're the place they're aiming to go for. They need some direction. Maybe your prisoners need to see a place a bit more restrictive like mine, in order to say, "Well look, let's negotiate, we won't go overboard because we don't want twenty or thirty to go to Albany." ' So I think there is room for the difference.

The awareness of such differences has implications for the ways in which the members of staff in different prisons view themselves and one another, and by extension their construction of what being a prison officer means. Each body of staff tend to construct a model of good practice out of their own experience. Such models are mixtures of principle and pragmatism: they are partly about what is right and partly about what 'works' in their own case. To this extent their own model can be used to disparage other prisons, sometimes on the basis of a rather stark and simplified view of what happens elsewhere. Yet a similar argument may also be used, on other occasions to argue that there is a need for diversity.

Uniformed Staff: identities and commitments

The Control Review Committee (see chapter 1) argued that relations between prisoners and staff were of fundamental importance in addressing the issue of 'control' and that a great deal therefore turned on 'getting that relationship right' (1984: para. 16). As we have already suggested, this leaves a great deal to be determined about what constitutes such 'relationships' in prisons. Not the least of these problems is that there are divergent, and to some extent conflicting, definitions of what it *means* to 'get it right'.

One way of approaching this issue is to begin by identifying some of the values and precepts which uniformed staff hold as to the proper ways of approaching and dealing with prisoners. This involves both differentiating between the emphases and commitments current in different prisons, but also attending to the points which are held in common and which constitute, as it were, the baseline of the experience of working in a high-security prison.

The values in which uniformed staff take most pride, and which they regard as underpinning their ways of working, tend to have to do with 'common sense', 'maturity', and 'fairness'. These are key terms for prison officers. The difficulty arises in showing exactly what is meant by them, and how they relate to everyday practice.

These are evidently very 'ordinary' virtues—designedly so, because their continuity with the solid practicality of plain folk (as distinct from the jargon of intellectuals and the scheming of mandarins) is part of what staff are asserting in using them. It is for this reason very easy to overlook the enormous importance that prison staff attach to them in articulating their sense of what is of value in the role of prison officer. It may also be in part for this reason (as we have argued elsewhere: Hay and Sparks, 1991a) that prison officers contine to have such difficulty in bidding for public recognition or esteem: they have no specialized language that supports a claim to expert knowledge. But these very terms *because* they belong to ordinary language are open textured and pregnant with implications: it is never self-evident what 'fairness' is—still less that it means the same thing in a prison as it does in some other place.

When asked 'what makes a good prison officer in this kind of prison?', staff in both Albany and Long Lartin offered a remarkably consistent range of answers. The salient terms suggested, roughly, two main areas of concern. These were, first, the kinds of *individual personal attributes* which staff felt to be necessary in order to withstand the daily demands and pressures of the job and, secondly, aspects of *personal style required to establish appropriate relationships with prisoners*. Uniformed staff are the people who have the most frequent dealings with prisoners and in some of the most difficult circumstances. Not surprisingly, they therefore regard their interaction with prisoners as being at the very heart of issues of security and control.

With regard to the first of these points (individual personal attributes), prison officers lay great stress on resilience, evenness of temper, and good humour. They tend to summarize these attributes using the terms 'common sense' and 'maturity'. Whilst most differentiate between maturity and age, there is also a widespread misgiving amongst experienced staff that too large a proportion of new or young staff is problematic. This results in part from the very widely held view that being a prison officer cannot be taught, but only learned by long experience or given by innate aptitude: being a prison officer is ultimately a matter of worldly wisdom:

It's no good ordering them. It's not as though we're in the army. But we've still got to use tactics to get the work done. If you're abrupt with prisoners the work gets done slower. You need diplomacy and patience.

(Long Lartin Officer)

Similarly, great stress is often laid on a sense of humour and other social skills:

You definitely need tact, sense of humour, a lot of insight and to a certain extent compassion. To see a classic example of a sense of humour used by staff you have only to stand by the hotplate. We don't dish the food up, we *sell* it. Many times when the meal has been on the dodgy side if it hadn't been for the staff selling it with comments like 'if you don't eat it we'll put it in your property box' then there would have been real trouble. You've got to be quick, to use your mouth correctly. A lot of staff don't and it can lead to assaults on staff.

(Albany Officer)

On the second question—of personal style and relationships—one begins to broach some more specific and substantive issues. The high level of agreement on general qualities results in part from their very generality: everyone agrees on the conventional virtues. This makes them no easier to state specifically (and to borrow Giddens's terminology again it seeems apparent that some of the most characteristic skill that prison officers exercise are carried in 'practical' rather than 'discursive' consciousness: see chapter 2). Thus in answer to the question 'Is it possible to say what qualities make for a good prison officer in this kind of prison?' one officer at Albany replied:

Not really. You've got young blokes who are very good and you've got older blokes who don't really want to know at times. You have to have an ability to mix with prisoners. You can't be prejudiced. You need plain common sense more than anything else. You've got to take each case as it comes.

It is for the very reason that prison officers see the job as revolving around 'plain common sense' that they often find it difficult to articulate exactly what it involves. Indeed, they tend to dislike attempts to formulate it:

Because of the length of sentence of many of the inmates the staff are going to spend an awful long time with those men, and as a result they've very quickly got to develop managerial skills. Most of them don't even appreciate that they've got this ability. A lot of them will say that they don't manage men, they only do a basic job. But for my money they do an extremely good job at managing men.

(Albany Senior Officer)

Much of prison officers' activity is taken up in talking to prisoners and coping with the contingencies of daily events. However, the question of approach to prisoners is open to particular disagreements about the *appropriateness* of different kinds of relationship and practice. Views on this issue varied between our two prisons, especially in respect of the degree of closeness or distance which it is right for staff to adopt *vis-à-vis* prisoners and on problems of flexibility versus consistency. This, in turn, varied in relation to the kind of regime which officers were expected to run, and hence the particular demands which the managerial philosophy of the prison made upon them. Prison officers are acutely conscious that working in prison routinely generates moral dilemmas and decisions which carry practical consequences. These everyday dilemmas are very much a matter of concern and debate among staff. On the question of closeness one officer remarked:

A lot of staff do get themselves involved. We take an interest in an inmate. If you see a bloke is down, and you go and ask him what is the problem, then you will find that others will come to you later. They will sus you out, and think 'Well, he is sympathetic to sorting out problems'.

(Long Lartin Officer)

Other officers stress that initiating and sustaining communication with prisoners is essential:

Most important you've got to be able to talk to an inmate no matter what he's in for, or what his attitude is like. Always say good morning. Some don't respond, so you leave it for a few weeks, then you try again. Some officers will see this as being soft. I don't. You can do the job without antagonizing.

(Albany Officer)

Some officers, however, express a note of caution in getting too involved with prisoners:

I'm a believer that familiarity breeds contempt. I can't agree with being on first name terms. I've known staff post money to prisoners' wives.

(Albany Officer)

Meanwhile questions relating to fairness, consistency and discretion are also fraught with problems. Staff frequently refer, as a general guiding principle, to treating all people equally:

If you are fair, you give them what they are entitled to, and make sure every inmate gets the same. Don't give it to one and take it from another.

Make sure you're seen to be fair to every inmate whom you mix with. They'll accept you, and they'll say, well—they may call you names occasionally whether you've given them everything or not—but they'll still respect you at the end of the day for being fair.

(Long Lartin Officer)

However, officers also affirm that certain situations are not always clearly defined and they often speak (indeed we would suggest that it is one of the terms that crops up most often in conversations with dispersal prison staff) of a number of 'grey areas':

It's always vague. You've got to take into account the characters involved, the member of staff, the inmate, and also the circumstances . . . In general everybody knows the limits and people will know when they've gone over them. You are not always dealing with people who behave rationally anyway. You can treat two people exactly the same, and one will still complain that he has been treated badly. There can't ever be two identical instances. It's always going to be a different time, place, and circumstance with different actors in it.

(Senior Officer at Long Lartin)

There is thus a large measure of agreement on basic features of what it means to be a prison officer. Nevertheless, there were also some marked differences between the views of staff at Long Lartin and Albany on particular aspects of appropriate practice, and on the maintenance of order and methods of control. It is to such divergences that we now turn.

Institutional Differences

Officers at Long Lartin were inclined to argue both that Long Lartin was a *better* prison than others in some fundamental ways, but also that it derived a benefit in terms of control from the deterrent effect on prisoners of risking being sent elsewhere. They thus tended to propose that Long Lartin should be seen as an 'honour' prison—allocation to it should be earned by good behaviour:

The majority of inmates say that Long Lartin is still one of the best prisons in the dispersal system . . . They shouldn't be in Long Lartin if they misbehave and they should be sent to a stricter prison. Coming to Long Lartin should be earned.

The tenor of the above view is indicative of a widespread belief among main grade staff at Long Lartin that the dispersal system should be graduated. In this sense, what is earned should also be subject to forfeiture:

I believe that there should be a system of graduation where you have different prisons with different regimes. The top one should be very relaxed and the bottom one strict and more restrictive on the inmate. If an inmate were to abuse the system then they step back down the ladder. If they are at the bottom and *still* abusing the system, they go somewhere where an inmate is locked up twenty-three hours a day with an hour's exercise. I'm a great believer in that system, not as punishment but as control.

Albany officers, on the other hand, attributed the troubles of 1983 and 1985 precisely to the failure of a 'liberal' regime. They considered that Albany had confronted its problems whereas others had fudged or evaded theirs. They argued that staff in 'open' regimes could not be 'in control' by any definition which they accepted. When speaking of Long Lartin, for example, one senior officer remarked:

All you can do is compare it with other prisons. An inmate once he's been at Albany shudders at the thought of going to Long Lartin. We know the protection rackets that are going on there. You can't stand on your own two feet there. There's power struggles, with little gangs, which doesn't occur here . . . You can do your bird better in Albany than in Long Lartin. Because of the freedom at Long Lartin there are even no-go areas. A man can do his bird privately better at Albany than he can at Long Lartin. You're either part of it, and if not, you can be trodden on.

In the view of Albany officers such open conditions encouraged unacceptable practices and accommodations. In reference to Albany's own past, one principal officer observed :

In the old days the word 'no' was very rarely heard . . . There was constant harassment: give me this, I want this etc. Every emphasis was on a placid approach. Officers are now more in charge of the situation and more able to convey to the prisoner what he really feels. Officers are able to give more individual attention to individual prisoners. There's far more authority which I believe is as it should be, giving personal attention to control their problems and the running of the regime rather than it was before.

In talking of the changes at Albany a main grade officer expressed surprise that:

The rest of the dispersals have not come into line with us. It has cut staff assaults tremendously. It has stopped a lot of inmate related fights. When there was a free regime there was a lot of bully-boy tactics. Now it has stopped. The cons don't dislike the new regime. Not all, but the majority.

It is our observation that there were real differences, including differences of interpersonal style and relationship, between the two prisons, and that these did indeed relate to aspects of policy in each prison. But these were only general tendencies, and there was a considerable range of variation within each prison. Moreover, the dynamics which led the members of staff in each prison to depict their own and one another's behaviour in these emphatic terms also concealed many points of convergence between the two institutions. These included considerable scope for disjunction between professed general attitudes and actual particular points of practice for individuals. Thus, Albany staff were almost unanimous in regarding staff–prisoner relations at Albany as mainly being good—and in insisting that there was no contradiction between firm control and adequate or even cordial relationships. They also acknowledged that an adequately stable mode of life for all concerned in long-term prisons required a substantial degree of co-operation from prisoners, and that such co-operation must be won in various ways. These included not only the regular delivery of activities and services but also, and more intangibly, humour, coaxing, attention to prisoners' needs and requests and so forth. Indeed there were a number of features of the regime at Albany—pre-release courses, shared working with probation staff—which, if not more highly developed than at Long Lartin, were at least their equal and which had been strongly supported by members of the uniformed staff at Albany:

Personally I don't just want to turn the key. I would like to see a lot more done for long-term prisoners, more evening classes, education, and discussion groups. A lot of them get fed up watching murder movies every night. In the groups we run we try to get them to see other people's points of view—to have logical arguments. It does spin off onto the landings.

For some officers such groups not only provided prisoners with much needed information and the opportunity to develop personal life and social skills, but they also served to enhance the quality of relations between staff and prisoner. In the words of one main grade officer:

My experience in working in pre-release means that you are able to achieve the higher degree of personal contact with a prisoner. It stays and it's beneficial. One of the greatest things we've found about doing that sort of work is the effect it has in relations between prisoners and staff on the landings. The prisoner does change his attitude and outlook. Staff may criticize, but they also remark that they see a difference in prisoners having done courses with us, and their relationship becomes better.

So far we have argued that there were indeed differences in the commitments and priorities felt and valued by staff in these two establishments, but that these were also variegated and complex. We now turn to explore the consequences of these matters for the nature and exercise of control, especially in relation to the enforcement of rules and the imposition of sanctions. Meanwhile, in the next chapter we go on to relate these variations to their most important outcome, namely the viewpoints of prisoners and the experience of incarceration in Long Lartin and Albany.

Rules and sanctions

Until now we have discussed some variations in the views of staff on questions of what kind of staff–prisoner relationships were *appropriate* in each prison. In each case, these perspectives on the question of 'relationships' were also fundamentally concerned with issues of *order*. In both prisons it was clearly recognized that questions of stability in long-term prisons extended beyond the overt exercise of 'control' to incorporate matters of interactional style, staff's views on their own roles and identities, and the realities of everyday dealings between staff and prisoners.

These perspectives constituted some of the informal 'rules and resources' (cf. Giddens, 1984) on which prison staff drew in defining their practice and their own codes of conduct in dealing with prisoners. These positions also represented some of the conventions or frameworks within which rules and sanctions in the more formal sense, as a body of requirements and prohibitions, were interpreted and applied. One may conjecture, therefore, that there would be some variation in the ways in which the Prison Rules, as a formal code with nominally universal effect, were deployed in different times and places. However much governors and administrators may have advocated consistency, these rules continue to have a sufficiently 'open texture' (Twining and Miers, 1982: 213) to be quite varied in their interpretation and effects.

The enforcement of rules is a central aspect of the 'dialectic of control' (Giddens, 1984: 16) as it exists in any institution at a particular time. Staff exercise control in the sense that they enforce rules and impose sanctions with compulsory force over prisoners. At the same time they also know that they cannot act upon every breach of rules and regulations. The scope of the rules is in principle so wide that they may be seen as being violated *all the time*. But to take formal disciplinary action at every opportunity that presents itself places in jeopardy the kind of relationships they are also trying to cultivate (and on occasion provokes a more drastic reaction). And, as Sykes was so well aware, prison staff may conclude that the game of asserting maximal control is not worth the candle: it sacrifices too much co-operation in mundane tasks and becomes disruptive of routines and 'normal' practice.

A degree of discretion is therefore *inherent* in the enforcement of rules in prison, notwithstanding any declared intention to achieve complete consistency. What varies is the nature and extent of such discretion in relation to other features of the social organization of particular institutions. Thus:

1. In that every application of a rule also involves interactions between people, the ease with which one party can enforce a rule varies in relation (i) to a prior relationship (and the distribution of power in that relationship) and (ii) what is normal or customary in similar cases.

2. The degree of emphasis which is attached to any particular rule is likely to vary as a function of the kinds of anxieties, concerns or priorities which predominate in a given institution.

Rule enforcement is thus related to the 'model' of imprisonment which is operative in a particular institution. There have been a number of attempts in prison studies to produce typologies of such models. Barak-Glantz (1981) has suggested that these may be (1) 'Authoritarian', (2) 'Bureaucratic-lawful', (3) 'Shared Powers', or (4) 'Inmate Control'. This typology is of some use descriptively, insofar as it identifies some different possible states of affairs in the 'dialectic of control'. All English long-term prisons are, formally, of the 'bureaucratic-lawful' type. However, there is a range of variations within this. Differences in rule enforcement between such prisons in England and Wales are not so great as between, for example, prisons in different jurisdictions within the United States. They are bound by the same codes and requirements. Nevertheless, insofar as they differ somewhat at less formal levels—in response to their own historical evolution, in the occupational cultures of the staff—they are likely also to differ at the level of rule enforcement. These differences will incorporate both the grounds on which a prison stakes its claim to exercise legitimate authority and hence also the kind of social relations between staff and prisoners which it posits as appropriate.

We now go on to explore some of these convergences and differences between Albany and Long Lartin. Staff at both Albany and Long Lartin told us frequently about the necessity of declaring and enforcing a 'line' of acceptable and unacceptable behaviour. Yet staff commonly also emphasized the fluidity of lines and rules. Rules, they argued, are broken all the time, and it would be impossible to act upon every single infringement. Therefore there is an inherent space for discretion, calling for careful judgement, and the evaluation of each case on its own merits. The aim of such professional judgement, they suggested, is to maintain an appropriate sense of proportion, and to avoid needless antagonism.

Enforcing the 'line' for one main grade officer at Albany involved certain shared understandings between himself and the prisoner concerned. Thus he himself must have:

The right attitude, not stepping over the very thin line with inmates.

Whereas:

It's the same for inmates who if they step over it get nicked . . . I've always been one for storing things. There's no greater weapon than saying to an inmate on the second or third time he tries something, 'I'm not that daft, I let you go on that one, and on the other one, but now you're nicked.'

The interesting question, however, is how and where this line is determined, negotiated, and drawn. And here rather different considerations may come into play in different prisons.

Long Lartin

The fluidity of rules was a particular preoccupation for staff at Long Lartin, given its regime and traditions. For one main grade officer there was always a need to attempt to 'play down' conflictual situations. This called for skill and a carefully formulated approach:

Cool it down. That is how you handle the situation. You've not got to lose control. If you lose control, you've lost it. If you can manage you've got to keep the dialogue going as well. This is where it helps to know the prisoners and the wing that you're on. You can say to somebody, 'Hey, what's the problem?' And he'll say such a thing isn't right. 'OK we'll sort it out.' Somebody else tries to come in and you say, 'Just hang on a minute, I'm talking. We're trying to sort out this problem.' And they recognize that you've started to solve it.

The sense of proportion needed (and the danger of creating what is deemed to be unnecessary antagonism) is illustrated thus:

They're only allowed so much cash in their possession. This particular prisoner had 20 or 30 pence over, so technically you've got the right to nick him for having excess cash, but it's not worth it. I asked him what it was all for, and he said he was collecting money for tea and sugar. They shouldn't run a tea scheme. He was the Yes Boss, No Boss, I didn't know Boss, Long Lartin type. I warned him not to let it happen again and if it did I would have to nick him, but if they become stroppy, then you have no option but to nick them. It depends on the inmate's attitude at the time.

Similarly, one senior officer remarked:

You've got to get a feel about how the wing is. There are times when you reel in a bit, and there are times when you've got to let some line out. There's always a balance. Perhaps I have quite an influence with the staff by saying they've really got to do something about that this time, or you can swallow it this time. Or I'm sure the bloke will come and apologize quite soon, and that quite often happens. In general everybody knows the limits, and people will know when they've gone over them. If they don't get nicked, I think they'd probably think they were lucky.

To this extent, Long Lartin staff argued, life in a long-term prison necessarily generates 'grey areas' in which a dilemma exists between, on the one hand, the need for vigilance and for staff to exercise control and, on the other, the necessity of sustaining a certain level of co-operation and consent. This, they argued, involved acknowledging a degree of personal autonomy for a prisoner group who are adults and, by definition, serving long sentences. There is thus, staff asserted, a direct relationship between the nature of rule-enforcement and the quality of life for prisoners which results.

Staff also insisted that these considerations made working in Long Lartin a more difficult, demanding and delicate task than in other more 'structured' or traditional penal environments:

Working in a disciplined, or a fairly disciplined service there's black and there's white. What they can have, what they can't have, what decisions you make on your own, what decisions are made on your behalf or whatever, are fairly structured and laid down. Here you feel you're on uncertain ground . . . You feel as though you're a sponge and absorbing things. The accepted thing about a dispersal is that they can say what they like and get away with it. But in reality they can't. They'll only get away with what you allow them to get away with even with a liberal regime.

(Principal Officer)

We found this to be a common theme:

Q   A number of people have said to us that they think it's more difficult to work in a more relaxed regime. Do you think that's right?

A   Much more. If you've got the guidelines it's dead easy. It's the vast areas of grey in the middle that are the minefields. . . . That's where you stand or fall. Personality and character will carry you through, not the rule book. You have to point out that we're a living unit, that he's got to spend at least two or three years with this inmate. That he's got to live with him daily, and if he makes a decision, then he's going to have to justify it. If he does nick the inmate, then he's got to be certain it's fair otherwise the inmate will never again relate to him for a long period.

(Principal Officer)

The point bears repetition that staff at Long Lartin, whilst agreeing that their *particular* way of doing this may have made the extent of the 'grey areas' greater or at any rate more obvious, were on the whole convinced that the elements of complexity and ambiguity were *intrinsic to all* long-term prisons (unless, presumably, they resorted to a complete 'lock-down'). There are a number of interesting points of comparison between these two viewpoints and those of Albany staff.

Albany

The views of staff at Albany and Long Lartin did not represent a simple polarity. In the same sense that the 'core values' of staff overlapped, so also did positions taken up with regard to rule enforcement. Hence, Albany staff professed many of the same views as prevailed at Long Lartin. This was particularly true in relation to the use of personal social skills to take the 'heat' out of potentially critical situations. On this question officers had in mind the possibility of exacerbating the problem by enforcing the rules too rigidly. In the terms of one senior officer:

We're governed by rules, and there is a saying that exception proves the rule. The most important thing is to know when that exception should be used. The good prison officer will bend the rules for good reasons, for the right reasons.

This need for flexibility and discretion in implementing the rules finds much support among uniformed staff. In a principal officer's words:

You cannot be a strict disciplinarian in these sorts of places. You've got to learn to work in the grey area to maintain stability. You've got to be out-going and not frightened to approach prisoners. Officers have got to learn man management—coaxing the inmates without them knowing what they're doing.

Moreover, for some Albany main grade officers the ability to do this without nicking the prisoner or engendering further conflict was a source of pride:

In my 12 years I think I've placed 5 people on report. I could have placed 305, 505 on report. Three of them I had to because they escaped out of their prison cell and 2 of them I was obliged to because I couldn't do any-thing further about it. They didn't listen to reason. I'd given them the opportunity to conform and they wouldn't. I can understand the inmate telling me to piss off when I tell him to get up and get ready for work. Now I wouldn't nick somebody for that, but some people do. If I tell somebody to get out of bed and 10 minutes later he's not out of bed, and tells me to fuck off, then I would nick him. But I haven't had to have that sort of experience. I've never been assaulted. I've never backed down from anybody and I feel if you handle a situation correctly you don't need to use the power of the Governor. If you can't do it yourself, you're just get-ting the Governor to do your work.

However, there was also a much stronger feeling among Albany staff of the need to minimize the indistinction which resulted from the inescapable grey areas. This case was made with reference to:

1. The experience of riot, and the demand that staff exercise control;
2. The safety of prisoners and staff;
3. The requirement of regularity in regimes, routines and activi-ties, and the value placed on everyone 'knowing where they stand';

4. Greater stress on the need for consistency in the interests of fairness.

Thus, Albany staff argued that a degree of stringency in rule enforcement also produced greater clarity, so that prisoners *knew* the boundaries of what was acceptable and what was not. This, for many officers, was in marked contrast to the state of affairs prior to the implementation of the post-1985 regime. Thus:

We have regained control. At one stage there was no control. They did what they pleased within the prison providing they banged up at bang-up time. They wandered around the wings in groups. That's stopped now . . . Once you get a pattern of rules and regulations and you enforce them fairly, I think people accept them.

(Main grade officer)

And in the view of a principal officer:

Most inmates prefer a structured regime where they know exactly where they are, though they won't admit it. Some of them say they like it in Wandsworth where they're banged up all the time.[3] You would think they would prefer a prison where they're unlocked all the time, but that's not always the case. Everybody accepts the regime now. It was in place when I came, and it has got more well-oiled during my time here. The new inmates accept it because they have never known anything different. Staff and inmates have to talk to each other more. The inmates seem more settled as well. I think they prefer a stricter regime in some ways. At least they know where they stand.

Discussion

Both these general rationales (flexibility and drawing the line) set up a number of dilemmas and problems, which we raise briefly here and return to in subsequent chapters. Each principle—that flexibility was necessary and that it was essential to establish a 'line' of acceptable conduct—was accepted by staff in both prisons, but with appreciably different emphases. We suggest that a number of relevant aspects of prison staff outlooks can be 'mapped' in terms of the distribution of positions on the question of flexibility, and also on the question of the appropriate degree of closeness or otherwise in staff–prisoner relations (discussed earlier). Indeed per-

---

[3] A large local prison in London.

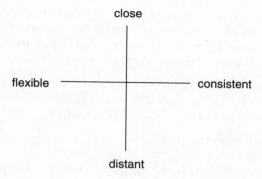

FIGURE 4.1. Dimensions of interactional style used by prison staff

haps one could conceive of these issues in terms of a hypothetical matrix composed of two orthogonal scales, as shown in Figure 4.1.

This diagram[4] claims to identify not persons but rather some positions they take up in relation to dilemmas generated in social situations in prison. Individuals will move their position within the diagram. Yet, conversely, it may also be possible that there are systematic variations in the positions which members of different institutions take up, resulting from the consolidation of policies or occupational cultures over time. For our own part, on the basis of our research observations, we would locate the predominant opinions of Albany staff in the NE quadrant (close staff–prisoner relations; consistency) and those of Long Lartin in the NW quadrant (close staff–prisoner relations; flexibility).

For Long Lartin staff this position raises, *inter alia*, the following questions:

1. Does a preference for a discretionary and individualized justice create inherent scope for discrepancy and unfairness? Is it the case that an apparently more 'liberal' system may also be more arbitrary, or that a strongly discretionary emphasis may produce a lesser regard for 'due process'?

2. Was there truth in the allegation that the terms on which order was negotiated at Long Lartin were fatally problematic, involving 'collusion' between staff and powerful prisoners, or the

---

[4] We prefer the fluidity of this matrix to some of the 'typologies' or 'ideal types' claiming to enumerate 'adaptations', which are commonplace in prison studies.

'appeasement' of prisoners' demands, and thereby increasing the scope for illicit activities (gambling, drugs, extortion)?

3. Was the level of victimization and exploitation of more vulnerable prisoners consequently higher?

Questions posed by prevailing practice at Albany, on the other hand, related to the level and style of 'control' and rule enforcement which was current. Might these really be:

1. Inappropriately stringent for a dispersal prison, or at any rate, too inconsistent with the rest of the system?

2. Successful in resolving the problems they claimed to address?

3. Counter-productive in terms of prisoners' withdrawal of consent or goodwill?—or, at least, did they present obstacles to positively enhancing relationships?

Some outstanding questions also include, to what extent were these professed rationales actually empirically demonstrable in terms of different levels of sanctioning? Was the practice of each institution in fact more similar than was claimed? However this may be, what effect do such outlooks in fact have on the generation and management of 'control problems'?

We propose to illuminate these questions, first in chapter 5 by considering prisoners' perspectives on aspects of the social order of Long Lartin and Albany and, secondly, in chapter 7 by introducing both statistical comparisons and case studies with the aim of furthering the understanding of the incidence and management of 'control problems' in the two prisons at an empirical level.

5

Social Relations II: Prisoner Perspectives

Introduction

In chapter 4 we discussed aspects of staff perspectives on their jobs, roles, identities and concerns in Albany and Long Lartin. In this chapter we consider prisoners' viewpoints on:

1. Regimes and the material conditions of their confinement in Albany and Long Lartin;
2. Their views of staff;
3. Their views on one another and coexisting;
4. Their views on how each of these relate to the incidence and management of 'control problems'.

Under these headings we shall be addressing a number of questions: what do prisoners want, expect or feel entitled to, in both the material and social conditions of their confinement?; what do they identify as sources of tension in their relations with staff and with one another?; where do they regard 'control problems' as originating, and how do they think they should be handled?; to what extent do such perceptions vary between the two establishments?

These questions to some extent parallel those posed in chapter 4 about staff perspectives. In large measure our method has been to address certain recurrent questions as they have been explained to us from the sometimes differing, convergent or opposing vantage points of prisoners and staff, and to construct our own understanding of what 'the issues' are out of the points of connection and disagreement between these accounts. What we find, we believe, is a certain consensus—across manifest boundaries—as to what *matters* in prison life, but degrees of dissensus over how the resulting problems and dilemmas should be interpreted or addressed. None the less, it is the evidence of perspectives which, if not 'shared', certainly figure in the discourses of both staff and prisoners which lead us to the view that the notion of legitimacy (as outlined by

Beetham) is indeed relevant to an understanding of social relations in prisons.

The prison 'community'

Prolonged confinement in enforced proximity with others in a situation governed by specific institutional rules and norms is the fundamental fact of long-term imprisonment, in relation to which its many subsidiary features must be understood. As we know, Sykes has argued (1958) that confinement inherently generates a number of 'pains' or 'deprivations' which are central to the experience. These 'pains of imprisonment' have been summarized as involving: the deprivation of liberty; deprivation of goods and services; the deprivation of heterosexual relationships; the deprivation of autonomy; the deprivation of security (Sykes, 1958: 63–83). Of these, the 'deprivation of security' is the hardest to specify but is perhaps most closely linked to the day-to-day texture of prison life, and of 'control problems'. It relates to the prisoner's physical safety, 'face', and performance:

> The prisoner's loss of security arouses acute anxiety, in short, not just because violent acts of aggression and exploitation occur, but also because such behaviour constantly calls into question the individual's ability to cope with it, in terms of his own inner resources, his courage, his 'nerve' . . . These uncertainties constitute an ego-threat for the individual forced to live in prolonged intimacy with criminals, regardless of the nature or extent of his own criminality.'
>
> (Sykes, 1958: 78)

We take it that Sykes's stylization of the 'pains of imprisonment' holds good to the extent that it identifies some real and important features of prison life. However, like the other typologies common in prison studies, it is not exhaustive; the categories blur into one another in practice; their specific features and relative importance to prisoners may vary between times and places. The existence in general of certain 'pains' does not in itself specify any particular consequences in the circumstances prevailing in particular institutions.

In stressing prisoners' adaptations in aiming to mitigate the pains of imprisonment Sykes devotes most attention to prisoner–prisoner relations and to the special features of the inmate society. However, whereas we also regard these dimensions as very important we have a number of further concerns. We are centrally concerned with the emergence of 'control problems' in English dispersal prisons. These by definition incorporate staff–prisoner interactions, at least through the application of rules and sanctions. We are therefore interested in prisoners' views of staff and of the legitimacy of the rules by which their lives are governed, as well as with the 'society of captives' itself. Nevertheless the 'pains of imprisonment' are likely to be related to 'control problems' in a number of identifiable ways. These include responses to the material conditions of life, *sub rosa* attempts to distribute and trade in scarce commodities, orientations towards formal regimes, perceptions of staff, and sources of antagonism between prisoners.

Material conditions of life: goods and services

Even on a brief acquaintance with life in long-term prisons one cannot fail to notice the importance which both prisoners and staff place upon the regular provision of goods and services and on aspects of life which the outside observer might regard as mundane or even trivial. If the prison does not adequately provide a minimum expected level of visits, letters, food, clean clothes and bedding, or recreation, it risks a hostile reaction from prisoners.

The importance of visits to prisoners, for example, is difficult to overstate:

If you mess about with a guy's visit even the most placid guy gets upset . . . visitors have [to travel] sixty miles, maybe more . . . you get two a month . . . that's two periods in a month that you can say 'I enjoy myself' . . . that's all I live for, my visits . . .

This being so, and generally true, any disruption in the regime regarding visiting can have severe consequences—and any break in this routine and arrangements relating to visits can precipitate critical situations. Breaks in the routine delivery of goods and services engender disappointed expectations. Such circumstances may result from practical, administrative difficulties (shortage of staff or space) or from policy changes (more stringent searching of visitors, for example, in the wake of the Gartree helicopter escape of 1987 or the Whitemoor break-out of 1994) or indeed from simple mistakes. Whatever the reason, if the visit fails to arrive, the failure is received as arbitrary and unwarranted:

Once you get your visits cut down it starts to get your back up—why are your visits cut down? Why? What's different from last year to this?

Visits are part of the prison routine, but they are also a necessary interlude or relief from the routine. Even though the visit itself may indeed be problematic, stressful and emotionally demanding, prisoners continue to look forward to the next visit, and visiting retains its central importance:

If you're going to get fed up, you're going to get out of order . . . because there's guys on here all day, day in and day out, year in and year out. And they're wasting away. They get wound up and wound up, and they have a bad visit, and the next thing they've punched somebody or stabbed somebody.

A case in point of these general concerns occurred in Long Lartin during our research. In a failure of communication between departments in the prison a prisoner had not been told that his visit had been cancelled. Like many others, he had taken pains to spruce himself up for the occasion. One prisoner observing the incident noted:

So in this instance, the guy's been wound up. His visit's not come. So he picks on a guy a foot bigger than himself . . . It was just over the knocking of a tray . . . the next thing the other guy's come rushing back at 200 miles an hour with a knife being thrust at him.

A similar sequence of events took place in Albany just prior to our fieldwork period, in which a prisoner became intensely frustrated over arrangements for visitors coming from Ireland. This resulted in a serious assault on a senior member of staff.

These incidents raise a series of considerations of more general relevance to which we will return throughout. First, the rationing or scarcity of goods and services which prisoners value, and which is inherent throughout prison life, inevitably focuses an extreme degree of attention and concern on them. Second, from their dependent position, prisoners therefore expect smoothness in administrative processes, efficient communication and delivery of services in areas which are important to them. Third, moments of crisis may result from breaks in routines and the disappointment of expectations. Fourth, any action, decision or mistake may have unintended and unforeseen consequences and repercussions. The Albany incident seemed to have been premeditated, at least in the sense that the prisoner was prepared to wait to take his revenge. However, in the Long Lartin incident, the prisoner's reaction was sudden and explosive. It contained the possibility of escalation into a widespread disturbance because of the degree of sympathy among other prisoners, who saw the incident as resulting from a failure of the prison, and who were therefore particularly alive to the way it was handled by staff. In this regard, however, it is also worth noting the sympathy felt by staff for the prisoner concerned. Staff expressed anger not towards the prisoner but rather the hapless probation officer whom they blamed for not transmitting the message that the visitors would not be coming.

Food is a frequent source of complaint and grievance, for somewhat similar reasons. As we have noted above, staff are conscious of the sensitivity of mealtimes, and often comment that they adjust their own behaviour to cater for this. Meals involve queues. Taking institutional food on plastic plates and carrying it back to a cell is a visible reminder of the fact that one is in prison, which contrasts sharply with some of the associations of food in the outside world—as a domain for expressing personal preference and pleasure, with a central place in familial social relations. Prison food is thus a sign of dependency, and as such acts as a focus for a range of diffuse stresses and grievances:

They want you to sit here like cabbages and anything you want you've got to go to them for. . . . They give us a choice of three meals, and each fucking one is shit . . . But when you're doing a sentence like this, man—you notice. You say 'I'm not getting my right rations'. Then you've got to make a scream-up about it. When you make scream-ups it just falls on deaf ears . . . The cons complain about the food but they eat it, instead of nobody eating it . . . Once everybody keeps taking it, geezers are going to keep serving it, so you're fighting a losing battle.

The serving of food at the hotplate is, then, a moment of particular potential tension within the daily routine. Staff fear a collective refusal of food. More commonly than this, however, a prisoner's irritation over food, whether its quality or the size of his own portion, may act as a catalyst for an outburst of frustration, manifested either against the staff or in antagonism with other prisoners.

The expectation of grievance over food is now institutionalized in the form of a complaints book, although prisoners are usually fairly cynical about this. Staff are prone to expect more complaints than praise:

Can I give you an example of the system? The food here is reasonable. One day we received a meal that you couldn't have got better in any transport cafe . . . It was well cooked. It was well presented . . . so I said, 'Right, I wish to put down in the food book that the food was decent, because I'm quick enough to go in there when there's something wrong.' 'You can't do that.' So I said 'Why not?' He said 'It's only for complaints.' And I said, 'I don't wish to complain, I wish to say "thank you very much, it was very nice" '. So he said 'Fuck off.' And that to me sums it up.

The most important way in which long-term prisons have acted to forestall or alleviate problems resulting from food is through the provision of cooking facilities on the wing which prisoners use during evening association. For prisoners cooking signifies a small extension of personal autonomy, an involving use of time and an opportunity to make things with or for friends. Clearly the wing kitchen is itself a potential source of trouble not only in the access it provides to hot water, knives and so forth but also because antagonisms may result if certain individuals or groups are seen as trying to dominate or monopolize the facilities. Nevertheless, the benefits it provides, in alleviating one of the pains of imprisonment and its attendant conflicts are seen by both prisoners and staff as outweighing any such potential problems.

It would be possible to extend discussion of these relations between the provison of services within routines, pains of imprisonment, and the incidence of 'control problems' at greater length, for example in relation to the provision of meaningful work, education, letters, and so forth. Indeed, we will return to these issues in discussion of specific incidents. However, these brief discussions of visits and food are sufficient to establish a fundamental point, namely that the regular provision of certain services is central in determining prisoners' feelings about their quality of life, and the quality of such services (or more particularly interruptions or problems in service delivery) can have an important bearing on the incidence of grievance and conflict. Equally, the reverse of this may also be the case in that the regular and efficient delivery of services helps to cement, but does not guarantee, the stability and legitimacy of routines.

Goods, privileges and possessions

The range of items which prisoners are entitled to have in their possession, and how and from whom they are allowed to receive them, was at the time of our research specified under Standing Order Four (dispersal prison privileges), in the form of an itemized list.

Prisoners know and appreciate the fact that these provisions are traditionally more generous in the dispersal prison than elsewhere. Nevertheless, there are a number of features of the administration of these privileges which prisoners find it difficult to accept. On some occasions this results from the sheer obscurity to the prisoner of the reasoning involved, the apparently innocuous character of the item concerned and the resulting difficulty in getting what seems to him to be an adequate explanation as to why he can or cannot have it (cf. King and McDermott, 1990):

I got particularly annoyed over one application I made to have an item of jewellery which they refused. This particular [Grade V] who was in charge of stuff in possession said it was too valuable, and my argument was that when I got here I saw people wearing items of jewellery in excess of the value of the one I wanted.

It is a feature of prisoners' dependency, and the relative scarcity of material goods, that they are very alive to such inconsistencies or discrepancies in the behaviour of the authorities:

May I point something out, please? I have here a knife which I shall place on the table. It doesn't have a protective cover. You could slit someone from arse-hole to breakfast with a knife like that . . . Now, I go down the education block and I have to carry that knife because I wish to sharpen the pencils. Now, I'm not allowed a pencil sharpener because it has a blade in it. I had to buy the knife instead.

These perceptions have historically come into sharpest relief in terms of what may be allowed at one time or place but not in another, especially in relation to real or perceived differences between prisons. The clearest instances occur, and the relation to possible control problems is closest, in the course of movements between prisons, especially where they are sudden and involuntary (see below, chapter 8). Thus, it is not uncommon for the prisoner's experience of a new prison to begin with a heated argument:

So I arrived in the reception and I've got this (Prison Department sweat-shirt) on . . . 'Can we have that sweatshirt?' I says 'why?'. 'Well, we don't issue them in here.' So I says 'so what, like, it's a fucking prison issue sweatshirt isn't it?'. 'Well you can't go through with that on'—but he's giving me the glare as well, and I've got a raging headache after this ten hours on the coach, and I've got this hired thug there mithering me for a prison issue sweatshirt. And I couldn't have a teeshirt that was in my box 'cos it had 'Long Lartin' stamped on the back of it . . . So I took *all* my clothes off and slung them at him. I said 'You can have the fucking lot, 'cos all that's prison issue . . .'. So I goes and sees the Governor next morning, and I says 'Tell me, if I'd come in this prison yesterday with a sweatshirt on with "Nike" splattered all across here, could I have had it?' He said 'Yes'. So I said 'Why can't I have a prison issue one with a PD stamp on it?' He says 'because they're not issued'. I said 'I don't believe this . . . you're supposed to be an intelligent man. I could come in here with a civilian sweatshirt, so that if I escaped no one would know the difference . . .'. 'That's right.' 'But a prison has *given* me a sweatshirt as part of my kit with a PD stamp on it, and I can't have it!' Well he couldn't do anything else then, 'cos I've just kicked him in the balls haven't I? So he gives it me. This is it. So then they took it off me at Durham next . . . [we all laugh].

Each of these stories was related to us humorously, as a joke against the absurdity of the position. The humour, though, is retrospective, and it recalls what was at the time a real frustration. It is a shrugging of the shoulders, but also a serious point about the experience of powerlessness. Nor is it necessarily helpful from the point of view of the prison's legitimacy to be seen to be acting in a laughable way.

These examples raise a number of important issues and acute dilemmas:

1. On the one hand there is a readiness among staff to recognize prisoners' frustration in this area. On the other hand enforcing the privilege list and simply giving prisoners 'what they're entitled to' can often look to staff like not only the safest but also the fairest procedure. Staff fear setting precedents which might form the thin end of the wedge of prisoners requests, but this does not make it easy to justify to prisoners or implement the application of a rule on any specific occasion. (All of this Mathiesen would lead us to anticipate—see chapter 2.)

2. Similarly staff commonly defend certain restrictions as having a serious basis in questions of safety (fire risks, potential weapons) or security. Moreover, under conditions of scarcity almost any valued item can in principle become a tradeable commodity. To the extent that staff have an interest in minimizing trade and its associated networks and differentials of power, they will seek to regulate goods and services. Hence, whereas they may recognize a need not

to dabble in the minutiae of the lives of long-term prisoners and, moreover, acknowledge that a few creature comforts are both permissible and desirable, this can on occasion be countermanded by the sense of a need to retain 'control', and to demonstrate that they have it.

Prisoners are well able to recognize these arguments and, on occasion, take the staff point of view. Even after the privilege list had been painstakingly and minutely formulated by DPSG (the then standing committee of dispersal prison Governors) it remained 'open-textured' enough to permit both accidental and deliberate variations in application (cf. Twining and Miers, 1982: 213). Nevertheless, applications of the privilege list which are either inadequately explained, or discrepant and uneven, or which are incremental restrictions on an existing situation are likely to be regarded by prisoners as petty, arbitrary and frustrating. This is related, in prisoners' eyes, to the status of 'privileges' themselves:

One of the problems is that we only have privileges, we don't have rights in prison, apart from a bed and three meals a day. So you accumulate these privileges, in the form of official privileges. Over a period of time you get extra furniture, *two* sets of knives and forks, *two* plates and *two* dessert bowls, which are all useful things to have, and you make use of them. You're only actually entitled to one of everything. Now, over a period of time, these things accumulate and life becomes a little more comfortable as a result of them . . . But when the occasion demands, the prison authorities can come down on you and say 'you shouldn't have that' and you can end up on a charge . . . There's no system of custom and practice. You can't say, 'Well I've had them for six months and in that time I've been seen by a number of officers who haven't taken exception to it'. But when the occasion demands they can make a charge out of it.

Clearly the regulation and distribution of goods and 'privileges' sets up a number of dilemmas for the prison, and problems for the prisoner. One of the most important of these is that historically the non-recognition of rights has necessarily increased the scope of staff discretion. Yet each exercise of discretion, in the context of prisoner–staff relations, is potentially problematic, especially if prisoners perceive habitual or deliberate differences between prisons in this regard, or if they regard their own treatment as being out of step with prevailing practice in their own prison.

ace in goods which have been legally acquired but informally redistributed, classically tobacco, for example. Beyond this, however, lies the whole area of goods and services which are formally forbidden: the *sub-rosa* economy of the prison (cf. Kalinich, 1980). This includes drugs, home-brewed alcohol (hooch), and gambling.

Among prisoners these forms of trading are closely tied to the pains of imprisonment. For users they offer diversion, recreation or forgetfulness. For dealers they signify a source of income, and hence increased comfort and influence. As we have noted, in chapters 2 and 4, there is scope for variation and ambivalence in staff responses. Can such practices ever be eradicated? Should the attempt even be made? What level of policing is therefore appropriate? Certainly, it has long been held (with the partial exceptions of hallucinogenic drugs and, latterly, the fear of the spread of the HIV virus through needle sharing, the possible arrival of crack-cocaine, the dangers of alcoholic poisoning and aggression related to hooch) that the primary problems have not been medical or directly behavioural. Rather they have mainly had to do with the generation, flow, and distribution of money and commodities—i.e. with the market itself and its consequences. Under conditions of scarcity prices are inflated (at least in proportion to incomes) and rates of interest and exchange are high. To this extent market conditions in prison include an intrinsic mechanism of indebtedness.

From the prisoner's standpoint it has been argued (for example by McVicar, 1982) that any problems resulting from these markets are accepted by prisoners as the necessary price to be paid for relief from the pains of imprisonment. However, this is a more complex question than it looks. At the very least, the extent to which prisoners share McVicar's angle is likely to vary in relation to the position they occupy in markets and their attendant social hierarchies. Moreover, from our observation the character of the markets and of policies of policing and regulation appear to vary quite markedly from prison to prison. Thus, we will treat questions of contraband in the course of separate accounts of prisoners' perspectives on social relations in Long Lartin and Albany respectively. To this extent, we will seek to relate these and other general concerns to a comparative account of prisoners' views of the situations prevailing in these two settings.

Until now, we have introduced in general terms some issues which are of widespread interest to prisoners and which are inherent in the fact of long-term imprisonment itself and its associated pains or deprivations—visits, food, privileges. Whilst particular manifestations of these basic features of life may vary, they constitute problems with which every prison has to struggle, and which every prisoner experiences in some degree. We will now turn to discuss in more concrete terms some particular features of prisoners' perspectives on daily life in Albany and Long Lartin, and on which the differences between prisons are perhaps more marked. These are prisoners' expectations of and responses to regimes and staff; their feelings of solidarity, antagonism or otherwise towards one another; their sense of physical safety and danger and their views on the incidence and management of 'control problems'.

Long Lartin

Prisoners' views on staff and regimes

It is difficult to represent adequately the full range and complexity of prisoners' viewpoints and experiences. Prisoners speak from diverse vantage points, which vary in relation to their prior experience, their sentences and offences, their degree of optimism or otherwise regarding their current position and prospects. Nevertheless, while it is of fundamental importance to seek to take account of this diversity, and its consequences, it is the case that common themes recur in many prisoners' accounts of their views of Long Lartin, as of other prisons.

Perhaps the most important of these themes on which there is widespread agreement was that Long Lartin was in some significant way different from other prisons. Unsurprisingly, for those who had only previously experienced local prisons Long Lartin represented an enormous change. However, the perception of difference was also shared by a number of prisoners who had spent time in other dispersal prisons. For most of those prisoners who were well travelled in the system, which would include a high proportion of those on Category A, Long Lartin's reputation as a relatively relaxed place to go was already well-known:

I knew. It's common knowledge within the prison system, for prisoners like us, who've got common sense, who just want to do their bird easy and go home, that this is the place to get to. I knew all about it before I even arrived here. I still wasn't prepared for it really . . . this is *streets and streets* in front.

Such views were perhaps held most strongly and in their purest form by men serving long determinate sentences who would often be referred to as 'gangsters': indeed the perception that this was so engendered a degree of cynicism from observers elsewhere in the system who were unsympathetic to Long Lartin's 'ethos'. That is, for hostile critics the fact that some experienced prisoners were known to prefer Long Lartin was treated *ipso facto* as evidence that its regime had 'bought off the gangsters'. We return to this problem below.

However, it is also important to note that these positive evaluations were not confined to 'gangsters'. A number of lifers, including some sex offenders, made out similar arguments:

I put in two petitions to come here . . . I put in a petition to the Home Office and said I wanted to come to a less militant prison [than Albany] because all I was interested in was doing my time as quietly as possible . . . A lot of people had told me about Long Lartin . . . they said it was very free and easy, very relaxed, the relationship with staff was very good, you were treated very well, the staff left you alone and you'd have to do something pretty bad to get nicked.
—And that's right is it?
Yes, that's true. Yes.

A number of men serving very long determinate sentences or life sentences said that coming to Long Lartin had provided them with an opportunity to, as it were, retire from conflict with staff and to do their time in a quieter way, perhaps because some of what they regarded as provocations were less in evidence:

What happens is, especially if you're doing a lot of bird, you can just slip into laying back and letting things go by, whereas, and I'm being blatantly honest here, every waking moment at Albany and other prisons I was looking for a way out, making keys, making bits to help me escape. Here . . . you tend to slip into a sort of lethargy and just let it pass by, and *not* mainly because of drugs—though cannabis does an awful lot for prisoners, keeping them quiet, which is why a lot of blind eyes are turned towards it. You let things go. I haven't thought of making a fucking key for ages. But now and again you have to pull yourself up because you're going their way, accepting everything and letting it be done. Perhaps that's what it's meant to do.

All but two of those prisoners whom we interviewed who had also spent time in other dispersals compared their previous locations unfavourably to their current position at Long Lartin. We will return later to the discussion of prisoners who specifically *disliked* Long Lartin or who encountered particular problems there. At this juncture it is sufficient to note that not only did many prisoners regard Long Lartin as different from and preferable to other prisons, but for some these differences were large enough to constitute something of a shock:

And so when people come from another prison, the comparatively liberal regime here throws them. I've known people who've come here and they've felt it's 'too free', in inverted commas, and they've wanted to go back into the block or they've wanted to get transferred to another prison. I find that a ridiculous thing but I understand why that is the case, because they are used to a very sharp, constrained, restrained environment. And when you put them in here and they're given just a little bit of extra space, it throws them.

What specific differences, then, did prisoners identify, beyond a general sense of 'liberality' in 'atmosphere'? In part these were straightforwardly material. At the time of our study Long Lartin provided comparatively comfortable conditions of life, relative to other prisons. There was a comparatively generous provision of gym; opportunity to associate outdoors in the evening in summer; a relaxed view was taken of prisoners wearing their own clothes, including on visits; cell association was permitted; bang-up times were relatively short; there was relative freedom of movement within the corridors at certain times.

However, it seems to us doubtful that the provision of such 'goodies' in itself is sufficient, or sufficiently different, to explain fully prisoners' predominantly positive evaluations of Long Lartin. Rather, many of their comments refer to specifically social dimensions of their relations with staff. Indeed, prisoners at Long Lartin did not characteristically differentiate sharply when they were talking about the delivery of 'regime' and when they were talking about staff behaviour.

It may be that prisoners did not differentiate sharply in this way because it would be difficult, perhaps false, to disentangle the order of priority between a certain level of material provision and the particular posture or set of values held by staff in the day-to-day running of the prison. Thus, from the prisoner's point of view, being able to wear his own clothes signifies an increase in his personal autonomy, and the staff outlook which allows him to wear his own clothes arises from a recognition of that autonomy. Similarly, the ability to move unescorted from A to B within the corridors suggests a relatively unobtrusive form of regulation and a degree of trust, though it also indicates a degree of self-confidence on the part of staff that any trouble which might result can be dealt with. Knowing that he is controlled in the last instance, the prisoner may be none the less glad not to be controlled minutely.

Prisoners most often described this situation as being less 'petty' than other prisons they had known:

In some ways there's not a great deal of pettiness here. This is the difference I've seen between this place and some other prisons I've been to. Although there's greater security here, there's a lot less pettiness in terms of things like dress, in terms of how you've got your cell—things on the wall . . . They may take the attitude, well all these guys are doing a long time and we've got all this immense security so they can't get out . . . so therefore we'll do away with the other petty rules, because that's just adding insult to injury in a way.

To this extent a comparatively positive orientation towards the prison and its regime tends also to go hand in hand with a similarly favourable evaluation of staff. One prisoner, a 'gangster', with considerable experience of conflict in other dispersals described a gradual change in his orientation towards staff:

As I told you yesterday, before I came to this prison I wouldn't *dream* of calling a screw by his first name . . . but I come here, I was in for a few weeks, I saw everybody doing it and being a bit older now I thought why buck it? . . . It's funny but over a period of time it takes away any barrier. When you're a number you're just like that table, you're an item, but when you're a name, you're a person. If they treat you like an animal or a lump of wood, you act like one. If they treat you like a human being you behave like a human being. You're polite. You don't hassle. It's just a different ball game.

Other prisoners corroborated this view that relations between prisoners and staff in Long Lartin were indeed different from their previous experience, deliberately so, and that this has a range of consequences for the nature of 'control':

A fairly successful attempt has been made to, not remove, but soften the barriers between inmate and staff. By that I mean I've seen inmates talking to staff far more deeply than in other prisons . . . The conversations that people have, say on the landings or in the office, with staff, would be frowned upon in many other prisons.

In the eyes of some prisoners such 'softening' suggests a different approach to what one can have, do, and say:

In most nicks you know the line which you don't cross. Here the line is not straight, it's curved. That fluctuation is one of the reasons this place hasn't gone up, because you've got so much flexibility. In a sense you don't know how far you can actually go before you really come a cropper. Elsewhere if you've got *x* amount of kit over the amount you're supposed to have, you're nicked. Here you can get away with it. And if you get a bad letter at lunch-time you can rant and rave, calling officers names. You can get away with that here as well. I wouldn't say the cons run the nick. They have a large say, but on the bottom line it's the staff who are running the nick . . . you get the feel that you've got some involvement, and you're not just a ball being rolled from one to another.

It is worth noting here that prisoners confirm a point made in chapter 4; namely, that staff at Long Lartin adopted a 'flexible' approach rather than a 'consistent' one. However, it is also clear that at least part of this testimony, with its allusion to a state of uncertainty as to 'how far one can go' can be construed, from other vantage points, as a source of anxiety, if not an outright criticism. This was a particular theme among prisoners who did not 'settle' at Long Lartin, or who encountered trouble there. For such individuals the apparent fluidity of rules at Long Lartin constituted a set of 'mind games' which, insidiously and unsettlingly, failed to let you 'know where you stand'. Prisoners in this position felt vulnerable to the whims of staff and unprotected from sources of threat among other prisoners. Nevertheless, for most prisoners to whom we spoke, including some who had encountered serious problems elsewhere, Long Lartin seemed to hold out the hope of what one of the latter called a 'mutually acceptable compromise'.

One prisoner who had spent a great deal of time in segregation and been generally regarded by staff in a number of prisons as an intractable 'control problem' commented:

I suppose it's the most liberal and relaxed dispersal prison that there is at the moment, and the emphasis is more on seducing people into conformity, as opposed to brutalizing them into conformity. The objective is ultimately the same: they want you to conform but there are various ways of doing it.

One way is the block at Wakefield; another way is Long Lartin, normal location . . . it's a strategy that I'm well aware of. . . . In terms of why Long Lartin in particular, why it's easy for someone like me, basically because I'm allowed a greater degree of free space.

Clearly, these perceptions are at some distance from any simplistic belief, which may have had currency among staff in other prisons, that staff at Long Lartin had relinquished control to prisoners. Rather, prisoners at Long Lartin recognized that a particular style of regulation was in operation, but that it was one which offered them what they regarded as elements of a more viable *modus vivendi*. This involved the recognition that, in the last instance, Long Lartin was capable of acting with the same suddenness and force as any other prison, and that such demonstrations that power finally resides with the staff were not rare.

Prisoners therefore held in tension the twin recognitions that, on the one hand, Long Lartin's liberal reputation had a real basis and a range of important consequences for the quality of everyday life but that, on the other hand, they should not be deceived as to the consequences if and when they committed infractions which the prison considered serious. Such a view indeed is readily borne out by an examination of the use of administrative control devices (10/74 procedures, as they then were, and Rule 43 (GOAD)) and disciplinary 'awards'. For whatever reason (and we will discuss these points in more detail in chapter 8) Long Lartin did not make significantly less use of sudden involuntary transfers under CI 10/74 than other dispersals, nor was it notably lenient in imposing other sanctions.

Thus, as one prisoner put it:

They still put you in body belts if necessary . . . If they have to go hard, if they have to go to the edge, they do go to the edge. They come kitted out and strap you up and take you. So I don't think there's much difference between this and other prisons there.

In a similar vein another prisoner commented:

They say that they would like the ethos of this prison to be a lot different than it is at, say, Parkhurst which is a traditional prison culture, and in a sense is based on violence by both staff and prisoners. They say they don't want that culture expressed in this prison, and when they see particular groups of prisoners with that particular culture that threatens the ethos of this prison, they will break it up . . . that is the justification they will use.

Q So does that mean that on occasions the liberal regime is actually
quicker to act to ship people out?
Certainly, and it can also be more brutal in many ways . . . I've found that
in so-called liberal institutions like this one, when they decide to use a bottom line against individuals, it really is no different than anywhere else.

For those prisoners who have experienced these measures, or felt
the threat of them, or witnessed their use against friends, this kind
of awareness can severely qualify their assent to notions of Long
Lartin's specially 'liberal' character. None the less for most prisoners most of the time these issues were not in the forefront of their
awareness. Rather, many prisoners expressed views supportive of
the regime to an extent which, on the basis of their prior experience and expectations, they found surprising.

However, during the period of our research there was also a very
widespread feeling that the regime was in a transitional phase—that
it was being 'reined in' or 'stolen back' and that this was among
the Governor's intentions. This was partly a result of the visible
increase in security measures in response to the Gartree escape.
These measures included the construction of a compound with anti-
helicopter wires on the playing field, and a 'cage' round the exercise
yard. Considerable disruption, especially to outdoor evening association resulted during building work. Partly it was a reaction to
increases in bang-up periods and delays in receiving visits which
prisoners attributed to the change-over to Fresh Start working patterns; partly an attribution of strategic intent either to the
Governor or alternatively to the POA.

The prison was thus in a ferment of anxious debate whose main
themes included that either the Home Office, or the Governor, or
the POA wanted to bring Long Lartin 'into line' with other dispersals and that this involved withdrawal of privileges and harder,
more intensive policing. This in turn gave rise to a number of pre-
dictions, including that there would be a riot, that the Governor or
the POA wanted to provoke a riot as an excuse for introducing a
tougher regime, and that there would be no riot because prisoners
had seen through this strategem.

Certainly, however, there was real anxiety, and a real strain on
trust. Prisoners felt strongly that their responses were being used as
a bargaining chip in the internal politics and industrial relations of
the Prison Service. On occasion prisoners would allege that staff
wanted them to cause trouble in order to underline their argument

that staff numbers provided under Fresh Start were inadequate, or in order to press for the return of overtime. Most particularly there was a nearly unanimous view that if Long Lartin were to lose its liberal reputation and become 'just like any other prison' then it would also lose its hold on co-operation and good behaviour, especially in relation to the 'straight' prisoners' toleration of the 'nonces'.

Prisoners' views on one another

It is conventional to argue that having to live in close and unavoidable proximity with other prisoners is one of the pains of imprisonment. Sykes treats this as having primarily to do with the 'deprivation of security'. For some individuals the situation of danger and uncertainty which Sykes describes clearly exists, even to the extent that some people who are not seen as falling into one of the categories which would render them particularly vulnerable, occasionally seek the solitary safety of the segregation unit.[1]

Yet Sykes's characterization cannot be applied without modification to the prison environments we have observed. Contact and association with others is not simply a pain, it is also one of the main consolations of imprisonment. The views which prisoners hold on living together and the conditions of their coexistence, are far more complex and ambivalent than the conventional view seems to suggest, and they vary considerably in relation to experience and status.

[1] Problems of 'voluntary' segregation, although a major preoccupation within the prison service, have received scant research attention or sustained treatment in general publications, at least until Sampson's (1994) contribution. Gostin and Staunton (1985) briefly summarize a number of important issues: 'In as much as prisoners ask for Rule 43 segregation out of fear for their safety, their choice cannot be said to be freely made, nor does it show a desire for solitary confinement *per se* . . . It is unjustifiable that a prisoner whose physical safety cannot be secured in normal prison conditions should have to face the sole alternative of having his mental well-being put at serious risk in solitary confinement.' (1985: 85–6)

It remains the case, however, that for a variety of possible reasons, some prisoners who are not at special, immediate physical risk *also* seek periods of solitude, away from the press of life on 'normal' location. This should not be taken to minimize the rigours of solitary confinement, only to indicate the social stress which dealing with other prisoners and staff in existing regimes represents for some prisoners (cf. King and McDermott, 1989) and clarify their apparent preference for the simplicity and predictability of the segregation unit. In such cases the 'problem' for the prison lies in persuading the prisoner to leave what one such individual described to us as his 'Trappist' lifestyle, especially given that at least one form of sanction or leverage usually available to the authorities, segregation, has nil deterrent value for that prisoner.

Certainly, living together includes sources of stress, anxiety and conflict. Prisoners speak of prison wings as being very public places, in which there is a good deal of display and role-playing. The problems of keeping up appearances, and of living constantly in company which is not of one's own choosing are of as much concern in themselves as the threat of physical violence. Indeed, many prisoners refer to the need to avoid allowing irritation to spill over into violence as calling forth a degree of patience, toleration and forbearance:

whereas here [in Long Lartin] you're actually living together, so although people may have differences of opinion they tend to put that to one side and get on with the business in hand of actually surviving on the wing. For instance, we've got Palestinians and Jews on the same wing here. They don't get on. They don't speak. They can't continue their war in here. It just wouldn't work, so they just keep away from each other. They ignore each other and get on with day-to-day living. That's all you can do really. Otherwise you'd be looking over your shoulder twenty-four hours a day.

Partly because of the potential consequences, most people are at pains to avoid overt conflict:

Because fights round here do get nasty. It's no kindergarten. If you have a fight with somebody you've got to win or lose, and either way you've got to be friends afterwards. A lot of blokes do.

This in no way denies that there are many dimensions, divisions and lines of demarcation between prisoners which are potentially conflictual, some of which may indeed have a systematic and discernible character—offence, race, religion, politics.

The patterns of stratification (of power, influence, access to scarce resources) which are constituted by these dimensions are complex and shifting. Simple analogies with class structures, which conceive of the 'gangsters' as a 'ruling class' and 'nonces' as a '*lumpenproletariat*' (cf. Genders and Player, 1989), cannot be applied unproblematically. There are a number of reasons for this. First, given the extent to which ultimate power remains predominantly in the hands of the staff it is not clear that *any* group of prisoners can be described as a '*ruling* class'. Second, it is not always plain how far the 'gangsters' seriously *attempt* to 'rule' the lives of other prisoners, although they may be ready enough to use force or threat to consolidate their influence or collect debts. Rather, being a 'gangster' entails achieving a certain status and recognition among the other prisoners and, to some degree, the staff. Achieving the status of a 'face' (or leading figure) confers certain benefits. These include: being left alone, having preferable jobs, holding more material possessions, being treated with a certain consideration by the staff, perhaps to the extent of being consulted in limited ways by managers. But for the most part these benefits have to do with mitigating the pains of imprisonment rather than achieving 'rule' as such.

To this extent, the 'gangsters' will seek to achieve such concentrations of privilege and influence as they can, and to maximize their scope as far as possible without calling forth an adverse reaction from the authorities. There is thus often a mixed relationship of conflict and co-operation between the most successful prisoners and prison authorities, which necessarily contains the possibility of overt crises in 'control'. Yet both sides sometimes claim that there is also an inherent tendency for the 'gangsters' to regulate their own activity, because they know that it will be tolerated only at certain levels. Their power is thus rather conditional. As one prisoner, who could reasonably regard himself as a leading 'gangster', commented:

You can't fight the system. You can't. It's no way. You might win a little fucking skirmish, but you don't win no fucking wars in the end. It's all a game, isn't it? Think about it, it's all a game. They're kidding us and we're kidding them.

The gangsters' power is also somewhat conditional from the point of view of other prisoners. Not all prisoners acquiesce in acknowledging the gangsters' status. Certain individuals who are 'non-aligned' make it clear that they have no intention of accepting orders from or deferring to other prisoners. Others commonly speak of 'plastic gangsters' overestimating their own position and influence.

Thus, the picture of the distribution of power and influence between prisoners in Long Lartin which we would wish to draw suggests not so much a rigid 'class structure' but rather a somewhat more fluid pattern of groups. Such groups (or 'firms' or 'cliques') were based on friendship or ethnic or regional affinities as much as 'business'. Some groups, such as those constituted by Irish Republican prisoners were unquestionably tighter, more hierarchical and more lasting than others. Certainly, this was one group with whom others would be reluctant to tangle. In general, however, such groups were not exclusive. Their membership changed as prisoners left or arrived, whether because of the normal flow of prison life and careers or because the authorities, noting a group achieving a certain ascendancy, acted to break it up. The frantic activity of exchange and antagonism between such groups constitutes what is known, in 'normal' times, as 'stability'.

The primary division within the body of prisoners is between those who regard themselves as 'straight' prisoners and those whom they consider 'nonces' (by which they usually mean men who have committed sexually-motivated offences against women or children). This much is well-known. Hostility towards 'nonces' from 'straight' prisoners is routine. It is usually expressed in straightforwardly vehement moral terms, and is described in such a way as to emphasize a sense of frustration at having to share their living space with men whose crimes they consider monstrous.

By tradition 'nonces' are expected to know their place and to keep out of the way of 'straight cons.'. On these terms they may be left alone:

I'd rather mix with somebody like myself, an armed robber or somebody who's been on the streets, than share my life with somebody who's ripped kids apart. I get emotional talking about it, so I won't. If you've got to live with them just blank them. Let them have their own little life at the bottom of the shit pile.

The conventional wisdom among straight prisoners at Long Lartin was that the 'nonces' were tolerated for two main reasons. First, they were considered too numerous to attack. Second, the game of nonce bashing was not considered worth the candle of getting shipped out of the prison. Long Lartin folklore considers this to have been the basis of a 'contract' (though not quite of the kind that Woolf later had in mind) between prisoners and prison managers—the price of the liberal regime and the soft policing was that the nonces were to be left alone and on normal location:

The weaker and lower elements of the criminal strata get on better here because they're left alone more, because that was the carrot that was held out as part of the agreement. And I think that works to a general degree. You still get one or two incidents, but not so many as you get in other prisons.

To this extent nonces (hereafter vulnerable prisoners) were conscious that they were being extended only what one of them called a 'grudging tolerance'. The extent of this tolerance and the circumstances under which it might be breached or withdrawn remain to be established in subsequent sections—both in relation to prisoners' general views on control problems and in respect of specific incidents. For the time being certain points should be noted. First, the 'Long Lartin strategy' as articulated by Jenkins (1987) is inherently not without problems in that the toleration of sex offenders by others is premised on a certain chronic tension, engendered by the 'straight' prisoners' feeling or allegation that they were 'surrounded by nonces', or that Long Lartin was a 'nonce's nick' (nothwithstanding that prisoners whose current offences included sex in fact only constituted some twelve per cent of the population: see Table 3.4).

For some prisoners this feeling took the form of a belief that the prison was 'geared up for the nonces' and a perception that 'they' receive preferential treatment and protection. Under these circumstances the routine hostility could take on a more overt character:

B wing is a weird place. There's a lot of nonces on it. Providing they do what they're supposed to do, which is stay behind their door and out of the way, and I don't have to see them then that's fine. But when they start to march around and they think that they're the top kids . . . no, no, I'm not wearing that.[2]

Meanwhile, the attempt to secure coexistence on normal location also inherently gives rise to opportunities for the frictions to be made manifest. To this extent, the attempt to survive on normal location as a designated 'nonce' was still a real struggle, marked by verbal abuse and occasional physical intimidation—and a curtailment of activity. At Long Lartin vulnerable prisoners often did not feel inclined to venture into television rooms, for example. A number of them suggested to us that the geography of the wings, their nooks and crannies, and what they saw as the intermittent and ten-

[2] It was true at the time of the fieldwork that B wing included a somewhat higher proportion of prisoners with sex in their current offences than other wings—19% as compared with an average for all wings of 12%, and only 5% in one wing. Whether this was an outcome of policy, or a direct outcome of a particular wing Governor's efforts at sustaining vulnerable prisoners on normal location, or an accumulation of voluntary inter-wing movements is impossible to determine conclusively. Certainly there was a development on B wing towards a somewhat more visible grouping of vulnerable prisoners prepared to resist any attempted or perceived intimidation. This is important in the background to the events reported in chapter 7 as 'incident no. LL1'.

tative policing by staff of TV rooms and certain spurs meant that they were constantly aware of a need to tread carefully. Some vulnerable prisoners shared a marked preference for remaining on the ground floor, close to the wing office. A proportion of vulnerable prisoners still found it necessary to seek the austere protection of 'the rule'. Meanwhile, a small (but perhaps increasing?) number, perhaps at the outset of a long sentence, were determined not to accept the social status, and its attendant risks, which had been marked out for them and chose to resist by making a pre-emptive strike against those whom they saw as their persecutors or potential aggressors. One or two of the latter had consciously cultivated a reputation as 'psychos', people who would meet violence with greater violence. Such stances can do much to confound assumed identities. A reputation for the efficient use of force does not sit easily with the stereotypical passivity attributed to 'nonces'. It may to some extent countermand that 'master status' and allow the individual concerned to be known more as a belligerent loner than as one of 'them'.

Prisoners' perspectives on 'Control Problems'

The maintenance of order is highly complex: within an 'orderly' or 'stable' situation there is constant activity. In some usages 'order' may seem to connote quietness or stillness. In the context of the prison, as indeed in most other settings, such a conception is inappropriate. Thus, 'stability' in Long Lartin meant not the absence of either antagonism or offending behaviour, but their containment and channelling into manageable forms. Staff–prisoner relations are marked both by interdependency and conflict. Similarly, prisoners themselves are a highly differentiated body of people whose relations with one another incorporate a variety of tendencies towards co-operation, and antagonism.

In this section we will differentiate between those problems which prisoners saw as arising out of their experience of prison routines, regimes and relations with staff on the one hand, and on the other those which resulted from their dealings with one another.

Staff–prisoner problems

Even the most cursory inspection of Governors' adjudications and awards reveals the preponderance of charges which are brought under paragraphs 18 and 20 of Prison Rule 47 i.e. 'refusal to obey a lawful order' and 'in any way offends against good order and discipline'.

These provisions cover a multitude of different possible situations, of widely varying seriousness. It is difficult to place much weight of inference upon them as indicating a 'real' pattern of behaviour. One outcome of this, however, is that the application of these rules themselves in their present form is itself a source of disgruntlement among prisoners. Their 'open texture' (cf. Twining and Miers, 1982: 213) lays them open to charges of inconsistency, whimsicality and arbitrariness from prisoners. Prisoners routinely dispute their legitimacy. Meanwhile questioning the legitimacy of an officer's order is one way of getting 'nicked'. It is not difficult to argue, from a prisoner's point of view, that the application of these rules includes elements of a 'double bind'.

In common with their general perceptions *vis-à-vis* 'pettiness' prisoners at Long Lartin did not on the whole perceive these rules as being applied with quite the same frequency as they had experienced elsewhere. Moreover, as we have noted in chapter 4, this was to some extent in accordance with the views of Long Lartin staff, who stressed their reluctance to give a 'direct order', and hence precipitate an offence, except as a last resort.

Whereas Long Lartin may in general, and with some important exceptions, have enjoyed a comparatively high degree of perceived legitimacy among its captive population, it none the less could not escape certain problems which are inherent in custodial institutions. The organization of time and activity which prisons impose and the regulation of minute aspects of life in prisons generally means that prisoners and staff will repeatedly find themselves in conflictual situations (cf. Sykes, 1958: 22).

Disobedience, non-co-operation, and refusal are in this sense intrinsic dimensions of 'control problems' in prison. Among the commonest areas in which this is apparent are the refusal to go to work, delaying prison routines, swearing at or threatening staff. Whilst these problems are endemic most of them are also slight and mundane, or at least would be thought so in almost any social setting other than a total institution. Yet, even in a 'liberal' regime the prison is likely to be reluctant to brook direct opposition to orders or interruptions to the regime, thus regarding itself as obliged to take disciplinary action. Instances of non-acquiescence tend always to be seen by staff as containing the potentiality of escalation, therefore, either because they may take on a collective character or because the consequences which ensue seem to the prisoner to be out of proportion to the original incident, thereby inciting further protest. For some individuals this results in a further withdrawal of goodwill, and a cycle of worsening relations.

These concerns relate in turn to prisoners' views of prison officers. A number of prisoners expressed to us a preference for older officers because they regarded them as being 'sensible', or as having a greater sense of proportion, or as being more conciliatory in tone and demeanour than some of their younger colleagues (cf. Cooke, 1991):

You can sometimes get a situation where the older officers, the very experienced ones, are more relaxed in their attitudes, and treat you better, whereas you get the young ones who are very, very keen to get on with the job—rules and regulations, and perhaps they're more likely to nick people and are less diplomatic with people.

These comments raise issues of both fairness and personal style in prisoners' expectations of staff. For prisoners 'unnecessary' nickings, undue searching, inadequate information and inconsistency are all 'wind-ups'(cf. McDermott and King, 1988). From the prisoner's perspective among the worst things a member of staff can do is to wind a prisoner up on purpose, to provoke him or 'dig him out'.

The problem of compliance thus in fact leads to some of the most intractable 'control problems'. On the one hand the prisoner may disobey a series of instructions if he regards the initial one as having been unreasonable; meanwhile, in order to maintain supremacy and/or 'face', staff member(s) may feel compelled (perhaps reluctantly) to act with a severity which is, in turn, delegitimating from the prisoner's perspective.

Prisoner–prisoner problems

Clearly, not everything which the staff define as a 'control problem' is seen as such by prisoners. Certain areas of life which the staff see it as their role to regulate are seen by prisoners as belonging in legitimate or private domains. Examples might include the giving and receiving of goods which can be variously interpreted as either bartering or gifts (and hence against Prison Rules), and the resolution of personal disputes or conflicts. The pressure towards self-regulation among prisoners thus has several sources: the avoidance of disciplinary action; a preference for private justice and the taboo against 'grassing'; the feeling that prisoners' dealings with each other are private matters in which staff attention is unwelcome. It is unmanly to involve staff in one's dealings with another prisoner.

Equally prisoners recognize that many of their transactions with one another are formally illicit and that staff are obliged to take an interest; this is what the rules of the game dictate. The self-regulation of certain activities—for example, brewing or gambling and, to an extent, the distribution of drugs—springs from a need for discretion to preserve the 'goodies', to sustain prisoners' obligations to one another and to avoid provoking staff to react. To flaunt one's activities is considered foolish because it obliges staff to take action. However, prisoners do not deny that from time to time this complex of mutual obligations and conventions breaks down or spills over into conflict. Most prisoners place considerable stress on the importance of being 'sensible'. Being sensible means pursuing a quiet life, maximizing perks and pleasures, not upsetting the apple-cart, doing 'one's own bird'. Prisoners who are not 'sensible', who disturb the quiet life and who bring the staff into play may be censured by other prisoners, and receive scant sympathy when they are punished (cf. Sykes, 1958 on the 'ball-buster').

These considerations are of general relevance in long-term prisons. However, we would argue that they were perhaps particularly pronounced in Long Lartin where prisoners' sense of their relatively privileged position and of the advantages of maintaining the liberal regime called for a high degree of self-regulation, not least because *opportunities* for dispute or trouble were also correspondingly greater. Age was an important dimension in this. Some older prisoners, who saw themselves as 'settled' at Long Lartin and who had established a position they wanted to protect, were irritated by the boisterousness of 'kids'. The expression 'You shouldn't put a boy in a man's prison' was a virtual proverb. It was also a threat. It implied that the 'boy' was riding for a fall, whether from staff or, more ominously, from other prisoners.

Most prisoners, we have been assured repeatedly in every prison, want to 'do their time quietly and go home'. Most are involved in illicit dealing only peripherally and insofar as it eases the pains of imprisonment. They refuse to dramatize the extent to which they are in conflict with one another and stress that most of the time they succeed in coexisting. Nevertheless prisoners will also acknowledge that strains exist, some of which may have a systematic character. To this extent, although we do not regard it as very fruitful in the present context to attempt to provide distinct categories or typologies of prisoners' 'roles' or 'adaptations', the differentiations which prisoners themselves draw between real 'gangsters', 'plastic gangsters', 'ordinary cons', 'nonces', 'kids', and 'psychos' suggest real differences of interest and preference.

The incidence of specific control problems in Long lartin and Albany is the subject of chapter 7. For the present one may note that among the sundry reasons for trouble which prisoners identify are: long-standing personal antipathies, exacerbated by enforced prolonged proximity; noise; cell thefts; pressures which relate to the outside world. However, the two subjects which are cited most often are debt, resulting from drugs or gambling, and relations between sex offenders and others.

Debt is indeed the area which is most often cited as a source of trouble:

Cash, basically. There is an alternative economy that turns into tobacco and bread. I mean money and stuff. People can or cannot get into debt— that sort of stuff will generate some friction. The trade is where the problem is at, people who get into debt and cannot pay. There's also a whole strata of gambling, and when things don't match up, the shortfalls in those areas generate serious friction. Then there's the general frustration . . . that can overspill into the interpersonal relationships in prison . . .

The true extent of debt, and its consequences, are difficult to ascertain. For some prisoners debt is acknowledged, but is not seen as presenting a serious problem. One prisoner argues:

If I go in over my head, say 20–30 quid in debt, I just say 'I haven't got it yet', and he can have it when I've got it. And that works out . . . If somebody owes me money it's to my detriment to bash them, because I ain't going to get any money in the end anyway—just give me 50 pence a week.

What is both apparent and crucial is that Long Lartin had a cash economy (as well as the exchange of goods in kind)[3] and that the sums of money involved were quite large—certainly in proportion to the debtor's ability to pay. Such sums could be counted on occasion in hundreds of pounds. Moreover a cash economy is inherently

---

[3] That is to say, prisoners received their weekly wages in ordinary currency, and also drew their private cash allowances in the same medium. By contrast (see later discussion) Albany operated a cashless credit system for both these purposes.

likely to expand, both because there is no theoretical limit to how much one might want or accumulate and because the amounts circulating can be increased by money flowing (illicitly) in from outside. Prisoners who have experienced debt problems do not usually see the matter in such simple or benign terms as those quoted above. Thus, one prisoner who was known by others to have access to large sums in cash commented:

Then the drug dealers started to take over. A hell of a lot of money was generated through drugs, not just one syndicate . . . It was a terrifying situation to be in.

Another prisoner expressed similar anxiety:

You've got to be a dodger in a dispersal . . . You've got to duck and dive. You've got to be cunning. The inmates are like packs of wolves . . .

Some strongly expressed negative views of Long Lartin were held by prisoners who had been dealt with as active 'troublemakers' and who felt they had been summarily or unfairly treated. More particularly, however, as the above comments suggest, some of the most trenchant views were held by those who felt they had been victimized, who argued that the Long Lartin regime permitted an untoward scale of trading and credit and, moreover, who did not regard themselves as having enjoyed adequate protection.

Prisoners are subject to competing pressures. On the one hand the desire to minimize the pains of imprisonment, the demands of friendship, the need to retain status and reputation, and varying degrees of anger and antagonism towards 'the system' and the conditions of confinement it imposes all lead the prisoner into potentially conflictual situations. Conversely, the widespread desire for a quiet life, the pressure to achieve early release, the question of physical security all provide strong incentives to avoid trouble and co-operate with staff. These contrary demands give rise to widely felt ambivalences and mixed feelings, which prisoners may seek to resolve in variable ways (as Mathiesen, 1965, has observed).

Albany

Many of the considerations which we have already outlined apply equally to life in Albany. The social position of long-term prisoners is in many ways fundamentally similar in all long-term prisons, and the competing pressures to which they are subject are similar in kind—relations with families; legal and financial problems; problems of living together. On occasions, prisoners would say to us, with a shrug, questioning the utility of our work: 'Prison's prison, isn't it?' Yet, it is also true that Albany and Long Lartin (and indeed each of the other dispersals, past and present) were institutions of which prisoners did report somewhat distinct experiences and perceptions.

Prisoners arriving at particular prisons usually have some notion—derived from rumour, grapevines, travellers' tales—of what it will be like. This was perhaps particularly true of Albany. Albany's reputation, for example amongst prisoners on remand in London gaols, has historically been particularly bleak and frightening. As one prisoner put it:

You don't want to go there, you don't get your visits, people walk about with blades all the time, you talk to people in the wrong way and you get stabbed.

Or again:

Rumours were that Albany wasn't one of the better places to go. If you got Albany you struck rock bottom.

Several prisoners had heard that Albany was the prison to which 'the hard core' or 'the young subversives' or 'troublemakers' were sent. One prisoner reported that his allocating officer at Wandsworth told him 'Albany was a shit prison'. One prisoner summarized his reaction: 'Dread and woe, dread and woe'. More particularly, such stories could lead the new arrival to believe that he may have to 'tool up' to protect himself:

It was pictured to me as kind of like a war zone. I was told that the procedure for when I got to Albany was to get a razor and a wedge for my door in order to protect myself, because violence was rife . . . I tried to avoid coming here.

Albany, then, had a hard reputation amongst at least some prisoners, and perhaps also staff in other prisons. The exact dynamics by which such reputations are spread and maintained lies beyond the scope of this analysis. Nevertheless, some of the consequences of the reputation are relatively clear. Many prisoners came to Albany unwillingly and in fear. Evidently this presented the prison with a number of problems. For example, some prisoners on arrival at

Albany would refuse to go on normal location and insist on remaining in the segregation unit.

However, most people quickly realized that the degree of violence and threat from other prisoners which they had been led to expect in fact bore little relation to the reality of everyday life in Albany. Not surprisingly this came as something of a relief:

Seventy five per cent act in a sensible way . . . only a minority don't. A lot of people want to get on with their hobbies, fight their appeals, or get to another prison—they have accepted life here.

The hard reputation also extended to expectations about the regime and the attitudes of staff. Here again, at least some prisoners reported that Albany did not altogether match up to its reputation:

It's a much more relaxed place than I expected. We're given a certain amount of leeway and much more general freedom. I remember when I first came here I saw an inmate really like giving it to Mr Bloggs in his office. I thought, 'Christ, if this'd been Wandsworth they would have strung him up' . . . That impressed me. In terms of general freedom this has much more, but I can only compare it to Wandsworth.

Nevertheless, although the reality of Albany was experienced as less draconian than the mythology, it was still widely and traditionally regarded as an unfavourable location among dispersals. This was partly the result of its geographical location and the 'damn water' which visitors have to cross, and partly an orientation towards the regime.

Prisoners' views of regimes and staff

For prisoners coming to Albany whose previous experience of imprisonment was confined to the large London local gaols their arrival at Albany plainly represented a welcome improvement in their material and social conditions. Nevertheless all prisoners could hear the reports and views of those who have spent time elsewhere in the system, especially given the frequent 'traffic' between Albany and Parkhurst which is adjacent. Some prisoners had been in Albany before 1985, and reports circulated about the extent of the subsequent changes. The extent of the legitimacy which such prisoners were prepared to grant to Albany's regime was limited by such comparisons:

In fact Albany and Parkhurst are two different worlds. At Parkhurst officers don't hound you, they don't make life any more difficult than they
have to. Sports facilities are better and there are more opportunities. After
work you can do as you please. It's very liberal . . . Staff treat you as a
mature person, willing to talk to you with respect and decency . . .

At least one prisoner who had been in Albany prior to 1985
insisted:

They were running a more relaxed regime then. You could move around
the wings freely, and shower when you wanted. There was a better relationship with staff then . . . What changed all that was the fight on B wing
. . . a couple of staff got involved, then the whole prison shut down. . . .
People were told it was only going to be for a period, but the regime stuck.
They said it was a riot in the prison, and it wasn't. They overreacted.

Such comparisons could give rise to a sense of grievance and
unfairness, either because Albany was felt not to be running like a
'proper' dispersal or out of a sense of indignation at having to live
with the consequences of others' actions in the past. Thus, one
prisoner commented:

They call it a dispersal. Forget the word dispersal. It's a controlled state. I
feel the pressure. Other people do too. As soon as you get three or four
grouping together in a little clique, they're split up.

Others go further:

The system says Albany is a rehabilitation prison. It isn't. It's an out and
out punishment prison. From what other people say, who've been to other
dispersals Albany is the worst one. It's a glorified block.

Certain prisoners gave more concessions to staff viewpoints, whilst
still contending that Albany should now return to a more liberal
mode of operation:

There used to be gangs. Now there aren't, because of the way the prison is
being run to a certain degree. It's annoying in a way. As soon as a group
of people get together in here, the tendency is to split them. Sometimes it's
genuine friendship . . . but it's understandable, because in the old days
there were posses, certain spurs you just didn't go down unless you were
invited, when this was Britain's toughest gaol. It's a pussy-cat gaol now.

Others felt similarly. One argued that he 'realized the reasons
behind' the introduction of the new systems, but:

Now I really don't think it's necessary, because I don't think you've got a
potential riot situation. [People here] are not going to risk getting into a

riot, and just the general atmosphere of this place doesn't need it. You'd probably get more peacefulness by letting them be more free.

We regard these views as broadly representative of the bulk of prisoners to whom we spoke. The theme that Albany should be seen as a 'punishment prison' was quite widespread.

However, these critical views were by no means unanimous. At least one prisoner with extensive experience of other dispersals said Albany is 'the best prison I've ever been in'. In particular at least one old prison hand felt that prison should be tough:

People come into prison for punishment, but they think they're coming to a 5-star hotel, with all the luxuries. Prison is not like that and shouldn't be. Doing bird in this day and age is too simple. If they make a prison too relaxed then they soon lose control.

This was clearly a minority view, however. On the whole there was a weight of opinion which agreed in identifying particular features of the regime as unnecessary or unjustified. These included principally:

1. the number of times during the day that prisoners were banged up and the consequent sense of being hurried along (for example over showering) and;

2. the restriction of numbers on evening association.

These restrictions contravened prisoners' expectations of what the appropriate conditions for long-termers should be. They restricted prisoners' scope for choice and limited their sense of having any control over their environment further than most of them regarded as being necessary. The fact of being banged-up during the day when no work was available was particularly resented. Again, Albany was compared unfavourably by prisoners with Parkhurst in this respect. Meanwhile a number of prisoners insisted that they did not in fact wish to go on association every night but wanted to retain the ability to choose when they would do so. Subsidiary restrictions, such as access to the gymnasium and canteen, were seen as flowing directly from the primary limitations of time out of cell and control of movements.

When asked why they thought these conditions existed, prisoners tended to attribute them to the 'paranoia' of the staff, or indeed directly to the Governor himself. The arguments which prisoners put forward about controlled unlocking aimed to rebut the staff's justifications of it. Thus:

Q The argument is that it cuts down the amount of trading and gambling and keeps that in bounds.

A If they can't see the guy because he's banged up, they'll see him the next morning. So it makes no difference.

Q It protects prisoners who are under pressure from other prisoners.

A He can be got at going to work next morning.

Q So what do you think the real reason is for it?

A It's down to the no. 1 Governor. I'm baffled by the thinking.

Hence, prisoners argued, the policy was premised on an exaggerated assumption of their deviousness and desire to cause trouble:

If prisoners wanted this nick to go up, they'd find a way to make it go up . . . I'm sure they think we sit and plot to burn this place down. Most people just want to get on with their bird and be left alone. Of course you do get anarchists but the majority just want to do their bird and get out.

More than one prisoner regarded the system as both vindictive and counter-productive:

The regime is stupid, irrelevant, and mindless. Most of their rules are not designed for any specific purpose other than for bashing you over the head every day of the week to remind you you're in prison, in punishment . . . The so-called controlled unlocking creates the very reverse—ill feeling, discontent, and disharmony.

Or again:

I just think that people doing a long time should be given a bit more freedom than what they are getting. You're getting *bitter* people in these prisons.

One particular source of annoyance to prisoners was their belief in inconsistencies in the way the regime was operated, not only between wings but even between different landings on the same wing:

I've heard the other wings are slacker about locking up—more humane. Trouble starts over the banging up.

Prisoners in the 'main' prison and those in the vulnerable unit each believed that the others enjoyed more favourable conditions than they did. The sense of living under a 'controlled state' focused particular attention on perceived inconsistency, whether between prisons, or between areas within the same prison—irrespective of whether prisoners' perceptions of practices in other prisons were accurate or not, or whether prisoners at Albany indeed idealized life in Parkhurst or Long Lartin. The more closely the policies of the prison impinge on intimate or precious areas of their lives the more deeply such feelings of injustice or constraint are felt by prisoners. In particular, given the importance which they attach to visits, differences in practice between prisons will always be noted by prisoners. Thus, for example, the fact that prisoners in Parkhurst could receive visits in the morning and afternoon of the same day, or wear items of their own clothing on visits, while Albany prisoners could not, were apt to become topics of grievance. At the same time, as we have already suggested in relation to Long Lartin, prisoners experience mixed or ambivalent feelings. On the one hand they want staff to show discretion, flexibility and 'common sense'. On the other they feel that rules should be applied uniformly across the board (cf. Mathiesen, 1965). This in turn conditions their attitudes towards staff and staff conduct.

Prisoners' views of staff

We find it interesting that prisoners at Albany frequently differentiated between their views of the regime and their relations with uniformed staff. This stands in contrast to our observations at Long Lartin where, as we have noted above, prisoners rarely made this distinction sharply. On the whole, and with some important exceptions and qualifications, prisoners' views of staff at Albany were markedly more positive than their views of the 'regime' or 'system' as such:

This particular prison is completely and utterly different from the others. I've got no complaint against the prison officers themselves, it's the system as a whole that seems ludicrous.

Indeed, some prisoners went so far as to say that they did not believe that prison officers necessarily wholeheartedly wanted to run a restrictive regime or go 'by the book' in interpreting rules and regulations:

Q   Would you see the rules and regulations being largely at fault, rather than individual prison officers' attitudes, and what is the relationship between these two things?

A   I think a lot of prison officers think the rules are petty and stupid, and they admit openly that they don't like carrying them out, but they've got to because their job's at risk.

Q   And that's the majority?
A   Yes.

What is interesting to note, here, is that prisoners who adopted this line seemed to be unaware not only that Albany's uniformed staff and its management were largely in accord with regard to the appropriateness of the current regime, but also that uniformed staff, especially through the contribution of the local POA branch, had played a significant part in its initial formulation. Nevertheless, a number of prisoners tended to explain the situation they identified by reference to factors beyond the staff's control. In this case they usually viewed the staff as being either dominated by the Governor or subservient to the dictates of 'faceless bureaucrats' in the Home Office who had no idea at all what prison life was actually like:

The officers on the wing are all right. They know what's what, they're on the front line. It's never them. It's the people who are normally behind desks in security who haven't got a clue, and don't particularly care, who pass orders that upset everybody else, and these people here unfortunately have got to then untangle it all.

Similarly:

They say they agree with us, but what can we do? It's the Governor. I really do believe they're scared of this Governor. He has got a very big reputation.

Thus, the staff with whom prisoners were most familiar, the ones with whom they shared their time and space, were often not seen as the source of the 'problem'. Policy did not originate with them. More often the people to blame were seen as standing somewhere in an ascending hierarchy of distance and power. For some the security staff were 'big, bad wolves bringing grief'. Very often it was the Governor, and beyond him the bureaucrats and politicians. Quite often prisoners commented that staff would regrettably 'cop it' or be 'in the firing line' for trouble springing from frustrations not of their making. They just happened to be 'there'.

    Prisoners did not necessarily want to cultivate excessively close contact with staff. For many prisoners the defining feature of a good prison officer was one who leaves you alone as much as possible and, when contact is necessary, is civil, good-humoured and fair. Thus:

I really try to avoid speaking to officers unless I have to. I respect them for what they do, but I think they're still opposition. But I do think you can be polite to each other, that's where the sense of humour comes in. There are definite boundaries as an inmate that I can't cross. . . .

There is 'us' and 'them', and my policy is that of the nick: you don't talk to officers unless you've got a reason.

In general, prisoners at Albany seemed to prefer dealing with staff who would do what they could to help prisoners, not lock up unnecessarily, display a sense of humour, not promise what they could not deliver, were prepared to be slagged off, did not 'play mind games', and did not 'wind prisoners up'. Prisoners mistrusted staff who were seen as unduly keen. As such they often expressed a preference for staff who were just 'doing their jobs', earning their pay and going home, because such staff were considered less likely to be motivated either by ambition or by a personal animosity towards convicts. Some prisoners explicitly recognized the difficulty of prison officers' tasks. It is notable that, notwithstanding a widespread dissatisfaction with aspects of the regime, most prisoners none the less considered that there was an acceptable relationship between themselves and most members of staff.

This is perhaps all the more surprising given the frequent reporting by prisoners of what they regarded as 'petty' nickings. This being so they tended to attribute such nickings and other 'wind-ups' to an identifiable minority of staff. Prisoners characterized the staff they disliked as being overzealous, erratic, rude, confrontational, untrustworthy and rigid. They refered to feeling hounded, singled out, and wound up. They resented staff who appeared to take pleasure in locking them up, or who made jokes they did not find funny. Thus, the most vehement objections by prisoners were usually directed towards what they regarded as undue or vindictive exercises of power:

There are a couple of officers I could directly pick out who seem to deliberately go out of their way to frustrate or aggravate inmates . . . There are officers that seem to take pleasure from banging people up as soon as they've had breakfast—'Get behind that door'—and won't unlock until five minutes before you're going to work . . . Some deliberately come on the landings to antagonize people. They pick their victims—they're not silly there.

Some felt themselves provoked to react:

They like to humiliate people, and I won't stand for that sort of behaviour from them. So I stand firm, I'm not going to let them humiliate me . . . There are certain officers who are not like that, but if there's one officer who's got a character amongst the others, who's got a strong personality, he influences them very easily. I've noticed that.

This is partly to do with whether or not one gets nicked:

You wouldn't believe the sort of nickings you get here . . . There's one hated screw, not on my landing, been hit with a brick in the face—he's so petty.

Partly it is a matter of feeling placed under pressure, crowded or pursued. In this sense it is also a matter of personal style or manner:

There's one screw here called Bloggs who could cause a riot in the prison—he wants to bang you up without giving you any time to slop out . . . only about 10 out of 300 are bad . . . bad officers and bad inmates should be got rid of immediately.

Some prisoners indeed felt that other staff may have shared their dispproval of bad staff practice, as the following examples suggest:

We've had one occasion where we had to go downstairs and ask them to remove a member of staff who'd been antagonistic towards us. And they did, because they don't want trouble.

On one occasion the very worst officer on the landing was following me around everywhere. I called him a wanker—and he nicked me. Every day this particular man is called a cunt to his face, and he doesn't do anything about it! The Block PO, when he asked me about the incident—I told him I called Bloggs a wanker. He just said 'But that's exactly what he is' and walked off shaking his head.

In sum, prisoners held a number of views in tension. They may have chafed under aspects of Albany's regime, but on the other hand it was not as bad as they expected. Perhaps, we conjecture, low expectations, borne of the hard experience of remand in the London gaols combined with Albany's grim reputation there, made it easier for them initially to reconcile themselves to its actual conditions of life. On the other hand, the comparisons which were drawn with other dispersals, or with Albany's own past, tended to reinforce the view that Albany's current regime was restrictive.

Meanwhile, insofar as they had to put into operation an unpopular set of control measures staff were seen as doing unwelcome things and enforcing rules which prisoners regarded as 'petty'. At the level of generalities this tended to encourage a view of staff–prisoner relations which was more polarized into 'us' and 'them' than, say, at Long Lartin. Yet, prisoners were none the less prepared to agree that most of the staff with whom they had daily contact were 'OK' or 'all right'. Rather, they attributed most of their problems either to the dictates of the Governor or to the whims of certain 'power mad screws', bent on making their lives a misery.

There is a deep irony at the heart of the relations which staff and prisoners have with one another in dispersal prisons. At times prisoners have told us of experiences of humiliation, powerlessness, abuse, and fury—sometimes silent, sometimes vocal. At such times their relations with staff are marked by systematic antagonism and resentment. The terms which prisoners use—'mind games', 'wind-ups', 'digging out'—all express feelings of being taunted or baited and being powerless to respond. At one level prisoners and staff are clearly in opposition. And yet prisoners and staff also have what Christie (1989) calls 'thick' social relations. They share the same physical and social space. They cannot sustain a state of submerged warfare all the time. They develop familiarities. They banter. There are acts of concern and kindness. It is a situation marked by contradictions. Certain kinds of 'control problems' inherently emerge out of such contradictions.

Prisoners' views of one another

It is apparent from figures on the respective populations of Albany and Long Lartin (see Table 3.4 in chapter 3) that there were a number of significant differences between them during our study. In general, the Albany main prison population included more people under twenty-five, more black people (around twenty-five per cent of its population was Afro-Caribbean), more prisoners with firearms offences, fewer lifers, more people serving shorter sentences, and a relatively large proportion of people from one geographical area (Greater London).

Just as young people in the general population commit more offences than other age groups, so it is widely held that young adult prisoners present more control problems. By this it is usually meant that they are more likely to receive more frequent Governor's reports (cf. McEwan, 1986). Overall, Albany held a population which by virtue of its age and ethnic composition as well as high proportion of violence and firearms offences would be thought of by many in the Prison Service as particularly difficult or problematic, in comparison with that of Long Lartin or Wakefield, for example. Moreover, Albany could be said to lack the 'steadying' influence of lifers. On prevailing assumptions one would thus be led to expect, as we expected, a high level of racial tension, relatively frequent fights and assaults, and frequent reports for insubordination. *Prima facie* these assumptions appeared to receive support in Prison Statistics (see Tables 3.1 and 3.5) and were mirrored in aspects of Albany's reputation throughout the dispersal system, including in accounts previously given to us by prisoners who had been there.

How did these views correspond to prisoners' perceptions? Many of those factors which are posited as representing sources of trouble between prisoners are *not* commonly seen as such by prisoners themselves. Indeed, as we will go on to suggest, prisoners at Albany presented themselves as a more homogeneous group, experiencing fewer *chronic* sources of tension and antagonism with one another, than seems to us to have been the case at Long Lartin. We will return to the implicatons of this point below.

The most striking instance of this point is presented by prisoners' views of the race question. Very few prisoners from any ethnic group reported hostility from prisoners of other ethnic groups as representing a significant problem. For example, one black prisoner when asked to identify the principal sources of trouble between prisoner and prisoner replied 'very silly things like football and arguments like cell thieving rate highly, and debts' but did not mention race. In the twelve interviews with black prisoners in the 'main' prison, none of them volunteered racism from other prisoners as a serious problem, and most discounted it even when prompted. These are the views of, mainly, young black men most of whom were born in Britain, who recognized the profound impact of racism but who in their present circumstances preferred to minimize its centrality in their lives and emphasize instead their shared experience and concerns with other prisoners.

In any case, they tended to argue, the numbers of black people in Albany represented a certain security. On the one hand they resented the sense that a disproportionate number of black people were sent there, seeing it as a discriminatory practice by allocating officers at the London prisons. On the other hand this guaranteed a

resource of mutual support and affinity and diminished any consequences which would result from being in a 'minority' status. To
this extent black prisoners may not have suffered a sense of racial
threat because they were conscious of themselves as a major presence in the prison. One indicator of this was that many of them
described the ratio of black to white as 'fifty-fifty', when in fact it
was about 1:2 in Albany main prison. Thus, prisoners sometimes
observed that race used to represent a serious issue amongst prisoners, but that this was no longer the case:

In the 70s, early 80s, there was about 20% black inmates here, and then
there was a lot of racism by cons and officers. Now its fifty-fifty. You can't
start doing it now . . . If you had 10% black people in here, the attitude
would change, but they can't do that now because they know there's too
many people would rebel against it . . .

Matters were rather different for Asian prisoners, who reported a
diversity of problems. They tended to see other groups of prisoners
as having more in common with one another (and the staff) than
with themselves. There were frequent language problems.
Meanwhile they rejected the Prison Department's categorization
which grouped together as 'Asian' people of different, and often
antagonistic, national, regional and religious commitments, thereby
demonstrating to them its failure of understanding. Moreover they
often felt that they were ignored for precisely the same reason that
they were commonly described as 'model prisoners', namely that
they suffered their position in dignified and stoical silence.

There was, then, certainly amongst black and white young
Londoners a *modus vivendi*. There were sporadic incidents which
incorporated an interracial dimension (see below, chapter 7). The
only visible element of race-related hostility which seemed in any
sense systematic came from some of the older white prisoners. This
usually took the form of complaints about the noisiness of the
youngsters in general and 'boisterous' blacks in particular. It also
went along with a resentful allegation that black prisoners would
protect black sex offenders, thereby preventing the white 'robbers'
from ridding themselves of 'nonces' on the wings. At least one
older prisoner, in commenting that Albany's regime suited him fine
because it held out the prospect of the quiet life added 'of course
you wouldn't get the spades to agree with what I'm saying'.

Association at Albany, given the prohibition of cell association, the cultural prominence of the younger prisoners, and the physical layout of the wings was a livelier, louder, more bustling event than at Long Lartin. At Long Lartin people disappeared either into the TV room or into one another's cells to re-emerge only at bang-up time. The only people visible on the wing would be a few darts players, a small card school, and the occasional individual ironing his kit. People came and went to the gym, canteen or outside association under their own steam and in ones and twos. At Albany on the other hand there was constant sound from the kitchen and TV room. Prisoners wanting to go to the gym or canteen congregated at gates, bantering with one another, hailing friends from other wings, and pleading with staff to let them through.

In these circumstances a distinctive, powerful, older 'gangster class' was difficult to identify. Neither the weight of numbers of the young, nor the arrangements of the routine lent themselves easily to the formation of a power élite. Older prisoners tended to gather in the relative peace and quiet of the small television room at the back of the wing, or in the wing laundry or to cook. They were irritated by the 'kids' and not infrequently preferred to stay banged up rather than always go on association. Some older prisoners were socially isolated and looked rather forlorn. One or two spent more time talking to staff (or to us) than to other prisoners, twenty odd years their junior.

'Control problems'

The 'control problems' which prisoners reported constituted a familiar group: debts; relations between 'straight cons.' and sex offenders; cell thefts; noise; sporadic instances of bullying, mutual antagonism, and fights; moments of resistance to instructions or demands of staff which were viewed as illegitimate; annoyance over bad food or delayed visits.

As at Long Lartin, prisoners did not want to exaggerate the extent of such events. Instead they emphasized the normality of daily mundane routines and reminded us that most of the time there was mutual toleration and co-operation. Indeed they pointed out that most of the time social relations in the prison seemed to them more harmonious than in analogous institutions of the outside world:

People are remarkably tolerant. I would say any club or police station has more problems than this place.

On the other hand, prisoners also felt that the 'silly, stupid little things' which constituted the bulk of problems between themselves were perhaps exacerbated by the controlled regime:

There's not a day goes by when I don't feel frustrated and angered, and all the time you're bottling it up, and that's why sometimes people go off at the smallest of things because it's a build up.

Similarly, the lack of things to do during association periods or of places to get quietly away from the hurly-burly were often cited as reasons why prisoners got on top of one another:

Long-termers shouldn't be under this kind of pressure . . . people are just dying to get banged up some nights, because they're *so bored.*

A number of older prisoners used this as the basis of an argument for a 'stage' system of increasing privileges according to behaviour and length of time served. In so saying they hoped to be relieved of the irritation they felt at being amongst the 'kids' and so that they could then enjoy a quieter life, more liberal conditions and less competition for scarce resources like cookers or the choice of TV programmes:

A lot of the hassle has gone out of this prison, but it comes back as soon as they get the wrong people. . . . My rows have always been with other inmates, like over booking the cooker . . . Now I don't argue over it . . . [cell association] would be all right, but you've got to have the right bods on the landings.

Thus, although the majority of prisoners objected to controlled unlocking and argued that 'if there's more relaxation, then there's less tension' a few, predominantly older prisoners, approved of it as providing structure, control, and an opportunity for peace and quiet 'behind your door'. This argument was only seen as holding good for current conditions; they did not regard controlled unlocking as inherently necessary.

Of the more discretely identifiable 'control problems', debts deriving from drugs and tobacco were again regarded as the most important. Bringing drugs into the prison, arranging lines of supply, keeping them hidden and the transactions (and proceeds) secret from staff were all quite refined and highly developed procedures. Staff were both constantly vigilant and at the same time resigned to a certain level of use, at least of cannabis. Most prisoners subscribed to the view that drugs 'keep the lid on' the prison and

hence also tended towards the opinion that staff were not fundamentally committed to stamping them out. Accordingly there was a
'cat and mouse' character to the policing of drugs. Prisoners
expected staff to temper their zeal in searching for and investigating
the supply and distribution of drugs. Hence, an unannounced or
'unfair' search was bitterly resented.

Most drug distribution in Albany was probably more accurately
characterized as 'user-dealing' than as 'baroning' or big business.
Prisoners acknowledged that there were occasions when people got
into debt and went down to the block to escape, and even accepted
that this was a legitimate concern of the staff. On the other hand,
and in contrast to Long Lartin, prisoners at Albany were not paid
in cash, nor were they officially allowed to have any cash in their
possession. Of course payment can be made in a range of ways
other than cash—in kind or via outside bank accounts or families.
However, on the whole, prisoners insisted that there was very little
cash in the prison. This was a marked difference between the two
prisons. It was one area where a particular policy difference seemed
likely to have a marked impact on behaviour, not because it
reduced the total consumption of drugs but because it limited the
size of the prison economy.

This being so, we may conjecture that the likely outline of the
drug market in Albany differed from that in Long Lartin in a number of ways. First, it seems probable that the supply was no less
plentiful and the demand equally high. The proportion of people
who would use cannabis and other drugs routinely 'on the out' and
who could get them via friends and relatives might, if anything,
have been larger, given the age of the Albany population and the
high proportion of people from one area, London. At the same
time the ability to pay was highly likely to be lower. Hence the
price was almost certainly lower, the scale of debts quantitatively
lower and the incentive to try to corner the market correspondingly
less. There were probably, therefore, a larger number of smaller
suppliers operating more informally via friendship networks than in
Long Lartin. The concentrations of money and influence were thus
almost certainly smaller. Similar considerations apply to gambling.
Most prisoners said they did not know of any large-scale regular
bookies and said that most stakes were laid in Mars Bars rather
than cash. Does any bookie want to accumulate thousands of Mars
Bars? The scale of operations in both cases would seem to be

smaller, more *ad hoc*, and less professional. This does not mean to say that drugs did not result in problems, however:

A lot of people borrow dope on credit, and they may genuinely not be able to pay the following week when they should do. So then people start getting heavy-handed. People that rely on somebody go and do something on the strength of that, which they shouldn't do, but they do, and so it goes on. He owes me, you owe me—a vicious circle . . . It's a serious problem. You hear rumours about people getting cut over a half-ounce.

Ironically, therefore, if people at Albany were indeed 'running for cover' over debts, they may have been doing so for amounts of money which would be thought too trivial to bother with in Long Lartin.

With regard to sex offenders, prisoners in the main wings at Albany voiced the routine hostility with equal vehemence as those elsewhere. Sex offenders at Albany constituted just under seven per cent of the population on the main wings. They might, therefore, be seen as a vulnerable minority. However, identifying and harassing sex offenders did not seem to be a preoccupation among the 'straight' prisoners. The statuses ascribed to different crimes are occasionally difficult for the outsider to understand. In part this stems from perceived inconsistencies in sentencing and treatment, and in part from gut feeling:

I don't want to spend my time around rapists and people who beat up old women. I want to be with *normal* prisoners, armed robbers and people who do nasty stabbings.

As at Long Lartin, from time to time such animosities spilled over into personal confrontations. What is interesting is that there had been a perceived change in the extent to which Albany's 'straight' prisoners actually acted on their hostility. Prisoners often said that in 'the old days' cells would be burned out and 'nonces' rapidly intimidated off the wing. However they were often at a loss to explain quite why things may have changed and offered only vague reasons such as the need to behave in order to get out, or at least off the island. This was in contrast to Long Lartin where prisoners were encouraged to behave in order to stay put to benefit from the regime. White prisoners claimed that black sex offenders received protection anyway. Others talked of the power sex offenders and others could wield through 'notes in the box' in engineering the removal of anyone who was threatening them. They spoke of the solidarity of the 'straight' cons. having been disrupted by successive sex offenders being 'slipped in' to the wing. Sometimes these remarks were presented almost as excuses, as reasons for not pursuing the sex offenders as was done in 'the old days'. Some prisoners seemed, as it were, to be letting themselves off the hook of the obligation to have a go at the 'nonces' which social pressure traditionally demands. They must still be seen to be hostile, but for the most part they did not have to act out the hostility. However, some will continue to act on their hostility, and vulnerable prisoners remain at risk. Meanwhile the presence of the vulnerable unit as a distinct entity may have diverted a certain amount of attention from the vulnerable prisoners in the main wings and allowed ample scope for the venting of verbal aggression and scapegoating. The level of actual violence in Albany against vulnerable prisoners was not, so far as we could ascertain, very high.

Summary

We have indicated a number of points of view which prisoners took up in relation to the experience of regimes and staff and their feelings about living with one another. The issues which prisoners identified as bearing on what they considered to be 'control problems' were of the same general nature in both prisons, but they suggested different levels, distributions and emphases within these broad categories. In general terms prisoners at Long Lartin were markedly readier to acknowledge the regime as legitimate, but those who disliked it did so with a rare passion. Views of Albany were less disparate. Few relished being there; most disliked the more overtly controlling aspects of the regime, but saw it as a burden shared in common by everybody. With exceptions for a few officers whom they roundly denounced Albany prisoners did not translate their irritation with aspects of the regime into active hostility against staff; and they saw many of those problems that did arise as inevitable outgrowths of extended and close confinement rather than attributing them to systemic failures of the regime. In chapters seven and eight we go on to discuss particular features of the incidence and management of troublesome situations in these two prisons, with reference to a number of actual sequences of events. First, however, we examine aspects of one very particular social world, namely the Vulnerable Prisoner Unit at Albany.

6

The Vulnerable Prisoner Unit at Albany

Introduction

In many prisons the risk of harassment or attack upon certain prisoners by others presents a series of very difficult questions. Traditionally, prisoners convicted of serious sexual offences (especially those involving violence towards children) have stood in particular danger. Such people are known by most prisoners and many staff as 'nonces'. Those considered to have informed to the prison authorities or the police ('grasses') are also especially at risk, as are some prisoners unable to meet debts incurred in drug or gambling deals. These groups have come to be known collectively as 'vulnerable prisoners'. It is now frequently affirmed by a range of informed observers including a former Chief Inspector of Prisons (Hennessey, 1986) and Lord Justice Woolf (1991: paras. 12.185–12.215) that the state of affairs which has arisen hitherto in which vulnerable prisoners, including some who are serving extremely long sentences, take indefinite refuge in segregation units under Prison Rule 43,[1] ought not to be allowed to continue forever. Rule 43 is inherently problematic as a means of providing protection for prisoners: it generally imposes severely restricted conditions of daily life (by association with its other function as an administrative control measure); it carries a stigma from which it is diffi-

---

[1] As we detail elsewhere, Prison Rule 43 has two primary aspects. It permits the Governor of the prison to segregate ('remove from association') any prisoner if in his or her view it is in the 'interests of good order and discipline' to do so. We return to this use of Rule 43 in ch. 8. It also empowers the Governor to keep the prisoner apart 'for their own protection' (whether or not at their own request), and it is this use with which this ch. is concerned. Prisoners who have recourse to this protective measure are commonly referred to simply as 'Rule 43s', and they refer to themselves as living 'on the Rule'. For some of the many legal and procedural controversies that attend both aspects of Rule 43 see Livingstone and Owen (1993); Richardson (1993).

cult for prisoners to break free; and it has traditionally been a crude instrument, setting up a stark choice between tenuous survival on normal location and lonely and austere segregation (Sampson, 1994). The problems associated with vulnerability are of long standing, though they have intensified in recent years, especially as the number of convictions for sexual offences and the lengths of sentences imposed by the courts have both increased. Given the presence in dispersal prisons of many of the most publicly notorious individuals, and those with the longest sentences, these difficulties have probably been felt most acutely within the dispersal system. Moreover, it has been suggested that deteriorations in general prison conditions (King and McDermott, 1989) can exacerbate existing tendencies amongst other prisoners to scapegoat and persecute vulnerable groups (Sampson, 1994). Conversely, the same circumstances may reduce the incentive for vulnerable prisoners to 'front it out' on normal location (Hay and Sparks, 1992). In any event, the numbers of prisoners seeking protection increased substantially during the 1980s, to a total of around 3,000 by 1990 (Woolf, 1991; Sampson, 1994).

All this sets up conflicting demands and proposed solutions. The general drift of insider opinion has become increasingly *integrationist* in recent years (Home Office, 1989), even if this results in the curious prospect of officials encouraging prisoners to lie about their offences as the price of survival on normal location. It is a point of principle for many prison managers and staff that vulnerable prisoners should be sustained as far as humanly possible on normal location: these are long-term prisoners, entitled to corresponding privileges and conditions. To act in any other way, many prison governors would feel, is to capitulate to unacceptable pressure from other prisoners. On this view sufficiently active management and supervision can achieve the reintegration of vulnerable prisoners into the general population for many purposes (principally work and education) even if a degree of separation remains in cell areas. Experience at Long Lartin could be cited in partial support of this argument, as could other initiatives outside the dispersal system, for example at Littlehey Prison in Cambridgeshire (Woolf, 1991: para. 12.191, Sampson, 1994; see also Appendix B). It is doubtful, however, whether the sorts of conditions which would favour full integration of vulnerable groups have been widespread in English prisons in recent times. And the question remains as to

what quality of life is indeed enjoyed by those who do 'survive'—
the risks and anxieties to which they may be subject remain part of
the hidden underlife of prisons. At present tens of thousands of per-
son-days per year continue to be spent in segregation units by those
who can no longer take the pressure.

A second line of approach to the problem has been to establish
separate units for vulnerable prisoners which at least approximate
to conditions on normal location. One such Vulnerable Prisoner
Unit (VPU) was in operation at Albany at the time of our research.
(Indeed, since the period in which our fieldwork was conducted
Albany has left the dispersal system and developed a specialism in
the management of vulnerable prisoners.) The Vulnerable Prisoner
Unit strategy is itself not free from problems. The defining feature
of unit populations is their vulnerability rather than their offences,
even if a majority of those within such units are long-term sex
offenders. In this respect, for all that their internal conditions of life
offer prisoners a far greater prospect of 'normalization' than life
'on the Rule' ever would, Vulnerable Prisoner Units are plainly in
origin a managerial strategy of segregative control and risk management, rather than an initiative which is in the first instance
concerned with developing a treatment orientation towards sex
offending (albeit that many of those who work within them would
see them as presenting this opportunity). This can have some ironic
effects. One is that, for example, at the time of its initial creation
the Vulnerable Prisoner Unit at Grendon was the only part of that
prison *not* specifically oriented towards addressing offending
(Gomershall, 1991). The treatment dimensions of this issue are
beyond the scope of this study; our concern centres upon the social
relations within a Vulnerable Prisoner Unit as a special case of
long-term confinement. However, as we will go on to show, the
lowly place of treatment within the Unit at that time was drawn
repeatedly to our attention by both prisoners and staff.

The Vulnerable Prisoner Unit (hereafter VPU) was established as
a regional resource in 'E' wing in 1984. Prisoners within the Unit
did not have the status of Rule 43, though they had almost invari-
ably been subject to 'the Rule' immediately prior to arrival. A second wing was added in 1988 following the refurbishment of 'D'
wing. At the time of our study the VPU thus occupied two-fifths of
the prison. The corridor linking the Unit and the 'main' prison was
gated. Prisoners from the 'main' prison only passed through the

area reserved for vulnerable prisoners *en route* to or from the segregation unit (and hence under escort). The Unit was thus in large measure self-contained. It had its own workshops and exercise area. Prisoners from the Unit had to enter the 'main' corridor in order to reach the hospital, classrooms, library, canteen, and gymnasium. At such times movements of prisoners in the 'main' prison were 'frozen'. This caused some degree of logistical complication, nuisance and irritation for all concerned. It is a curious fact of prison life that whereas we were repeatedly told that there were 'vulnerable' prisoners living on 'A', 'B' and 'C' wings, once a particular group has been identified as *the* vulnerable prisoners, it becomes necessary to keep them rigorously separate from all others. A number of problems also existed *vis-à-vis* differential access to the prison's resources, facilities, quality of work and so forth. Although these questions are not our main concern it is none the less important that the vulnerable unit at Albany, however separate, was *within* Albany with all the complications that that entailed, among which was the sense amongst prisoners in both parts of the prison of a competition for scarce resources. Among the many reasons why Albany could not contemplate the possibility of another riot, it was put to us, was the prospect of the mayhem that might ensue between prisoners from the two parts of the prison:

In the Armageddon scenario, it's a disadvantage . . . because it's one more thing that has to be worried about and dealt with, because prisoners in D and E would certainly have to be first protected, and secondly evacuated if we lost control of the place.

(Grade III)

The population of a VPU is, clearly, likely to be unusual within the general dispersal population. As shown in chapter 3 (Table 3.4), the Albany Unit held a larger proportion of Category 'A' prisoners than the main prison, and more lifers. Its average age was higher. It also had an unusual range of sentence lengths, the shortest of which were around three years. There were a number of anomalies which would qualify the widely-held view that the VPU had a 'quiet' or 'passive' population. For example the number of prisoners on 'E' wing with previous convictions for robbery (32%) and violence (55%) were slightly higher than in the main prison. Similarly, by no means all prisoners in the VPU were sex offenders, although they tended to be seen as such by other prisoners.

A significant proportion were there for other reasons, for example because they had been identified as 'grasses' or insolvent debtors. The consequences of this particular 'mix' for life in the VPU were among the particular concerns of both staff and prisoners in describing and discussing it.

The managerial policy of the prison was that routines and regime activities should be as nearly as possible identically enforced and provided in both its parts. However, as we will go on to note, this was not always perceived as being precisely the case within the VPU.

Staff perspectives

Among the factors which had an important influence on the outlooks of staff working in the VPU was their prior experience of working in the 'main' prison. Although the VPU had a degree of physical and operational separateness from the 'main', it was nevertheless part of Albany. It had the same 'plant', it followed the same formal regime and was part of the same managerial structure. Staff in the vulnerable unit were thus able to make two kinds of comparisons. First, they compared their current position to Albany's institutional past. Second, they described their present working practices with reference to contemporary conditions prevailing in 'the main'. To what extent can it be said that working in this somewhat different environment also contributed towards a different conception of oneself and one's role as a prison officer from working in, or returning to, the 'main' prison? The Governor of the prison commented:

The pleasure for me has been the way that staff have been prepared to work with vulnerable prisoners. The fear was that you'd only get a few staff who did not want to stay with the macho prisoners; but in fact there's been lots of volunteers. When we told the 'D' wing staff 'they're not going to be big hairy prisoners, they're going to be vulnerable sex offenders', and we gave them a chance to leave that group if they felt they couldn't live and work with vulnerable prisoners, not one man pulled out.

Clearly, implicit in this is an expectation that staff may feel reluctance or distaste at the prospect of working with vulnerable rather than predominantly with 'straight' prisoners. Indeed it was the case that some staff continued to have misgivings whilst working alongside certain prisoners because of the nature of their offences, and certainly some of them mistrusted anything which smacked of giving them 'preferential treatment'. In this they argued that their feelings of abhorrence were only those of ordinary people in the population at large. One way in which prison officers in this position defined their 'professionalism' was in maintaining a correct and fair posture irrespective of their private feelings. As one officer admitted: 'deep down I don't like them'. Another went on to say:

I tell new officers: don't go playing cards with the cons. They can't see any problems.

Q   What is the argument about playing cards etc.?

A   They say 'he's only a fucking nonce—he's nothing'. When in fact he's raped and murdered a little kiddie. He's been in the public eye, he's fucking hated. And here he is, playing cards.

Q   Does the nature of the offence which people have committed make it harder for you to treat them with professional courtesy?

A   No. There's a line. He gets everything he's entitled to whatever he has done.

However, there are a number of reasons why staff might also prefer working in the VPU. Amongst these, as the Governor also clearly recognized, was that for some 'battle-weary' staff it represented what they regarded as a quieter, less pressured, less dangerous, and less confrontational mode of working than that to which they had been accustomed in the past. This was generally viewed as a legitimate respite.

These views stemmed from a general expectation that vulnerable prisoners as a group were quieter, more compliant and presented fewer 'control problems', especially concerted or collective ones, than prisoners in the 'main'. Thus, as one officer working in the VPU recollected:

I've been in the front line for years . . . I worked down the segregation unit back in the 70s, early 80s, when we had the hard time. Every time you opened a door you got a bucketful or a punch in the mouth. It got to you.

For most staff, working in the VPU also went beyond the simple sense of relief at the prospect of a quieter life. A number of staff insisted that the particular characteristics of the population provided further opportunities for enhanced job satisfaction in that they felt able to form more satisfying and constructive relationships with prisoners, and to offer prisoners who would otherwise be languishing on Rule 43 in some segregation unit a certain quality of life:

It's hugely different. Staff can come into this wing or D wing and *talk* to prisoners quite freely and prisoners will relate to staff as people much more sympathetically than they will on the main. There's not the same stigma amongst them to shun people who do that. On the main a prisoner would find a great deal of peer group pressure if he were to talk freely to staff. It makes it easier because inmates are much more approachable. But in a sense it's harder because you have to cope with the interpersonal relationship in a much more in-depth way.

In general staff held that the characteristics of the population and of the relationships they had formed with them worked in favour of a more thoroughgoing form of control than was usually achievable in the 'main'. Among the reasons for this, they cited: the individualized, non-solidary nature of the population and, hence, the lack of a clear staff–prisoner opposition; the dependency of some prisoners and the speed and quality of the intelligence staff received in case of any incipient trouble; the deterrent effect on prisoners of the risk of being shipped out back to Wandsworth or elsewhere. They saw this state of affairs as standing in contrast to the sense that historically at Albany staff had had to labour to retain control of a disorderly population, and that the risk of a riotous outbreak still existed. Staff in the vulnerable unit felt that they 'had' control or were 'in control' in a more profound sense than was possible on the 'main'. One officer commented: 'In this wing you say jump and they jump. They do anything you want them to.' Another said:

In D and E, you can ask or tell inmates to do something and they do it. I've never known that for years in the main prison . . . I don't think the control's too heavy. It's not as heavy as what it was on the main when we first went to the control situation.
Q   How would you describe the atmosphere on this wing?
A   I think it's good. I think we strike a right balance . . . a balance between the regime and the relationship, between them and us.

The sense of being in control resulted in a welcome self-confidence for staff. They argued that this enabled them to create and sustain a 'relaxed' and 'easygoing' atmosphere within the wing whilst not loosening their grip on control or allowing the observance of the controlled regime to 'slip':

It is easier in the vulnerable unit providing we keep a tight rein on inmates, tighter in D and E than in the main prison. There's more of a united front [among prisoners] in the main prison to wear down the discipline and rules, but in the vulnerable unit protest is usually individualized. You can relax, but you shouldn't relax the rules—if you relax the rules beyond what is reasonable and safe, you take risks with your own safety and the safety of the inmates under you.

(Principal Officer, E wing)

One theme which emerged among staff of all grades in the VPU was the need to work to retain a vigilant regime. Meanwhile the prevailing quiescence of the prisoners enabled staff, they felt, to retain the regime which they saw as appropriate to a greater extent than could be achieved in the main prison. A principal officer observed:

We still feel we're in charge here. But in the other wings, if you talk to the staff, some of them will say, 'No, we've lost it'.

Three main reasons were put forward as to why staff considered it important to retain the feeling of a 'tight ship' in the vulnerable unit. These were:

1. Parity with the rest of the prison. Staff held that it was important that prisoners in the VPU should neither suffer inferior conditions nor be seen to be 'getting more' than the population of the main prison. Hence, they argued, they should observe the precise letter and spirit of the Governor's instructions about the regime.

2. Vulnerability. It was argued that the most vulnerable prisoners remained at risk even within a vulnerable unit and that the relatively strong may be able to 'throw their weight about' with comparative impunity if not strictly regulated. Furthermore, some staff argued that 'weak' or 'vulnerable' prisoners may have an inherent need for support, structure and supervision, for example in respect of suicide prevention.

3. Prevention of homosexuality. The combination of the staff's perception of the physical and emotional 'weakness' of a proportion of the population of the VPU and the high incidence of offences of sexual violence amongst them engendered a particular preoccupation with the prevention of homosexual contacts. This was a clear managerial policy, of which the Governor of the prison commented:

It wouldn't be good for the unit . . . if we were somehow allowing people to be corrupted or the staff had been corrupted by allowing it to go on, and with AIDS around, I've tended to use the placard, 'Look chaps, aren't we better off? We don't know what kind of sexual excitement may arise and what violence might follow, if we were just turning our backs and walking away down the spur and letting them get on with it.' And what about when the first case of AIDS comes out, how will we feel then? So I really had that one up.

This third issue—the policy on homosexuality—seems to have been observed down the line of management, and ironically tended to produce a perceived need to retain a *higher* level of supervision in the vulnerable unit than might be either feasible or applicable elsewhere. A principal officer commented:

Restrictions have got to remain in place to a greater extent in this wing. The last thing you want is two of these inmates getting into the same cell together, which is sometimes allowed up there [on the main]. Homosexual activities: we've got to make sure that that does not happen in here, and the staff are very good at ensuring that it doesn't happen.

This argument was bolstered by the perennial feeling that the prison was poorly designed from the point of view of achieving successful, unobtrusive supervision. The feeling among staff in the VPU was that whereas in the 'main' prison a compromise could be struck between the need for surveillance and the demands of normalization of the environment, in the VPU supervison took first priority. For one senior officer the design of the prison was:

shocking, because you see on rule 43 protection we have to protect them from themselves, and as I explained to you before the problem with this in Echo wing is that for instance the gardens party . . . they're entitled to a shower. When we say entitled we mean, yes, they should have a shower, because you would expect one and so would I. Now we can't just let them go up like the main prison and have a shower, they must be supervised . . . and in this wing *everything* must be supervised right from the word go, TV room, everything, because we know what they would be up to. And also, another thing that people don't realize—to *enforce* sex. You can't assume that all these would voluntarily jump into each other's cells or into bloody bed with each other. They wouldn't. I mean Bloggs is one who is in literally for raping prisoners. So the design is bad, very bad to supervise, but we do it by strict routines.

These rationales account for the apparent paradox that prisoners in the VPU who were generally viewed as being quieter and as presenting fewer 'control problems' and, moreover, with whom staff insisted that they had a good 'rapport', effectively received *more* stringent regulation and supervision than did prisoners 'on the main'. It was universally the view of Albany staff that because an individual is 'docile' does not mean he is not also dangerous. Arguably, the situation arose partly because a closer form of 'control' was consciously sought and partly because such measures were not met with the kind of resistance which mitigated their impact on 'the main'. To return to the theoretical vocabulary introduced in chapter 2, the 'dialectic of control' differed markedly as between the two parts of the prison. Whereas in the mainstream of the dispersal system there is an implicit recognition that prisoners represent a certain *bloc* of influence, of whose responses account must be taken, in the VPU matters were otherwise. Staff there felt that the form of regulation that they wished to impose could indeed be imposed, with little need for compromise.

The character of 'control' was not universally regarded as unproblematic, however. Some staff were acutely conscious that a routine expectancy of *not* meeting resistance, and a consequent habituation to exercising power, could lead them or their colleagues into acting in ways which they regarded as questionable. For example, in answer to a series of questions beginning 'what makes a good prison officer for this particular environment?' one member of staff responded:

We all deal with things differently. It's important to speak to inmates in E wing as human beings. There should be mutual respect.

Q   Do you need to be honest and genuine with prisoners?
A   Yes. You just have to be yourself, and be fair and just.
Q   Is it easier to be these things on E wing than on A, B, and C?
A   Yes, definitely.
Q   Does the worst side of human nature come out because it's E wing, you say 'No' and you can't be bothered—does this kind of attitude creep in?
A   Yes, it does.
Q   Even though it's easier to be respectful, polite, and do the job in a professional way?
A   Yes, you'll always get someone who takes advantage of his position.
Q   Why do you think that is?
A   Because there's a certain amount of bully-boy in a percentage of people and it will come out. They see a weakness and they will take advantage.
Q   Is that something you disapprove of?
A   Definitely.
Q   Have you ever had to speak to someone about it?
A   I've had words with certain people here.

Another member of staff, who considered himself a disciplinarian with a preference for firmness and clarity, nevertheless reported a number of worries about how some staff responded to coming into D and E wings:

I firmly believe that they've had years and years working up on the main wings and they get down here and think, 'fucking hell, I don't believe this . . . I shouted at him and he never shouted back' . . . and then one thing develops into another you see, and that's easy, that is . . . the power can go to your head easy. It's happened in here, not just in D wing . . . there's a couple of staff, I've drawn them on one side, and not just me others have as well, and said 'look, there's no need for that'.

This applies perhaps particularly to the treament of those whom both prisoners and staff see as the 'noddies' or 'divvies'—the least intelligent and self-confident prisoners:

Staff coming here who are newish . . . they could easily adopt the attitude of strong-arm, bullying—fuckin 'ell, you know, this is easy . . .
Q And that worries you does it?
A It worries me with these young boys, I tell you, the young ones in terms of service, not necessarily age, because . . . I said to one only a couple of days ago, 'Look old son there's no way would you speak to . . . you're talking to a *man*; he is a man; whatever he is, he is a man' . . . You certainly wouldn't get away with it on the main.

Officers were thus conscious that the relatively unchallenged power which they enjoyed in the VPU stood in danger of becoming overweening. This was a topic of internal debate and called for a felt need for self-policing and self-criticism. This was also noted by the Governor of the prison:

Every now and again you get the feeling that an officer is a bit more nit-picking down in E wing about something than he would be in the main prison. I think quite often his colleagues would say 'Now steady on old son. We *do* want this to be neat and tidy and we *do* want them to wear the right clothes but don't go overboard on it and don't think you could try it on any other wings. So temper it a bit.'

We will note some instances of prisoners' experience on this question below.

It is also true that, notwithstanding the arguments outlined above about prisoners' vulnerability to one another and the prevention of exploitative sex, some members of staff did not feel that the current stringency of 'control' was altogether necessary, or not inherently necessary for the current population. Those who took this view argued that only the presumption of the necessity for parity with the 'main' prison prevented a modified regime being considered:

I think we could let all these out without locking them up every five minutes. We have to be seen to be doing the same on here as on the main.

The vulnerable unit was in a sense still in its infancy. Its long-term purposes, it seemed to us, remained to be clarified and developed. Working with vulnerable prisoners was still a new, and in some ways, strange and challenging experience for many staff. In the course of this experience a number of staff were drawn towards using terms which remain unfashionable in some quarters—rehabilitation, therapeutic. A number of staff looked towards the psychiatric orientation of Grendon rather than to the 'humane containment' of the dispersals for their guiding model. The prospect of working with this particular group of people seemed to some of them to offer a greater opportunity than their experience of working in the main prison of extending their role as prison officers towards constructive engagement with offending behaviour.

From our own observation one cannot avoid the sense that the 'quietness' which existed in the VPU could extend to a feeling of moroseness, dejection and aimlessness amongst some of its captive population. Yet it was also the site within the prison in which there was a feeling of potential, vision and optimism. The governor (Grade V) with responsibility for the unit drew attention to the continuing dangerousness of a number of prisoners in the unit, and his feeling that a responsibility existed to seek to address it. The unit should in his view be able to offer its population 'association and work' which had hitherto been denied them but also, he pointed out:

There are 18 Cat. As on E wing. That is a lot of dangerous people. There are a number of people coming up to release date, beyond which we can't keep them, unless they're sectioned. This has made me wonder what we're doing while they are here to make them less dangerous when they are released. We're not doing very much. I want to start to develop an initiative whereby we look at individuals much more—we've got psychiatrists, a medical department, a strong psychology department and staff themselves are quite interested. They've done lifer training, pre-release course training and are quite skilled and young. Of 65 people on the wing the vast majority could be helped to some extent.

All members of staff in managerial positions within the unit considered that the factors which obstructed the development of a 'therapeutic' regime and those which made for such 'control problems' as they experienced had a common root, namely lack of clarity in the allocation of prisoners to the unit. By this they meant that since prisoners become 'vulnerable' for different reasons they constitute a far from homogeneous group. They suggested that the presence in the wing of those who were 'robbers' or 'bandits' who simply happened to have encountered problems in the mainstream dispersals meant that:

1. a significant proportion of the population were not amenable to the kind of regime activities the wing managers would like to initiate; and

2. such prisoners were able to exercise intimidatory power over the 'truly' vulnerable, unless a stringently controlled regime remained in force.

This gave rise to a call for a clearer definition of the aims and purposes of the unit, including a wish to differentiate between a '43 unit' and a 'vulnerable unit'. The wing Governor observed:

We're still used as a Rule 43 unit, not as vulnerable prisoner unit, because they've failed at some other establishment. For example we've got one character who was at a Cat. B training prison for twelve months, who was suspected of strong-arming and of taking and supplying drugs there. He was moved from there to a local, who got in touch with South East Region. He turns up on our doorstep. We accepted him. He had to come on the Rule 43 wings. He's a most unsuitable person for a vulnerable prisoner unit. He's a bully, he winds everybody up, he gets people to do his dirty work, and still makes implied threats continually. He's not a vulnerable prisoner, he's a thug. We can't do both. Either we run a strong regime for the vulnerable prisoners with the ideal of making them a less dangerous proposition for when they get out, or we run a control-type regime to deal with people like him.

In a similar vein we asked a principal officer 'How would you go about devising terms of reference for people making allocations to a vulnerable unit?':

Basically you're looking at sex offenders, immature types of people, possibly even mentally subnormals who are all vulnerable people when you put them in a mix with the rest of the inmates. If we could select those out, and bring them into this unit, we'd be doing a damn sight better than we are at the moment. We've got too many ex-bully boys—people who've got into debt and dived for cover. They're not vulnerable. If you move them on to another establishment, they'd survive quite happily.

However, it seemed likely to most of those with whom we spoke that a tension in the area of allocation to the vulnerable unit would continue to exist between, on the one hand, the unit's own priorities and its preferences at the level of its own internal order and, on the other, the functions it performed for the system as a whole. The exigencies of allocating prisoners considered at risk were likely to continue to determine the population of the unit, whether or not they were considered 'vulnerable' in the sense intended by managers within the vulnerable unit. The Governor of Albany commented:

I see quite a bit in minutes of meetings about how we must get clear with Region what the allocation criteria are. I can understand that, and I applaud it . . . If we push Region into their proper role, which is to give us the people who've been selected, they will inevitably find that they have got some prisoners who are vulnerable *not* because of their crime, but because they've grassed or because they've fallen into debt . . . I think however much you test Region on the allocation you'll find that's either written in, or they pop them in from time to time.

There is thus a persistent ambiguity. The problem arises as to the exact relationship between the unit and the prison in which it was located and, beyond that, to the dispersal system as a whole. Over twenty per cent of its population was Category A; yet some staff in the unit referred to the 'main' prison as the 'the dispersal side'. On the other hand one might argue that a diverse population within VPUs need not necessarily be a wholly detrimental thing, in that it seems closer to rationales underlying the dispersal system as a whole both at the levels of securing co-operation and of 'leavening' the mix of lifers and men doing extremely long sentences. Or does one replicate chronic problems of the dispersal system on a smaller scale, thereby demonstrating inherent tensions within dispersal policy?

What is clear is that a particular difficulty existed in adjusting or controlling the population in the unit through either normal 'progressive' moves or disciplinary transfers (cf. the parallel problems experienced for rather different reasons at the Barlinnie Special Unit: who should come?; when?; how long should they stay?; where should they go on leaving?—see Bottomley et al., 1994). Vulnerable prisoners have historically been hard to place in constructive ways. Thus, although the unit might lay claim to benefiting from the deterrent prospect that ejection meant a return to Wandsworth, this was a drastic solution, and to resort to it frequently would be to subvert the very rationale for the unit's existence.

In sum, in comparison with the 'main' prison staff in the VPU reported a lower incidence of most 'control problems'. Few incidents of the kinds reported in the next chapter originated there. Numbers of assaults, levels of drug dealing, and absolute amounts of debt were relatively low. This might be taken as a lack of empirical support for the necessity of a stringent regime, on any other grounds than parity with the 'main' prison. Conversely it *was* taken by staff as a vindication of current practice, while the VPU was also held to have its own special problem (the 'policing' of homosexual acts) which justified a restricted regime and high levels of staff supervision. The unit also faced a number of other problems which were more particularly related to its own characteristics and its position in relation to the mainstream of the dispersal system.

Prisoner Perspectives

The majority of prisoners arriving at the VPU came there from the austere conditions of Rule 43 in other prisons. It is worth bearing in mind what this has often meant in recent times. The following is part of the testimony of a prisoner who was on Rule 43 in another prison at the time we spoke to him:

Only a sex offender knows what it's like to do time under these conditions . . . I get abuse every night, shouted at me through the pipes and through the doors about being a nonce and a sex offender. I get it from officers here . . . You're only out one and a quarter hours each day, actually mixing with the staff, and you're happy to be banged up for the other twenty-two and three-quarters hours just to get away from them . . . I'm uncertain about everything. I've never been so uncertain in my life. Three times now I've thought about suicide . . . I've had urine thrown over me, shit thrown at me, people trying to attack me in the course of being moved from one nick to another . . . I've got another six years. I've lost two and a half stone in weight since I've been in here. [Why won't they] look at me and say this man is a bad sexual offender, let's put him in a proper unit, not one where I'm locked up all day, nor where the staff are not professional, who don't want to know sex offenders, but where there's work. I'm not the only bloke . . . Nobody cares about sex offenders . . . If they're not going to hang me let me do my time, but they won't; this is where they put me. It's not just me it's *all* sexual offenders . . . Sometimes it rains here which means I'm banged up all day . . . Sometimes I want to talk to someone. A week can go by and you can not *actually* have a conversation with anyone, just a brief couple of words. For sixteen months of my sentence I've had more or less solitary conditions—it's no way to treat someone at all. Maybe it sounds like I'm whining.

Many of the prisoners in the VPU at Albany had similar stories to tell. For some, conditions similar to those recounted above constituted virtually the whole of their prison experience. For such men, therefore, conditions in the VPU at Albany were likely to be the most advantageous they had experienced. As one of them commented 'Albany is a paradise after Wandsworth'.

At first sight such prior experiences and subsequent reactions tended to confirm the impression held by staff that many prisoners were glad, even if not as they might fondly think 'grateful', to come to the VPU. Certainly, it is possible to find comments from prisoners which seemed to corroborate these aspects of staff viewpoints. Thus, for example, one prisoner who was considered something of a 'moaner and whinger' by staff observed:

This prison is all right . . . the unit is run pretty well . . . The atmosphere here is non-trouble . . . the atmosphere here with inmates and staff is very good on the whole, it's a very relaxed unit, easygoing.

Coming from an alleged 'moaner' this seems like quite a testimonial. Meanwhile, one of the non sex offenders in the VPU observed that he intended remaining there for some time because it meant 'freedom from pressure . . . this is an ideal prison if you want to do your time without any trouble'. Another prisoner who had also experienced life in the 'mainstream' on a previous sentence also commented:

I've never been on the Rule before but I can see in one way it's much easier, quieter—if you can handle that self-esteem that's been diminished.

For the most part prisoners concurred with staff views in several particulars: that relations were stable within the wing, that staff were 'in control' and that there was little or no overt trouble. The comments of a number of the 'robbers' and other 'straight' prisoners on the wing suggested that, after an initial period of adaptation to living in close proximity with sex offenders, they often came to see advantages in being in the unit, over and above the protection it offered them in their own situations. It represented the opportunity of a quiet life in the sense of not having to 'mix it' or compete or maintain face as in 'the main'. They had, in effect 'retired'. A number of robbers thus acted in a quite ungangsterish way.

However, there were a number of ways in which these apparent agreements on points of fact had very different meanings and consequences when looked at from the prisoner's point of view. Thus, the fact that a more stringent form of regulation could be achieved within the VPU and that there was little prospect of concerted resistance served to remind prisoners of the weakness of their position. The prospect of being moved was similarly demoralizing. The obverse side of the relatively 'advantageous' character of the VPU as compared with their prior experience was that prisoners felt that they couldn't complain or otherwise risk incurring the displeasure of the staff. That is, prisoners in the VPU, especially lifers, felt themselves to be at the mercy of the staff to a larger extent than most prisoners in 'the main'. This in turn shaped the kinds of complaints and grievances which they nursed, and which they revealed to us. These often had to do with having to suffer in silence. They included a sense of injustice which derived from the feeling that staff could act in ways which they would not 'on the main'. Prisoners suggested that, owing to the sheer scale of the disparity in power, some members of staff were inclined to act in ways which were arbitrary and whimsical and to give expression to their personal dislikes.

The feeling that this state of affairs resulted in a number of distortions in the 'normal' relations between prisoners and staff was expressed in a number of specific ways. The first was that some staff were unable or unprepared to conceal their dislike of sex offenders. Some prisoners expressed suspicion of staff's true feelings:

Although there are good staff on the wing, there are far too many that you know their real feelings are just below the surface, and that feeling is prevalent every day of the week. You may be playing darts or cracking a joke and all the time you know really that guy wants to harm you . . . this is called 'the noncery' by most staff. [They say] 'the beasties', 'the animals', 'that nonce' and they seem to delight in reading our files . . .

Thus, although there were grievances about the regime itself, and the feeling existed of a discrepancy between the VPU and 'the main' in this regard, these were not the primary complaints. Indeed there was something close to an inversion of the situation which prevailed on 'the main'. Whereas prisoners on 'the main' objected to certain features of the regime and yet took a relatively benign view of most staff, prisoners in the vulnerable unit tended to take a philosophical or resigned view of the regime as such, which was anyway as staff correctly pointed out vastly preferable to some of the alternatives, and to reserve their strongest criticisms for particular features of staff behaviour. One theme in such criticisms was that, within the confines of the unit (and given the particularities of the power relations which existed there) the behaviour to which prisoners objected could on occasions take on a peculiarly personal and idiosyncratic character. In this regard, prisoners argued that within the unit it was possible for the attitudes of particular members of staff to have a disproportionate effect:

In a place like this you only need one person and it upsets everything. For instance, on the landings you have three members of staff. Two can be absolute diamonds, which is often the case. They're OK. They're professionals. They get on with the job. You get one bad one and instead of the other two telling him to back off they close in and protect him. So it doesn't have to be a majority. There are a couple who do lead it, and they're *known* for it. There's no secret about it that they hate us, and the only reason that they're in this wing is because they've been slung out of every other wing, because they cause so much trouble . . . They've progressively ended up in our wing, because we're the quietest and don't cause any trouble. And of course those bully tactics and that prejudice comes out.

As we have seen from staff accounts it may very well be that the 'professional' members of staff did indeed disapprove and censure the others, but this was usually in private. Criticizing a colleague, even if the criticism was actually voiced, was a backstage activity— and hence inherently unlikely to be apparent to the prisoner. Equally, we do not consider that there is a great analytic gain in building a 'rotten apple' theory of problems in staff–prisoner relations within the unit, or in other penal contexts. However it seems probable, on the basis of the observations of both staff and prisoners, that social arrangements in the vulnerable unit were such as to demand particular discretion, vigilance, and intelligence on the part of staff if their mode of control were not to become uniquely overbearing. This in turn would seem to call for a high degree of professional self-control or mutual control amongst the staff. These issues arise from the systematically disempowered social position of vulnerable prisoners:

There's no defence for us, to go anywhere else. So we're stuck. We're trapped. We're literally a captive audience and they exploit that because they *know* that because we can't go anywhere else, we have to conform, accept whatever the regime is, knowing that there's little or nothing we can do about it. And that's it, and you just have to put up with it. Consequently that leads for a minority [to be able] to get whatever pleasure they can out of it.

Prisoners in the unit knew that they did not constitute a body or interest group with any effective power. However, this did not mean that there was complete impunity for any member of staff to 'ride roughshod' over the feelings of prisoners. Indeed, as one or two prisoners on 'the main' also observed, the lack of solidarity amongst prisoners or of any capacity to seek collective representation or redress, can make more likely an *individualized* reaction of a fairly extreme kind (cf. Mathiesen, 1965). One prisoner commented:

It keeps going down hill. Officer Bloggs thrives on it. He gives out details of my record. He throws it in my face in front of other people. One day there will be a reaction. Someone will go berserk. He'll push too far one day and someone will turn round and attack him.
Q How do you control your feelings?
A You bite the bullet. Tell the wall what a bastard it is. I've *got* to. I can't afford to go mad in here.

One particular case in point of these problems lay in the area of race relations. This is a fundamentally important question in itself, here as in all penal settings, but the particular form it took within a vulnerable unit is also illustrative of the specific distributions of power which existed there. There seems to be a particular danger, in settings where staff are clearly in control and which are manifestly stable and peaceable and, moreover, apparently friendly, of neglecting the possible impacts and consequences of what is said. This is true of remarks about people's offences but also, and more particularly, of racist humour. Thus one member of staff felt able in an interview with us to point to his frequent use of race in jest, and the fact that it would not be acceptable 'on the main', as a demonstration of the successful control and cordial relations existing within the vulnerable unit. He took it that because such banter appeared to be taken in good part it must be not only inoffensive but also signify something positive. No prisoner, black or white, shared this interpretation. In fact some of the most vivid indignation about racial jokes was expressed by white prisoners who saw it as expressive of a particular presumption of untrammelled power. Thus:

I keep hearing 'Nigger, come here.' I find it very offensive. The black guys take it with good grace because they haven't got a leg to stand on if they object.

Similarly:

If you're black, you've got a problem, and if you're a black sex offender, you've got a double problem. It starts as a joke, but it's a *testing* all the time, to see how far they can go. You have to nip it in the bud and say 'I'm not into that.'

Or again:

I feel embarrassed when a black guy is ridiculed, sometimes badly. But now I've got used to it. The black guy doesn't turn round and say, please don't call me that any more, and finish with it. They still laugh, but they're seething inside.

For the black prisoner the question is both simpler and more important:

I feel the majority of the time when the staff call an inmate a black arse or a nigger they don't realize how close they come to being *hurt* on the wing. Put yourself in the prisoner's position. He's all tensed inside. He's doing a twelve year sentence. He's got *plenty* to lose. He's got kids outside. He wants to go outside . . . On the out they wouldn't even be able to utter a word like that . . . It's like a game, isn't it? You play ball, we'll play ball. But . . . in here it would always be an unfair game. . . . If I turned and reacted every time they passed a racial comment I would be here for ever.

Clearly, such sources of anger and irritation did not very often result in overt control problems. However, it is a problematic feature of a mode of control if prisoners feel that humour and ridicule are being used systematically to demean them and, as the prisoner quoted above points out, the possibility of provoking a control incident thereby always remains. This is in explicit contrast to the situation that prevailed in A, B, and C wings, or in Long Lartin, where the dangers of needless provocation, race-related or otherwise, were specifically recognized in staff discourse and practice.

Prison managers and staff felt, as we have noted above, that there was particular scope within the vulnerable unit to develop activities and to foster closer and more cordial ('thicker', in Christie's terms) social relations between prisoners and staff than elsewhere in the prison. In this respect, on an evaluation of social distance, they may bear closer comparison with features of relationships at Long Lartin than with the 'main' wings at Albany. Indeed we heard evidence from both prisoners and staff that such relationships could and did develop. However, it is also apparent from the example of offensive humour that there is a special danger of presuming too far upon any such relationship. In particular, the more powerful party may simply fail to see the damage which may result.

One particular problem which this raises is the degree of scepticism which some prisoners came to feel about the viability of shared working and personal officer schemes or other innovations. Many prisoners in the unit wanted close relations, supported innovation, and expressed a keen demand for activities directed towards offending behaviour. One prisoner stated:

I've got a problem. I know that. Unless somebody comes along we're never going to know if it's a problem that could be solved. I'd die next year—I would have said tomorrow but give me a year—if I could change. I would give that up just for a year of the kind of life that I see is out there . . . In truth, yeah, ninety-five per cent of those who are up there are very broken men, very hurt, very ashamed, and would like to change given a chance. But we can't do it on our own . . . I've got no objection to an officer objecting to my offence, because it is *offensive*. I've got no objection to him thinking that. But it's when he carries it over, and reacts because of that, it's back to the professionalism.

Moreover, however much demand existed for rehabilitative activities it seemed very likely that prisoners' objections to aspects of the conduct of some staff would stand in the way of their readiness to participate. Thus, for example, one prisoner expressed deep suspicion of the idea of prison officers being trained and assigned as case officers for lifers because it represented to him 'an elevation of power which could be abused'. He continued:

Certain officers here, you couldn't put them in that position to train them *at all* because there's no compassion, no understanding. There's a lack of tolerance. They're bullies and they're thugs. It's common knowledge who they are.

The continued existence of such feelings would present an obstacle to the development of the sorts of regimes and programmes which many prisoners and staff both favoured and supported. In that they did support such objectives prisoners criticized actions by either prisoners or staff which seemed to jeopardize the stability of the unit and its future development. Thus, although there was disagreement among prisoners as to the rights and wrongs of the cases of particular prisoners who had been removed from the unit, none the less there was agreement in principle that staff should act to remove those whose activities genuinely disrupted the orderly pattern of life in which most people felt they had a stake. Most prisoners also agreed with staff that there was an additional danger in somebody beginning to 'strong-arm', and that this should be prevented. However, this did not mean that prisoners agreed that they merited or required all aspects of the form of regulation to which they were subject. Nor did they feel that a similar unit would necessarily be run in the same way outside the context of Albany. Indeed they expressed most of the same objections to the regime as were voiced on all the other wings, with the additional insistence that there were in any case fewer control problems within the unit which would justify a high level of regulation.

Most prisoners asserted that such control problems as did exist within the unit were 'petty', interpersonal altercations and fights, of the order of things which are bound to happen in any enclosed community. The unit accounted for a disproportionately small number of the total adjudications and incidents reported within the prison (see chapter 7). Whilst these were usually similar in kind to those which took place 'on the main' they were both less frequent and generally less severe.

In sum, both staff and prisoners did identify positive features and potentialities within the unit, and there was considerable agreement as to what these were. For many of the staff the unit offered special scope for creative and satisfying ways of working. For prisoners the unit represented a break in the vicious circle of life on Rule 43 as they had previously experienced it, and at least a glimmer of hope for the future. There were numerous members of both sides who agreed on the positive potentiality for group work and prisoner programmes aimed at addressing offending behaviour and who would have welcomed the opportunity to work co-operatively towards those ends. Such agreements on the legitimacy of objectives are not very often found in prisons. By the same token, however, the absence up to that time of such desired developments in any very systematic form, and the priority within the VPU policy accorded to safe 'warehousing', confounded what some prisoners and staff regarded as a legitimate expectation.

On the other hand there also seem to have been particular dangers, stemming from sometimes inappropriate and careless staff conduct, based on a perhaps mistaken assumption that there would be no resistance or reaction from prisoners. There is a debate within probation circles about whether current 'confrontative' styles of working with sex offenders permit a form of 'legitimised nonce bashing' (Sheath, 1990), in which advantage is taken of a privileged position to repudiate and humiliate the deviant other. If such a tendency exists, how much more extreme might its expression be in the context of the long-term prison? Given the close physical confines of a VPU, the lengths of sentences, the stringency of the regime, it seems in any event that the 'depth' (Downes, 1988) of imprisonment is greater there even than in other dispersal prison settings, and the possibility of 'normalization' correspondingly more remote. If the possibility of abusive relationships is to this extent systemic, it must be guarded against with special and self-conscious vigilance. It would be a peculiar irony if, having set up units for the protection of vulnerable prisoners, such prisoners then felt themselves to be uniquely taunted and aggrieved within them.

7

Control Incidents: the Incidence and Management of Trouble

UNTIL now we have looked in general terms at social relations in Albany and Long Lartin. We have attempted to give some sense of the kinds of order which prevailed in each prison and the means used to sustain it, and to say a little about the conditions under which such order is disrupted or strained. However, as briefly explained in chapter 3, there was also a second and more 'pointed' aspect to our work. In addition to our general interviews, and observational work, we looked in detail at certain defined 'control problems' and 'control incidents' in the two prisons, using both documentary sources and 'specific interviews' in which we tried to reconstruct—from the perspectives of various relevant actors—how some recorded 'control problem incidents' in both prisons had developed. In this chapter, we begin to explore these issues. The chapter is divided into three main sections, the second of which is the most important. First, we explore in a tentative way some data relating to the temporal and spatial aspects of control incidents. Secondly, we consider in detail the main 'control incidents' that occurred in Albany and Long Lartin over certain specific periods, and we examine in what ways (if at all) these incidents might be regarded as related to the more general kinds of 'order' and 'control' (see chapter 3 for definitions) that the two prisons sought to establish. Thirdly and finally, we examine various statistical data that might be regarded as related to 'control problems', to see to what extent they corroborate or otherwise the picture that has emerged from the detailed discussion in the second section.

As a follow-up to this discussion, chapter 8 will go on to consider so-called 'movements from normal location': that is to say, the occasions on which the prisons' *response to* 'control incidents' took the form of deliberately moving a prisoner away from his present location, to some other place such as the segregation unit or another prison.

Time and Space

One aspect of the incidence of 'trouble' in prisons that has come to interest us concerns *where* and *when* incidents occur. We have come to see this aspect of control problems as rather revealing for what it indicates about how the ordering of social relations in prisons depends on the regulated use of space and the rigorous scheduling or timetabling of activity (the prison 'routine'). It is not hard to discern that our interest in these matters has developed very much from our growing conviction that Giddens's (1984) 'structuration theory' has much to offer to students of prisons (see chapter 2).

As we saw in chapter 2, Giddens has taken particular pains to show that the reproduction of *any* institutionalized form of life depends upon the fitting together of individuals' paths through time–space. In many circumstances, but especially perhaps in prisons, what *counts as* an orderly situation has much to do with whether the timing and spacing of activity does or does not conform to a set, routinized or predictable pattern (a feature of carceral institutions earlier highlighted in their distinct ways by both Goffman and Foucault). As we have noted, for Giddens the domain of study of the social sciences *is*, fundamentally, 'social practices ordered across space and time' (1984: 2).

Prisons tend to be insular and often claustrophobic places. They have a special topography, provided by the division of the institution's internal space into its functional units. This much is true of any office or factory. But in the prison those divisions are not merely about convenience or efficiency. They have the purposes of preventing escapes and imposing control; and they take the austere physical form of gates, fences, bars, 'sterile areas', and so on. The prison officer's progress around the prison is an endless sequence of lockings and unlockings, openings and reclosings; and the prisoner's is one of waiting and passing through, again and again. This intensive control of *space* links inextricably with the regulation of *time*. To be in one's proper place in prison means being where you are permitted to be only when you are permitted to be there. As a prisoner there are numerous places to which you may not go at all, unless summoned there for some exceptional purpose. Similarly there are many places where you *must* go, but only at certain moments; and at other times you *must be* somewhere else. Canter (1987: 214) notes that

The whole system of events associated with imprisonment contains a network of human activities inextricably linked to places in which these activities occur. The prison building is the instrument of incarceration.

The design of prison buildings plays a central part in shaping the nature of the day-to-day routines and the doings of staff and prisoners who have to live and work in them, although prisoners and staff may attach very different meanings and significances to the environment they jointly inhabit. For example, one important study (Canter and Ambrose 1980) found that prisoners were more concerned with conceptualizing their space in terms of personal and group activities, whereas staff tended to think about space in terms of achieving staff goals: moving prisoners easily, being able to monitor their behaviour for control purposes, and for prisoners to have appropriate facilities. Moreover, it would seem that 'the significance of design [becomes] more important as the security level of the prison [increases]' (King, 1987: 120). Yet despite these important observations and a wealth of attention to *historical* aspects of architecture (seminally Foucault, 1979a; but see also Evans, 1983, Ignatieff, 1978) the importance of prison design to the contemporary problem of penal order has received little serious attention, apart from occasional discussions of the 'control' benefits of the 'new generation' prisons that have emerged in the United States (King, 1991). Having said that, it is also important to note that architecture never fully *determines* behaviour; even when one is locked in a cell a small degree of choice of activity remains, and within a given prison building very different kinds of social order can be developed at different historical periods (cf., for example, Ignatieff, 1978, on nineteenth century social order in Pentonville Prison, London, by comparison with the mid twentieth century sociological study of the same prison by Morris and Morris, 1963).

In what follows, we seek to do two things, both in a very tentative manner. First, we describe in a general way some of the specifically spatial aspects of life on the wings at Albany and Long Lartin; and secondly, we present some data (for Albany only) showing that disciplinary incidents in the prison were anything but randomly distributed in space and time. Because our interest in spatio-temporal matters developed from our reading of structuration theory, which in turn developed in creative interaction with our fieldwork experience, we did not from the outset seek to collect relevant spatio-temporal data on control incidents; hence, our data on these matters is limited (see further below) but nevertheless—we would argue—revealing and interesting.

At the time of our research Albany had five wings (see Figure 3.1), running off a single broad corridor. Gates at the back of each wing opened on to a 'back road' leading to the exercise yard, playing fields, and workshops. As we have noted, two of the wings, D and E, formed a completely separate Vulnerable Prisoner Unit, which because of its location in Albany was able to accept category A prisoners. This presented a number of logistical difficulties for the staff, resulting from the determination to keep the two bodies of prisoners separate from one another; these difficulties included, for example, the exclusion or 'freezing' of prisoners from A, B and C wings from the main coridor when VPU inmates needed to use that corridor.

Internally, each wing had four storeys. Association took place entirely on the ground floor. Each wing contained one large and one small TV room, a table tennis room, offices, and a single spur of eight cells. Above were three storeys, each housing twenty-four cells in a cruciform layout. Access to each floor was by an enclosed stairwell. Problems of visibility, supervision, and ease of movement posed by the stairwell were a constant source of anxiety to staff. There was also fairly widespread dissatisfaction with the internal layout of the wings. Staff and prisoners tended to agree that space was extremely restricted for any prisoner who wanted to do anything other than watch television endlessly, and that association periods were both more tense and boring as a result. Some of the consequences of these issues as perceived by both staff and prisoners have already been commented upon; others are detailed below.

The system of electronic locking and unlocking of doors was abandoned in Albany in 1985 and the use of keys was reintroduced. Staff overwhelmingly regarded the system of manually unlocking prisoners as vastly preferable (because it produced more human contact, and thus better staff–prisoner relations), though they agreed that the consequent lack of access to night sanitation for prisoners was regrettable.

Long Lartin (see Figure 3.2) meanwhile had six wings (containing a total of 420 cells) built around a central square. Also contained within the main building were the gymnasium, library and educational facilities, kitchen, hospital, chapels and segregation unit. Long Lartin's 400 prisoners were divided in roughly equal numbers between its six wings. In general architectural terms, Long Lartin has much in common with Albany. Like Albany, but in stark contrast to Victorian prison buildings, corridors and wings have low ceilings and quite large windows. In many features the two buildings resemble schools and hospitals built at the same period. Staff and prisoners at Long Lartin also criticized, although perhaps with less vehemence and unanimity, the internal layout of the wings and the facilities on them. Ceilings were low, cells small, and floor space limited. Lines of sight for staff supervising prisoners' activities were marginally better than at Albany because each landing at Long Lartin had only two spurs running off an open space. Association periods at Long Lartin often seemed very quiet in comparison to Albany because most prisoners were either in the TV room or in cells (their own or another's), reappearing only for lock-up.[1]

The dispersal system is not overcrowded. Maximum security prisons have, in general, more space than others and have historically allowed a greater degree of freedom within their walls. It is instructive to note, however, that prisoners in Albany and Long Lartin lived in conventional cells (which, at the time of the research did not have integral sanitation) and that space available to them in the prison was not only extremely limited but also highly regulated and monitored. At another level, staff in dispersal prisons confront many of the same logistical problems as their colleagues elsewhere concerning the clothing, feeding, and arranging of work and education for a large group of people within a rather inflexible routine.

More generally, those working within the dispersal system are faced repeatedly with the ambiguities and anxieties inherent in the task of balancing the demands intrinsic to the maintenance of high level security (usually translated as meaning restrictive and heavily surveyed environments) with the obligations which ensue from the principle that long-term prisoners should be entitled to a degree of latitude, autonomy, and time to themselves even when these may be denied prisoners elsewhere. Clearly different positions can be taken

---

[1] It will be recalled that 'cell association' was permitted at Long Lartin, but not (formally, at any rate) at Albany.

up in response to the variety of moral and practical dilemmas that flow from attempting to reconcile these potentially conflicting aims. The differences between Albany's routine and that of Long Lartin (as outlined in earlier chapters) reflect somewhat divergent views on how the routinization of prisoners' day-to-day life should be organized and managed, and how the resources of time and space are to be utilized to achieve certain desired aims and objectives.

How does all this relate to when and where control incidents occur? As we have noted, our interest in this question was late in developing, and by the time we sought specific data it was possible to find it only for Albany.[2] However, we were fortunately able to analyse the time and location of the 670 disciplinary offences recorded for Albany in 1988 (see chapter 3 for other aspects of this data).

TABLE 7.1. Disciplinary offences at Albany, 1988, according to the day they were committed

	No.	%
Monday	126	18.8
Tuesday	121	18.1
Wednesday	93	13.9
Thursday	94	14.0
Friday	78	11.6
Saturday	64	9.6
Sunday	94	14.0
Total	670	100.0

Table 7.1 suggests that disciplinary offences do not occur randomly on different days of the week ($p < 0.01$). Rather numbers of recorded offences appear gradually to reduce throughout the week, reaching their lowest point on a Saturday, before the rate rises again on Sunday. Paradoxically, there are often greater numbers of prisoners milling around at any one time during the weekend than on other days in the week, which would commonly be seen as *increasing* the opportunities for troublesome situations to develop.

---

[2] Data had been kept only imperfectly in notebooks in Long Lartin, and we were unable to construct retrospectively a full data set. For Albany, we were able to use the detailed computerized data on disciplinary incidents that was developed by psychologists in the prison from 1988 onwards.

How, then, might one go about accounting for the day-to-day differences?[3]

One argument that might be advanced is that the smaller numbers of recorded offences at the weekend were simply the result of fewer staff being on duty then. Many breaches of the prison rules may thus have gone unnoticed or at least passed without formal sanction. Alternatively staff might feel reluctant to police the wings as systematically and with as much rigour as they might during the week without the support and backup of a significant number of people (weekend staffing rosters are low). Maybe there is just more latitude given to marginal misbehaviours at weekends in prisons as in other social settings. Whilst each conjecture has some plausibility, none provides more than a partial explanation. It is quite likely that the differences are the result of both staff and prisoners behaving somewhat differently according to the day of the week. Prisoners and staff are just as likely to resent Monday mornings as the rest of us, perhaps rather more so. Despite, in many key respects, each and every day in prison being much like any other, prisoners (like people outside) view the weekend as being qualitatively different from the remainder of the week. The weekend does indeed offer benefits—more visits, increased leisure time, greater access to the gym, more scope to gamble on televised horse-racing, to name but a few. More generally, prisoners clearly welcome the break from the weekday routine, and respond accordingly. As for prison staff, set free (to an extent at least) from the onerous and instrumental task of moving large numbers of prisoners around the prison, they are more likely to engage prisoners in cordial banter at weekends. In such circumstances they may be reluctant to interpret the rules too strictly, and may impose sanctions only as a last resort. In sum, what these data may seem to imply is that both prisoners' attitudes towards breaking the prison rules and staff attitudes towards the policing of the wings were influenced, at least in some measure, by the day of the week.

The same Albany data set allows us to explore whether disciplinary offences are more or less likely to occur at particular periods of the day, or in some locations more than others (see Table 7.2). With the exception of the VPU, the categorization of the areas (see

---

[3] Because these data were compiled after the completion of our fieldwork at Albany, we were not able to explore staff views on how the differences might be understood. Explanations at this distance can therefore only be tentative.

TABLE 7.2. Disciplinary offences at Albany by time of day and place for 1988

Time	Main	VPU	Seg. unit	Work shops	Class- rooms	Ground	Other	Total No.	%
07.45–08.14	8	2	23					33	4.9
08.15–08.59	26	5	5				8	44	6.6
09.00–11.10	138	24	31	27	1	17	10	248	37.0
11.40–12.09	24		6			1	2	33	4.9
12.10–13.29	2		1					3	0.5
13.30–14.14	20	1	4	1		1	1	28	4.2
14.15–16.10	66	4	7	12		8	23	120	17.9
16.40–17.14	17	4	3			4		28	4.2
17.15–17.59	7		1					8	1.2
18.00–20.30	54	11	3	1			7	76	11.3
20.31–07.44	31	1	17					49	7.3
Total No.	393	52	101	40	2	31	51	670	100.0
%	58.7	7.8	15.1	6.0	0.3	4.6	7.6	100.0	

top of table) finds its equivalent in other dispersal prisons, including Long Lartin. The time periods that are shown equate to the important periods in Albany's daily timetable (see Table 3.2).

Of the 670 disciplinary offences committed in Albany during 1988, 553 (82 per cent) were committed by prisoners housed in the main prison. Of the remainder, 75 (11 per cent) of the total were committed by prisoners in the vulnerable unit and 42 (6 per cent) by prisoners in the segregation unit. Of course, there were more prisoners held in the main prison than the VPU, but nevertheless the contribution of main prison inmates to the recorded disciplinary figures was wholly disproportionate.[4] These data tend, therefore, to confirm the analysis in chapter 6 concerning the more 'controlled' nature of social relations in the VPU.

[4] Calculating exactly how disproportionate is unfortunately rather complex. At the time of our fieldwork, the ratio of prisoners in Albany 'main' wings to those in the VPU was approximately 3:2 (i.e. corresponding to the number of wings in each section of the prison), and this ratio held at the beginning of 1989 (see Table 3.4 in Chapter 3). However, at the beginning of 1988 one of the VPU wings was completely out of action (for health and safety reasons), and it so remained for much of the year, then gradually filled up. The *average* number of prisoners in the VPU for the whole of 1988 can be taken as approximately 90 (this is derived from Albany's official ADP for 1988, given in Table 3.1, minus the normal population of the 'main' prison as shown in Table 3.4). Assuming these data to be correct, then the 553 disciplinary offences committed by 'main wing' prisoners in 1988 represent an average of 2.4 offences per prisoner in the year; while for the VPU the corresponding rate was only 0.8 (i.e. 75 offences for an average of 90 inmates).

In terms of the location of offences, 59% of all offences (71% of those committed by prisoners from the main prison), were committed on A, B, and C wings; and a further 23% were committed in the VPU or in the segregation unit. Clearly, the great majority of incidents leading to disciplinary offences occur in residential contexts rather than in workshops, classrooms, etc.

It can be seen that nearly two-fifths of all disciplinary offences (37 per cent) were recorded as having occurred in the morning work period (this was twice as many as in the corresponding period in the afternoon, though that was the next most troubled time). More specifically, conventional wisdom in prisons has it that incidents are most likely to occur at particular moments such as unlock and 'bang-up', the journey to and from work, and at mealtimes; and this is confirmed from the data. Note, for example, that although over half of all offences occurred in the two main time periods set aside for work (see above), very few actually took place in workshops or the classrooms. Indeed, 50 offences (7.5 per cent) were recorded as having occurred at or immediately around 09:00, the time when prisoners set off in the morning for work, education or the gym, while 41 offences (6 per cent) were committed at or immediately around 14.15, the corresponding starting time for the afternoon period. One may add that 33 offences (5 per cent) were recorded at or around the morning unlock period. These three very specific 'critical' times of the day thus accounted, between them, for nearly a fifth of all disciplinary offences in the prison.[5]

Evening association is the time when prisoners are able to engage with one another under less exigent constraints than at other times in the day. Whilst the emphasis is, by definition, upon recreational activities it is also a time when people can meet to continue arguments, and in some cases settle old scores; it is also a time when arguments may flare up over competing demands for the use of particular facilities. It is thus reasonable to assume that a fair proportion of rule infractions will be committed during this period, and this proved to be the case, 11 per cent of offences being recorded for this time. Evening lock-up can also be understandably a fraught time for all concerned. It is a dubious matter of pride for some prison staff to claim that they can lock inmates up in a

[5] Note the strong relevance to these data of Giddens's emphasis on the social importance of 'routines' and (though in a wider definition than the one he employs: Giddens, 1984: 60) 'critical situations'.

matter of a few minutes. For inmates, lock-up time is characterized by a variety of responses. Some prisoners amble back to their cells in quiet reflection. Others frantically attempt to seal their last deal of the day, secure a final cigarette or cassette tape from friends who may be located at the other end of a long wing. Staff, meanwhile, cajole, threaten, and engage in the cut and thrust humour that is so much their stock in trade. Most of the time such strategies 'work', at least at the instrumental level. But staff are anxious to get that job done: it has its own tension, *and* they want to go home. Prisoners who, deliberately or otherwise, delay lock-up are likely to find themselves on report. A significant proportion of 'evening' offences arise at the close of the prison day.

These various data and comments are no more than suggestive starting-points. However, they are highly congruent with emerging data on offences in the outside community, showing that such offences 'cluster' in 'hotspots' much more than has often been recognized (see for example Sherman et al., 1989). Taken together with the insights of structuration theory (see earlier discussion), it would seem that the patterning of prison incidents in time and space, in relation to prison routines (indeed, to the *different* routines in different prisons, and on weekdays as against weekends) is a matter worthy of fuller research attention.

Specific Incidents

From the time of the formulation of the original research proposal for this study, it was clear to us that it would be necessary and appropriate, as a central part of the research, to take a careful look at a defined series of 'control incidents' in each of the two studied prisons. The main aim of this part of our work, it was anticipated, would be to try to relate the general understandings that were developing about the regimes, and the nature of 'order' in each prison, to actual incidents that had occurred. To maximize the research value of work of this kind, it seemed necessary to inter-view key 'participants' in the incident (offender(s), victim(s), per-haps some onlookers, managers who had to deal with it, etc.), to gain a rounded understanding of how the incident had emerged, and how it had been dealt with. To avoid entangling ourselves in possible legal complications, it was eventually decided that we would interview only *retrospectively*, i.e. after the incident had been fully dealt with by the prison's disciplinary procedures, administrative responses in terms of moving prisoners from normal location (see chapter 8), etc. These intentions were put into practice in the following way. In each prison, we drew up (from official records) a list of events which had been officially recorded as 'control incidents' over a period of four months shortly before the commencement of our interview programme. In respect of these events, we made efforts to speak to everyone recorded as having been primarily involved (and sometimes we spoke also to persons who—it became clear to us— had been involved in some important way, but who were not named in the official descriptions of the incident). The aim of these interviews, it must be emphasized, was not for us to try to arbitrate what 'really happened' in any particular case. Rather it was to seek to understand the relation between particular happenings and the competing explanations, experiences and objectives of different parties, in the social context of the prison in which they occurred.

In approaching these data, there are a number of provisos which need to be borne constantly in mind. The first is that, as we have noted at several points, prisons have historically identified different priorities and had different emphases in the kinds of behaviour they seek to control or prevent. One may go so far as to say that they seek to create and sustain somewhat distinct forms of social order. In so doing they may also vary in their use of control measures. A comparative understanding of these issues is one of the primary concerns of this book. Prisons have also historically had somewhat different practices of recording and response. Thus different sets of control 'incidents' in the files of different prisons are composed of the interaction between distinct sets of real events and different practices in response to them at the levels of discovery, ranking according to seriousness, and recording. This variation makes serious comparative work extremely difficult. It would, for example, obviously be unwise to seek to draw strong inferences on the basis of prison records alone or to assume that they are either complete or identically compiled.

We took events officially defined as 'control incidents' as a starting-point for research because we were (and are) interested both in the kinds of events which take place, *and* in which of them are seen as important enough to warrant responses. This does not mean that we are misled into thinking that we are necessarily comparing like with like in each prison. Indeed if prisons 'produce' different kinds and numbers of incidents this may be highly instructive in understanding differences in their styles of regulation and control. In short, we were interested in organizational behaviour and managerial decision making in relation both to the possible generation and to the handling of incidents, and that being the case there was good reason to focus on a set of incidents administratively defined as such.

The Prison Service has sought to systematize the reporting and coding of control incidents through the use of Circular Instructions (at the time of our fieldwork, CI 32/84), which differentiate between 'major' and 'minor' incidents, and stipulate the appropriate courses of action in relation to each. Even so there remains considerable scope for interpretation and variability. For example there is latitude in the decision to charge interpersonal violence as 'gross personal violence' (Rule 47(3)) or 'assault' (Rule 47 (4)) or simply fighting. At the time of our research this decision determined whether the incident in question was to be coded as a 'major' or a 'minor' one.

What then is a 'control incident' for the purposes of our research? We have already offered a definition in chapter 3. That broad definition allowed that an 'incident' or 'control problem' might be any situation or event in response to which staff felt obliged to take controlling or disciplinary action. We suggested in that chapter that such incidents are of three main kinds, namely episodes of interpersonal violence; incidents related to the *sub rosa* prison economy and its related hierarchies; and moments or campaigns of silent or vocal protest or non co-operation. In this section we will be dealing mainly with a subset of such events, using a narrower operational definition. These are happenings which were regarded as distinct and serious enough to warrant recording as major incidents under the relevant Circular Instruction. Our self-imposed (but, we would argue, in research terms vital) task of interviewing the main participants in a defined class of control-related events for each prison meant that we were obliged, for practical reasons, to limit ourselves for the purposes of this chapter to this narrower definition.

In more practical terms, at the level of creating a sample our decisions were influenced by three particular considerations. *First*, we thought that it was only possible in 'specific interviews' to ask people about events and situations which had already been recorded and processed (though without taking the official version as definitive). The danger was that, had we done otherwise, we would have put the prisoner, ourselves, and prison staff in the untenable position of having to confirm or refute mere rumours, allegations, and suspicions. More importantly, whilst such interviews might well have been interesting, it was unlikely that people would have been particularly candid; and so we offered people the opportunity of raising such experiences in 'general' interviews instead. *Secondly*, despite the constraint on the number of interviews we could attempt, we wanted to look at incidents over a long enough time-scale to be reasonably confident that they were not wholly untypical of the kinds of situations generally arising in the respective prisons. *Thirdly*, we considered it unwise, given that we were relying on people's firsthand accounts from memory, to try to address events that had taken place more than a few months before.

In this light, as already indicated, we decided to look systematically at 'serious incidents' recorded as having occurred within the four months immediately prior to a given date during the fieldwork in each prison. We set out to interview all named participants in each of the relevant incidents. We discounted incidents which were still subject to internal or police enquiries, or which were of a purely 'security' nature. Nor did we look in detail at routine drugs finds. This procedure generated samples of five incidents in Long Lartin and seven in Albany. In Long Lartin we succeeded in interviewing all named prisoners, while in Albany we succeeded in nine out of thirteen instances. The resulting sets of incidents are as follows:

Long Lartin

LL1   Two prisoners (one category A lifer, one category B determinate sentence prisoner) were scalded by hot water thrown by another (category A lifer) in a wing during evening association (at 18.40). The incident seems to have been a pre-emptive attack by a prisoner, identified by others as a 'nonce', against those he saw as potential aggressors. Extensive action was taken in response by the prison; most notably five prisoners were removed from the wing, three were transferred subject to CI 10/74 (see chapter 8 for details of this procedure), and two prisoners were permanently transferred. Two prisoners received hospital treatment.

LL2   Damage and noise during a protest in the segregation unit (at 13.30). This was part of the aftermath of incident LL1. Two prisoners (one category A, one category B) were removed under restraint on CI 10/74.

LL3   Prisoner (category B) assaulted officer in kitchen (at 10.55) Prisoner held in segregation unit pending adjudication by the Board of Visitors.

LL4   Assault by one prisoner (category B, lifer) on another (category B) using blunt instrument in a wing (at 10.00). One prisoner received five stitches in the prison hospital. The assailant was removed to segregation unit pending adjudication by the Board of Visitors.

LL5   Stabbing by one prisoner (category A) of another (category B) in a TV room on wing (at 15.10). Victim required hospital treatment. The assailant was subsequently transferred under CI 10/74.

Albany

A1   Fight between two prisoners (both category B determinate sentences) in a wing at morning unlock (07.30). Following adjudication one prisoner moved wings.

A2   Fight between two prisoners (both category A lifers) in a wing kitchen (at 19.30). One prisoner moved wings following adjudication.

A3   Fight between two prisoners (both category B, determinate sentences) on exercise yard (at 11.04). Prisoners returned to wings after adjudication.

A4   Fight between two prisoners (both category B determinate sentences) during association on a wing (at 15.25). Following adjudication both prisoners returned to the same wing.

A5   Fight between two prisoners (one category A lifer, one category B determinate) in TV room on a wing during association (at 14.20). Following adjudication and apology both prisoners returned to the same wing.

A6   Fight between two prisoners (both category B) in a wing (at 11.40). Following adjudication one prisoner moved wings.

A7   Fight between two prisoners (both category B) in canteen queue (at about 19.30). Following adjudication one prisoner returned to the wing, one remained in segregation on Rule 43 (GOAD).

It is notable that in both prisons events coded as control incidents are, in terms of our threefold typology (see chapter 3), primarily instances of interpersonal violence. The single exception is incident LL2, which is a 'demonstrative act' of angry protest. This predominance of violence is scarcely surprising. Whatever the underlying causes of the problem, it is the moment of violence which is often treated as constituting the 'incident' as such. One purpose of the specific interviews which we discuss below is to understand and contextualize the sequences of events which preceded each 'incident', as well as its management and aftermath.

Obviously, in view of the small size of our samples, one important question that arises concerns whether the incidents can be regarded as typical of each prison. We can respond to this legitimate concern in two main ways.

First, we devoted much of our attention in general interviews (see above chapters 4 and 5) to asking prisoners and staff what were the main causes of control problems and what kind of situations resulted. We also asked many times whether people thought that the recent past had seemed to them in any ways unusual in these respects. Although there was a good deal of unease at Long Lartin during the period of our fieldwork over post-Gartree security measures, neither prisoners nor staff felt that overt control problems were at a specially high (or low) level. Meanwhile at Albany the consensus among staff was that, in comparison to its recent institutional past, the prison was 'very quiet'. In short, we could find no reason to suppose that the particular periods we were looking at were uniquely troublesome.

Secondly, we sought to strengthen our 'specific interview' sample by placing it in a broader context, derived from a consideration of data in prison records. Table 7.3 summarizes all recorded 'control incidents' (serious or otherwise) which were recorded under CI 32/84 in Albany and Long Lartin over a two-year period, organized in terms of our threefold typology of control problems. This table embraces a wider set of incidents than our 'specific interview' sample, in two senses: *first*, the data cover twenty-four months instead of four; and *secondly*, because the definition of an 'incident' is broader (see further below). Nevertheless, we would argue that the events in the specific sample broadly correspond in both number and kind to the sort of situations shown in Table 7.3 as having been notified as 'control incidents'; and this strengthens our confidence in the specific interview sample.

How should Table 7.3 be interpreted? It is important to note that the records on the basis of which it is compiled were kept somewhat differently in the two prisons. Long Lartin kept separate files of 'major' and 'minor' incidents, roughly corresponding to paragraphs 6 and 16 of C1 32/84. Drugs finds were thus logged together

TABLE 7.3. A comparison of incidents reported to prison department head-quarters, Albany and Long Lartin prisons, 1987 and 1988

	Albany				Long Lartin			
	1987	1988	Total	Rate*	1987	1988	Total	Rate*
Interpersonal violence								
Assaults/fights (prisoner–prisoner)	28	19	47	15.3	8	10	18	4.4
Assaults/fights (prisoner–staff)	11	10	21	6.8	2	3	5	1.2
Total	39	29	68	22.1	10	13	23	5.6
Challenges to authority								
Demonstrative acts (for example: collective or individual smashing up, barricading cells, fires)	9	4	13	4.2	10	3	13	3.2
Collective or individual refusals and resistances	9	8	17	5.5	2	6	8	2.0
Total	18	12	30	9.7	12	9	21	5.2
Informal economy								
Drugs finds	17	23†	40	13.0	14	14†	27	6.7

* = Rate per 100 prisoners over the two year period (17 months in the case of drugs finds).
† = Data to 31.5.88 only. No data beyond that date in 1988 for Long Lartin; in Albany the total for the year was 61.

In addition to the above the following miscellaneous incidents were reported:

Long Lartin

1987 (5 incidents)
2 cases involving suspected explosives (one harmless, the other a hoax)
1 case involving the loss of equipment (a knife)
1 suicide
1 attempted suicide

1988 (3 incidents)
2 cases involving medical emergencies
1 case involving the loss of equipment (a pair of scissors)

Albany

1987 (6 incidents)
3 medical emergencies
2 home leave failures
1 assault on a prisoner by a visitor

1988 (8 incidents)
3 home leave failures
1 refusal to hand over an item not allowed the prisoner
1 food refusal
1 concealment of a blade
1 visitor in possession of some 'vegetable matter'

with minor incidents of other kinds. Fights, fires, demonstrative
acts and so forth occurred in both files, presumably differentiated
by gravity, though the criteria for this differentiation did not seem
to be hard and fast. Albany, on the other hand, had one book for
'incidents' generically, and another reserved for drugs alone. The
figures reported in Table 7.3 incorporate the sum of both major
and minor incidents at Long Lartin as compared with all 'incidents'
(including drugs) at Albany. It is reasonable to ask whether the two
columns are strictly comparable. Might it be, for example, that
some incidents in the 'minor file' at Long Lartin would not be
thought worth recording in the 'incident' book at Albany?
(Conversely some events in the 'minor' file at Long Lartin are open
to being interpreted as quite serious in their implications.) We can
provide no conclusive resolution to these or other 'dark figure'
problems (though see the final section of this chapter for further
relevant data). However, we can say that the figures represent the
soundest comparison possible on available information.

Each of the categories recorded in Table 7.3 raises its own issues
for interpretation. Thus, the figures for drugs finds reliably indicate
the numbers of known occasions on which drugs were found; but
as with other offences relating to goods and possessions (inside and
outside prisons) this is highly dependent on policies of searching
and policing. In both prisons numbers of finds per month vary
markedly depending on whether there was a concerted effort taking
place (a 'blitz') to restrict the availablility of drugs. (The disparity
between Albany's figures for 1987 and 1988 is unlikely to be explicable in any other way.) Similarly, comparisons between incidents
involving challenges to authority, dissent, disobedience etc. are also
problematic. Such challenges and resistances take place constantly.
Only a proportion of them ever become 'nickings' and only a few
of those are recorded as 'incidents'. Whether this is the same proportion in each prison is impossible to judge with any certainty.

However, we think it is likely that the figures regarding incidents
of interpersonal violence in the two prisons are more directly comparable. Fights and assaults often come to the attention of staff,
and when they do they are highly likely to be recorded and
processed. Equally fights and assaults are distinct events, easily recognizable as 'incidents'. It is true that not all fights are recorded as
incidents—charges for fighting in any one year are significantly
higher than fights or assaults which find their way into the incident

books. There is still a process of decision making involved in defining a fight or assault as an 'incident', therefore. However, we have no strong reason to suppose that these decisions were made on different grounds in the two prisons.

The question thus remains of how to account for the higher number of incidents of interpersonal violence in Albany than Long Lartin, a difference which is greater when the existence of the VPU is taken into account (since the VPU generated few incidents, yet is included in the population figures used as the denominator when calculating rates). There are a number of possible considerations and arguments which would need to be considered in answering this question. These include at least the following possible explanations:

1. The difference might result from the fact that Albany had a younger and more violent population (see chapter 3);

2. Differences in regimes, relationships, and perceived quality of life perhaps resulted in more frustration and aggression at Albany than Long Lartin;

3. Perhaps, however, the true rates of violence are more similar than they appeared and that more instances of aggression went undetected at Long Lartin than at Albany.

We do not seek to resolve these issues at this stage, though we shall return to them at the end of the chapter. Rather, we hope now to provide a better context for the discussion of such issues by reference to qualitative questions about the severity and importance of particular incidents, the interpretations made of them by participants, and the relation between specific problematic situations and the style of control prevailing in the prison in which they happened. For these reasons, we will now present in more detail some issues arising from accounts of the twelve incidents in the specific interview sample.

Twelve Control Incidents

As we have seen, in terms of the threefold typology of control problems the incidents within our specific interview sample were, with one exception, cases of interpersonal violence. However, it is clear that within the category of interpersonal violent acts there is a considerable range of situational and motivational differences, as well as of degrees of seriousness. In approaching these issues, we shall discuss incidents occurring in Albany and Long Lartin together in the first instance, and go on to consider their separate implications for the two prisons subsequently. We deal with the incidents in ascending order of complexity, in terms of their relations to underlying or systematic problems of order.

'People Flip'

The simplest category of incidents are those which are momentary outbreaks of violence between two people. Such incidents may be highly situational, and according to the participants' accounts do not require any special explanation in terms of their interpersonal antecedents or background. Rather than forming parts of running feuds or conflicts between groups such incidents are usually characterized by the participants as momentary, unpremeditated, unexpected episodes. They are often explained by references to pains and pressures of imprisonment—the sense of living on top of one another, irritation over queuing or noise, feeling 'wound up' and anxious for other reasons—rather than to any very specific underlying interpersonal or group dynamic. Such incidents are often regarded as being 'closed' afterwards, and people tend to deny bearing any grudge or continuing ill will. We regard incidents A1, A2, A4, A5 and A6 as being of this kind in having some or all of the above features. In such cases prisoners often summarize the circumstances which made them 'snap' on a particular occasion and/or in a particular place. For example, this prisoner said that he had encountered very little trouble since his arrival in the prison:

I have only had one row since I have been here and that was over something petty. Sometimes you just feel trapped . . . It can be [made worse by living on top of one another] but usually it blows over very quickly on these type of wings [VPU] . . . We just clashed over a towel . . . If you lose control there's nothing you can do about it.

(Incident A2)

In this case the triviality of the precipitating cause is freely acknowledged by both parties, but this does not diminish the suddenness and violence of the moment itself. Thus, the other party to this incident commented:

I moved the towel in the kitchen so that I could sit down and he went berserk. I'd never seen him before in my life. I thought 'we've got a right one here'. I had to wallop him. I just couldn't believe it.

Other prisoners stressed not only how events can assume a significance out of proportion with the reality of the situation but also how easily people can overreact when such situations occur:

I'm the kind of person . . . I don't like mornings. I wake up grumpy. This particular morning somebody woke me up [by rattling a door] . . . Sometimes, you know, you've just got to go. So I had a fight with him, went down the block, came back up and went on another wing. It was a little thing.

(Incident A1)

In this instance the rattling door was being shaken by a neighbouring prisoner trying to draw the attention of the staff to his desire to be let out of his cell. The prisoner who had been rattling his door attributed the incident directly to the Albany regime which he viewed as giving rise to a sense of persecution and build-up of tension such that some people reacted violently. He summarized trouble between prisoners in terms of confinement, frustration, impatience and a sense of injustice. The fact that he was rattling his door (which in turn led to his being hit) was, he thought, directly related to his difficulty in accepting being banged up. This prisoner was also involved in incident A7 (see below).

Incident A4, meanwhile, involved two friends who were playing backgammon:

I was dropping the dice. He told me to roll them. I told him not to tell me what to do, and we had a fight . . . we told the Governor we were friends, and he allowed us back on the wing, as long as there were no repercussions.

One of the participants in this incident denied that there were any underlying or sub-textual tensions involved; he insisted that it bore no particular relation to any special features of the prison nor to other anxieties, and that the two parties remained on friendly terms.

Incidents A5 and A6 are somewhat more complex and problematic than those cited so far. We have little reliable information relating to incident A6. One of the participants insisted that it was purely a clash of personalities sparked off by a quarrel over noise. Staff, on the other hand, strongly suspected that there was an unacknowledged drug-related debt involved. We were unable to resolve this conflict of interpretations.

Incident A5 on the other hand can best be understood with reference to the respective positions in their sentences of the prisoners involved. The two prisoners involved were of widely differing ages and sentence lengths. The 'victim' was a young, black determinate sentence prisoner. The 'assailant' was a category A lifer. The younger prisoner provoked an angry response from his assailant by telling him to go and watch his preferred television programme in another room. The 'victim' explained what had happened to him in terms of the pressures and 'wind-ups' of prison life both generally and as they particularly affected the assailant: 'people flip', he commented. The 'assailant' was awaiting a long-promised transfer 'home' to a prison in Ireland after fifteen years in prison. One interesting feature of the incident was the degree of sympathy expressed by staff for the feelings of the assailant, and their view that the incident could be largely attributed to bureaucratic slowness in responding to and processing his case. More generally, staff also expressed sympathy for the reactions of older prisoners irritated by the behaviour of the more numerous youngsters.

Incident A3 is unusual amongst Albany incidents in that it involved a degree of premeditation. The assailant freely admitted that he was seeking to settle a score resulting from his prior acquaintance with the 'victim' on 'the out'. He had already packed his things in preparation for a stay in the block before confronting his antagonist. He did not regard the prison itself as bearing any responsibility, nor did he have any complaint about the fairness of the treatment he subsequently received. Honour having been satisfied, the assailant had no wish to prolong the feud any further.

Fear and Loathing

We will now go on to consider aspects of incidents LL1, LL3, LL4, LL5, and A7. This broad group of incidents seem to us to call for a somewhat greater effort of interpretation, to have been more ramified in their implications, and to have posed more difficult dilemmas for managerial decisions and policies. (Incident LL2 will be considered as a consequence or sequel of incident LL1.) These are incidents which can only be understood with reference to their antecedent histories and which seem to be clearly embedded in the social relationships prevailing in the respective prisons.

Incident LL3 is the only case of an assault by a prisoner on a member of staff in our sample. On the face of it the incident was precipitated by the officer unexpectedly placing his hand on the prisoner's shoulder:

I'm not saying he punched me or anything, but he laid hands on me. He grabbed hold of me from behind, and I didn't know who it was. I reacted. I hit him with my elbow in the face, without even looking, then turned round and I've hit him once more. End of it. That's it.

Neither party viewed the incident as having been preceded by any specific interpersonal animosity. At the same time the prisoner clearly felt that the officer concerned had made a serious error of judgement, and in effect precipitated the incident by breaking a *de facto* taboo on unwanted physical contact:

The manhandling bit, especially in this prison, is something you just don't do. You don't grab anybody from behind and bring your hand down with any force on someone's shoulder. A screw should know better. I didn't know at the time it was a screw, it could have been anyone. It's a violent place, the amount of people that get stabbed here in a year, you don't know what's happening, and I reacted, and that's basically what happened.

In the prisoner's terms, then, the incident is to be explained by his unusually acute sense of living in a dangerous place, and his proneness to react accordingly. There is a clear disagreement in interpretation of this incident. From the officer's point of view his placing the hand on the prisoner's shoulder was intended as a calming gesture at a moment of agitation whilst the prisoner was complaining about the quality of his food. The officer saw the prisoner's response as out of character. Its being out of character contributed to a widespread view amongst the staff that the incident would not have happened had the prisoner not already been under pressure, probably through being heavily in debt. Indeed the possibility could not be excluded that hitting an officer might have served the strategic purpose for the prisoner of having himself removed from the wing to the segregation unit. Whilst the prisoner rejected this interpretation he nevertheless referred to a serious debt problem:

Somebody in the office had said that I owed *x* amount of pounds out, which might or might not be a lie . . . let's say I owed somebody £600 . . . There's lots of reasons for debt—smoke too much and can't pay for it. Let's say they took somebody off the wing who was selling it to somebody else, and they [i.e. the staff] swagged it before he collected the money. He's in a hole, isn't he? He can't get the money for the people he owes it to . . .

Even if the facts of this case are impossible to establish, it is illustrative of some of the pressures to which prisoners can be subject in the face of debts, and suggestive of their possible scale in a highly developed prison economy such as Long Lartin's.

Incidents LL4 and LL5 resemble those dealt with earlier in that they are constituted by a moment of violence between two prisoners. However they differ from them insofar as they had clearer and more complicated antecedent circumstances, they involved the use of weapons and hence were also regarded as more serious by the prison authorities.

From the victim's perspective incident LL4 was occasioned by the assailant's (misplaced?) sexual jealousy. The incident provides a vivid insight into the kinds of tensions which can develop between members of a group of friends within a prison wing, and the way in which violence can flow between socially proximate individuals. The victim of the assault recalls:

This bloke . . . I didn't like him, but I said I'd be friends. He got together with another poofter called Bloggs. He believed that another guy and I were living together which we weren't, and he got jealous. One day I was going upstairs when I glanced up and a hammer bashed me on the side of the head, and also on the chest, and he said 'I'll kill you, you bastard, I'll kill you.' I couldn't believe it.

As is always possible in such incidents (incidents LL3, LL5 and A7 for example) there are differing accounts of points of fact. For example in this case the assailant admitted having caused the victim to require stitches but (successfully) denied having used a hammer. Moreover he insisted that he was attacked first with a mop bucket. However, whilst the assailant's account is more inexplicit with regard to motivation there is nevertheless a measure of agreement that the incident resulted from the strain on personal relations in confined conditions. It is worth noting also that the depth of personal feeling involved here may have been accentuated by the issues of privacy and opportunity which arise under a regime which permits cell association. The assailant describes his feelings:

It was just that we were on one another's backs all the time. Every time I went in my mate's cell, he'd be there as well. He felt that I was getting in his way, I thought he was getting in my way. He worked in the same shop as well. We all sat and had tea. We were on decent terms—we weren't the best of pals but we weren't arch-enemies. We got very stand-offish towards each other, and it just came to a head.

Unlike some of the simpler incidents cited above an event such as this has an ongoing control dimension. Whilst the assailant remained in the prison (in segregation, under investigation) there was always the possibility that he might come back up onto the wings, a prospect which the victim not only feared but refused to countenance:

I've got hate in me now. I will kill that bloke. They said they would bring him up . . . I've told the Governors and my solicitor that if I see that bloke I will kill him. Without hesitation or compunction I will kill him.

For the assailant's part, meanwhile, whilst he denied having any fear of reprisals he nevertheless expressed relief at remaining in the block for the time being:

It's just that I've noticed that since I've been down here how much more relaxed I am than when I was up there. I've seen the amount of people come down every morning and the kind of things they get placed on report for . . . so rather than have that I'd rather stay down here, . . . I don't get into any fights down here. If I get into a fight, being a lifer I can get two or three years added on. So it's better for me to be down here. So I'm happy.

In a similar way incident number LL5 also stems in part from the dynamics of acceptance and exclusion within a particular circle of prisoners in a wing. There are many points of difference between the 'assailant's' and 'victim's' accounts of the episode, nor will we attempt to resolve these differences. The victim described events as follows:

I was in my mate's cell and [he: i.e. the assailant] comes in and asks my mate for a cigarette . . . he wouldn't ask me. So he went away. I would have refused him anyway because he's a nonce. My mate was called down to the doctor and I went over to another friend's cell . . . The next thing I see is this guy [the assailant] nipping in to my mate's cell and closing the door behind him . . . so I asked him what he was doing, and told him to get off the landing and not to show his face . . . A couple of weeks later I went into the TV room, and he was sitting in the corner. When he saw me he got up, ran over to me and stabbed me with a kitchen knife.

The only real point of similarity between this and the assailant's account is in the location of the incident:

It happened while I was watching TV. He [the victim] called me a black something. That's why I got transferred on a 10/74. No one saw the fight, which he started. He invited me to fight, but I didn't want to . . . . He went to the hospital on account of his face. Next thing I know I'm transferred.

The only explanatory background detail provided by the 'assailant' was that he felt he had been racially abused:

He [the victim] felt he could say and do as he pleased to black people and that they're cannibals, uncivilized, come from the bush, play jungle body music. It started with my music. The person in the cell above banged on the floor all night.

Notwithstanding the differences between these two accounts it is not difficult to see sources of possible hostility. The 'victim' had already identified the assailant as a nonce, an intrusive presence and a possible cell thief. The assailant knew that his music had irritated other people and was experiencing racial hostility. It is interesting to compare this incident with incident LL4. Whereas in incident LL4 the issues include tension within a tight social group accentuated by jealousy and animosity between two individuals, incident LL5 revolves around the exclusion of a socially isolated individual from an existing social network and his apparent obliviousness to the fact that he had been repeatedly rebuffed. He seems to have violated a number of important conventions, about privacy, personal property, and social distance, especially by entering other people's cells uninvited. Although these are serious incidents involving potentially lethal weapons one can readily see ways in which they are an extension of a chronic problem of irritation with one another which prisoners describe as generally present (cf. chapter 5). Whether the circumstances prevailing in one prison rather than another increase the likelihood of such underlying tensions resulting in incidents of this kind is an important issue, to which we will return below.

Incident A7 bears a more than passing similarity to incident LL5 in that it involves a socially isolated and vulnerable (in this case white) individual attracting the anger of another (in this case black) prisoner. The incident concerned an altercation in a canteen queue. The vulnerable 'victim' insists:

A black person hit me in the face and told me to get to the end of the queue. He was sitting in a chair, not in the queue. He had no right to tell me what to do, so I hit him back.

There are two subtexts involved in this incident. First, like incident LL5, it is a trans-racial confrontation. Secondly, it involves a vulnerable prisoner who was considered 'strange', if not mad, by other prisoners. The allegation of butting into queues is always a potential source of friction, but it seems to us likely that it might not have attracted the same response if it had been done by a more socially or physically powerful prisoner. Moreover, the vulnerable prisoner (the 'victim') stood his ground. Thereafter, whilst both parties were initially segregated the vulnerable prisoner was subsequently kept in segregation (on Rule 43 GOAD) for a much longer period, because of the potential control problems which might follow from the perceived belligerence of his defiant posture:

They're saying I'm down here for protection. If they're asking me if I'm afraid to go back on the wing the answer is I'm not.

The Governor of Albany clearly felt the combination of a prisoner who was odd, small, vulnerable and defiant posed him with a serious managerial problem:

Some staff say he's very odd, and he has wobbly days—emotional and psychiatric. But in terms of the medical textbook it doesn't signify madness. It's a discipline issue . . . He can't go on the wing because the fellows would have a go at him and they would really injure this guy, because he's got nothing about him. But he'll have a go, so he's going to be a punch bag. He's got no feelings of self-preservation, so we'd better give him a chance and move him on.

There is an irony here, notwithstanding the unpredictable reactions of the particular prisoner in question, which reflects on the policy of maintaining vulnerable prisoners on normal location. That is, if a vulnerable prisoner is to achieve a quality of life which is remotely comparable to that of other prisoners he may have to withstand verbal hostility and provocation, yet in resisting he may be seen as causing a control problem and perhaps be defined as a 'control problem prisoner'.

Incident LL1 has in common with incident A7 the fact that it includes an act of resistance, or pre-emptive aggression, by a vulnerable prisoner. Incident LL1 is perhaps the most complex and serious of those in our sample, not only in terms of the episode itself but also in its repercussions and implications.

The origins of incident LL1 can be traced back to the arrival at Long Lartin of two brothers whose trial for a sexual offence had received enormous coverage in the press and on television. They were brought to Long Lartin virtually straight from the court following sentence, as Category A prisoners. After a short period of observation for suicidal intentions, they were placed together on normal location. Their arrival there was never likely to be a trouble-free experience. The younger brother commented:

We went to Long Lartin the day that we were sentenced . . . and because our case was so widespread and popular the cons there assumed straight-away 'That's it, we've got to give them a hard time' . . . Sex offenders in Long Lartin—the so-called plastic gangsters, they didn't like us, they were always causing trouble for us and grassing us up to the screws, trying to get us into more trouble . . .

Serious friction thus developed between the brothers and a number of others, exacerbated by the status and reputation of one antagonist in particular. Under pressure, but against the wing Governor's advice, the younger brother elected to ask for protection under Prison Rule 43 (see chapter 6):

because of him and all his gangsters. I'd had too much and decided to get my head together by going on Rule 43. In the seven days I was down the block I straightened out, but then when I went back on the wing [he] started again. So I decided that going down the block was no solution. The only way to do it was to do him.

Having made this resolution, and after one particular provocation, the younger brother sought the advice of another sex offender who had survived on normal locaton for an extended period, in part by succeeding in developing a reputation for his physical prowess. The latter prisoner recalled:

I told him to do something about it, because if he didn't you're going to have a life of misery. They're all going to be at you. Right from the very start you've got to show them that if they want trouble they can have it. This is the reality. When you're put in a position like that you've got to do something, because these people will kill you if they have the chance, not because of any moral indignation about what you've done but because it's the culture in prison that they've got to have someone to look down upon.

This conversation extended to the choice of method, a jug of hot water, which would be designed to hurt and humiliate without endangering life. From the point of view of the prisoner cited here the threat of violence was also strategic in an attempt to get the prison to move the primary antagonist. Hence, he told the staff beforehand that something was likely to happen. The position of the staff would have included a reluctance to have their course of action determined by threats from either party. Staff are faced with a dilemma between, on the one hand an imperative to prevent trouble occurring and, on the other, an unwillingness to be seen to capitulate to the 'blackmail' of threats by prisoners, on the grounds that this would encourage the strategic use of threatening behaviour.

The incident itself consisted in the younger of the two brothers throwing a jug of very hot water over the primary target, whilst he was having his hair cut by another prisoner, scalding both of the latter. This was thus a very public event, in full view of staff and other prisoners. The state of affairs culminating in incident LL1 had at least the following consequences. The two brothers were removed to the segregation unit. Whilst in the segregation unit the older brother was attacked by another prisoner, requiring several stitches in his ear. They remained in segregation for some time and were eventually permanently transferred to another prison. Meanwhile on the wing, tension had become very high. The victim of the scalding seemed to the wing Governor to have increased his active hostility to sex offenders and could give no reassurance that 'he would not have a go at them again'. The wing Governor's position was that there was going to be a full scale 'anti sex offender campaign':

Sex offenders on the wing grouped closer together because they appreciated why [the assailant] did what he did. Their view was that it was about time that they stood up and didn't stand anything from people like that. That's the increasing problem. Sex offenders aren't always weak and inadequate. And that was the tension which led to [the victim's] removal, because it was creating a very unpleasant atmosphere in the entire wing. A lot of ordinary, basically reasonable inmates complained about it, warning us that if we didn't do something there would be a body. And that was why he [i.e. the 'victim' of the scalding] was removed.

The latter removal also had a series of consequences of its own, most particularly incident LL2. As far as the prisoner in question was concerned he—the victim of incident LL1—had been placed in 'an impossible position'. He felt deeply aggrieved at the incident itself, at the thought that his assailants might even now be returned to the wing, and subsequently at his own removal from normal location:

They informed me that they were going to bring him [i.e. the assailant] back onto the wing! If he did come back I'd have no option but to seek revenge in some way, which I really didn't want to do . . . If I'd thrown hot water at someone I would have been gone the next day. They suggested that they understood my point of view and the guy wouldn't be brought back. But the following day I was moved . . . I was very very bitter . . . and I caused considerable damage to the cells. And again they had to remove a few of us involved with body belts and ankle straps.

Incident LL2 constituted this man's protest at what he saw as the iniquity of the situation, and in which he was joined by at least one other sympathizer within the segregation unit. They were both thereupon removed from Long Lartin on CI 10/74 (see chapter 8 for this procedure). On the wing, meanwhile, some of the 'victim's' friends felt a sense of injustice at his removal. This was indeed acknowledged by the wing Governor:

It was very difficult because [the younger brother] was the assailant, and on the simple laws of fairness he should have been moved out and that would have been the end of it . . . He admitted he'd gone over the top in the way he did it . . . But if [the victim] had let it go he would never have gone out on 10/74 afterwards. But it did engender a lot of anti sex offender feelings.

In this developing situation managers felt that the problem could only be resolved by further action, resulting in two more of the friends of the victim in LL1 being removed from the prison on 10/74. These were the 'barber', who was in any case forthright in his dislike of sex offenders, as well as another friend who had expressed anger at the circumstances of the 'victim's' removal from the wing.

Some Reflections

We have discussed twelve incidents, ranging in complexity and seriousness from a momentary fracas between peers to an important confrontation whose consequences touched numerous people. Although all but one of these recorded incidents have a moment of interpersonal violence at their centre, they none the less vary enormously in their character and implications, nor are they amenable to a single explanation.

One of the most important questions which this research raises concerns the ways in which each incident is related to the prison in which it occurred—could one, for instance, equally well imagine any of them taking place in the other prison, or elsewhere? Is it coincidental that incidents LL1–LL5 (i.e. in Long Lartin) in general look more complex and potentially serious in their implications than incidents A1–A7 (ie in Albany), with the partial exception of incident A7?

A further set of questions arises concerning the avoidability of such incidents in relation to policy choices and managerial decisions. These are real and important questions, but they also broach counter-factual and hypothetical conditions, making them almost impossible to answer conclusively. However, on the basis of the information presented here we would argue that in general the incidents at Long Lartin, as might be expected from perspectives gained in general interviews (see chapters 4 and 5), seem to suggest a more differentiated and complex set of social relations between prisoners, perhaps incorporating more entrenched hostilites.

Albany, on the other hand, as is visible from Table 7.3 (and see also Table 3.5) had more violent episodes on A, B, and C wings—it appears from recorded data to be a quantitatively 'more violent' prison. Yet qualitatively on the evidence before us such a generalization seems questionable. This problematizes the notion that Albany 'had more control problems', just as it does the idea that Long Lartin had few—and at the same time the two sets of data taken together may call into question each prison's premise that its then-current regime reduced the level of 'control problems'. Equally, this whole discussion calls into question the utility of any assessment of the level of control problems which takes the available figures for granted.

What would these points imply? It may be that, contrary to conventional wisdom, it was Long Lartin which in fact housed the more potentially problematic combination of people, not in terms of the day-to-day use of force but in terms of what situations were conceivably possible on occasions. This may be compounded by differences in opportunity. As Long Lartin managers openly agreed it was significantly easier for anyone who was so minded to engage in trouble under 'open' than under more 'restricted' conditions. But this is a complex cost-benefit problem, since rationales for the regime included its not provoking—or defusing—conflictual situations.

Conversely, the greater age/offence homogeneity at Albany may in fact have served to limit the scale of violence, though not its frequency. This might have been more particularly true given:

1. the apparent diminution of race as an overt problem between prisoners (see chapter 5);

2. the actual and symbolic consequences of the presence of the Vulnerable Prisoner Unit, in both removing potential victims and focusing routine hostility *outside* the main wings; and

3. violence was more often between peers, and more likely to be resolved.

At the same time one still has to explain the higher numbers of incidents at Albany. Conjecturally, the elements for an explanation would include:

1. the youth of the population;

2. the possibility of higher levels of detection and formal action at Albany as a function of its less 'soft-policing' policy;

3. specific situational frustrations, whether resulting from Albany's island location or from particular features of the regime, such as resentment of banging up.

With regard to this last point, it was noticeable that only at Albany, within our samples, did any participants in the incidents actually account for their actions in terms of 'pressure' or 'wind-ups' originating with the regime as such.

Points such as those indicated above raise the question of differential kinds of opportunity for trouble to take place in the two prisons. For example, there is a possibility that the interaction between Albany's population and its regime generated a high likelihood of 'sporadic' violent incidents, but reined in their seriousness by successfully inhibiting the development of some social networks, and by increasing the likelihood of early detection. It should also be noted that the combination of the three factors suggested above (youth, less soft policing, and regime frustrations) would be consistent with Albany's much higher rates of recorded disciplinary offences for disobedience and disrespect (as shown in chapter 3). Long Lartin, on the other hand, may have provided the time, space and privacy in which some potential incidents dissipated, and some were ignored because of the 'soft policing' policy, while others fermented and eventually became quite major incidents.

Each of these possibilities seems consistent with the kinds of incidents known to us. They relate closely to the modes of control sought and practised in the respective prisons. Thus, by analogy with the general literature on crime prevention in the outside world (see Rosenbaum 1988), Albany had developed an emphasis on situational aspects of control, centred upon the reduction of opportunities for engaging in problematic behaviour—by controlling movements, limiting numbers unlocked, maintaining close supervision and attempting to keep people occupied—in addition to seeking to foster good relationships. Long Lartin, on the other hand, in addition to surveillance and policing, had a highly developed policy of 'social' prevention, centring on relaxed staff–prisoner relations, good access to gym and exercise, and an appeal to prisoners' rational self-interest in remaining in Long Lartin, through the availability of advantageous material conditions (compare in these respects Barlinnie Special Unit: see Cooke, 1989).[6]

Neither of these strategies existed in pure form, but each related to definable points on the continuum of possible modes of control and kind of order in prison. Long Lartin and Albany both stood at some mid-point in the continuum between absolute situational control (Marion, USA) and consensual social control (Barlinnie Special Unit), and the differences between them are often falsely emphasized. Nevertheless it seems true both from the accounts of managers, uniformed staff and prisoners as well as from differential actual features of incidents that there was a degree of difference in the contribution which situational and social factors made to 'control' in the two cases. We shall return to some of the dilemmas which these distinct emphases generated for each prison, and for the analysis of conflict in prisons more generally in chapter 9. In the meantime, we want to explore whether other statistical data available to us—however imperfect—are consistent with the picture of 'control problems' in each prison that has seemed to develop, in this section, from our analysis of a set of specific incidents.

Illuminating Dark Figures?

As noted in chapter 3, in this project we have adopted a 'multi-strategy' methodological approach in which, while the primary research methods were qualitative (extensive observation and semi-structured interviewing), we tried to be as creative as possible in seeking out quantitative data that might help forward our research

---

[6] This analogy with social and situational crime prevention is developed more fully in chapter 9; see also Bottoms et al. (1990).

understandings. In the previous section of this chapter, we presented the results arising from our main methodological approach for understanding 'control problems' in the two prisons (i.e. the 'specific interview' sample and the larger context from which it was drawn). We now want to supplement that analysis by considering some quantitative sources that might potentially confirm or contradict our emerging interpretation of the data.

Three kinds of fresh quantitative data will be discussed, namely information on alarm bells, data from hospital records, and inmate requests for protection. We do not pretend that the data are conclusive, and the first and second sources in particular pose problems of interpretation. Nevertheless, we hope that the three data sources, considered together, will help to take forward the argument.

Alarm Bells

Data for alarm bells in the two prisons over relevant twelvemonth periods (distinguishing between 'genuine' and 'false' alarms), are shown in Table 7.4. 'Genuine' alarm bells were constituted overwhelmingly by fights or assaults between prisoners, and more rarely by assaults on staff as well as smash-ups or fires. A certain number of false alarms were produced by accidental pressings or technical malfunctions. Others were deliberately engineered by 'campanologist' prisoners, for whom the sight of staff charging around the prison offered amusement and an unwonted sense of power. False alarms tended to cluster on particular days. For example, of the forty-nine alarms in January 1988 at Long Lartin, eight occurred on a single day, seven of them within a thirty-seven minute period. (It is also important to note that this particular spate involved four separate wings.) The most plausible explanation of this occurrence is as an example of 'campanology' as sport: it conjures a vision of harassed prison officers racing from bell to bell in a way that must have been as infuriating to them as it was comical to the prisoners concerned.

We need to consider the data on false and genuine alarms separately. The most striking result in Table 7.4 is the very much higher rate of false alarms at Long Lartin.[7] As with other areas of

[7] Note that the Long Lartin–Albany rate difference as regards false calls was so great as to be essentially unaffected by the complications—discussed later for other data—regarding the respective contributions of the main prison and the VPU at Albany. For the record if we 'adjust' the false alarm rate for Albany 'main' prison in

TABLE 7.4. A comparison of alarm bells in Albany and Long Lartin over a twelve-month period

Month No.*	Total		Genuine		False	
	Albany	Long Lartin	Albany	Long Lartin	Albany	Long Lartin
1.	4	20	3	7	1	13
2.	4	19	4	7	0	12
3.	5	23	4	8	1	15
4.	6	22	4	6	2	16
5.	7	15	3	4	4	11
6.	3	20	2	8	1	12
7.	7	49	3	9	4	40
8.	5	17	2	4	3	13
9.	5	21	3	5	2	16
10.	5	36	1	6	4	30
11.	4	36	4	7	0	29
12.	9	23	3	4	6	19
Totals	64	301	36	75	28	226
Rate†	20.3	74.2	11.4	18.5	8.9	55.7

† Rate per 100 prisoners during twelve months studied.
* Albany data are for the calendar year 1988; Long Lartin data are for July 1987–June 1988

difference between the two prisons, the explanation for this finding may be partly at least in terms of opportunity. That is, it was much easier for a 'campanologist' to press an alarm bell falsely without being observed and detected at Long Lartin than at Albany. However, it also seems likely to us that a proportion of the recorded 'false alarms' were originally pressed in good faith either by prisoners or by staff. If so, this might perhaps suggest a higher level of anxiety among both parties on certain occasions in the more 'open' conditions at Long Lartin. It is also likely that 'false alarms' sometimes included situations in which something was indeed happening at the time the bell was pressed, but in which either the problem had been resolved by the time staff arrived, or the participants had scattered, or the bell presser (if a prisoner) did not want to make an issue of the matter once staff had arrived.

As may be seen from the bottom row of Table 7.4, when one allows for the difference in the size of the populations of the two prisons, the rate of 'genuine' alarms was in a ratio of approximately two at Albany to three at Long Lartin. However, as with

the same manner as for genuine alarms (see subsequent text), it rises from 8.9 (as shown in Table 7.4 to 11.2.

other statistical comparisons, a complicating feature here is the VPU at Albany, which produced many fewer alarm calls, just as it also produced many fewer disciplinary incidents (see Table 7.2). Although we cannot separate the Albany data in Table 7.4 into 'main' and VPU alarm calls, we do have other data which suggest that, at a time when the VPU was fully occupied, the 'main' prison produced 88 per cent of all genuine alarm calls from residential locations at Albany.[8]

If we apply this finding to the data for genuine alarm calls in Albany in Table 7.4,[9] and calculate a rate by reference to the population in A, B and C wings *only*, the Albany 'main' rate for genuine alarms in 1988 becomes 14.0 (in comparison with Long Lartin's 18.5). Thus, *the Long Lartin rate remains marginally higher*, notwithstanding that genuine alarm calls were mostly about assaults or fights (see above), and notwithstanding that Albany main prison's 'official' assault rate was higher than that of Long Lartin (see Tables 7.3 and 3.5, and note that both of these tables have rates for Albany calculated on a 'whole population' basis).

Neither the 'genuine' nor the 'false' alarm call data can be regarded as conclusive, but both clearly suggest that there might have been a higher level of 'backstage' activity in Long Lartin than was apparent from some of the more official indices of 'control problems'.

Medical Records

Davies (1982) interestingly suggested that some light could be thrown upon the hidden world of prisoner—prisoner violence by searching prison hospital records for evidence about prisoners' (otherwise unreported) injuries. We attempted to follow up this suggestion in our two prisons, although—in view of the fragmentary

[8] These data (for Albany only) are for the period July 1989 to July 1990. Alarm bell rates were by that date higher than those shown in Table 7.4, and were as follows: A, B, and C wings—73 genuine calls, 9 false calls; D and E wings—10 genuine calls, 1 false call; other locations—6 genuine calls, 6 false calls.

[9] This might be marginally charitable to the 'main' prison because—see note 4 to this chapter—the cells in the VPU were not in fact fully occupied during 1988, hence the true 1988 proportion of genuine alarms in the 'main' prison might have been higher than 88%. On the other hand (see note 9) the alarm bell rates were generally higher in 1989–90, and this increase could have occurred especially in the main prison, which (if true) would have affected the proportionate distribution between the main prison and the VPU.

nature of some of the hospital records—we cannot be confident that the data we obtained are wholly reliable.

The relevant data are shown in Table 7.5. They show only a small rate difference between the prisons as regard injuries to the hands.[10] Head injury data is perhaps a more appropriate data-source when looking for statistical indicators of 'dark figure' violence: hands can get injured accidentally more easily than heads, and head injuries are also more likely to be indicators of victimization than aggression. Hence, it is of interest that Long Lartin had a higher rate than Albany for head injuries (and this difference between the prisons remains even if one assumes that all the head injuries in Albany took place in the 'main' prison, and calculates rates accordingly: the Albany 'head injury rate' on this basis would be 4.4, still less than half as high as Long Lartin). Numbers are very small, and the data not necessarily very reliable; nevertheless, the data do (for what they are worth) again seem to be consistent with the hypothesis that there might be more 'backstage' violence at Long Lartin.

TABLE 7.5. A comparison of prisoners' injuries as shown in hospital records, Albany and Long Lartin 1988*

	Albany	Long Lartin*
Cuts, bruises, etc. to the head	10	39
Rate per 100 prisoners	3.2	9.5
Cuts, bruises, sprains, etc. to the hands	26	33
Rate per 100 prisoners	8.2	8.0

* Albany data are for calendar year 1988. Long Lartin data were collected for January–August 1988 *only*; they have been adjusted by a factor of 1.5 to provide comparability with Albany data (i.e., there were 26 head injury reports in eight months, shown here as an annual rate of 39).

Requests for Protection

Data on inmates' requests for protection under Rule 43 (see note 6 to this chapter) are shown in Table 7.6 for a twelvemonth period for each prison. In this table, since all the requests at Albany came

[10] Though if the rate for Albany is calculated on a 'main prison only' population basis (which will, of course, exaggerate the rate a little) it becomes 11.5.

TABLE 7.6. Segregation under Rule 43 (own request) in Albany and Long Lartin over a twelvemonth period*

	Albany	Long Lartin*
No. of prisoners making successful requests for 'own protection' (OP)	18	33
Rate per 100 prisoners of prisoners making OP requests	8.0	8.0
Times R43 (OP) used	20	52
Rate of R43 (OP) per 100 prisoners	8.8†	12.8
Average period spent in segregation	33 days	42 days

* For Albany, calendar year 1988; for Long Lartin, July 1987 to June 1988

† Calculated using population for A, B, and C wings only

from the main prison (it makes little sense to ask for protection under Rule 43 in a VPU), the rate shown for Albany is calculated in relation to the population of A, B, and C wings only.

The first point to note from Table 7.6 is that the overall rates of prisoners making 'own protection' (OP) requests was similar in the two prisons. This was so despite the facts that (1) Long Lartin had a more 'open' regime with more opportunities for placing pressure on vulnerable inmates, and (2) it also had a somewhat higher proportion of sex offenders in its population than Albany 'main' prison (see Table 3.4: the figures are respectively 12 per cent and 7 per cent). To that extent, Long Lartin could be reasonably satisfied with the data shown in Table 7.6. However, closer examination of the table shows also that there was a very different pattern, in the two prisons, between the total number of prisoners making requests and the total number of segregations. In Albany, 18 prisoners successfullly requested OP segregation, and only 20 OP orders were made—hence repeated OP stays in segregation were uncommon. In Long Lartin, however 33 prisoners produced no fewer than 52 OP segregations, an *average* of 1.6 each. Hence, the overall rate of OP segregations (as distinct from prisoners successfully making OP requests) was higher at Long Lartin than Albany, a rate difference that was attributable *solely* to 'repeat OP segregations'. All this suggests that, notwithstanding many of the successful features of

Long Lartin's open regime, there was a small group of prisoners who found the conditions extremely difficult to cope with, and required special protection from time to time. Such an interpretation is, of course, fully congruent with that which has emerged from the qualitative analysis (see for example chapter 5 and the data from specific interviews reported in this chapter).

We said at the beginning of this short final section to this chapter that the data to be considered could not be regarded as conclusive, but they might nevertheless help to confirm or otherwise our emerging interpretation of control problems in Albany and Long Lartin, an interpretation based primarily on the data from the specific interview sample. We reiterate that these quantitative data are in no sense definitive, but we believe that, all things considered, they strengthen and help to confirm the picture that has emerged from the specific interviews, and the surrounding ethnographic work based on general interviews and observation.

8
Movements from 'Normal Location'

Introduction

In this chapter we discuss the movement of prisoners from 'normal location' as an administrative device and control measure. The movement of prisoners is an area of deep controversy and contention between prisoners and staff. Most interventions which are available to prison authorities in response to emergent trouble—or as preventive measures—have to do with the movement of prisoners from place to place, whether within prisons (for example from wing to segregation unit) or between them. The suddenness of administrative segregations and transfers, and the traditional absence from them of due process, appeal or redress (all of which may seem vital to staff if such measures are going to fulfil their functions in emergencies) are among the grounds on which prisoners most often challenge the legitimacy of prison rules and administrative decisions. For these reasons the study of such movements is integral to the social analysis of prison control strategies, and of their consequences (be they intended or unintended, successful or counter-productive).

In this discussion we therefore consider movement from 'normal location' as a social process, whose dimensions include (1) the reasoning and decision making of prison managers at moments of incipient trouble; (2) the experience of such movements for the prisoners concerned; and (3) their further consequences for both parties.

Varieties of Movements

As we have seen in preceding chapters there are a number of social situations and events in dispersal prisons which are seen as constituting difficulties of control, some of which result from time to time in particular control 'incidents'. *Situations* (by which might be meant the formation of networks or groupings of prisoners regarded as in any way menacing or unstable) may however be regarded as very problematic by staff even where no *incident* as such has occurred. Incidents, on the other hand, may be isolated and momentary, and not clearly related to chronic control problems. Thus, drug dealing or gambling may be regarded as a primary control problem, even where it does not often result in specific 'incidents'. Something similar is recognizable in many more familiar settings: the fact that teenage John or Jane gets roaring drunk at a family wedding may by remarked upon by everyone (it is certainly an 'incident'), yet only be constructed as a 'problem' if it seems indicative of some latent unhappiness or incipient alcoholism.

Thus, the events which are seen as most serious, except by virtue of the sheer scale of injuries or damage which may result, tend to be those which are related to underlying problematic situations: the prison economy and its related competitions, systematic conflict between groups of prisoners, the continuing intractability or non-co-operation of some individuals, etc. Where a situation or incident is unresolved, or where staff or prisoners continue to experience tension or anxiety, Governors are presented with problems which may dispose them to take certain courses of action. The movement of one or more prisoners from their current 'normal location' whether temporarily or permanently, within the prison or to another one, is the primary power which Governors exercise in seeking to address the control problems which they confront. For this reason, the 'events' which we consider in this chapter are wider in definition than the specific recorded 'incidents' discussed in chapter 7, though they all fall within the definition of 'control problems' which we offered in chapter 3.

In considering possible control difficulties in their prisons, Governors have to make judgements about which of the options open to them is most likely to resolve the situation. In taking such decisions they have to take account of a number of considerations, which may be in tension with one another. These include, the security of the prison (i.e. breaches of the wall by persons getting *out* or drugs or weapons getting *in*); the stability of the prison; the views and feelings of staff; the nature and severity of the 'problem' as it appears to them and the quality of information which exists about it; the likely effectiveness of the action under consideration, including any possible adverse consequences, for example in the loss of goodwill from prisoners; the views of Prison Service Headquarters. Such decisions inherently raise problems of practical moral reasoning, consequences, and justifications.

We are concerned here primarily with the movement of prisoners at the Governor's discretion using administrative procedures, rather than periods of cellular confinement which are 'awarded' on adjudication within the formal disciplinary system (and which raise many further problems: cf. Maguire et al., 1985; Home Office (Prior Committee) 1985; Woolf, 1991; Livingstone and Owen, 1993).[1] As Woolf notes, amongst numerous others, those formal disciplinary mechanisms have themselves been continually controversial, given the rather draconian nature of the Governor's (and formerly the Board of Visitors') quasi-judicial powers, and their often-alleged departures from due process. But the scope of *administrative* powers to move or segregate, whilst no less controversial, has received less clear social analysis (King and McDermott, 1990, provide something of an exception). In any case, the boundary between these realms is far from sharp, as we shall see (not least given the catch-all nature of some disciplinary offences under Rule 47 (classically paragraph 21—'in any way offends against good order and discipline')).

The administrative movement of prisoners on control grounds may assume one of several forms:

Inter-wing movements: This is perhaps the mildest and least controversial measure under discussion, and it requires no special mechanism or procedure. Prisoners are sometimes moved from wing to wing, often following an adjudication or incident, as a prudential step. Inter-wing moves are one way in which prison managers may attempt to redistribute the population in what they see as beneficial ways, such as by breaking up particular groups, friendships or enmities, or by placing ethnic or linguistic minorities together. Because they are moves *between* normal locations, interwing transfers are rarely seen as punitive by the staff, although they are sometimes felt as such by prisoners.

---

[1] Data on punishments awarded for disciplinary offences in Albany and Long Lartin in 1987–8 are shown in Table 3.6 in ch. 3.

Rule 43 (GOAD): Prison Rule 43 has historically been perhaps the most often invoked, but also most contentious, administrative control mechanism in English prisons. Rule 43 provides that:

Where it appears desirable, for the maintenance of good order and discipline or in his own interests, that a prisoner should not associate with other prisoners, either generally or for particular purposes, the Governor may arrange for the prisoner's removal from association accordingly.

This comparatively anodyne form of words conceals a history of deep conflict, not least because the term 'removal from association' has usually meant confinement in the segregation unit for twenty-three hours a day under conditions approximately as severe as those imposed upon prisoners undergoing 'cellular confinement' as punishment.[2] Thus, whilst all advice to Governors has stressed that the use of Rule 43 for the purposes of good order and discipline (GOAD) is to be regarded as a purely preventive measure, it has none the less been experienced by many prisoners as a directly punitive (if not vindictive) one. This ambiguity was not much clarified by the outcome of this aspect of the litigation in *Hague*,[3] in which the courts did not accept either that the prisoner was entitled to a hearing in order to respond to reasons given for his segregation or that the Governor was under any obligation to prefer bringing a formal disciplinary charge over the use of Rule 43 even where he had reason to think that an offence had already been committed under Rule 47 (see Livingstone and Owen, 1993: 218–23). The reasons underlying the use of Rule 43 probably remain as various as they have ever been and it remains a deeply vexed measure, even if the latitude of Governors' discretion has latterly been somewhat diminished under Circular Instruction 37/1990.[4] Because the cases

---

[2] The then Chief Inspector of Prisons, Sir James Hennessy, commented in 1985 that conditions in segregation units 'can entail living under an impoverished and monotonous regime which may even be psychologically harmful' (HM Chief Inspector of Prisons, 1985).

[3] *R v. Deputy Governor of Parkhurst Prison ex parte Hague* [1992] 1 AC 67.

[4] CI 37/1990 (amended in 1991 to take account of Woolf's general principle that reasons should be given for decisions, especially where their impact upon the prisoner is adverse) asserted *inter alia* that the regime imposed upon prisoners undergoing Rule 43 should be 'as balanced and well integrated' with the rest of the prison as the preservation of good order allows and that prisoners should be given reasons for their segregation in writing 'as soon as possible or at the latest within 24 hours' (CI 37/1990, para. 15). CI 26/1990 also *extended* the period after which authorization for continued segregation must be sought from one day to three. Whilst this looked like a marked increase in the Governor's powers Livingstone and Owen point out

of the use of Rule 43 differ greatly, so do rationales brought to bear by Governors. We consider some of these later, before going on to detail some prisoners' responses to the experience of Rule 43.

Temporary Transfers: Governors of dispersal prisons have for many years had the authority to transfer a prisoner immediately to a cell set aside for the purpose in a local prison as an emergency measure. At the time of our study this power was exercised under Circular Instruction 10/1974 and this, although applied to many fewer people than Rule 43 (GOAD), was if anything still more controversial. CI 10/74 stated:

The purpose of this facility offered to dispersal governors is to provide a brief 'cooling off' period for a trouble maker who needs to be removed from normal location because of an imminently explosive situation caused by either his actual or impending disruptive behaviour, and for whom placement in the segregation unit is inappropriate or impracticable, either because the prisoner would still be able to exercise a disruptive influence from the segregation unit . . . or because the extent to which the prisoner provides a focal point for prisoner unrest would mean that the mere act of placement in the segregation unit could have a provocative and explosive effect on the rest of the establishment.

We found a good deal of evidence in our study (on which see further below) that the tepid language of 'cooling off' was sometimes markedly at variance with prisoners' reactions to the 10/74 procedure, and indeed that that measure was prone to more varied uses. It was, for example, not infrequently a prelude to a permanent transfer. Equally, it was well-known amongst both staff and prisoners throughout the dispersal system that certain prisoners (not many, but their reputations travelled before them wherever they went) were made subject to several 10/74s in quick succession (a phenomenon known to prisoners as the 'Ghost train' or 'the magic roundabout' and to staff as a principle of 'shared misery'), sometimes without emerging from segregation between whiles. Numerous uncertainties thus came to surround 10/74 as a measure. Was it to be thought of as an expedient administrative device, or as a punishment, or as a deterrent, or (as seems more likely) as an

that the prisoner would now usually be in possesssion of written reasons before any such extension arises. Whilst there is no *right* to a hearing there is now an expectation that the prisoner will be seen and his views sought; and failure either to provide reasons or to speak with the prisoner may result in a successful application for judicial review (Livingstone and Owen, 1993: 226).

uneasy amalgam of all of these, depending on whose perspective one adopted? Certainly there were numerous occasions on which prisoners did not 'go quietly', and it was not uncommon for a prisoner being sent on a 'lie-down' to be carried from the prison under physical restraint.[5] By the time our fieldwork ended CI 10/74 had become a very controversial measure. The Court of Appeal's decision in *Hague* followed soon after, in which it was held the *assumption* that prevailed under 10/74 that the prisoner would remain in segregation throughout his 28-day 'lie-down' bypassed the expectation that continued segregation in the new prison must be specifically approved by relevant authorities in that prison (see Livingstone and Owen, 1993: 222; Loucks, 1993: 103). Circular Instruction 10/1974 was wholly superseded by Circular Instruction 37/1990 which provided *inter alia* that decisions to transfer must be reasoned; that those reasons must be provided in writing if requested; that temporary transfer should not be used in place of a formal charge; and that segregation at the local prison should not be automatic. This measure was in turn replaced by Circular Instruction 28/1993, which extended the power of immediate temporary transfer to all Category B training prisons. Both of these alterations moved the temporary transfer system in the direction of greater formality and central co-ordination; but in so doing they confirm that temporary transfer remains an important control strategy, and a very sensitive one.

Plainly the replacement of CI 10/74 removed some of the more flagrantly discretionary aspects of the former position, and hence perhaps some of the scope for perverse outcomes. Nevertheless it is certainly arguable that space remains for conflict between the claims of managerial expediency (the view that there must be provision for an emergency transfer measure) and those of procedural justice.[6] To this extent some at least of the issues that arise from our interviews in this chapter remain current, despite formal procedural changes since the date of our fieldwork.

[5] Equally, there were no small number of allegations by the prisoners concerned that they would be met by 'reception committees' when they arrived at their destinations. Some of the more serious claims of outright brutality made by prisoners centred on either end of the journey taken in the course of a 10/74.

[6] See in this regard the evidence submitted to the Woolf Inquiry by Professor Roy King. King argued *inter alia* that there should be a disciplinary hearing before any transfer and that such transfers of this kind should be planned. Woolf responded by affirming the continuing need for an emergency procedure, albeit with improved procedural safeguards (1991, paras. 12.255–12.260).

Permanent Transfers: The permanent transfer of prisoners on control grounds shares with temporary transfer under Circular Instructions the fact the prisoner is physically removed from a given prison. In this respect the two raise similar issues, and we will discuss them in close conjunction. The key difference is that both CI 10/74 and its successors as emergency measures provide the Governor of a dispersal prison with the capacity to remove a prisoner immediately and without prior external consultation. Permanent transfers on the other hand involve negotiations (sometimes rather elaborate ones) with fellow Governors, Area Managers, and with the relevant sections in Prison Service Headquarters. Under these circumstances it is unsurprising that temporary transfer was sometimes used as a preliminary to a permanent move—it was much quicker and could be presented as a *fait accompli*. Permanent transfers have a different legal status from the special provisions of Circular Instructions; but this may sometimes have the twin advantages to the Governor of a dispersal prison that (1) the prisoner goes away for good and (2) it may not be necessary to acknowledge that this is being done specifically as a control measure. Thus, for example, when the discretion of the authorities to transfer a prisoner has been challenged in the courts it was held that decision makers should have due regard to the prisoner's personal circumstances but that 'operational and security reasons' supervened, into which the court declined to inquire.[7] This suggests that, although more cumbersome, permanent transfer in fact escapes some of the procedural limitations to which more specialized measures may be subject.

Transfer to a Special Unit: A further measure available to Governors is to propose a prisoner as a candidate for one of the 'special units' established in the wake of the Control Review Committee's report (1984). At the time of the commencement of our fieldwork, the units at Parkhurst and Lincoln were already open, and candidates were being assessed for the unit at Hull. The specific contributions of special units to the orderliness or otherwise of the long-term prison system are beyond the scope of the present study (but see chapter 1; see also Home Office, 1984; Bottomley and Hay, 1991; Walmsley, 1991; Bottomley et al., 1994). It is integral to the principle of 'special' units that they are reserved for a

[7] In *R* v *Secretary of State for the Home Department ex parte McAvoy* [1984] 1 WLR 1408.

small number of the most persistently 'difficult' or 'intractable' individuals (on differences of view over the making of such assessments see Williams and Longley, 1987 and King and McDermott, 1990). It has not been uncommon for Governors to complain of difficulty and delay in having 'their' candidates accepted for the units. Whilst there may be some basis for this perception, and the numbers of prisoners who have passed through the special units has by definition been small, they remain at the time of writing one component of the patchwork of control strategies.[8]

Prison managers characteristically describe the courses open to them in terms of their appropriateness to an ascending scale of the seriousness or intractability of problems. To move a prisoner between wings is not so large a step as to place him on Rule 43 (GOAD). In turn, to segregate the prisoner is not so large a step as to remove him from the prison altogether, whether temporarily or permanently. In each case a threshold of some kind has to be passed before particular actions are deemed appropriate. Governors are also conscious, amongst other considerations, of a need not to be seen to be overusing their powers, not least because some of the measures open to them rely on reciprocity with their counterparts in other prisons.

One question which arises with regard to each of these measures concerns the consistency or otherwise of their use. On the one hand discretionary and administrative measures are *designed* to be used flexibly as circumstances are seen to demand. Yet, as we have seen, consistency is one of the chief terms that prisoners use to assess the fairness or legitimacy of the treatment they receive. Prison managers often seek to avoid undue inconsistency, whether on principle or from fear of inciting an adverse reaction. If it turns out that the measures in question are used in varying ways, this poses certain problems for the justifications offered for their use; and it may increase the scope for the sense of grievance among prisoners (not least since many of those who do experience these measures personally already have extensive knowledge of their use elsewhere in the system). There is thus an extensive set of considerations that the

---

[8] The unit at Lincoln has since closed, and has been replaced by one at Woodhill prison in Milton Keynes. Woodhill also houses a Special Assessment Unit whose functions include both (1) the attempt to make allocation to Special Units more systematic, and (2) to answer Governors' complaints that they have been unable to transfer prisoners into the special unit sub-system sufficiently speedily.

Governor of a dispersal prison must take into account in deciding how to address the problem that he or she perceives.

In the remainder of this chapter we will examine the use of each of these kinds of measure, drawing on examples and illustrations from our fieldwork. We will compare the problems of decision making that confront prison managers with prisoners' experiences of the other face of these measures.

Movement as Control

Movements between wings

The movement of prisoners between wings is the least drastic and controversial form of 'control movement' available. It is a movement *between* normal locations rather than a movement *from* normal location. Thus, although it may be considered disruptive or uncalled for by prisoners, it is not usually considered detrimental enough to arouse strong protest. It is often thought of by managers as purely precautionary. For example, it was a well-established policy, at Albany in particular, to move one or other prisoner to another wing on return from the segregation unit following a fight. In such cases some controversy might result if it was the perceived 'victim' who was moved, because prisoners dislike any measure being taken 'against' them if they do not accept that they have done anything to 'deserve' it. As is generally the case with administrative control measures, problems can arise when the prison and the prisoner are speaking different languages: the prisoner uses a vocabulary which is mainly about justice, whilst managers use a vocabulary which is mainly about prudence and practicality. These problems may arise in particular where different wings within the prison are perceived as having differing characteristics in terms of either regimes or populations, so that the move may be construed as specifically punitive. Moreover, prisoners are sometimes moved because they are thought to be 'keeping bad company'; this is often a bone of some contention because prisoners may attribute such transfers to the prison's 'paranoia' in interpreting groups of friends as 'cliques' or 'power groups'. On the other hand, a proportion of inter-wing moves in our study were at least partly voluntary, especially in Long Lartin where prisoners could apply to move wings as a relatively formalized matter of course. Equally, prisoners who were felt to have been misplaced on a particular wing because of personality, offence or language difficulties, might be moved to another wing in order to try again. The high concentration of Asian prisoners on one wing at Albany was an outcome of such a practice.

Rule 43 GOAD (Managerial Perspectives)

The Governor of Albany described the considerations relevant to a decision to use Rule 43 GOAD, including a reluctance to see the measure imposed unnecessarily:

I try to get staff to look for specific things that offend against the discipline code, because I think it's better to have an instance in which the bloke clearly offended [so that] punishment will be accepted as reasonable. I believe that Boards of Visitors and politicians are very worried about the Prison Department's use of Rule 43 GOAD. I keep telling everybody here that there might well come a day when there's a very big political battle about this. So we'd better make sure that wherever humanly possible, if a bloke is in bad trouble, to get him on report for refusing an order, or abuse. Let's try and have a momentary halt in life, but if that's not possible, and it's slipping very quickly, and it looks very dangerous to the stability of the place and somebody might get injured, then I'm prepared to say, 'Rule 43, GOAD'. I've done it today.

(Governor I, Albany)

Evidently the Governor of Albany is pointing here to a feeling that extensive discretionary powers are necessary, but politically and legally controversial. This imposes restraint in their use, and a preference for disciplinary action where possible. On this logic the administrative use of segregation only becomes appropriate where the formal disciplinary code has been exhausted, or where the matter is so urgent as to call for immediate intervention. Equally, as well as using the disciplinary system as such, this also suggests the need for continuing attempts at persuasion, negotiation, and other informal means of influence before administrative segregation becomes unavoidable. Moreover, from a managerial point of view, even once a prisoner has been placed on Rule 43 GOAD and is in the segregation unit, effort is required to get him out again, and this necessitates a continuing attempt at resolution—on terms acceptable to the prison—whether simply as a result of the passage of time, or as a result of undertakings given by the prisoner, or through a positive change in his circumstances (a change of wing or workshop, for example). Clearly Rule 43 looks formally like an incapacitative (or 'situational') measure. But it is also, for practical purposes, a compliance strategy: once Rule 43 has been invoked the prison and the prisoner are embarked upon a negotiation over the terms on which he may come out. Rule 43 is thus sometimes thought of as a sort of bargaining counter or method of 'leverage' in a process of negotiation with the prisoner, even if from the prisoner's perspective it may resemble blackmail rather than dialogue. Nevertheless (indeed partly for this reason) some prisoners remain on Rule 43 for very extended periods without mutually acceptable resolution. For a fraction of these the segregation unit can become, in effect, their 'normal' location, in which case (ironically but not infrequently) the prisoner's refusal, or reluctance or inability to *leave* segregation becomes 'the problem'.

The Governor of Albany provides an illustration of the process within which a decision to use Rule 43 GOAD may be embedded. These include negotiation, and the attempt to pre-empt possible escalation, whilst leaving open the possibility of some form of settlement:

Twice he'd refused to work. We did all the talking in the wing and all the persuading we could, to try to get him to say that under certain conditions he would. He didn't, and threatened what he would do. We also know that he went round trying to threaten and intimidate other prisoners into group activity, and political activity against the system. People could have been hurt. I don't think he's made any accommodating noises whilst he's been in the block. So I've put him on Rule 43, trying to use it as a negotiating point with him, and to say 'until you give some signs that you're prepared to meet us in some ways, I'm going to lock you up, because I think you're dangerous'.

(Governor I, Albany)

In certain cases, Governors also recognize that the excessive or inappropriate or continued use of Rule 43, however much they regard the measure as a necessary one, can become counter-productive. This may be because it is part of a spiral of deteriorating relations between the prisoner and the prison, or because it results in a situation in which a prisoner who is in any case having difficulty 'settling' on normal location is, by virtue of being in the segregation unit 'on a continual wind-up, living in a punishment unit', as the Governor of Long Lartin put it. Or it may simply mean that the segregation unit is constantly full:

GOAD only really solves a problem if it either persuades the inmate to stop mucking about or leads to him being transferred away. If neither of those things happen you end up with him under your feet in the segregation unit, and you can only do that a few times. We keep getting lifers who don't want to be here . . . who will, if we let them, become long-term inhabitants down there . . . If people don't make efforts to empty the seg. then sooner or later it will become totally blocked and there won't be room for anyone else.

(Governor IV, Long Lartin)

On a manifest level the benefits and problems associated with Rule 43, and the considerations relevant to its use, are described in similar terms by managers in Albany and Long Lartin. However, it would appear from the data in Table 8.1 that there are some empirical differences in practice.

TABLE 8.1. A comparison of segregation under Rule 43 (GOAD) in Albany and Long Lartin over a twelvemonth period*

	Albany	Long Lartin
No. of prisoners segregated	42	57
Rate of prisoners segregated per 100 prisoners	13.3	14.1
Times R43 GOAD used	46	66
Rate of GOAD use per 100 prisoners	14.5	16.3
Duration of segregation (in days)		
0– 10	5	36
11– 20	5	14
21– 30	7	1
31– 40	6	1
41– 50	5	2
51– 60	3	3
61– 70	2	1
71– 80	3	1
81– 90	4	2
91–100	0	0
101–150	4	2
151–200	1	2
201+	1	1
Total	46	66
(Average no. of days)	(55)	(28)

A number of points of interest arise from Table 8.1. First, the absolute level of use of Rule 43 GOAD in both prisons is rather high: nearly one in seven prisoners in each prison was so segregated in a twelvemonth period. From the prisoner's point of view, this is a substantial risk level, and helps to explain some of the feelings that were generated about this procedure.[9] Secondly, there was not much difference between the two prisons in the overall frequency with which Rule 43 GOAD was used (Albany's marginally lower rate rises if one corrects for the existence of the VPU, with its lower rates on all 'control problems', but reaches only 20.4 even if one makes the assumption that *all* administrative segregation in Albany was from the main prison). Thirdly, and perhaps of greatest interest, it is apparent from Table 8.1 that the largest difference between the two prisons is that the great majority of those made subject to Rule 43 GOAD in Long Lartin (50 out of 66, or 76 per cent) remained in segregation for 20 days or less at a time, whereas at Albany the corresponding figure was only 10 out of 46 (22 per cent). Both prisons on the other hand had a small number of people who remained for *very* long periods of over 100 days.

How should one explain Long Lartin's more pronounced use of short-term GOAD? It seems to us that there are three possible explanations:

1. Long Lartin was, for whatever reason, more 'successful' in returning people to normal location sooner;

2. Albany was more sparing in its use of Rule 43 for problems which could be resolved within a relatively short period of time;

3. Long Lartin transferred more of its potential long-term Rule 43 'candidates' out of the prison sooner, whether temporarily or permanently.

We were unable to resolve this issue empirically; each of the three explanations may well have been true in varying degrees. However, it is worth noting that Long Lartin had six 'normal location' wings, whereas Albany had only three 'main' wings and two 'vulnerable' wings. It would thus have been much easier logistically for Long Lartin to take people out of segregation by trying to place them on another wing (though the degree of freedom of movement by prisoners at Long Lartin perhaps lessened the effectiveness of

[9] Note however that the data for 'number of prisoners segregated' and 'times R43 GOAD used' differ only slightly: hence repeated use of Rule 43 on the same prisoner was rare (though other measures, notably temporary or permanent transfer, might of course be used). Compare in this respect the data for R43 (OP) in Long Lartin: see Table 7.6.

inter-wing transfers as a control measure). Equally, it seems at least possible that there was some relationship between the policy of the prison as regards disciplinary or 'control' transfers with other prisons (see further below) and its use of Rule 43 GOAD. To this extent the import of each of these 'administrative' control measures can only be properly understood in relation to one another.

Rule 43 GOAD (*Prisoners' Perspectives*)

Prisoners' objections to Rule 43 GOAD were roughly of two kinds. First, they argued that it is emotionally destructive, especially in that the individual may not know with any certainty why he has been segregated. Second, they contended that it offended against natural justice or fairness. These issues were often in practice connected, in that the sense of injustice exacerbates the stress of isolation. Thus, one prisoner at Albany expressed a degree of uncertainty as to why he was on Rule 43:

There's got to be some justification for being here . . . They've got to explain to me why they're trying to make me out to be a nutter or something when I'm not . . . At times it seems they're setting me up or framing me up. Why don't they come out to my face and tell me these things? I can't see an end to it, but what can I do?

Prisoners without recent personal experience of Rule 43 may take a view which is more straightforward and abstract:

They put you on this GOAD and there is no recourse to it. It is a right of the prison to put you on it. It was done to Bloggs who was asking for extra visiting orders. The Governor gets intimidated if you ask him a question and he has no answer to it. Once you come into these places you haven't got any rights.

One prisoner at Long Lartin who had very extensive experience of Rule 43 GOAD made a number of distinct, but connected and important points. In the first place, he argued, in the absence of successful 'negotiation' the prisoner may find it preferable to remain in the block:

One of the fundamental reasons why I spent so long in solitary confinement was that I felt that my dignity and self-respect had been under attack, and in many ways I felt that probably the segregation unit, which was a very spartan environment, was somewhere where I could retain some degree of dignity. At least they would leave me alone. For the purpose of

long-term survival I had to retain some degree of individuality, because if
that went, really it would be a form of death.

Nevertheless, he suffered from the feeling of not knowing why this
was happening:

All the time I'd been placed in segregation I'd never been told *why* I was
there. I felt that I was being victimized. I was being given no reason. And
basically I felt that any concept of natural justice as far as I was concerned
had been thrown out of the window. So I started to protest . . .

Interestingly, however, this prisoner, at the end of a particularly long
and bitter experience of Rule 43, did not completely condemn the
measure, but rather asked for more stringent safeguards on its use:

I'm not condemning the use of measures which in their eyes have got some
legitimacy. All I'm saying is that there should be some inbuilt procedures
and some degree of natural justice should apply when they're taking these
measures. Because they're no small measures. To lock somebody down in
solitary confinement for years on end, which is a direct violation of anybody's human rights—it's no small measure. There *must* be some sort of
safeguard for that person's rights. There are none whatsoever at the
moment.

As we have seen, since our fieldwork there have been procedural
improvements to the use of GOAD, notably as regards the giving
of reasons (see note 4 to this chapter). The procedure, however,
retains some strongly discretionary features and it seems unlikely
that in the eyes of prisoners it is now seen as fully just.

Temporary Transfers (Managerial Perspectives)

If the decision to use Rule 43 GOAD is difficult and sometimes
counter-productive, the use of temporary transfers under Circular
Instructions is perhaps still more complex and problematic. One
Governor grade articulated what we may describe as an orthodox
view on the appropriate application of CI 10/74 (as it then was) in
the following terms:

We think very critically about using it when we do. If we remove someone
from normal association and he then continues to pose a threat, either by
virtue of his influence on other people in the segregation unit, or because he
is still in communication with other parts of the prison etc., then he would
go. It's usually to do with group activities rather than individual. . . .

(Grade IV, Albany)

There are several clear implications here. First, on this view 10/74 was to be resorted to after other solutions had been tried, including the removal of the prisoner from normal location on Rule 43. Second, it was a measure whose primary application was to those regarded as 'troublemakers' or 'subversives' or 'leaders' and whose continued presence anywhere in the prison was felt to be destabilizing. On the other hand the same individual, having just stated his belief in the necessity of the measure, went on to describe some of its related problems:

People used to get sent on lie-downs for lots of spurious reasons. When you have the power to determine whether prisoners stay or go it becomes an excuse for not doing an awful lot of other things . . . It's a fatal power to have, because it means that people never bother to tackle anything.

This is the argument that prisons should 'consume their own smoke' in its pure form. Most Governors' comments accepted in some degree a tension between what they saw as the necessity of the power to remove a prisoner suddenly from the prison, and the propensity for a useful measure to be overused. To this extent many of their comments on rationales for using CI 10/74 also took the form of defining and delimiting the 'proper' circumstances in which it should be used. Thus, the Governor of Albany seemed to suggest that the principal, if not the *only*, reason for invoking the 10/74 procedure concerned the likely reactions of others to an individual's continued presence, rather than, for example, an attempt to modify the individual's behaviour. Thus, the decision was not taken on the spur of the moment; other means were to be tried first; and the use of temporary transfer was only justified by its effectiveness in staving off probable widespread trouble. For example, the Governor alluded to the fact that there had been no 10/74s from Albany in the six months prior to our interview (see below, Table 8.2):

I realize that for a few months we haven't sent many people on 10/74, but I haven't had the feeling that there's been a groundswell to have mass indiscipline, and therefore it's not been necessary . . . there was a time if you were going to put an IRA bloke down the block, you *had* to send him away, because all the others would either come flooding down or they would get involved in an incident. They haven't been doing that, in fact they've been doing just the opposite . . . Similarly, Bloggs has been away twice. I've had him on a piece of string, because I knew he didn't want to work and was finding every reason why he shouldn't. Yet if I didn't ensure that he was challenged with work, there would be a whole range of other blokes who'd see themselves as aspiring top robbers who'd try and do the same thing . . . There was a time when I'd been a bit worried that [he] would start smashing things up on the wing. But it hasn't happened.

Q   Is that why he's still here?

A   Yes.

Not everyone takes such a strategic or purist view. One manager, for example, in reply to a question about administrative powers versus considerations of justice and due process presented a strongly utilitarian argument:

This is a difficult argument, because in a place such as this sometimes you have to act quickly. And then I'm a firm believer that the rights of the majority take precedence over the rights of one or two individuals . . . I think ultimately you have to look at the greater good. For example, I transferred a couple of life sentence prisoners out of here which has probably been prejudicial to their careers, but it's protected the careers of a greater number of lifers. I feel sometimes you have to sacrifice someone to protect the regime for the majority, and I have no regrets about so doing.

(Grade V, Long Lartin)

This view is also quite close to that of many uniformed staff who tended to stress the use of the 'lie-down' in providing respite for staff and other prisoners from the presence of individuals whom they found troublesome. Uniformed staff were more likely than governor grades to argue that the 10/74 procedure could be used more frequently and that some prisoners should not return. Such views arose directly from the problems which staff confront in dealing on a daily basis with prisoners in troublesome situations, and they gave voice to a sense of frustration. They thus sometimes did not differentiate sharply between 10/74 and other transfers:

As far as I'm concerned I can't prove it. He's already been placed on report for dealing in LSD and heroin, and he's still at it. I would then say, 'if you don't stop it you know what the consequences are', and if he didn't stop it then ghost him. I'm not saying it's right and I understand that, but you must also expect that a person like me is not going to do that on a vindictive basis, and I'm not going to abuse it. Before we reach the point where I would ask for somebody to be 10/74'd the indications would be very strong, and it would be a tool that I can use to help to defuse a potentially difficult situation.

(senior officer, Long Lartin)

Another senior officer in Long Lartin presented a similar argument:

Q   From a prisoner's point of view, they might see action based on suspicion, without hard evidence, as being illegitimate and unjust. What
would your view be on that?

A   I've got to survive as well as they have. I can sympathize with it, certainly. If you can get a written agreement and they'll follow it all the
time and play the game clean, then so will I. But that's not always
going to happen. So I don't see why I should be the only one playing
the game cleanly.

Or again, in response to the same question, an Albany principal
officer insisted upon the need for pre-emptive action, irrespective of
considerations of justice and evidence, to prevent among other
things conflict between prisoners:

You can't do it any other way. Otherwise you'd finish in anarchy. At the
end of the day the prisoner would be the sufferer because their justice is
not down the block and seven days remission, their justice is a bottle of
scalding water.

Meanwhile, wing staff found prisoners who appeared to them to be
both recalcitrant or litigious and aggressive extremely wearing, and
articulated their need for a break from such people. Thus, the same
principal officer argued:

[He] is a persistent pain in the arse, continually fighting the system. He
produces little work, tries to take the smaller person on and agitates. In his
case it's a twenty-eight day relief for staff in the wing.

All the arguments made out in support of temporary transfer concern *realpolitik* problems. As the viewpoints summarized above
indicate, such measures are called for, and indeed used, in a wide
range of different circumstances; and the vehemence and violence
aroused in some of the situations in question bears little relation to
the mild language of 'cooling-off periods' of official formulations.
Moreover, the fact that the 10/74 procedure was often invoked following specific events, quite apart from the conditions in which it
was undergone, tended to mean that as far as both prisoners and
staff were concerned it was being used punitively, whatever its
overt justifications.

The Governor of Long Lartin expressed a number of the dilemmas and difficulties involved in the 10/74 procedure:

It's something which used to go very much against the grain for me,
because there's a degree of 'I know he's at it but I haven't really got

enough evidence to do him for it, so I'll lift him anyway.' But if you get all worried about justice and evidence and all that stuff then I think you're in trouble with 10/74s . . . Now, whether they need to go on a 10/74 or to another prison or just to normal local population, that I think is arguable, but I would just go back, in terms of justification, to the original Radzinowicz comment that nobody should apologize for having to move people out, either into seg units, or into other prisons, in order to maintain what it is that he believed you could create in a prison . . . and I think that is part of the balancing act that you do . . . There comes a time when you've just got to get them out of the way, and it can be seen, it *is* seen, as unjust . . . But it may not be a lot to do with justice. I just have to live with it.

(Governor I, Long Lartin)

At the level of general justifications, both Governors connected temporary transfer to the problem of dealing with the wider prospective implications of certain situations or dynamics which they identified as emerging within the prison. However, it may well be that the identification of such situations, and hence the practical application of the procedures varied between the two prisons. This could have resulted from differences in the emergent situations themselves, or from different emphases within managerial philosophies or styles, or from differences in the structural positions of Albany and Long Lartin within the dispersal system.

Some of these structural features included the following. There was a general presumption from the point of many prisoners and staff that Long Lartin was a more favoured location than Albany by reason of geography and reputation, even if this was not an officially shared perception. This had a number of informal but real consequences:

1. At Long Lartin staff of all grades, and some prisoners were inclined to argue that it should be considered an 'honour' prison, and that therefore continued presence there should be in some sense deserved and/or that prisoners (whatever their past reputations), who wanted to come to Long Lartin in order to 'settle' or 'behave' should have the opportunity to do so. They consequently tended to argue that people who crossed certain boundaries or threatened to 'spoil' this opportunity for others should in effect 'forfeit' their right to remain and should be summarily removed.

2. Long Lartin staff also argued, in connection with their desire to retain an 'open' or 'liberal' regime, that circumstances at Long

Lartin necessarily permitted more opportunities to disrupt the routine or exploit other prisoners and that the prison should therefore act promptly in expelling people who continually did this.

3. In consequence Long Lartin staff further argued for the deterrent value of the 10/74 procedure in as much as they assumed that prisoners' rational self-interest would make them want to remain in Long Lartin, and hence temper their activities accordingly. Uniformed staff in particular thus felt that the 10/74 procedure should be readily and visibly available to them.

4. Conversely, Albany was conscious of having been traditionally regarded as an unfavourable location. The 'deterrent' value of the 'lie-down', especially when it involved a prisoner going to a London prison, was thus viewed as more problematic. Albany managers were thus careful with regard to the perceived danger of 'rewarding bad behaviour' by the use of temporary transfer.

5. Moreover, and in contrast to Long Lartin, justifications for the 'controlled' regime at Albany revolved around its success in minimizing opportunities for disruption. To this extent, if the regime was to be seen to be 'working', occasions when it was necessary to remove people from the prison should be reduced.

6. Meanwhile, the proximity of Albany to Parkhurst (another dispersal prison, immediately adjacent to Albany) made possible a whole alternative policy, involving fairly frequent movements in both directions. It was possible for the two prisons to exchange prisoners on what were formally not disciplinary transfers. It was thus easier, and arguably more satisfactory, to remove a prisoner from Albany segregation unit to Parkhurst than to send him on 10/74 to the segregation unit of a distant local prison.

There were thus a number of reasons for anticipating that Albany might be more constrained in its use of 10/74 than Long Lartin. What does the empirical evidence actually show?

Table 8.2 indicates that both prisons used the 10/74 mechanism fewer times in 1988 than 1987. Overall, Long Lartin sent more men away both absolutely and relative to the total population. However, as with previous tables, this is a misleading comparison since no one was sent from the VPU at Albany, and when the total figures are calculated relative to the main population in each prison, the total rate of use for the two prisons was in fact similar. This simple rate calculation, however, does not give the full pic-

TABLE 8.2. A comparison of CI 10/74s for Albany and Long Lartin in 1987 and 1988

| | | Albany | | Long Lartin | |
		1987	1988	1987	1988
Jan.		—	3	1	1
Feb.		2	—	3	1
Mar.		3	1	3	—
Apr.		2	—	3	3
May		1	5	—	1
June		—	—	3	2
July		3	1	2	4
Aug.		4	1	1	2
Sept.		—	—	2	2
Oct.		—	—	2	—
Nov.		—	—	2	1
Dec.		—	—	3	1
Total		15	11	25	18
Rate per 100 prisoners (whole prison)		5.0	3.5	6.3	4.4
Rate per 100 prisoners (main prison only)		6.6	4.9	n/a	n/a
Prisoners returned:	No.	11	9	11	(*)
	%	73	82	44	(*)

(*) No data available for full year: 8 out of 12 (67%) returned to end July.

ture. At least part of the point of the use of 10/74 was the symbolic message it conveyed to the other inmates and to the staff in the prison, and in this respect two other aspects of Table 8.2 are particularly worth noting. First, Long Lartin's use of 10/74 was more *regular*—there were only 3 of these 24 months when no one was sent on 10/74, as against 13 out of 24 months at Albany (whilst by contrast 5 men, or nearly 20% of the two-yearly total, were sent from Albany in one month, May 1988). Secondly, more of those who were sent from Albany returned there (see bottom row of table). It thus remains possible that Long Lartin management were prepared to invoke 10/74 more willingly and for a wider range of purposes.

The greater irregularity of use of 10/74 at Albany also gave rise to a curious situation for our research, in that the four month period in each prison in which we sought to do detailed analysis and 'specific interviews' (see chapter 7) yielded samples of ten cases in Long Lartin (April–July, 1988) but none in Albany (September–December, 1988).

Our interpretation is that Long Lartin used CI 10/74 more regularly, and with fewer prisoners returning because the prison found it more useful in pursuit of the kind of order they were seeking, and met fewer constraints in doing so. Long Lartin were thus more likely to use the procedure for a wider range of purposes and to call on more diverse justifications for invoking it. By contrast, Albany appeared to tend to restrict their use of the measure to a more limited set of conditions involving impending serious disturbance. (They may have used it for other reasons as well, but infrequently.)

These data are best read alongside the information on the use of Rule 43 (GOAD) (see Table 8.1). Here it will be recalled that Albany made greater proportionate use of longer-term segregation. It would seem that a number of possible 'candidates' for 10/74 (i.e. people who might have been 10/74'd from Long Lartin) remained at Albany in segregation on Rule 43 (GOAD). That is, they were in effect being 'laid-down' in the block rather than in another prison, or alternatively they may have been transferred to Parkhurst.

These conjectures and inferences from Table 8.2 are best illuminated using qualitative examples, drawn from specific interview data. The perspectives included here incorporate both Governors' descriptions of their decision making and rationales, and prisoners'accounts of their experiences of 10/74.

The following cases provide illustrations of some of the various events in which people were made subject to 10/74 in Long Lartin. Some of these events are also related to the incidents summarized in chapter 7:

Case 1. The victim of the attack in incident LL1 (see chapter 7) was eventually sent on 10/74 following his involvement in a demonstrative act of protest in the segregation unit (incident LL2). Three other people were also sent on 10/74 in connection with these events, all of them members of the victim's 'side'. All returned. This seems to represent a fairly 'classic' case of the procedure being used as some sort of 'cooling off period', close to the spirit of the official formulation, with a view to forestalling what was seen as mounting tension both in the wing and in the segregation unit.

Case 2. The assailant in incident LL5 was subsequently sent on 10/74 prior to being transferred permanently to another dispersal prison. The victim of the same incident was also sent on 10/74, but not immediately, and following a separate allegation of 'agitation' after the prison's attempt to bring an HIV positive prisoner onto normal location. He did not return but went to another Category B prison. These may well both be 'preventive' uses of 10/74 rather than retributive ones, but they can hardly be interpreted as 'cooling-off' periods from the point of view of the sending prison, inasmuch as neither prisoner came back (unless the decision not to have the prisoners in question back was taken after the event of their being sent on 10/74).

Case 3. Two prisoners from one wing were sent on 10/74s and subsequently transferred to other dispersal prisons in the wake of a variety of allegations of 'subversion' and 'intimidation' and, as the Governor summarized:

It's just that such groups believe that they've got more power than they really can be allowed to have from a management point of view. So therefore at times it's got to be broken up.

In this case the allegations included that:

it's all to do with . . . drugs, and running a book and fear, and you suddenly realize you've got to use a knife to cut it out, and almost start again. And it has to be big enough to make the impact that you mean it.

(Governor I, Long Lartin)

Again, this sequence of events cannot be adequately described as involving a 'cooling-off period'. Rather it was an attempt to achieve a conclusive resolution of a particular situation. We went on to ask the Governor how the decision was made whether such prisoners should come back:

It's probably down to the old one of feelings. Do we think he would resettle? Is it something where we would want resettlement? . . . Bloggs is a shit . . . He certainly shouldn't be in a place like this. I've laid him down two or three times over two years. As far as I'm concerned he has not shown in that two years a capacity to settle down in here. He's always at it.

This case seems to combine a number of elements in which 10/74 served, at least, the purposes of risk-reduction and the pre-emption of possible further trouble: preparation for a permanent move (which was conceived in terms of 'desert', given the previous chances to settle) and an 'exemplary' demonstration of power.

Case 4. Another use of 10/74 which may have had a retributive component concerned the alleged sabotage of the laundry by two prisoners, who subsequently returned to Long Lartin. There was a widespread feeling among prisoners that 'examples were being made' of the two people concerned, and a related sense of grievance on their behalf. It was never definitively established that they had been responsible, and managers later acknowledged that they may have been mistaken in 'lifting' the individuals concerned.

Case 5. Finally, we interviewed two people who were made subject to 10/74 at least partly because they were long-term occupants of the segregation unit at a time when it was nearly full. In both instances the 10/74 provided an immediate way of liberating space in the segregation unit. In one of these cases the 10/74 seems to have been in preparation for a projected permanent transfer. The other concerned a prisoner who was regarded as a 'nuisance' by staff, who was described by the Governor as a 'mad litigious prisoner', and whose occupation of the segregation unit was considered unjustified and a 'problem' in itself. In this instance the use of 10/74 may have been in part strategic in an attempt to persuade him to go on normal location on his return to Long Lartin.

Several of these examples raise the question of under what circumstances people sent away under 10/74 might or might not return to the sending prison. The Governor of Long Lartin, in line with the wording of the circular, voiced a strong presumption that in principle people should come back, and that both prisoners and staff should know that:

once you went, it didn't mean it was the end of you. Really, you could go away, you could have your bottom slapped, but you could come back and you could resettle down again. Whereas in the past . . . if you went on a lay-down you were automatically transferred to somewhere else. Now, I don't believe that that is acceptable . . .

This might appear to be at odds with the fact that so many of those sent on 10/74 from Long Lartin did not return (see Table 8.2). However, several considerations should be borne in mind. The circular itself referred to its use in emergencies or crises. What seems most likely is that it was being used as a means of acting swiftly to remove somebody from the prison in what the management saw as an emergency, at which point the decision as to whether or not he should return may well not have been taken. It may only have been determined subsequently that a 'cooling-off period' was not a sufficient means of solving the original problem.

Equally, the fact that a prison used the 10/74 procedure, and may have done so for a variety of purposes, did not mean that a good deal of effort was not also devoted to resolving problems informally, internally and preventively in a significant number of cases. This was sometimes explicit presented as seeking to pre-empt the necessity of using 10/74. There are examples of this from both Albany and Long Lartin.

Thus, in Long Lartin, the Governor described a situation in which he had received many Security Information Reports naming a particular prisoner as being to the fore in extensive gambling and extortion and 'getting above himself'. The Governor felt that 'the pressure to move him was very great'. The Governor spoke to the prisoner twice, letting him know that he had a good deal of information about his activities. As a result:

After that he disappeared into the woodwork. My paranoia dropped mainly because he screwed his loaf and he backed off. And he's still here and things are going all right.

Similarly, the Governor of Albany spoke of the case of a prisoner whom he regarded as being 'at the centre' of the distribution of drugs in the prison. The prisoner in question was the object of deep suspicion from both wing and security staff and was named frequently in Security Information Reports. Again, the Governor spoke to the prisoner and kept him for periods on Rule 43, but declined to transfer him. He argued that it would only have become necessary to transfer the prisoner if he had had a 'following' on the wing who had felt obliged to 'perform on his behalf' whilst he remained in the prison.

The 10/74 procedure was one whose use centred on 'hard cases'—difficult, unresolved or critical situations. There was almost always an extensive set of prior events, but the application of the procedure itself could come as a stunning surprise to the prisoner. The 'cooling-off period', insofar as this was ever the main objective of the actual use of temporary transfer, often looked very different from the point of view of the recipient, not least because it came at a late point in complex sequences of events in which there was par-ticular scope for different and opposing interpretations. Thus, we now turn to examine the perspective on temporary transfers of some of those who have experienced them.

Temporary Transfers (Prisoners' Perspectives)

The views of prisoners with experience of temporary transfer centred on the questions of its justice and its effectiveness. The following accounts are drawn from interviews with the prisoners involved
in the cases outlined above.

Prisoners disputed the justice of their treatment on a number of
grounds. First, they objected to the fact that commonly no charge
had to be laid or proven, leaving them no opportunity to rebut allegations. This was also connected to the frequent grievance that no
real explanation was provided for what was happening. These features offended the concept of natural justice by which prisoners
often assessed the fairness and legitimacy of the treatment they
received. Secondly, prisoners suggested that the process of removal
itself, in that it was disorientating, disruptive, lonely, and sometimes
physically rough, was disproportionate to the problem or infraction
in question; yet since it was not supposed to be a punishment no
formal account was taken of proportionality. Thirdly, prisoners
insisted that, since it had regard to suspicion rather than proof, the
decision to send someone on temporary transfer was based on
'prison paranoia' and 'prison politics' rather than reasoned judgement. They especially resented the feeling that staff were prepared
to act on 'notes in the box' (i.e. anonymously passed information).
This, they felt, gave an enormous power to someone who wanted to
'grass them up', a move that might result from a personal grudge or
a strategic intent to get them out of the way, for some other, self-
interested reason. Prisoners who had a certain reputation, of whom
staff were wary, felt especially vulnerable to being 'ghosted' on slender evidence or pretexts (cf. King and McDermott, 1990).

Thus, a sense of grievance and frustration often resulted:

The terrible thing here is that staff will take an informer's word, because
of the reputation of the inmate, and act on it, whether it's true or not . . .
They won't tell you what you're down there for, or what the charge is.
Then they tell you it's not a punishment, but you're still on solitary. So
[you think] fuck them, I'll give them something for me to be down here
for: they open the door and they get a pot of shit in their face. (Case 1.)

Or again:

You've got a lot of notes going in the box here. People say, he's selling
drugs upstairs, he's got a bucket of hooch down, he's going to do this or

that against the system, he's talking about this. Sometimes they invent things that haven't taken place. I think you'd find the number of notes in the box staggering. When they believe the word of an informer I find that very disturbing. (Case 4.)

For some, the sense of injustice remained, even granted that some device or mechanism was necessary:

I think it's a grossly abused procedure. There are no procedural safeguards for a start. Nobody's saying that a prison system shouldn't put anybody into solitary confinement under any circumstances. Obviously there must be some measures that it can use to maintain, as far as it's concerned, the good order and discipline of the institution. Whether I like it or not there are various individuals walking around the prison system who are extremely dangerous to other prisoners as well as the staff. So far as they're concerned there is probably adequate reason for using the 10/74. But like anything else in prison it's a rule that's arbitrarily abused. (Case 1.)

Some prisoners drew a direct connection between the grievance which resulted from the sense of injustice and their feeling that the 10/74 procedure was ineffective or counter-productive:

Being sent away for twenty-eight days is going to make me more antagonistic. These cooling-off procedures only wind you up more. They take you out of the dispersal prison and cart you off to some stinking local and think that it calms you down. So you're returning with a worse attitude because you've had twenty-eight days of crap. (Case 3.)

Equally, some prisoners felt that, although not a disciplinary measure, the appearance of an administrative transfer on their record worked against their future prospects just as much as if it had been one:

I don't agree with the 10/74 system at all. I don't think it does any good. Men come back bitter and twisted. A lot of them don't come back, they get reallocated elsewhere. It disrupts the routine you've got. You feel you've been victimized. I've got that on my record now, and when I go for my lifer review, they're going to say, 'Look at this, suspicion of sabotage under 10/74'. It's another black mark. (Case 4.)

Another prisoner described the difficulty of resuming life at the sending prison after a period on 'lie-down':

For the first month after I came back I wouldn't talk to anyone. I stayed behind my door. It retrogrades people, whether you've misbehaved or not.

There is no need for the expense, whether you've offended or not. It takes six screws and a van to shift me or any other 'A' man, sometimes with a full police escort with motor bikes. It's a waste of time and money. What does that cost to send you and then send you back afterwards? Nothing comes out of it except more bitterness. (Case 1.)

The theme that temporary transfer was a 'waste of money' which didn't achieve its objects was widespread. Most prisoners were prepared to recognize that some forms of segregation or separation were necessary and legitimate, but questioned the particular utility of 'ghosting' as a method:

It's a total waste of fucking money. It's not necessary. If they want to separate you, they should just put you down the seg. unit and not necessarily for twenty-eight days, and come down and *discuss it* with you. If you had two antagonists that couldn't live in the same environment one or both of you would have to go somewhere else *permanently*, not just for twenty-eight days, because that doesn't do anything. (Case 1.)

However, a significant minority of those we interviewed were prepared to admit, if not the legitimacy of the procedure, at least that a change of scene or circumstances might have had some benefits for them. The nearest we found to a vindication of the 10/74 procedure by a prisoner was the following comment:

The reason why we went was because we opened our mouths to the Governor and voiced our opinions about what we were going to do. He's got to run this place. It was a control exercise, really. Maybe I did need a cooling-off period. I don't know. (Case 4.)

On the other hand the same prisoner also observed:

It made me feel very sick. Not angry, a bit annoyed. It put a bad strain on the officers who took me down there, because I've known a couple of them several years. They were only doing their job. Now that I've come back one or two of the officers feel a bit uncomfortable and I do too. It tends to make you want to erupt more when they do that to you. I think it's a waste of time. Pointless. (Case 4.)

Another prisoner expressed a similar ambivalence—on the one hand acknowledging some benefit from the experience, but compromised on the other by resentment of the procedure itself:

I was getting bitter and twisted, but I know now that that's not the answer, and after that 10/74 it's opened my eyes up a bit. I'm a bit more placid now. I don't want to know trouble, prison politics. But I still feel as though I've been dug out. (Case 4.)

For a third prisoner the 10/74 actually seemed preferable by virtue of his desire for solitude and his straightforward hatred of Long Lartin:

I'd rather stay here, because I'm left alone. I get my hour's exercise, and the food's good, and I get no pressure from staff . . . It's no punishment to me. I've just flopped . . . It all depends where you do your 10/74. You go to Wandsworth, then it's a punishment. (Case 5.)

Nevertheless, this view was still held in tension with a repudiation of the procedure itself:

The lie-downs don't solve a thing. The law of 10/74 is a farce. It causes problems to the prison you go to, to your family and friends if they want to visit you. You lose property. Half of it is torn and broken when you get it back. They consider that you're just a pain in the arse to the system, but they are the ones that manipulate the system. (Case 5.)

Permanent Transfers (Managerial Perspectives)

Unlike 10/74s, of which records were kept, we found it impossible to quantify with any certainty the extent of permanent transfers made on control grounds. This was particularly true of Category A prisoners, whose moves tend by definition to be between dispersals, and who are always liable to be moved summarily. Many permanent transfers may incorporate a 'control' element, without being sharply differentiated from others. The clearest cases in point of permanent transfers on control grounds were those which immediately followed a movement under CI 10/74, although we have also been able to identify a number of other illustrative examples. Managers occasionally contemplated 'one for one swaps' with other dispersals (particularly as between Albany and Parkhurst) although they were reluctant to do this because they knew that they would also receive a 'problem' in return.

In fact there was a measure of inbuilt reluctance to undertake permanent transfers on grounds of control, in part at least because managers at each dispersal felt that they *ought*, as a matter of professional pride, to be able to handle whatever problems were presented by particular prisoners. At the same time managers may come under pressure from staff to rid them of prisoners deemed to have definitively 'failed', or whose continuing presence provoked anxiety, or otherwise threatened to sap morale. The issue often focused on the problem alluded to above by the Governor of Long Lartin, namely whether 'resettlement' was possible or desirable. Permanent transfers became likely once (1) the authorities felt they had 'had their fair share' of a particular individual, or (2) where relations between the individual and the prison in question (meaning, that is to say, its specific personnel) were thought to have broken down irretrievably, or (3) where the prisoner was regarded as being involved in a 'control problem' which was intractable within the confines of that prison. Points (1) and (2) seem to have applied in relation to Case 3 above, for example, whereas point (3) applied to the position of the assailants in incident LL1 (see chapter 7).

Permanent Transfers (Prisoners' Perspectives)

Although ostensibly a more far-reaching measure, permanent transfers did not usually provoke quite the same resentment from prisoners as did the use of CI 10/74. They were regarded as a more legitimate prerogative of the prison, and on the whole as less personally damaging. Prisoners who were regarded as having 'caused' trouble were also often 'in' trouble in their relations with staff or with other prisoners. To this extent a permanent transfer sometimes represented a resolution to a situation which was also troublesome from the prisoner's point of view, and an opportunity to start afresh:

In a way I'm glad . . . I just stay behind my door anyway now, because I'm not going to give them the opportunity to say anything about a clique again, like at Long Lartin. I'm not going to get involved. I'm not going to give them that opportunity. (Long Lartin to Full Sutton.)

Or again:

The AG approached me and told me that he knew I had had enough of Albany and asked if I would like to go to Long Lartin. So I agreed. I don't think I'm labelled a troublemaker here. (Albany to Long Lartin.)

One prisoner who was regarded as being at risk from other prisoners in Long Lartin, meanwhile, said:

One day I will expose Long Lartin for what it is, and the people for what they did there . . . Every prison should be like this prison [Frankland]. I couldn't say a bad word about it. The prison staff are highly trained,

observant, pleasant men, apart from one or two duds . . . They're not bullies. They don't continually pressure people. Here you can live with a little
bit of dignity. (Long Lartin to Frankland.)

A permanent transfer may be seen as either punitive or preferable
depending on where it is from and where it is to, where the prisoner's home and family are, and so forth. If it is not regarded as
unduly vindictive (as the transfer of a northerner or Irish prisoner
to the Isle of Wight may be, for example), it may be easier for a
prisoner to reconcile himself to a permanent move than to the
impermanence and disruption occasioned by a 'lie-down'.

In sum, there were very few prisoners who did not at some level
recognize the right of prison managers to separate or segregate prisoners and to act to avert crises. Conversely, there were perhaps
fewer still, at least amongst those who had experienced them, who
did not raise questions about the justice and effectiveness of the
measures concerned, and especially the 10/74 procedure as it was
then constituted. Many staff, meanwhile, recognized these as real
problems, but regarded them as being overridden on occasion by
the pressure of events and the need to take, and be seen to take,
swift action. Prisoners were aware that the official discourse styled
10/74 was a 'cooling off period' but it was difficult for them to see
it in this light because of the circumstances in which it was applied
and undergone. Prisoners indeed often acknowledged that considerations of due process were likely to be so overridden under force of
circumstances. They found this unsurprising in itself. However, the
particular resentment reserved by many for the 10/74 mechanism
pointed to the gap that fell between the blandness of the official
rhetoric of cooling-off periods and the reality of the experience, and
which they identified as hypocrisy. To this extent prisoners and
staff at least agreed, in contradistinction to the official discourse, in
recognizing that in practice 'ghosting' was likely to incorporate a
punitive component. Even where the intention of the sending prison
was not directly punitive, and may indeed have been entirely preventive, the application of 10/74 involved, in many cases, the inflic-
tion of very painful experiences.

Special Units

Our research had, in one sense, little to say empirically about
the use of 'special units' as a control strategy, because very few

prisoners from Albany or Long Lartin had been or were being sent to the units. Our final research report to the Home Office (Hay et al., 1990) did, however, contain a number of observations of a more general kind about special units, seen from the perspective of extensive qualitative research in dispersal prisons. As our observations in this regard were—in part—directly quoted in the Woolf Report (Woolf 1991: 324), it is appropriate to reproduce an edited version of them here; they take the form of four main observations:[10]

1. Given the way that most dispersal prison governors seem to operate, the special units strategy can be said to have a limited relevance to their day-to-day operational needs. Governors normally try (commendably enough) to 'hold' and 'contain' potentially difficult prisoners within the structures and regime of their particular institution, to the maximum extent possible. That is what the system requires them to do, and that is what they normally attempt . . . However, sometimes it is decided that a particular prisoner can no longer be coped with in that particular prison—but then the operational logic often seems to demand that he should be shipped out of the prison *quickly* (to nip a situation in the bud, prevent unrest spreading to other prisoners, etc). The (rightly) slow and deliberate special units selection procedure simply does not mesh very well with these twin operational imperatives.[11] Perhaps that is why the total number of special unit places required *in real terms* by dispersal prison governors is now considerably less than that suggested by prior research based on the hypothetical existence of special units (see Home Office, 1987: p. 26) . . .

2. Our research demonstrates the importance of the overall social context of the prison in relation to the issue of 'control problems': many such 'problems' are clearly seen, in Albany and Long Lartin, to be either immediately situational or to result from structural dynamics which are not reducible simply to the personalities and dispositions of particular individuals. There is a danger that the whole small-unit strategy might overstate, by implication, the extent to which 'control problems' in dispersal prisons are *simply* the product of 'difficult individuals'. Out of abundant caution, we had better make it clear at this point that we are not denying that some individual prisoners are habitually more troublesome than others—that is obvious to anyone who spends any time in long-term prisons. What we are saying is that the social and situational

[10] In these paragraphs, all italicized words and phrases were similarly emphasized in our original report.

[11] Note, however, that this was written before the introduction of the Special Assessment Unit at Woodhill (see note 8, above).

contexts in which these 'troublesome individuals' live are *also* very important in the generation of the phenomenon known as 'control problems': and that the small units strategy, *precisely because it is about 'selecting out' difficult individuals for special treatment*, runs the danger of institutionally obscuring this important fact.

3. Additionally, it should be observed that special units are, by definition, only for *serious* or *persistent* 'control problem prisoners', and many of the individuals in our 'specific incident sample' would therefore not in any case be candidates for special units. This emphasizes the point, made by RAG, that 'in the nature of things long-term prisons will always contain a proportion of difficult individuals, and their staff will always need to possess the skills to deal with' the resultant social situations, even when the special units are in full operation (Home Office, 1987: p. 26).

4. The various considerations raised [above] between them highlight one single point of some significance. This is that, whatever the possibilities offered by the special units strategy, the fact remains that perceived 'control problems' in long-term prisons usually originate in the social settings provided by 'normal location' in the dispersal system, and *a primary focus of debates about control problems in long-term prisons should therefore concern the character of 'normal location' (or different kinds of 'normal location') as a social environment.* There is a real danger that the inevitable [official and research] interest generated by the introduction of special units may come to obscure this important point.

More specifically in relation to the administrative control measures that are the focus of this chapter, one of us subsequently added the following comment:

The administrative control measures open to dispersal prison governors [Rule 43 (GOAD), CI 10/1974, etc.] . . . cannot be said to have been given full consideration by CRC . . . but in the wings and workshops of the average dispersal prison they loom infinitely larger than the special unit system.

(Bottoms, 1991: 12)

Concluding Comments

Although carried out some time ago, and before some important procedural and legal developments in the regulation of control movements, this discussion has highlighted several issues of enduring interest and concern. The use of administrative rather than strictly disciplinary measures in response to some forms of actual, impending or perceived trouble is a prerogative that prison managers are unlikely to relinquish, even if a number of interventions from the courts and from Lord Justice Woolf's report have nudged the English prison system in the direction of somewhat greater formality in recent times. In common with other features of regulatory and sanctioning systems in prisons internationally (see example Loucks, 1994), but in a more pronounced way, these measures have a strongly discretionary and expedient aspect. This is in some senses seen as integral to their value to prison managers; but it is also the source of their most problematic, and on occasion counterproductive, features. The use of such control measures occurs at moments of particular tension within the everyday social relations of the long-term prison, and they are themselves often the focus of contention. This is a topic which brings into sharp relief the dilemmas between the claims of expediency or utility and those of justice or consistency which are chronically present in prisons, and it is a field in which the legitimacy deficits that routinely attend the governance of prisons are revealed in acute form.

This in itself, as prison managers often know very well, *limits* the utility of their most utilitarian measures, and counsels restraint as to their use. It may mean that powers which were more formally accountable and procedurally explicit might in a sense be more effective. This has indeed been the drift of policy in recent years, if only within sharp limits (and note that even the 'liberal' Woolf rejected proposals on temporary transfers which would have constrained Governors' discretion further).

All of this also suggests, and it has been a preoccupation of our work almost throughout, that whilst various sorts of 'special' relocations of prisoners seem to be constant features of prison control strategies, these are nevertheless less basic to the maintenance of order than is the character of everyday life on 'normal location'. To focus only on the nature of the *responses* to difficult situations (whether in the form of old-style segregation or newer-model special units) can obscure the prior importance of the social and physical environments that prisoners and staff are required jointly to inhabit and the propensity of these variously to permit or prevent, provoke or assuage conflict and danger.

9
Conclusions

THE research which we have reported in this book presents an illustrative series of contrasts and comparisons between the nature, level, definitions, and handling of 'control problems' in two prisons within the long-term prison system in England and Wales as we observed them at the end of the 1980s. Our task in conclusion is to draw together the threads of argument and reflection which these seem to us to suggest for the development of a social analysis of the nature of order and disorder in prisons. Because we take the view that the task of social research is in large measure to *illuminate* (or to 'make better sense of') the social world as it is experienced on a day-to-day basis, we have taken some pains to ensure that our analysis evokes some of the particular features of the local cultures and practices of the two prisons in which we primarily worked as they then were, and to ground our discussion of the emergence of 'control problems' in a secure understanding of the daily lives and routines of those institutions. But Albany and Long Lartin in themselves have never been our exclusive concern (if they were then the significant changes in the English prison system since 1990—see chapter 1—as well as the changes of function, management, regime, and population that Albany and Long Lartin have themselves since undergone[1] might render our discussion of limited, and now little more than historical, interest). Instead we wish to reconsider our case-study in terms of the more general theoretical position on problems of penal order which we have now reached[2] and the policy implications which we take from it.

[1] Since our fieldwork was completed Albany has left the dispersal system. It became a Category B training prison with an expanded role in the housing of vulnerable prisoners. At the time of writing Long Lartin remains part of the dispersal system, but not of the smaller sub-system housing the very highest security risk prisoners. Both have since been the subject of inspections (HM Chief Inspector of Prisons, 1992; 1993) which were sharply critical in certain respects.

[2] In large measure our task here is to synthesize and develop the arguments which we have advanced in a number of earlier publications. These include Bottoms et al.,

In chapter 2 we raised a number of concerns that bear on the problem of thinking about the question of order in confinement. The several accounts expounded there by no means all point in one direction, nor deliver a settled body of conclusions that our discussion can 'read off' against our own evidence. They do, however, warrant certain provisional and precautionary inferences. First, and following aspects of the views of Sykes and of Mathiesen, there are distinct ways in which the patterning of social relations in prison (the deprivations they impose, the disparities in power which are evident) differ from those of other institutions, including other 'total institutions' such as hospitals, asylums, and barracks. They do necessitate a form of analysis which is sensitized to their particularity, their enclosure, their internal disposition of conflict and collusion. But secondly, as both Jacobs and DiIulio acknowledge, albeit divergently, their apartness is never complete. To this extent prisons are not *sui generis* for analytic purposes. Their particular and distinctive features are always special cases of the problems of action, structure, power and authority with which social and political theory are centrally concerned. Moreover, the differences which exist empirically between the prisons of different historical moments and of different countries necessarily betray the signs (in however transformed a fashion) of the particular economic, cultural, and legal circumstances of the surrounding society.

What we take to follow from this, and see as borne out in our own study, is quite simply stated but very complex when fully elaborated. It is unavoidably true that the social order of the prison is imposed and enforced. Prisons, especially maximum security prisons, entail deprivations and compulsions considerably beyond those ordinarily found in advanced industrial societies. Their 'order', to the extent that it exists at all, is neither spontaneous nor consensual. Even in a 'liberal' dispersal prison such as Long Lartin the dialectic of domination and subordination is very different from that which subsists in the 'open parts of society' (Cohen, 1985) or in institutions which have other purposes (hospitals, schools, armed services), especially those to which people in any sense voluntarily belong. Levels of surveillance and the managed control of activity in prisons are inherently high.

However, even if prisons provide a limiting case of 'power as

1990; Hay and Sparks, 1991a; 1991b; 1992; Bottoms, 1991; 1992; Sparks, 1994a; Sparks and Bottoms, 1995.

domination' (Giddens, 1984) in our kind of society (and our research confirms the comments of earlier researchers that *in extremis* that power shows itself in physically forceful ways), it does not follow that the naked use of force, coercion and violence is the most characteristic—still less most astute or desirable—form that power assumes there. On the most critical reading of the case, for example that advanced by Scraton et al. (1991) when they speak of the prisoner as having 'the full force of state coercion handcuffed to his wrist', this might be to say no more than that this power is simply kept in reserve as a constantly implied threat, only to show its 'true' face at given moments of conflict. We do not dispute (just as for example Sykes does not) that in the last instance this is literally undeniable. Our interpretation, however, of the deployment of power in the construction of penal orders is rather different, not least in the sense we attach to the way that prison staff 'represent' the state (a point developed below).

Empirically, our comparison between Long Lartin and Albany demonstrates, at a minimum, that even within one system at one time there are variable as well as constant features in the ways that order in prisons is conceived of and achieved. Thus, the continual tendency in prison studies to seek to show that there exists some essential and irreducible ideal type of The Prison is almost certainly misleading (this tendency goes back at least as far as Sykes and Messinger, 1960; in Scraton et al.'s account the prison's essence shows itself most truly wherever it is most violently coercive). It is more productive and more sociologically sensitive to think of a spectrum of possible ordering relations of which 'actually existing' prisons in any given society accentuate certain features.[3] Theoretically, our point is broader again. Briefly, we suggest, with Beetham (1991), that every distribution of power generates its own sets of normative expectations and criteria of legitimacy, and that its durability as a form of 'order' in large measure depends on these being fulfilled.[4] That is, the empirical differences between the

---

[3] Hence the title of our book is *Prisons and the Problem of Order*, in deliberate contrast to an older tradition represented by, e.g., the work edited by Cressey (1961) entitled *The Prison*.

[4] Or, at any rate, this is true of relatively 'open' societies, and it extends to include at least some prison regimes. In the prison context there are exceptions, and regimes can indeed be based on naked power (*macht* in the Weberian sense) rather than authority: as e.g. in the Victorian 'separate system' or the 'lockdown' regime at Marion Penitentiary, Illinois, in the United States Federal system (Ward, 1987).

institutional climates, regimes, 'control problems' and control measures at Albany and Long Lartin suggest that slightly different normative orders exist (from which certain 'microclimates' such as the Albany Vulnerable Prisoner Unit differ again). This is not to offer an apologia for either of these prisons, nor for any current practice of imprisonment in general. Rather it is to suggest an inherent connection between the 'problem of order' and the problem of legitimacy, to which prisons—far from being immune—are subject in ways that are both chronic and severe.

Legitimacy and Order

As we have argued in chapter 2 and elsewhere (Sparks and Bottoms, 1995) the main traditions in prison studies have dealt only sketchily with the question of legitimacy. Moreover, they have tended to do so from a position which assumes the _non-legitimate_ nature of power in penal social relations. This produces some strange alliances such that liberal realists (Sykes), 'radical pessimists' (Scraton et al.) and conservative pragmatists (DiIulio) implicitly concur in their assumption that prisons escape or exceed considerations of legitimacy. Even Beetham, whose conception of legitimacy is perhaps the most nuanced and intelligent of which we are aware (and which has fundamentally influenced our analysis), casually refers to imprisonment and slavery as two special cases of power so extreme as to evade his general scheme (1991: 27).

All of this of course contrasts strangely with the preoccupations of prison administrators whose discourse betrays a continual preoccupation with the legitimation of their own practice (cf. Sim, 1992). Within that 'language game' the converse commonplace is now routinely asserted—'prisons cannot be run by coercion' (Home Office, 1984: para. 16).[5] Our dissatisfaction with these polar oppositions is a matter or record (Sparks, 1994a, Sparks and Bottoms, 1995). Most academic commentary (with the notable exception of Mathiesen, 1965) excludes precisely those local, situated, and everyday contests over the legitimacy of prison regimes which we take to be theoretically central, just as official discourse frequently seems

[5] Though recently (as we observed in chapter 1) there has been a new tone in some official discourse, suggesting that there is sometimes _not enough_ coercion in prison regimes. For one aspect of discourse of this kind, see the concluding section of this chapter.

incapable of taking its own legitimacy deficits seriously. Our evidence, we believe, suggests that within the daily life of prisons matters are quite otherwise. Prison staff are in fact frequently rather keenly aware of the need to tailor their actions, demeanour, and demands in recognition of prisoners' customary expectations—and their capacity to resist. Equally, given the fact of their imprisonment, most prisoners have a quite precise sense of what they can and cannot legitimately expect. Our understanding that prisons embody some version of a normative order is not in any sense intended to imply consensualism. There is no necessary, neat functional fit between the positions and demands of prisoners and prison staff. Prisons are indeed, as Mathiesen has shown with particular clarity, 'disrupted' societies. They are ordered hierarchically and they involve routine compulsion. Yet as Beetham suggests, none of this argues against the relevance of legitimacy: indeed, it is the state's uses of force which *par excellence* necessitate legitimation work. Prisons may certainly (and literally) institutionalize conflict. But it is on the terrain of the prison's legitimacy that such conflicts are fought out.

One of the most important events in British penal politics of modern times was the riot and occupation at Strangeways prison, Manchester, in April 1990 and the epic report by Lord Justice Woolf which those events stimulated. In our view, in common with that of most commentators, the key feature of Woolf's intervention lies in its elaboration of the idea of 'justice in prisons'. Woolf's argument (one which differentiates it sharply from all preceding official discourse on prison disorders in Britain) acknowledges clearly that the intensity of the 1990 disorders, and the extent of the support they received, is only intelligible in the face of a widely shared sense of grievance and injustice:

A recurring theme in the evidence from prisoners who may have instigated, and who were involved in, the riots was that their actions were a response to the manner in which they were treated by the prison system. Although they did not always use these terms, they felt a lack of justice. If what they say is true, the failure of the Prison Service to fulfil its responsibilities to act with justice created in April 1990 serious difficulties in maintaining security and control in prisons.

(Woolf, 1991: para. 9.24)

Elsewhere Woolf went on to argue against the historically received view that prisoners' goods and services should be regarded as 'privileges', awarded or removed by discretion (for example para. 14.32ff.). He referred instead to the 'threshold quality of life' of all prisoners and to the 'legitimate expectations' that prisoners have of their treatment (for example para. 12.129). For him, serious attention to justice in prisons required the Prison Service to make available to prisoners at least (1) a humane regime (for example 'a dry cell, integral sanitation, . . . exercise, activities, association and food': para. 10.20) and (2) a reasoned explanation for all decisions adversely affecting individual prisoners, and fair procedures for dealing with prisoners' grievances and alleged indiscipline (ibid.). Throughout his report, including in the final paragraphs of the main text, Woolf emphasized his belief that such issues are fundamental to the stability of the system:

Our suggestions are directed to one of the themes which has run through this report, the theme of justice in prisons secured through the exercise of responsibility and respect. *The achievement of justice will itself enhance security and control . . .*

. . . Were these proposals to be followed, then we believe that they would substantially influence the way prisoners come to view the prison system. While not preventing all disruptions, they would marginalise those who claim they must resort to deeply damaging and costly disturbances on the ground that there is no other way to have their voices heard.

(paras. 14.437–14.438, emphasis added)

In our view what Woolf is outlining here (albeit at times only implicitly) is something akin to a theory of legitimacy. He believes, that is to say, that there are variable conditions which render it more or less likely that prisoners will accept, however conditionally, the authority of their custodians. What is novel here is not so much the insight itself (which, as indicated above, is frequently affirmed on prison wings and landings by prisoners and prison staff) but rather the insistence that official discourse should articulate and act upon it.

In policy terms, Woolf's concern with 'justice' results in proposals with two main emphases. He seeks to outline the components of a defensibly humane regime and he stresses the importance of 'just' procedures. Changes of the first kind include the provision of letters, home leaves, clothing, telephone calls and so on (paras. 14.1–14.275). Those of the second sort relate principally to the giving of reasons for decisions, defensible grievance and disciplinary procedures, the abolition of the 'dual' function of Boards of

Visitors, the recommendation in favour of a complaints adjudicator (or ombudsman) and so on (paras. 14.300–14.435; see also Richardson, 1994; Livingstone, 1994). In short, Woolf's approach combines, especially, two dimensions of problems of legitimation—expectations of the material standard of daily life and of fair treatment in the handling of disputes and troublesome situations. It would appear to be Woolf's view that these two taken together constitute the minimum sufficient bases for the restoration of legitimacy, and hence of order.

Whether this is a wholly adequate view remains open to dispute. It is arguable that Woolf remains conservative on the question of prisoners' explicit *rights* (Sim, 1992, 1994; Richardson, 1994). To what extent does the acknowledgement of an 'expectation' also create a right to its fulfilment? Moreover, Sim has argued that the 'hagiography' now surrounding Woolf as a heroic figure of British penology obscures a number of shortcomings in his diagnosis of penal legitimation problems. He suggests instead that Woolf is equivocal about the reliability of prisoners' evidence (1994: 35–6); that he lacks an account of the implication in the disturbances of the daily roles and practices of prison staff (ibid.: 37); that Woolf's language of prisoners' 'contracts' obscures the implicit coercion still pervasive within the system (ibid.: 41) and that Woolf connives with the 'paramilitarism' of the emphasis on 'Control and Restraint' training and penalties for 'prison mutiny'.

There are some, though by no means all, of these criticisms with which we agree. (On his last point, Sim fails to differentiate clearly enough between the recommendations made by Woolf himself and the gloss placed upon them after the event by the Government of the day.) In particular, it is clearly true that Woolf treads especially cautiously in respect of prison governors' discretionary powers of segregation and transfer (with which our research has been much concerned) and that he does not significantly limit these (paras. 12.254–12.260), despite some substantial evidence of their often problematic and sometimes frankly counter-productive aspects (King, 1990; 1994; King and McDermott, 1990; and see Appendix B).

Our research adds a further set of questions, also in part broached by Sim, relating to the internal regulation and ordering of prison life. Woolf's view is open to the criticism that it seems to presuppose that the combination of an improved level of material provision and the introduction of reasons for decisions and more procedural fairness in formal disciplinary and grievance procedures are *sufficient* to secure stable, orderly and legitimate prisons. But this seems to understate (albeit that Woolf is aware of it, see PROP, 1990; Woolf, 1991: para. 14.432ff.) the senses in which the institutional climates and local cultures of different prisons result from other, less openly visible sources—the demeanour and routine practices of prison staff, locally held assumptions about the appropriateness of certain kinds of relationship, the exercise of discretion—in short precisely those features of daily prison life which the sociology of prisons since Sykes has emphasized.[6] It may be precisely these aspects of imprisonment as a complex institutional form of life (the ones which most easily escape formal oversight and policy interventions) which more immediately condition the lived quality of daily experience (Ryan, 1992). Similarly, it is only in comparatively infrequent instances of formally stated grievances, litigation or concerted acts of resistance and revolt that prisoners consciously and explicitly take issue with some aspect of 'the system' as such. More commonly, moments of objection or resistance are experienced as local, individual, situated and specific—an individual slight, a personal sense of wrong, here, and now—even if an external observer can see that such moments have some sort of systemic character. By extension, prison staff know that it is they (or other prisoners) as individuals who will face the unhappy prisoner's wrath and refusal of co-operation (the 'potting', the food refusal, the cell barricade, the angry tirade) whether the incident grows out of their own conduct or is bestowed upon them by some distant edict of penal policy. And the generalized sense of grievance noted by Woolf probably results from the gradual accretion of many such moments.

What is therefore missing in most overviews of penal problems—arguably including Woolf's—is any developed awareness of the ways in which the broad outlines of policy and the local construction of social relations in prisons interact. In studies of policing, by

[6] Compare in this respect the remarks of the Prior Committee on the Prison Disciplinary System (Home Office, 1985a: 7–8), which in general showed a livelier awareness of these informal matters: 'Control in prisons derives from three elements: the quality of relationships between staff and prisoners; the provision of a wide range of purposeful activity for prisoners; and procedures that are demonstrably fair for enforcing rules and responding to complaints'. Note that the informal dimension of 'relationships' is listed first here.

contrast, such concerns are widely discussed. The notion of the police officer as a 'street corner politician' and the impacts of varieties of 'cop culture' in police/public relations have become commonplaces of academic discussion. Moreover they have fed increasingly into the language of policing agencies and police training themselves. But such 'institutional reflexivity' (Giddens, 1990) has been much less evident in relation to imprisonment. Instead there has been a sterile trading of assertion and denial. The official discourse asserts that prison staff will secure the 'willing cooperation' (Home Office, 1964: Prison Rule 2) of their captives; the radical language of critique denies that such co-operation is possible (Scraton et al., 1991: 63). We are left with a stark choice, posed in terms which are really quite insensitive to the specific interplay of legitimacy and delegitimation and its variation from prison to prison and place to place.

It is for these reasons that in chapter 2 we have given emphasis first, to Beetham's conceptual analysis of the legitimation problems that attend the exercise of power in general, and coercion in particular; and secondly, to Tyler's empirical account of conditions of legitimacy in people's encounters with criminal justice agencies. What Tyler's work particularly clarifies, it seems to us, is the *representational* dimension of such encounters. People view the behaviour of public officials as representing aspects of the system whose agents they are. Citizens seem to derive their view of such a system from the manner of their own treatment at its hands—its responsiveness, its fairness, its acceptability to them. In our view, the fact that disparities in formal power between prisoners and staff are greater than in almost any other institutional setting and that prisoners' dependency is likewise more pronounced (Richardson, 1994), means that such concerns are perhaps of greater significance there than elsewhere. We can therefore extend Woolf's argument that under inappropriate conditions 'a sentence of imprisonment which was justly imposed will result in injustice' (Woolf, 1991: para. 10.19) in the following way. Imprisonment (in common with but in a more extreme form than other contemporary forms of punishment) is the practical embodiment of the state's claim to moral authority in the delivery of justice. It cannot itself be legitimate if the grounds for allocating punishment in the first instance are not, or are merely insecurely and eclectically defined. But conversely, and more centrally to the present discussion, neither can the state's authority claims be sustained if the practice of imprisonment routinely belies them (whether in the material conditions of confinement—such as overcrowding, and sanitary arrangements; *or* in its formal and procedural aspects; *or* its 'cultural', relational, and discretionary features). In brief, prisoners (any more than anyone else) can hardly be expected to take the state's pretensions to moral authority and concern seriously unless the *representations* of that authority and those concerns, which they receive from the activities of prison administrators and staff, give them reason to do so.

At least within a democratic society, no abstract justification of penological rationales can indefinitely survive a practical failure to deliver regimes or standards that conform to its claims. Similarly the most assiduous work of prison staff can hardly overcome a failed or unprincipled policy. In that they are required to represent the state's position, chronic discrepancies between the rhetorics and realities of penal life can make the position of prison staff untenable. As Caird (1974) comments, from a prisoner's vantage point, the attempts of staff to dissociate themselves from the surrounding cant may not ultimately look very convincing. This is not, however, to argue, as Sim seems to do (1992: 285), that the regressive culture of the staff is therefore the primary problem. We agree completely that such subcultures can and do take root, and that when they do so their effects on the quality of life for prisoners, and ultimately perhaps on the prison's descent into disorder, can be disastrous. In our analysis regressive 'canteen cultures' are most likely to arise in one or other of two situations. They are likely when prison staff feel in a defensive and unsupported position—alienated from and afraid of prisoners on the one hand, distanced from and mistrustful of management on the other (Hay and Sparks, 1991a). But they are also likely when the local power of certain groups of staff is excessive or unbridled, and when the unopposed exercise of power becomes a matter of casual habit (Hay and Sparks, 1992). In our view the position prevailing in the Vulnerable Prisoner Unit at Albany during the period of our fieldwork stood alarmingly close to the latter extreme. But more fundamentally still, we are concerned that even when staff act in responsive and practically intelligent ways, their best efforts can still be undone by systemic problems. Yet to overstate the problem of the staff, as Sim in our view does, can itself be politically distracting. There is enough of a history in English official discourse of 'invective against prisoners' *and an* 'undercurrent against staff' (King, 1994: 61) to suggest that some interests within the managerial and political hierarchy will be only too ready to use staff-bashing as a way of getting themselves off the hook if offered the opportunity to do so.

In a sense this whole argument returns us to one of our key starting-points (see chapter 1): namely, the Control Review Committee's contention that 'relations between staff and prisoners are at the heart of the prison system and that control and security flow from getting that relationship right' (Home Office, 1984: para. 16). Our initial puzzlement about this position centred on uncertainty as to what a 'right' relationship would look like in a prison. Perhaps we are now somewhat nearer an answer. The attempt to sustain order through social relationships, in the context of radically unequal power relations,[7] has to be underwritten by an understanding of what those relationships represent. In short, the answer to the question 'what does it mean to get the relationship right?' is dependent on the prior question 'what are the political and moral concerns of a public authority which it claims to embody in its practice of imprisonment?' The task that remains for us is to sift some of the implications of these questions for long-term prison regimes.

That these are difficult questions has long been known. Since Sykes it has been virtually axiomatic that prisons formally claim near 'total power' but that in key respects this claim diverges from their actual mode of daily operation, save in extreme conditions. In imposing the power to confine, imprisonment also induces dependency. The fact that prisoners are in a dependent position imposes on state authorities duties of care for physical well-being and psychological survival that are qualitatively greater than those the state assumes over the free citizen. Some differing accounts of the historical development of long-term prison regimes summarized in chapter 2 draw divergent inferences from this. For DiIulio (1987) the primary issues are the provision of safe custody and the reduction of violence, combined with an increased emphasis on efficiency in the delivery of services. DiIulio believes, to summarize crudely, that Sykes-inspired attempts to reduce the 'total' character of

---

[7] Note, in this regard, that even the Control Review Committee, in its famous 'relationships' paragraph, also said that 'nothing can be allowed to qualify the need for staff to be in control at all times' (Home Office, 1984: para. 16; see also Fitzgerald, 1987).

dominative power and to operate via negotiated forms of order has resulted in a mephistophelean contract with inmate hierarchies. It has allowed a cynical exploitation of lines of divisions within the captive society. It has resulted in an abdication of prison managers' responsibility to rule their prisons judiciously, and has led to tolerance of excessive levels of violence and exploitation in pursuit of the quiet life of non-confrontation. (This is, in effect, what some Albany staff in our study alleged against Long Lartin; it is also, as we discuss more fully below, what Sir John Woodcock (1994) concluded had happened in the Special Security Unit at Whitemoor prison, leading to a major breach of security.) DiIulio thus interprets rather favourably the charismatic authoritarianism of an earlier generation of autocratic prison governors (Ragen of Stateville, Beto of Texas). Ultimately 'he who governs most, governs best'. We should cease to pretend that prisons are open to democratization. Only a 'control model' of quite assertive authority, observing due process rights and delivering high levels of 'amenity and service' is finally defensible. It is so because it prioritizes *safety* for inmates and staff above all else, and hence acknowledges that the first duty of prison administration is safe custody.

Jacobs in *Stateville* relates a somewhat different story. His 'mass society' perspective emphasizes the sense in which prisons are *within* society. They have moved, he claims, from a peripheral position (in which local chieftains like Ragen held sway) to somewhere nearer the societal 'core'. The prison wall has been breached—notably by legal action and by mass communication. The transition which Jacobs traces in Stateville from Ragen's autocracy to Brierton's 'scientific management' stance is not historically reversible, precisely because the changes which have taken place within prisons result from changes in the wider society. In that sense, whatever the virtues claimed on behalf of the autocratic model may have been in their historical context, that context is not ours. It is inappropriate to feel nostalgia for them. The style of authority on which they depended could not be legitimate now, not simply because—in prisons as elsewhere—the 'rule of rules' is more pronounced than formerly, but also because legitimation depends upon some degree of consonance with externally prevailing sensibilities (Beetham, 1991; Garland, 1992: 411). Modern prisons confine contemporary people who make contemporary demands; and contemporary social institutions, most notably the courts, have during the last half-century often significantly altered their responses to such demands and taken a markedly less 'hands-off' approach (cf. Bottoms, 1995: 23).

The principle claiming currency in English law that 'a prisoner retains all rights not taken away expressly or by necessary implication'[8] may stand drastically in need of interpretation (and indeed often be very conservatively interpreted) but it does impute a degree of citizenship to prisoners alien to earlier periods (Richardson, 1985; Gearty, 1991; Livingstone and Owen, 1993). Moreover, the exposure of prison management to external inspection and international obligations (Neale, 1991; Morgan, 1994) may be extremely partial and limited matters, but remain instances of the same general considerations. At least the small incursions of accountability and legal oversight into prison life permit us to ask some new questions. If prisons are inevitably different from other social settings, within what limits must this be the case? And on what grounds does any particular instance of such differences seek justification? We will return to some of these issues once more below. First, however, we must reconsider the implications of our study for understanding some of the ways in which prisons are indeed 'different', and the varieties of 'control' that may exist there.

Albany and Long Lartin Revisited: Situational and Social Dimensions of Control

If there is one dimension of prison life regarded by prison authorities as superordinate in justifying differential treatment and the use of compulsory authority it lies (as DiIulio is right to observe) in the arena of institutional control. The demands of safe custody and safe working conditions for staff, the regulation of institutions regarded as incorporating massive risks of disruption and violence on both individual and collective levels: these are the bases on which prison managers are most apt to insist that prisons are *sui generis*. Prisons are different, and must be differently run. They contain people against their will, in close confinement with others whose company they have not chosen, under conditions not of their choosing—'at bottom that is what it is about' (King, 1985).

[8] This statement was made by Lord Wilberforce in *Raymond* v. *Honey* [1982] 1 All ER 756. This case was a notable step in extending prisoners' access to the courts, and signalled the beginning of the end of the notorious 'prior ventilation' inhibition on prisoners' airing of grievances (see Livingstone and Owen, 1993: 20–1).

The special administrative (see chapters 1 and 8; King and McDermott, 1990) and judicial powers exercised by prison managers claim necessity on these grounds. Such powers to withhold privileges, extend periods of confinement (Criminal Justice Act 1991 section 42; Livingstone, 1994), segregate and transfer prisoners, have been modified recently but have not been radically altered since the date of our fieldwork. They remain levers towards the production of compliance, or the emergency exclusion of troublesome or undesired elements. Our own analysis has detailed examples of their use and has indicated cases in which their effect has been limited or merely displacing, and on occasions counterproductive.

Much of the debate on the 'special handling' of prisoners deemed 'disruptive' or 'difficult' (RAG, 1987; Bottoms and Light, 1987; Bottomley and Hay, 1991; Bottomley, 1994) whether via the use of 'special units' or (in the case of the United States) 'last resort' prisons (see Ward and Schoen, 1981) offers limited and sometimes discouraging conclusions. It remains the case that the primary device for the control of problematic situations in prisons is provided by some form of movement of prisoners within and between institutions, and that this is principally exclusionary or incapacitative in effect rather than positively oriented towards facilitating improved behaviour;[9] it also sometimes involves fairly draconian additional deprivations.

We doubt whether exclusionary/incapacitative movements of this kind should be relied upon excessively as a preventive device, by any prison system. Woolf (1991, paras. 9.32–9.33) interestingly made this point, drawing on evidence from our own research and from a comment by Dr Dan Grubin of the Institute of Psychiatry, University of London. Dr Grubin had reminded the Woolf Inquiry that prisons were places where people live (sometimes for substantial periods), and that moving house was known to be a stressful experience. We had given evidence to the Inquiry emphasizing (from our empirical work and from structuration theory) the importance of stable routines in the production of trust, security, and order, in prisons as elsewhere (see Appendix B and the papers therein referred to). Elaborating the point, Woolf commented that

---

[9] Though see the claims strongly made on behalf of the Barlinnie Special Unit in Scotland until its precipitate closure in 1994 (Boyle, 1984; Cooke, 1989; Bottomley et al., 1994).

'frequent moves for prisoners must make it more difficult to achieve such stable and predictable routines' (1991, para. 9.33).

It is difficult to deny that the movement of prisoners, as a form of risk management or 'preventive channelling', is sometimes justified (Bottoms and Light, 1987; Hay and Sparks, 1991b; Bottomley et al., 1994); and it is certainly difficult to envisage prison managers refraining from the use of such measures altogether. Yet the contribution of these strategies to the maintenance of order within a long-term prison system as a whole is subject to inherent limitations. The harder forms of methodological individualism which claim with any confidence to identify a distinct sub-population of intrinsically difficult prisoners (cf. Williams and Longley, 1987) tend repeatedly to over-predict the size of such a group, and to understate the processual and situationally specific nature of 'control problems' and their emergence within particular aspects of the regimes of long term prisons (King and McDermott, 1990; Bottoms, 1991). They have this in common with similar approaches to absconding (cf. Clarke and Martin, 1971; Banks et al., 1975) and suicide (Liebling, 1992). Also, within the prison systems of England and Scotland at any rate, the numbers of prisoners who have passed through such 'special' sub-systems have to date been small, certainly in proportion to the amount of academic and policy making attention, and indeed financial resources, which they have attracted. If one can defend the existence of 'special' units it will be in one of two ways. They may act as prefigurative experiments in different ways of living and different kinds of relationship (see Scottish Prison Service, 1990; Fitzgerald, 1987), though there may be as many cases where their lessons are negative and frightening as where they are progressive (Vantour, 1991). Secondly, they may remain defensible simply as devices for solving particular problems. Special units can—if they are 'special' enough, as the historical role of the Barlinnie unit suggests—sometimes offer a prisoner trapped in an intractable cycle of opposition with the authorities some sort of dignified escape route (cf. Sparks, 1994b). What they cannot do is magically to unlock the problem of order for a prison system as a whole. Their inherent and peculiar 'risk', if such it can be called, lies in being used as a distraction by those who would argue that just because prison 'control problems' are 'caused' by real individuals they are entirely individual in origin (see Player and Jenkins, 1994: 6–7; King, 1994: 47).

The main focus of preventive attention, therefore, must remain on 'normal location'—that is, on the everyday conditions of existence in the wings and landings of long-term prisons, within which 'control problems' primarily arise. This point was sometimes in danger of being lost during the English policy debates of the later 1980s and early 1990s (see Bottoms, 1991), but it is a conclusion of central importance. Given this, and the limitations of exclusionary/incapacitative movements as a preventive device, it is of some significance to think through more generally the possibilities for approaches to order maintenance in 'mainstream' prisons.

Prison Management as Crime Prevention

In considering the implications of our study of Albany and Long Lartin for the nature of order in long-term prisons we have found it helpful to draw analogies between styles of institutional management and approaches to crime prevention in other settings (for a fuller discussion of this aspect of our work see Bottoms et al., 1990). Conventionally, approaches to crime prevention are regarded as falling into two camps—the *situational* and the *social* (or 'community') styles. Each rests on rather particular assumptions about the nature of offending and the possibilities for collective action in reducing its incidence. Simplifying freely, the two approaches may be thought of as follows.

Situational crime prevention comprises:

1. measures directed at highly specific forms of crime;
2. which involve the management, design or manipulation of the immediate environment in which these crimes occur;
3. in as systematic and permanent a way as possible;
4. so as to reduce the opportunities for these crimes.'

(Clarke and Mayhew, 1980: 1)

The key term in situational outlooks is 'opportunity', and their stress lies on 'manipulating opportunities and inducements' (*op.cit.*: 5). Situational approaches may presuppose that many people will have a 'disposition' to offend where opportunities exist and benefits seem likely to follow, and that not much can be done to alter such 'dispositions', except by reducing opportunities and increasing risks in relation to offending. In the prison context 'situational' measures include emphases on direct and electronic surveillance; the searching of prisoners, cells, and (more controversially) visitors and staff;

the control of prisoners' movements; the removal of means and opportunities (such as limiting the use of tools within the prison, to prevent escape attempts; or of cash, to limit the scale of gambling and other economic activity); and of course the segregation or removal of prisoners from the main prison. With the possible exception of the last, each of these strategies appeared, at the time of our research, to be more highly developed at Albany than at Long Lartin.

Social approaches to crime prevention, on the other hand, assume that dispositions to offend may vary in relation to a variety of other social conditions. These may include the recognition of the legitimacy of rules, internalized inhibitions against offending, the fear of penalties, or of shame or censure and so forth. For one commentator their defining feature lies in the 'purposive concern to alter the social structure of particular communities' (Hope, 1994). In effect social crime prevention relates, for present purposes, to all attempts to reduce undesired outcomes which are pursued through the development or strengthening of social relations. To use a simple analogy from domestic life (the significance of which we shall develop later), whereas the *situational* prevention of chocolate thefts from cupboards by smallish children is achieved by locking the cupboard door, the *social* reduction of this activity is accomplished by various styles of parent–child interaction to do with socialization and the development of trust. In our research this was an abiding preoccupation of staff at both prisons, but was especially used by Long Lartin staff as the rationale for their particular style of working.

The positions of Albany and Long Lartin on these dimensions do not represent a simple opposition. Albany staff had a strong interest in sustaining relationships which they regarded as good, as well as in preventing 'trouble' through the reduction of opportunities. Equally, quite apart from its historical concern with encouraging certain kinds of social relations, Long Lartin still placed prisoners under a far higher degree of surveillance and supervision than would be conceivable for any group of adults outside a secure prison or psychiatric facility. Moreover there are many aspects of prison regimes that are ambiguous in terms of the social/situational polarity. The provision of high levels of activity (games, education, work) may be thought of by prison managers in largely 'situational' ways: they occupy prisoners' time and energy in supervised groups.

On the other hand these activities also have a clear 'social' aspect: if the prison offers prisoners opportunities that are of enough interest and importance to them the social climate of the prison is likely to be improved and its tedium and frustration alleviated. Nevertheless, we suggest that the social/situational prevention analogy does express real institutional differences between Long Lartin and Albany. Such differences broach a complicated set of costs and benefits. One question which arises is, how far are these modes of control in tension with one another, or could they be successfully reconciled? Such cost-benefit problems raise questions of value. In terms of the objectives they set themselves each prison could claim to have been fairly successful. The 'benefits' which were claimed differed between the two prisons. Hence, the stake for legitimacy or success was laid on somewhat different grounds. The 'costs' may differ in parallel ways. Thus it was readily admitted by Long Lartin managers, and our research has confirmed, that since the model of long-term imprisonment pursued at Long Lartin aimed to increase prisoners' self-determination and freedom of movement it also correlatively permitted opportunities for 'misbehaviour'. Moreover, such increased opportunity may particularly have increased the scope for incidents (especially prisoner–prisoner incidents) which were regarded as serious. In terms of our typology of 'control problems' this may mean, in particular, problems attendant on a highly developed economy and increased risks for vulnerable members of the population. Equally, however, there was *less* protest, disobedience, and non-co-operation with staff at Long Lartin than at Albany and fewer assaults on staff. Long Lartin may have strategically accepted a degree of risk that certain kinds of incidents or activities might occur without their jeopardizing the basic stability of the institution (see Hay and Sparks, 1991b). Albany, on the other hand, seemed prepared to accept a degree of unpopularity amongst prisoners for the sake of a higher degree of supervision and opportunity reduction.

From the point of view of prisoners' preparedness to acknowledge the legitimacy of each institution, meanwhile, we might summarize the prevailing positions roughly as follows:

Albany: At the time of our study Albany operated a regime which was stringently controlled relative to other English long-term prisons: this involved, in particular, restrictions on association and movement within the prison. Prisoners in general were well aware of this difference: indeed prisoners in Albany probably had a slightly exaggerated perception of their relative disadvantage. Accordingly, many felt aggrieved at having been located there, and felt that they had been given no adequate explanation of their differential treatment by comparison with their peers elsewhere. Some went further and interpreted their allocation as deliberately and personally punitive. Throughout the 1980s Albany regularly generated higher recorded levels of minor disciplinary problems (refusals to work, disobedience, fighting) than other dispersal prisons, giving rise at least to the suspicion that attending to the risk of disorder on one level might serve to exacerbate it on another (Hay and Sparks, 1991b); though the relative youth of the inmate population is also a relevant factor in explaining the rate of disciplinary infractions.

The Albany regime was therefore in the main rather unpopular with prisoners, except among older men who often welcomed its restraining effect on the noisiness and bumptiousness of the younger majority. However, with few exceptions (and somewhat against our initial expectations) prisoners drew a rather sharp distinction between the regime as such and the staff who administered it, whom they considered in the main to be reasonable, fair, 'just doing their job', and so on. Our impression was that, aware that they were administering a disliked system (albeit one which they strongly supported themselves) staff at Albany took some pains to counter their own potential unpopularity by cultivating a rather discreet and amenable interpersonal style. They did this in the hope—realized to some extent—that good relationships would help them retain a degree of legitimate authority. Moreover, the regime at Albany was quite highly procedurally explicit and relatively consistent in its operation, and emphasized good 'service delivery' in matters such as food and pre-release programmes. Assuming Tyler's views to be correct, all these factors may have helped limit the scale of the prison's legitimacy deficit (see further below).

Long Lartin: The regime at Long Lartin was widely regarded by prisoners as having a number of benefits over those of other dispersal prisons. Prisoners had significantly more time out of cells than at Albany, more association, more freedom of movement within the prison, more frequent access to the gymnasium. They also noted and mostly approved the staff's cultivation of a rather relaxed and friendly way of working and a light and unobtrusive style of supervision. The use of first names between prisoners and staff was fairly general, and staff took pride in being able to manage the prison without formally sanctioning every 'petty' infraction of the rules. Amongst the successes claimed for Long Lartin's liberal approach were the avoidance of riots, and hence an unbroken line of continuity with the founding principles of the 'dispersal' prison system (Sir Leon Radzinowicz's 'liberal regime within a secure perimeter': see chapter 1). It was widely accepted that a number of prisoners who had rejected regimes at other long-term prisons and been reckoned unmanageable had settled successfully at Long Lartin. It was also clear that Long Lartin used its rather favoured status in the eyes of most inmates as a device for influencing prisoners' behaviour. Thus the prison had enjoyed some success in integrating sex offenders and other vulnerable prisoners into the main body of the prison's population, calling on potential predators' fears of being transferred elsewhere. By the same token vulnerable prisoners were more ready to tolerate the risks involved in mixing with other prisoners for the sake of the perceived benefits of the regime. Yet it was also clear that such people were by no means free from fear. Moreover, the level of *sub rosa* economic activity (especially in the supply of drugs, and gambling) was rather high; there was evidence from hospital records and numbers of alarm bells to suggest that the level of backstage violence might have been much greater than the official picture of calm would indicate; and when incidents did occur those within our sample were more likely than at Albany to involve numerous people and the use of weapons. The history of stability (assessed in terms of the absence of large scale collective unrest), the favourable regime, and the generally approved staff practices lent to Long Lartin an appearance of much greater legitimacy in the eyes of the majority of prisoners than was the case at Albany. Yet it also seems probable that the regime gave rise to opportunities for trouble, and predation on fellow inmates, not found to the same degree elsewhere, and hence to some risks in day-to-day inmate life. It is certain, from our evidence, that some of the victims of predation felt not only afraid but angry and unsupported. Meanwhile some of those alleged to have caused trouble, and in consequence transferred from the prison on the Governor's authority, felt they had been unfairly treated procedurally. Hence there were two kinds of allegation raised by some prisoners against the liberal regime at Long Lartin: one concerning the provision of safe custody, and one concerning its scope for procedural discretion and consequent injustice.

Sykes might have had Long Lartin in mind when he wrote that:

The maintenance of order does not necessarily require that excess of caution which seeks to eliminate the possibility of any 'incident' without regard to the inmate's fearful loss of self-determination, if the free community learns to accept the fact that crime within the walls does not necessarily represent outrageous neglect on the part of the officials. In short, the authoritarian community of the prison does not need to be a harshly repressive one, but the demand for more extensive control than is to be found in society at large will continue, and we had best recognize it.

(Sykes, 1958: 133)

One question which arises in any analysis of the costs and benefits of the mode of control at Albany, meanwhile, is did it act with an 'excess of caution'? Staff at Albany made out a strong case that the regime imposed after the troubles of 1985 expressed a perfectly justifiable degree of caution. Whether every aspect of that regime continued to be necessary and justifiable by the time of our fieldwork is perhaps an open question. Certainly caution was valued among Albany staff. From that vantage point the 'risk' strategy which was seen as having been adopted at Long Lartin was considered inappropriate for practice at Albany, if not flawed in principle:

If you run a relaxed regime in a penal institution then you need to be eagle eyed about what is really going on . . . and I have no confidence in the ability of the Prison Service to run a regime in the long term which is relaxed and unoppressive and all those things, at the same time to control it so that the inmates are not abused. I think it would be a wonderful trick if one could do it, but I have no confidence in our ability to do it.

(Grade III, Albany)

From this point of view Albany had little alternative but to proceed with caution, but the benefits which followed from that caution were regarded as comparatively concrete. Meanwhile there was an accompanying scepticism about whether Long Lartin had really pulled off its 'wonderful trick'. Perhaps then the analogy with crime prevention breaks down at this point? Arguably what was at stake at Long Lartin was not so much the prevention of 'crime' as the avoidance of disorder, in pursuit of which a certain level of 'crime' may be tolerated (precisely the calculation which its critics would say it took too far).[10]

We certainly make no claim to resolve all the dilemmas which a comparison of modes of control at Albany and Long Lartin raises. In the last instance the comparison between Albany and Long Lartin presents a series of moral decisions and policy choices, because more than one version of sustainable 'order' has been shown to be possible in dispersal prisons. Meanwhile, Governors and others in both prisons suggested the necessity of limits on the tendencies which each contained. 'Situational' control, in its extreme form, becomes unacceptably oppressive and antithetical to any humane aim which a prison might claim to pursue. The spectre of the prison as 'electronic coffin' (King and Elliott, 1977: 3) still haunts the practice of long-term confinement. The option of 'lock-down'—what we might term the 'Marion question' (Ward, 1987) or indeed, at certain points in its recent history, the 'Peterhead question' (Scraton et al., 1991)—is always there as one pole of penal possibility. And as Sykes put the matter so long ago 'In a very fundamental sense, a man perpetually locked by himself in a cage is no longer a man at all; rather he is a semi-human object, an organism with a number' (Sykes, 1958: 6). 'Social' control, on the other hand, risks either becoming an insidious repertoire of 'mind games' or ceasing to be effective 'control' at all.

Our work has, however, led us to one general conclusion which we believe to be of some importance. Before addressing this conclusion directly we need to analyse the concept of 'social crime prevention' a little more carefully.[11] More often than not, people who have a clear opportunity to break the law do not do so. But, as Tyler (1990) points out, their reasons for such compliance may be

[10] There are plainly further analogies with debates on crime prevention and order-maintenance in other settings here, perhaps especially with the policing of public order problems. Note, e.g., Lord Scarman's well-known conclusion (1981) that the 'hard policing' of street offences in Brixton had in the longer term been disastrous for order in that locale. Note too that Scarman (not uncontroversially) placed order maintenance (or the preservation of 'the Queen's peace' as he had it) *above* the detection and punishment of crime in his list of police obligations. Similar issues arise in the debate over 'paramilitarism' in policing (Jefferson, 1990, 1993; Waddington, 1993).

[11] Our original work on 'social' versus 'situational' crime prevention approaches in prison (Bottoms et al., 1990) was developed before we had formulated our present view on legitimacy (see Sparks and Bottoms, 1995). Hence the 1990 paper does not incorporate the distinctions now introduced.

of several kinds (Tyler distinguishes three in particular, any one or more of which may be in play at any given moment). Let us consider these a moment in 'ideal-typical' form, using again the illustration of the child and the chocolate:

Compliance Mode A: Socialization
> The child is imbued by the belief that stealing, even within the house is wrong; hence she desists from taking the chocolate, even though the cupboard door is open.

Compliance Mode B: Legitimation
> The child believes that her parents (whom she loves) exercise a legitimate authority over her; hence she desists from taking the chocolate because they have forbidden it.

Compliance Mode C: Deterrence
> The child desists from taking the chocolate (the cupboard door being open again) because she fears being caught and punished, and the pain of the punishment will outweigh the pleasure of the chocolate.

Separating these modes of compliance empirically is difficult, but, in work based on surveys of the American public, Tyler (1990) claims to have done so. In particular, he claims to have identified a small but definite compliance effect attributable to *legitimation per se*. In the rather special context of the long-term prison, whilst individual differences in compliance as between different prisoners may certainly be attributable largely to prior socialization, the large-scale *resocialization* of the inmate population looks, to say the least, unlikely on past experience.[12] It seems probable, therefore, that the resources available to the prison for influencing the behaviour of its captives (in social rather than in situational terms) have mostly to do with *deterrence* or *legitimacy*. The instrumental/deterrent approach to human behaviour clearly underpins the 1995 moves, in England and Wales, towards prison regimes based on 'earned privileges' (see chapter 1), whereas Lord Justice Woolf's report was equally clearly interested in enhancing order through legitimation (see our earlier discussion). Prisons traditionally have some deterrent measures at their disposal, but the two prisons we

---

[12] That is, there is little reason to believe that prisons are so effective in inculcating moral beliefs that these alone are sufficient to lead prisoners to comply with their rules (the best source on this being Dickens's account of Uriah Heap's prison conversion in *David Copperfield*). But some such process is not actually impossible, as, e.g., Cooke's (1989) analysis of the gradual abandonment of violence by many former members of the Barlinnie Special Unit suggests.

studied had no novel or special ones on which they relied.[13] However, it is certainly the case that the management and staff at Long Lartin did adopt a social 'crime prevention' style, aimed at securing effects based on enhanced legitimacy. It was a form of statecraft grounded in the belief that one had to relinquish some manifest control in order to keep control in the long term (see Jenkins, 1987).

Let us now return to our 'one general conclusion'. It would seem from our research findings that Long Lartin's more 'social' crime prevention style gave its captive population cause to confer greater *legitimacy* on the prison and its way of working than was the case at Albany, and this seems to have helped Long Lartin to avoid major disturbances. The key qualification here concerns the resentment and bitterness amongst those particular individuals for whom 'it' had emphatically not 'worked'. It seems equally undeniable that some aspects of Albany's 'situational control' genuinely reduced opportunities for trouble. While some of these opportunity-reducing situational features of the Albany regime restricted prisoners' choices and lifestyles in a fairly major and intrusive way (for example association only two evenings in three) other situational features were much more neutral in these terms (for example the reduced place of cash in the prison economy). Perhaps, therefore, a creative general way forward for future thinking about control in long-term prisons would include:

1. To seek a 'social' crime prevention approach, aimed at enhanced legitimacy, to the maximum possible extent consistent with the adequate maintenance of order and supervision in each prison (and recognizing that prisons vary in the composition of their populations and their past histories of control problems) whilst;

2. within this framework, considering creatively how 'situational' dimensions of the prison environment could be adapted to reduce

[13] The 'traditional' measures include the disciplinary system and the sorts of administrative control measures outlined in ch. 8. Our point here is that neither prison regarded itself, nor seemed to us, particularly distinctive in this regard. Their more distinctive features involved the focus on *situational* control at Albany, and the *social* attempt to enhance order through legitimation effects at Long Lartin. The 'novel' measures we have in mind include the 'incentives and earned privileges' (and their correlative sanctions) now being introduced into English prisons. At the time of writing research is being conducted at the Institute of Criminology, University of Cambridge, to evaluate the impact of these. The research director is Dr Alison Liebling. We await the outcome of that work with great interest.

opportunities for control problems, without destroying the legitimacy of social relations and trust necessary for effective *social* control.

In other words, this approach seeks to maximize the effects of, and to blend where possible, 'legitimacy-based control' and 'situational control'. In attempting this task, for the sake of the prevention of harm to both staff and prisoners, it follows that the use of more neutral situational controls should wherever possible be preferred to the use of more personally intrusive ones. When they seriously begin to impinge upon individual autonomy and quality of life, situational controls chafe and vex and arouse frustration and annoyance. They continually remind the prisoner of his confinement and his subjection to close scrutiny and control. In a setting as fragile and contentious as a long-term prison they can erode its limited legitimacy, with severely counter-productive consequences. Moreover, there remain issues which no amount of ingenuity in devising situational controls can obviate. These are questions of the habitability of an environment in which people are required to pass significant portions of their adult lives, questions of fairness, and of the distribution of power.

These observations seem to hold out some hope of 'unpacking' the apparent opposition between the 'situational' and the 'social' aspects of the problem of penal order. At least they allow us to raise some educated speculations about current trends and developments. They counsel caution against any assumption that 'control problems' in prisons can ever be overcome wholly or principally by purely technological or architectural means. This may be especially important in a political climate where new high-tech, electronically sophisticated prison designs are proposed alongside proposals for cost savings through cutting staff–prisoner ratios, reducing interaction between prisoners and staff, and so on. (And this argument would speak, for example, to certain tendencies within privatization debates, at least to the extent that the 'efficiency savings' envisaged by some private contractors rely on such assumptions.) Wherever benefits do appear to have accrued from applying 'new generation' design principles these seem to have had as much to do with the prospects they offer for facilitating certain styles of social relationship and interaction as with situational opportunity reduction strictly so called (see King, 1991).

By extension, arguments over the nature of 'units', 'special units' and 'unit management' may be subject to similar considerations. The most convincing account of changes in problematic behaviour in special units (see Cooke, 1989) uses a broader and (somewhat confusingly) more inclusive definition of 'situational' effects than is common in the crime prevention field. Cooke means, in effect, that the prisoner is placed 'in a radically different situation'—in social or relational terms as well as in strictly environmental ones—and from this change of situation, longer-term benefits may in time be developed.[14] Proponents of special unit strategies, and of unit management more generally, can readily call upon notions of benefits from opportunity reduction—the separation of antagonistic groups, the protection of the most vulnerable, the removal of a prisoner from the original context of trouble, and so on. But they may still hold to the view that, beyond all this, a 'unit' is in the last instance a setting of interaction and a crucible for the development of novel relationships and outlooks. It is also centrally important to note that such perspectives cut through the prevalent assumption (attributable to DiIulio, for example) that the 'normalization' of prison life inherently leads to unregulated and anarchic violence.[15] The most 'normalized', prison setting in the United Kingdom, until its closure in 1994, was the Barlinnie Special Unit which, whatever other controversies surrounded it, was correctly celebrated for its avoidance of violence and confrontation despite holding a group of men reckoned by definition to be especially 'difficult'. Conversely it is the ordinary prison wing (holding eighty or a hundred diverse people, in close confinement with each other, with little to do and little privacy) that looks 'abnormal' on this reckoning. As the diffusion of riot and protest in British prisons since the mid-1980s has shown, quite 'ordinary' prisons (like Haverigg in Cumbria or Lindholme in Yorkshire or, most severely, Wymott in Lancashire) can also generate spectacular disorders. There is no determinism

---

[14] Cooke's argument is that, at Barlinnie, prisoners were first placed in a new and better situation which they did not want to leave—and they knew that violence led to expulsion. In time, however, through living in this more pacific environment, they tended to adopt a non-violent approach to problems as their own, and for many of them this seems to have persisted even after leaving the Unit. For a compelling autobiographical account of this kind of process see Boyle (1984).

[15] 'Normalization' is used here in the sense developed by King and Morgan (1980), i.e. the deliberate development of a prison regime incorporating as far as possible key features of 'normal' (non-prison) life.

that ensures that only a very tough or secure prison holding especially violent or desperate people can 'lose the roof' (see Cavadino
and Dignan, 1992: 27–30). Any prison can enter a crisis of order if
its resources of legitimacy are sufficiently thin, its social relations
sufficiently stressed or provocative, and its practices of risk management sufficiently unreflexive. But it does not follow, as DiIulio
seems to conclude, that the moment one 'lifts the lid' on autocratic
dominion the prison is necessarily on the slide into the state of
nature. It is the equation of normalization with *laissez faire* and
indifference which is so misleading.

The Structuration of Prison Life

It will be recalled that in chapter 2 we drew upon Anthony
Giddens's theory of structuration as a means towards grasping
more clearly aspects of the problematic nature of order in prisons.
We argued that Giddens's views helpfully combine attention to the
durability of institutions over time (including their constraining and
indeed compulsory aspects) with an awareness of social actors as
knowledgeable, reflexive beings. The structural properties of institutions, according to Giddens, are reproduced in and through the
activities of the people who compose them. It follows, for Giddens,
that most social practices will have a routinized aspect. Both the
survival of social forms and, he argues, the psychic well-being of
actors (their 'ontological security' and 'trust') depend in large measure on this. But routines are not the only kind of action; and in
any case they do not just 'happen'. Almost everyone, including prisoners, has some interest in the routine maintenance of the institutions and relationships within which they live. But people can also
act otherwise, albeit in constrained ways. They can also stop, challenge, refuse, subvert.

In prisons the capacity of the staff to achieve or impose a daily
routine is itself evidence of their power. To the extent that this is
done 'smoothly' (on a 'normal' day) that power remains largely
'unseen' (Giddens, 1984: 257). It is when that flow is interrupted or
challenged that the issue of power, and of who holds it, becomes
visible. Power may simply override opposition, thereby emphasizing
the dominance of its holders; or else its limits are more clearly
exposed and its basis renegotiated. In general terms, power holders
would rather avoid such challenges, though on occasions they may

find it necessary to reassert their position in open confrontation. Yet the avoidance of challenge itself may require flexibility and adaptation, in which case a subtle reconfiguration of power relations has already taken place. Giddens terms the various means whereby 'those who are subordinate can influence the activities of their superiors' the 'dialectic of control' (1984: 16).

There may be many contingencies which influence how dialectics of control are played out in any particular prison. In our study these include the histories and local cultures of institutions, their populations, their architecture, and, more generally, which of the risks inherent in the practice of imprisonment the decision making of prison managers seems to prioritize. More broadly again, they incorporate the external political and legal environments which surround the institution—the extent and explicitness of prisoners' rights and their access to channels for complaint and redress, for example. At bottom, both our reading of the sociology of imprisonment since Sykes and our observations in our own study lead us to conclude that the considerations implicit within the notion of the dialectic of control are endemic, and central to the problem of penal order. It follows, we have argued, that problems of legitimation and the sometimes concealed, sometimes very overt contests and negotiations that they entail are of focal importance to the sustainability and justification of prison conditions and regimes. The really knotty and unanswered question is just which (if any) actual or possible prisons meet the criteria which this suggests of practical viability and moral defensibility?

We are by no means confident that we have an answer to this question. But we do now have a sense of what the elements required for an answer comprise. We have compared two broadly similar prisons in one country. Yet even this narrow range of comparisons exposes some sharp dilemmas on the relations between legitimacy and order. We also know that historically examples of the failure of legitimate order in prisons are at least as frequent and as instructive as are examples of even qualified 'success' (Adams, 1992; Scraton et al., 1991; Woolf, 1991). Moreover, in chapter 2 we briefly raised the point that even amongst contemporary prisons in liberal democratic societies the range of possible states of order in prisons is quite wide (cf. King, 1991).

In conclusion, therefore, let us now briefly return to that wider spectrum of comparisons and reconsider it in terms of the categories which we take to be important. That wider spectrum of comparisons is schematically set out in Figure 9.1. Here we take a number of prisons of which we have some knowledge, either at first hand or from relevant literatures. We see them as being differentiated by (1) the level of *situational* control they impose; (2) the degree of *legitimacy* in the eyes of the confined on which each is predicated; (3) the modes of *social* control which each predominantly deploys; and (4) the status of the *prisoner* which each seems to us to assume. At one end of this spectrum lies Marion Penitentiary in Illinois, an 'end of the line' institution, famous for its extremely high level of situational control (Ward, 1987). At the other there are a variety of possibilities. On the one hand there is the rather successful (in 'control' terms) example of the Barlinnie Special Unit, whose practice is founded on a measure of internal democratization and consultation (Cooke, 1989; Bottomley et al., 1994). On the other there is the recently notorious case of Wymott prison in Lancashire where in 1993 the apparent absence of either adequate situational controls or of socially sustainable interaction resulted in a destructive riot (HM Chief Inspector of Prisons, 1994). In between stand the 'ordinary' long-term prisons that we have studied.

We do not wish to overstate the significance of this conjectural diagram, and we are content to leave the reader's inferences from it somewhat open. Our suspicion, however, is that those prisons which receive positive values on the dimension of legitimacy are likely in the long run both to be more stable and more defensible in principled argument than those which do not. Yet, at least in Long Lartin's case, the niggling doubt remains as to whether its lesser prioritization of situational control exposes some prisoners, and perhaps staff, to unacceptable levels of risk. What we have yet to encounter is a prison which receives positive scores on *both* situational control *and* legitimacy (though it is the purpose of King's (1991) comparison between one English and one American maximum security prison to demonstrate that this is indeed possible, as one should surely expect if one interprets situational control as increasing physical safety and psychic security).

In our view this discussion clearly confirms that Woolf was correct in his implicit stress on the need for prisons to seek legitimation from prisoners, and on the importance of humane regimes and procedural justice in the process of doing so. The earlier CRC

	Marion	Albany (VPU)	Albany (main)	Long Lartin	Barlinnie Sp. Unit	Wymott
Level of situational control	+++	++	+	–	– –	– –
Legitimacy?	– – –	– –	– (disputed)	+ (disputed)	++	– –
Mode of social control?	redundant?	high staff dominance	'rule of rules' routinization	civility discretion routinization	autonomy participation	'state of nature'
Status of prisoner?	dangerous object	docile object	dangerous subject	thinking agent (some dangerous)	participant	'wild thing'

FIGURE 9.1. A speculative model of some styles of prison 'control'

Report (Home Office, 1984) was also correct in its emphasis on staff–prisoner relationships, with important implications for staff training and conduct. We have sought to extend those concerns and to provide them with a developed theoretical basis. The perspectives on which we have drawn argue strongly both for the extension of procedural justice in prisons and for sensitivity to the relational and specifically social aspects of prisoners' treatment.

Legitimacy and 'Appeasement'

Our analysis, then, has led to a strong emphasis on the importance of *legitimacy* as a crucial concept in prison sociology, and also for prison adminstrators.

That being the case, we must, before concluding this volume, address a searching and important question. It is a question that was first addressed to us by a prison governor with strong academic interests,[16] when he read an early draft of what was to become our published journal article on legitimacy in prisons (Sparks and Bottoms 1995). The question is:

Does all this mean that legitimacy is just about pleasing the prisoners?

This question has assumed an added piquancy and urgency since it was first posed to us. The Woodcock Report on the serious escape from Whitemoor Special Security Unit in September 1994 (see chapter 1, also Woodcock 1994) nowhere uses the word 'legitimacy', but it seems reasonably clear from the analysis and recommendations in the report, and from its general tone, that the Woodcock Enquiry Team would ask the governor's question of us even more insistently than when it was first asked. This being the case, this is clearly a matter that we must address seriously and directly. We shall do so, *first*, by quoting our full original answer to the question; *secondly*, by outlining the Woodcock Enquiry Team's position on some key matters, and *thirdly*, by responding further to the important issues raised.

Our original reply to the question was as follows (Sparks and Bottoms, 1995: 58–9):

It is an important question, and one can easily see how it arises—not least for those who have explicitly or implicitly imbibed the Weberian view of legitimacy simply as subjects' 'belief in legitimacy'. But if, on the other

[16] Mr Suhail Ahmad, a governor in the Indian Prison Service, currently completing a Ph.D thesis on 'Fairness in Prisons' at Cambridge University.

hand, we adopt Beetham's formulation that power relationships are legitimated (in part) when they can be '*justified* in terms of [subjects'] beliefs', then subtly different considerations are introduced within the 'dialectic of control' (Giddens 1984) that continually takes place in all prisons. For Beetham's formulation injects a moral judgement into the dialogue, and the moral judgement will inevitably be grounded principally in the prevailing moral beliefs of the particular society in question. Hence, prisoners making far-fetched demands (for example, for luxury accommodation, or waiter-service at all meals) will be easily rebuffed by prison management, who will know that such demands have no basis of moral support in that society. By contrast, the protesting prisoner may not infrequently (as Thomas and Pooley, 1980 pointed out) be asserting standards and expectations of fair and humane treatment now taken for granted in the world beyond the wall (cf. again Tyler (1990) on the importance of fair procedures, and the representational importance of the behaviour of officials). Where this is so—or where the prisoner is able successfully to 'point the finger' at prison officials for not following their own rules or proclaimed principles (Mathiesen's (1965) 'censoriousness')—then paying attention to prisoners' critiques of prison regimes has to be judged as *not* being simply about 'pleasing the prisoners'; rather, such critiques may be pointing to moral issues which will, sooner or later, carry real social weight both within the prison system and in wider political debates.

If this is correct, then a defensible and legitimated prison regime demands a dialogue in which prisoners' voices (as to what is 'justified in terms of their beliefs') are registered and have a chance of being responded to. Moreover, (as Woolf recognized with a clarity unfamiliar in English penal debates), legitimacy, thus understood, demands reference to standards that can be defended externally in moral and political argument. In the first instance this stipulates attention both to procedural and relational dimensions of prison regimes; in other words, to the recognition of prisoners in terms both of their citizenship and their ordinary humanity. (More ultimately it also calls for accounts both of the justice of the laws and procedures which put them in prison, and of the rationales which claim to justify their confinement.) Where any of this can be achieved, prisoners are to that extent more likely to acknowledge the legitimacy of the regime, as the positive dimensions of our Albany/Long Lartin evidence show.

How well does this answer stand up to the facts subsequently reported, and the analysis contained in, the Woodcock Report? The report is long and detailed, but for the present purposes the following salient points may be highlighted:

1. Whitemoor Prison is a dispersal prison, opened in 1991, where 'the highest levels of security had been incorporated in a "green-

field" situation'. The Special Security Unit (SSU) was 'the most protected area of the whole site . . . it was seen as a prison within a
prison, with the label of "impregnable" often assigned to it'
(Woodcock, 1994: 2).

2. In September 1994, the SSU contained ten inmates. On the
evening of 9 September, while four of the seven officers on duty in
the SSU were playing a game of Scrabble, six of the inmates
escaped from the Unit. All managed to get over or through four
high perimeter security barriers, and to escape from the prison; all
were, however, recaptured the same evening.

3. To effect their escape the six inmates had managed to manufacture and store in the Unit a very large amount of makeshift
equipment. They also acquired from outside the prison, and successfully concealed, two pistols and ammunition which were used
in the escape. Subsequent analysis showed that many prescribed
surveillance and searching procedures within the Unit had not been
carried out, for a variety of reasons, mostly connected with inmate
protests or complaints about 'lack of privacy', etc. Had proper procedures been carried out, there was 'little doubt' that the escape
equipment would have been discovered in advance.

4. The Woodcock Enquiry Team's central conclusion was that
'two main underlying themes and beliefs' had 'affected the whole
regime at Whitemoor SSU'. The first of these beliefs was that the
physical properties of the SSU made it, for all practical purposes,
escape proof; hence, from the point of view of security *any* internal
regime could apparently be applied. Secondly, 'there was a deeply
held, inherent fear on the part of Grovernor Grades and above of
another Strangeways-style riot'[17]; and this led to 'a regime of non-
confrontation' where prisoners 'were able to push back the boundaries of acceptable practice at every opportunity' (Woodcock,
1994: 82).

5. The Report states that 'the word "appeasement" became
widely used' in the media (page 3) regarding the regime and privileges in the SSU; the Report itself nowhere formally adopts this
term, but it is reasonably clear that the Enquiry Team did indeed
believe that a policy of 'appeasement' of the inmates had been
adopted, though not quite in the same context as that word was

[17] 'Strangeways' is the local name for Manchester prison, in widespread use
within the Prison Service.

used in the media.[18] *Inter alia*, the Enquiry reported that the 'predominant ethos' within the Unit had become 'don't upset the inmates' (page 24).

6. The Report states approvingly (apparently with a much wider applicability than the regimes in SSUs) that 'improved practices for controlling prisoners are at present being addressed by the Service'. It strongly advocates 'a regime based on consistency and firmness'; this will not only be in the interests of prison staff, and good security, but will also provide 'the greatest measure of protection for the inmates, in particular those vulnerable to the power wielded by the more violent prisoners' (page 84: this clearly has strong echoes of the analysis of DiIulio (1987), though there is no explicit reference to this source).

7. Woodcock further notes that Whitemoor SSU was opened 'in the wake of the Strangeways riot and the Gartree escape'. (See chapter 1 for details of these incidents.) This, it is said, was 'a time of very mixed ideologies within the Prison Service', with an emphasis (post-Gartree) on 'increasing physical security to prevent escapes', but also a wish 'to provide the greater element of "care" and positive staff–inmate relationships which the Woolf Report had encouraged' (page 81). No mention is made of the Woolf Report's central emphasis on justice in prisons.

What are we to make of all this? Clearly the subtext is 'if you pay too much attention to what prisoners want, you appease them, and you will ultimately lose control of your prison'. Is this correct? Does it, in effect, drive a coach and horses through all our fine words on legitimacy (and those, implicitly, of Woolf, subtly shifted by Woodcock from a 'justice' to a 'care' ideology)?

Let us be clear that in part Woodcock is right. Assuming the facts to be correctly reported by the Enquiry Team, there were some clear failures of situational control within the SSU, for example:

1. It had become the practice for officers not to enter the exercise yard of the SSU because 'they had not felt welcome' by the inmates there (page 56). CCTV was relied on instead, but there was

---

[18] The media apparently linked the 'appeasement' allegations to alleged 'political motives' connected with the IRA cease-fire of 31 Aug. 1994; the Enquiry Team found no evidence of this. (Five of the six escaping prisioners were convicted IRA members.)

at least one known deficiency in the CCTV's physical coverage at Whitemoor, which was highly relevant to the escape (page 54).

2. Related to the above, staff in control of SSU CCTV cameras were dedicated SSU staff. Inmates apparently disliked any panning or tilting movements of the CCTV cameras, alleging they were being 'spied on'; and they would then 'challenge [the relevant staff] personally the next time they were on general duties' (page 56). Thus was created a degree of personal intimidation of individual officers, who knew that these particular prisoners 'had the resources and connections to carry out any threat they made, and the unflinching will to do so' (page 82). The simple situational device of a division of labour between CCTV staff and SSU patrol staff would have prevented this personal intimidation, but was not adopted.

3. There were official limits in place concerning the amount of private cash allowed to inmates; in practice, however, *no* cash limits for private cash were applied at Whitemoor (or other SSUs). This is a matter of some considerable importance, since some inmates in the SSU could call on considerable outside resources, and in the prison context—as Woodcock rightly notes and as our Long Lartin analysis confirms—cash 'has the potential to be a source of power to the holder' (page 66).

Despite all this, however, we have to say that in places Woodcock displays a somewhat cavalier attitude to the inmates' perspective. So, for example:

1. It is noted that there had evolved 'quite significant differences in practice' between different SSUs. This fact, it is said, was 'relentlessly exploited' by inmates, and in Whitemoor SSU at least 'the overall effect had been to bring down standards to the lowest common denominator' (page 75). No recognition is given to the important point that, from an inmate's point of view, *consistency of treatment* is one of the most important features of prison justice (cf. Mathiesen 1965). (For example, 'why should X, who is the same kind of prisoner as me, get Y if I am denied it?') The failure, if it was one, was clearly in part managerial rather than simply attributable to the 'relentless' character of the inmates.

2. As regards visits to inmates (a highly sensitive topic, as chapter 5 has shown), the Enquiry Team reports that 'due to staffing levels and limited space availability', all required search procedures

were often not carried out on visitors 'in an attempt to speed the passage of the visitor'. This was because 'it was customary for inmates to complain bitterly if they did not get their full 2-hour visit' (page 36). The language used in this last comment is, with all due respect, simply indefensible. Which of us, if a prisoner, would *not* complain if we had been promised a two-hour visit from a close relative, that relative had made a special (and probably long and inconvenient) journey to the prison, and then the visit had been cut by say, half an hour? Indeed, under the 'legitimate expectations' approach favoured by Woolf, this is precisely the kind of injustice that would in time result in a successful action in judicial review, with the court issuing a formal 'declaration' against the Prison Service.[19]

3. In an Appendix to the Woodcock Report, the text of a letter from the Director General of the Prison Service to the Home Secretary is reproduced. Written six months before the escape, the letter addresses a Member of Parliament's complaint about the so-called 'hotel-style conditions' in the SSU. The Director-General agrees that the surroundings in the SSU are 'marginally more comfortable' than the rest of Whitemoor dispersal prison, but justifies this in the following way: 'Some prisoners live in the SSU for many years. They have no access to staff or prisoners outside the Unit, workshops, education and training facilities, the library or the prison shop. . . . *From my own inspection, I know it is extremely claustrophobic . . .* [The improved facilities in the Unit] *provide a modest counterbalance to some of the more draconian aspects of the environment and regime*' (pages 141–2, emphasis added).[20] Nowhere else does the Woodcock Report convey any sense of the claustrophobic physical conditions in the Unit, but obviously these would be regarded by prisoners as a matter of considerable importance in terms of 'just conditions'.

We hope that this discussion, and these examples, provide an adequate clarification of the distinction that we drew in our earlier

[19] The visits in question, being two hours in intended duration, were beyond the statutory entitlement in the Prison Rules; had they been 'statutory visits', cutting them short would already be challengeable in the courts under judicial review, following Hague's case (see ch. 8).

[20] In considering this comment, it is worth noting that the then Director-General was not a Prison Service professional, but an outside appointee with a business background.

paper—in response to the searching and pertinent question rightly posed to us—between, on the one hand, 'prisoners making far-fetched demands' (for example 'don't patrol our exercise yard') and prisoners 'asserting standards and expectations of fair and humane treatment now taken for granted in the world beyond the wall' (for example 'if you've promised me and my visitor a two-hour visit, don't cut it short'). The central point is that (following Beetham) ultimately the concept of legitimacy has a moral content that links it very closely to the concept of justice. In a penetrating discussion of the concept of justice, the Oxford philosopher J. R. Lucas (1980) suggests *inter alia* that persons in power who are concerned to avoid injustice need:

1. to consider situations from the point of view of those who may be disadvantaged or disappointed by the decisions that they (the powerful) are about to make; and

2. to reach decisions that are adverse to citizens only for reasons that they (the citizens) ought rationally to acknowledge as cogent.

Following this kind of perspective, we concluded our earlier paper on legitimacy and order in prisons in the following way (Sparks and Bottoms, 1995: 60):

[E]very instance of brutality in prisons, every casual racist joke and demeaning remark, every ignored petition, every unwarranted bureaucratic delay, every inedible meal, every arbitrary decision to segregate or transfer without giving clear and well founded reasons, every petty miscarriage of justice, every futile and inactive period of time—is delegitimating. The combination of an inherent legitimacy deficit with an unusually great disparity of power places a peculiar onus on prison authorities to attend to the legitimacy of their actions. This underlines the necessity of acting legitimately in terms of formal rules at all times, and attending to those elements of shared moral beliefs existing between staff and prisoners (for example in terms of humane regimes, distributive and procedural fairness and supplying meaningful rationales for the exercise of power) so as to maximise the residual sense in which prison authorities may be entitled to call upon prisoners to confer consent.

None of this, however, means that one has to 'appease' prisoners. Following Lucas, decisions that are adverse to citizens (in this case, prisoners) should be made only for reasons that the citizens ought rationally to acknowledge as cogent; but some such reasons clearly exist, and sometimes the prison authorities will be right to say 'no'.

There is, in other words—and as Mathiesen (1965) long ago correctly perceived—a strongly moral dimension to the job of running a prison (and that remains the case despite the fact that modern managerialism—increasingly influential in prison services across the world—tends to downplay moral considerations in favour of approaches such as the actuarial: cf. Feeley and Simon 1992, Bottoms 1995). We hope that our emphasis on the importance of legitimacy to order in prisons will help to refocus attention upon these moral dimensions of penal practice.

It will have become apparent that neither of the two prisons in our study had achieved a fully satisfactory resolution of the dilemmas of securing order in a maximum security prison, nor of those of legitimation: it is conceivable that no such thing is possible. But the contrast between them does, it seems to us, clarify some of the dilemmas. It also perhaps opens up fresh issues for both prison administrators and sociologists to explore more fully in the future.

Appendix A
Order in Dispersal Prisons: Notes on a Research Process

In history everyone is right: the hammer as well as the anvil
Heinrich Heine

There is something of a genre of the methodological postscript in prison sociology. Sykes has one, so does Mathiesen. These may be more or less concerned with technical matters, or they may have a somewhat confessional tone. Doing prison research is by its nature a personally challenging and sometimes fraught experience, one in which some kind of final settling of accounts (if not indeed a need or desire on the researcher's part for self-justification) frequently appears important. Perhaps it is that the demands of responding to the situation so often seem to necessitate departing from the canons of orthodox research procedure. Or maybe researchers confronting their own final texts find some absence in them of the sense of 'being there' that they had hoped to convey. In any case it is clear that prisons research, at least of our style, has all the usual problems and pitfalls of field research in other settings, with a few very special ones of its own thrown in for good measure. One shies from breaking up a substantive text with the kind of fragmentary notes and comments that follow here; and embarrassment forbids presenting them 'straight' as a 'methods chapter'. It was all, the researchers murmur to themselves, more pragmatic, more improvised, more opportunist than that; and perhaps it had to be so.

This appended note, therefore, offers some late reflections on our experience of doing research in prisons. It does not claim to extend the large and sophisticated literature on qualitative or field research methods, certainly not in any prescriptive or programmatic way. And with one or two exceptions it refrains from commenting on the methods or accounts of others. It does, however, broach a number of difficulties we encountered and decisions that we took, the record of which may be of some value to others contemplating similar research in future.

We will point out some factors which influenced the initiation of the research, both in terms of the concerns of those who funded and sponsored it and of those of us who actually designed it and put it into practice. We will outline aspects of a firsthand account of some special features of doing interview-based research in prisons. Briefly, research in prison which sets out to tap the perceptions of both staff (of all grades) and prisoners faces some particular problems. It has as its aim the difficult task of investigating with equal sensitivity the views of all parties in situations of conflict. Its methodological starting point is similar in spirit to Heine's aphorism: the whole situation can only be grasped by attempting to 'take the point of view' of both parties. But just whether this is in principle achievable, and how making the attempt affects the role and commitments of the researcher are matters worthy of reflection. By way of conclusion we offer some brief comments on what 'model' of research this seems to suggest as being appropriate, in terms of how it might conceive its relations to its subjects, its subject matter, and its possible readers. This paper was origi-nally drafted almost immediately after the end of our fieldwork, with the experiences on which it draws still anxiously and nerve-janglingly close to us. It has lain like a guilty secret, largely untouched in the virtual state of existence of an unaccessed computer disc, ever since. Somewhat to our sur-prise, we have wanted to change its contents only slightly. It is a personal memoir, albeit one now very much 'recollected in tranquillity' rather than in the heat of the moment.

The Prison 'Community'

As we outlined in chapter 2, the tradition of sociological concern with incarceration, usually glossed following Clemmer as the study of 'the prison community', is of long standing. It includes some contributions which are rightly regarded as among the best monographs on social institu-tions available. Works such as Sykes's *The Society of Captives* (1958) and Goffman's *Asylums* (1968) have enjoyed a longevity which is unusual among the torrential flow of research reports in the social sciences, with their necessary attention to topicality and contemporary relevance, and the ephemerality that often flows from that. This is noteworthy in itself. Perhaps it suggests that, notwithstanding the pressure and contingency of events, certain fundamental issues in incarceration do not change very much.

We should be careful about this however. To rely on a tradition of 'clas-sic' studies may have some limiting consequences. It may mean failing to question and re-evaluate them. It may reduce our awareness of the issues to an ideal-typical notion of 'the prison' which is conceived of as being, at least in the Western liberal democracies, always and everywhere substan-tially similar. This is the weakest feature of Goffman's theory of 'total institutions' for example, as well as some of the uses which are made of Foucault's work. To view the 'classic' studies as amounting to a general theory may mean failing to differentiate between the social processes which take place in different types of prison, or in different prisons of the same 'type'. It is to lose the sense of time and place which the authors of those 'classics' were at such pains to capture. Not least, it may be that the classic monographs still enjoy their predominant position at least in part because relatively little work of similar quality has been done in the intervening years.

We think that this latter point is largely correct. In Britain at least patient, empirically grounded and theoretically informed contributions have been relatively few and far between.[1] Some of the reasons for this may not be hard to detect. They include the peculiar development of British criminology, its historically primary interest in juvenile delinquency and street crime, and its lack, until at least the 1970s, of a strong basis in sociological theory or ethnographic method. In prisons research, of course, there has also been the special problem of tense and uneasy relations between researchers and the sponsors or gatekeepers who control access and funding (see Cohen and Taylor, 1977). Moreover the pressing awareness of a deepening prisons crisis has proved almost distracting. The most urgent tasks have proved to be those of documenting facts about rising prison populations and deteriorating material conditions, examining sentencing decisions and justifications for the use of custody and designing or evaluating alternatives to imprisonment. In these circumstances examining aspects of social life within the prison itself, and especially adult long-term prisons, has sometimes seemed to take second place.

This situation has begun to change recently, and some of these changes provide the background to our research. In the first place there has been a renewal of scholarly activity which bears on long-terms prisons, including recent work by King and McDermott (1990; 1995), Scraton et al. (1991), Sim (1990) and Genders and Player (1989). Second, prisons themselves are never silent. They always generate talk and controversy. But at least until Lord Justice Woolf's more systematic intervention, an observer has had to piece the 'debate' together from its fragmentary sources. These include official publications, whether on the prison system as a whole (Home Office, 1979), the dispersal system in general (Home Office, 1984) or particular events within it (for example Home Office, 1977; 1982); the growing body of case-law stemming from prisoners' litigation (cf. Maguire et al., 1985: chs. 1–3; Livingstone and Owen, 1993); autobiographical accounts by prisoners and ex-prisoners (Boyle, 1977; McVicar 1979); arguments put

[1] The main exceptions to this include work by Morris and Morris (1963), Cohen and Taylor (1977; 1981), King and Elliott (1977), and more contemporarily King and McDermott (1990). Little British research, whatever its other virtues, can lay much claim to insight into the lives, commitments and identities of prison staff. Cohen and Taylor's depiction of the 'vulgar authoritarianism' of prison officers, e.g., is no great basis for sympathetic understanding (1977: 68).

forward by the Prison Officers' Association (POA); the work of prison charities; journalism. This is the disposition of forces in relation to which any research enterprise must orient itself and find its bearings.

The researcher entering a dispersal prison for the first time is in a weak and vulnerable position. It is a territory which has not recently been charted by earlier researchers, one whose language and conventions are almost wholly unfamiliar. Yet it is one that has a whole history of contention about which many of the protagonists, the researcher's nominal 'subjects', are intimately knowledgeable, whilst he or she is relatively ignorant. This is one of the first fundamental features of doing research in long term prisons. As anthropologists report, the researcher coming from outside is effectively an ignoramus, a potential object of sympathy or scorn. One begins, as Burgess puts it, as a 'clumsy alien' (1984: 11). We will return to the question of the researcher's role below, after having considered some prior questions in the formulation of our research design and strategy.

The Context and Design of Research in Dispersal Prisons

Any empirical research project in the social sciences whose concerns bear upon topics in public policy and administration must at some point consider its position in relation to existing fields of theory and debate and to the interests of its sponsoring agency. As Reiner has documented these considerations are relevant to the whole of recent British criminology (Reiner, 1988). Such concerns are especially vexed in respect of prisons where issues not only of funding, but also of protocol, access, co-operation, protection of sources and publication must be confronted in an acute form. Thinking through these questions is a precondition for both clarity and integrity in the conduct and writing of research. In officially sponsored research it may be (as it was for us whilst preparing the report which eventually mutated into this book) that even after some pondering the researchers find themselves unable to resolve all the relevant questions conclusively: what is going on in the 'customer–client' relationship within the bureaucracy?; exactly what kind of document do 'they' want, and for what precise purpose?; who within the apparatus does want the research and who may not?; is there pressure to arrive at definite conclusions or proposals in answer to questions which seem to remain open or intractable?; should the likely readers of the document be thought of as 'lay' people or specialists?; to what extent can writers of the document influence the uses to which it may be put?; who 'owns' the report?; more particularly, who 'owns' the data?; at what point, even in a co-operative, businesslike and mutually respectful relationship may the researchers' priorities (whether towards curiosity or critique) begin to depart from and perhaps conflict with those of the 'customers' or 'users' of research? Such questions are integral to the design of such research and the researchers' responsibilities. Certainly any-one doing research in prisons had better think about them, because they will be asked repeatedly by prisoners and staff. If officially-sponsored researchers are honest they will acknowledge, at least if they hope that the research will be of any use or effect, that their own curiosity cannot be the sole motor which generates the research. Nor should this be thought of just negatively as a problem: in fact it is part of the conditions of possibil-ity for the research. It is how they got there.[2]

Some features of debates about dispersal prisons which have preceded our research are already well known, if not notorious—and we need not rehearse them further here. They include the arguments which have contin-ued since the inception of the system over the issues of 'concentration' and 'dispersal' of prisoners deemed security risks and over the specialization of regimes for particular categories of long-term prisoner, especially those considered 'disruptive'. In particular there has been the conflictual history of the dispersal prisons themselves. Most investigations of the dispersal sys-tem, both official, and independent (cf. Thomas and Pooley, 1980) have had regard primarily to major crises of control, rather than to more mun-dane or chronic events and problems.

As we have outlined in chapter 1 the background to our own research lay in the ways in which these debates were deliberated first by the Control Review Committee and subsequently the Research and Advisory Group on the Long-Term Prison System, in whose 1987 report the need for a new activity of research, including our own was specified.

It would be easy for a critical critic to take the view that our research agenda was thus 'set' by a debate within the official discourse. Our view is rather that at that point the discourse had developed in such a way as to invite a sociologically imaginative response. It had become open to an observer to respond in a variety of ways. On the one hand one could examine the discourse itself, to identify its presumptions and commitments. To do this might help us to 'track' likely developments in policy, and to

---

[2] As Pahl observes one besetting problem for policy-related research which arises from this is that: 'If the everyday worlds with which we are most familiar are mainly those of the underdogs or, at best the middle dogs, we are forced to fall back on accounts of non-sociologists for an understanding of the top dogs.' (Pahl 1977: 130).

We have been fortunate in that some of the topmost dogs willingly agreed to par-ticipate in the research. We are particularly grateful for the co-operation of the then Governors of Wakefield, Long Lartin and Albany prisons during our fieldwork there. Even so, how one handles relations with the most locally powerful people is always a key question. Governors may feel entitled to be kept informed about 'how the research is going' in ways that potentially conflict with prerogatives that researchers would wish to guard jealously.

understand better the implicit ideologies, including the competitions and tensions between them, on which decision making of powerful people depends, (cf. Adler and Longhurst, 1989; Fitzgerald, 1987). Alternatively one could see propositions within the official discourse as a stimulus to a research project of a more directly empirical kind. This is how we viewed the CRC's well known statements about 'getting the relationship right' in prisons (Home Office, 1984: para. 16; see also para. 118). For us it meant an opportunity for researchers to go into the prisons and find out about the 'relationships' which existed there. In this kind of project one can ask what it would mean to 'get those relationships right'? What happens when they are not 'right'. How, when and why are social relations in prisons maintained, strained or broken down and with what consequences for the people involved? How are the relevant social processes and events undertaken and interpreted by particular groups of staff and prisoners? Do different things happen in different prisons, and if so why? These are some of the questions which prompted us in designing and conducting our research in the way we did.

'Control Problems and the Long-Term Prisoner': the Career of a Research Project

Even quite open-ended questions presuppose implicit theories, commitments and conjectured answers. So, what did we know, or think we knew, when we started? We knew that dispersal prisons had some special features including, in principle, that they were supposed to incorporate a 'liberal regime within a secure perimeter'. We knew that they had somewhat differing populations, histories, and reputations. We knew that the dispersal system had a history of sporadic upheavals and conflicts and we knew some of the explanations which had been put forward for these. We knew that the people confined in them were disparate in offence, length of sentence, age, race, religion and experience and that some of them might have antagonisms towards one another. We knew that this might create problems for us. We knew that we didn't know much, especially perhaps about the lives, identities, problems and activities of prison staff on which at that time very little work existed in Britain, with the exceptions of one important historical study (Thomas, 1972) and one recent attitude survey (Marsh et al., 1985).

We speculated that the existing literature about life in prison might be of limited help to us. Much of it was no longer recent, the best of it had been done in other jurisdictions (in America and Scandinavia), and very little of it addressed issues particular to everyday life in English dispersal prisons. We also knew however that the questions of order and conflict in institutions were among the fundamental concerns of all social enquiry and that we could not therefore confine our attention to work originating only in penology/prison studies as such.[3]

We knew that we anticipated the prospect of starting our fieldwork with as much foreboding as curiosity.

We thus began from a position of considerable uncertainty. After all, if a research project is genuinely directed towards new knowledge then there are limits to the kind of foreknowledge the researchers can have. Hence, the research would have to begin in an exploratory, even naive, spirit and this would influence the choice of methods.

However, whilst this starting point is unavoidable it contains considerable dangers. Quite often when researchers have gone into prisons they have found themselves adrift in the midst of a complex human community, full of events, incidents and characters. It is easy to be swamped by this complexity and variety. One wants to record every detail, every impression, every humanly interesting story and situation. Several problems can then arise. The researchers may gather too much information, with no very clear idea what to say about it or how to explain its importance to a potential reader. They may be tempted to produce a highly autobiographical account of the pleasures, fascination and miseries of the research process itself which risks becoming self-regarding and losing sight of its primary responsibilities to the people and institutions out of whose lives it is constructed. Under these circumstances the researcher can suffer stress, fatigue, and become, in effect, 'burned out', overwhelmed by a sense of the difficulty of the task, and unable to synthesize his or her impressions in an intelligible, accountable way. Perhaps riskiest of all, the researcher, whose position is inherently somewhat isolating, may become captivated by his or her involvement with particular individuals or groups within the prison and come to take on their point of view to the exclusion of others. Some of these dangers are exemplified in Mark Fleisher's account of his research at the United States Penitentiary at Lompoc in Northern California. In his book *Warehousing Violence* (1989) Fleisher recognizes that he effectively 'went native' with the guards:

From September 1985 to January 1986, I lost touch with my role as research anthropologist and began to think of myself as a correctional worker. My thinking about penitentiary research started to fuse with notions, opinions and beliefs of inmates and penitentiary staffers. I began to answer my own research questions, as if I were

---

[3] Recent contributions in social theory have demonstrated a renewed interest in and sensitivity to the 'problem of order' and the definition of 'power' (Young, 1987), as well as to the importance of the organization of time and space in social life. Each of these topics is of fundamental importance in understanding social relations in prisons. We have found elements of the recent work of Giddens (1984) especially helpful, as we have indicated in ch. 2.

a correctional worker. In other words, I became my own informant . . . I was becoming lost.

(Fleisher, 1989: 112)

Fleisher is very candid about this. Yet it is doubtful whether his subsequent resolve in which 'I regained my perspective, and from then on I kept my eye on research' is a sufficient insight into the ambiguity of his position. Anyone reading Fleisher's book, or any other prison research should be very alert to the precise position from which it is written. These considerations will have particular bearing on anyone undertaking research who is in fact a prison service employee or even who, like ourselves, has a more oblique relationship to officialdom.

We only became aware of Fleisher's book after our own fieldwork, although some of the issues it raises already preoccupied us. The most tenable solution available to us seemed to be to define a relatively specific set of research 'problems', whilst at the same time not foreclosing the range of perspectives or influences which might bear upon them, and provide their contexts.

To this extent we took as our primary task the examination, elaboration, and interrogation of the perspectives broached by the CRC report as these had already been glossed by the Research and Advisory Group on the Long-Term Prison System. A sociological interpretation of this loose research 'agenda' incorporated some of the following considerations which we built into our research:

First, there could be no simple opposition between 'quantitative' and 'qualitative' approaches. On the one hand, we had to document and enumerate *rates* of incidents falling under particular categories. These in turn might indeed be systematically related to quantifiable dimensions of regimes or populations. Nevertheless, the 'quantitative' dimension of the problem remained that which we would have to interpret and contextualize.

Second, even the 'hardest' of the quantitative dimensions is not a fact of nature but rather the outcome of complex social process of action and reaction, the definition and application of rules and sanctions, and practices of recording. It is a criminological commonplace that crime rates are subject to these determinations, but the same perspective has rarely been brought to bear on the internal disciplinary and regulatory mechanisms of prisons.

Third, the notions of 'control' and 'control problems' are thus not self-evident. As Young has pointed out the meaning of these terms in prison depends on 'what kind of order one is seeking' and the means used to achieve it (Young 1987). How do prisoners, uniformed staff, and Governors use these terms in their accounts of their activities and their relations with one another? How do these perspectives vary between prisons?

Fourth, particular 'control problems' or 'control incidents' are situations or sequences of events. They have antecedents and consequences. What range of actions and reactions fall under these headings? How do events or situations which attract the intervention of staff, and hence the status of 'control problems', arise in or depart from the 'normal' conditions of everyday life in prison? In what does this 'normality' itself consist; how is it maintained or restored? A 'control incident' may be anything which contravenes what Garfinkel (1967) calls the 'routine expectancies' of everyday life.

Fifth, a control incident sets in train a sequence of disciplinary or administrative actions. Foremost among these is the removal of a prisoner or prisoners from 'normal location' either as a punishment (or 'award') or as an expedient measure (under Prison Rule 43, or Circular Instruction 10/74, as it then was). What is the extent and variation in the use of these measures? What ethical, practical or legal considerations, and what process of decision govern their use? What are their intended and unintended consequences? How are they experienced by the prisoners concerned?

To recap: until now we have described how a number of general and rather diffuse concerns, interests and scraps of prior knowledge began to be resolved into particular research questions. We have also begun to note some pitfalls of prison research which we tried to avoid. We will now go on to summarize briefly an outline of the research we actually did, including some personal reflections on problems in the researcher's role.

Undertaking Research

We began from an awareness of a deficit in our knowledge and understanding. We also surmised that a fuller understanding of the 'quantitative' problem of 'control problems' in dispersal prisons might best be gained by 'qualitative' means, that is, by an effort of interpretation of the accounts which prisoners and staff might give us of their situations and actions. In short, we had to go and ask people what was going on.

We were looking for something like a 'grounded theory' (Glaser and Strauss, 1967) of 'control problems', albeit that we were uneasy about the apparent inductivism of some of Glaser and Strauss's propositions about how theory 'emerges' from data (Layder, 1993: 61). This meant a task of theoretical reflection on the concept of 'control' and its relation to related and more general terms, such as 'order'. It meant considering the meaning of such terms in use. It meant a constant interleaving of theoretical refinement and self-criticism in response to the knowledge gained from observation, talk, and the study of records and documents. It meant, in particular, trying to see systematic features of 'control problems' as constituted by the situated actions and interpretations of knowledgeable actors in their dealings with one another within the 'flow' of everyday life in dispersal prisons.

'Pilot' Work

We reasoned that these goals would require extensive preliminary or 'pilot' work. With this in mind we undertook four months of pilot work at Wakefield Prison during the winter of 1987–8. Beginning with a two week induction programme of timetabled visits throughout the prison we observed, chatted with prisoners and staff, asked questions, and tried haltingly to explain our presence and our interests. We spent time (and time is after all the primary currency of the prison) on the wings, in offices, workshops, on playing fields and in the gym, in the kitchen, in the chapel, in the segregation unit. We tried to be present at each of the moments by which the routine segments the day: unlock, breakfast, work, classes, lunch, work, tea, association, lock-up. We spent the weekend in the prison. We went when invited into what Goffman calls the 'back' regions for the staff—tearooms, the staff club, pubs. We learned a new vocabulary of technical terms: acronyms, argot, terms of abuse and affection. We tried to make sense of prison records and statistics and think about what we could do with them. Towards the end of this period, and on the basis of our provisional and tenuous knowledge, we began to conduct a number of open-ended and exploratory interviews. With hindsight many of these interviews now seem to us diffuse and rambling. But they were also rich and various. They suggested that most people would agree to be tape-recorded if they accepted the interviewer's good faith. They demonstrated that both prisoners and staff were able, in a private and sympathetic context, to speak with moving force and clarity about their respective situations, anxieties, problems, consolations, and relations with one another. In particular, they suggested that it was possible to refine our interview technique and formulate viable interview questions for the main study.

Main Study

Our theoretical premises, including that 'control problems' are both situationally specific and contextually variable, gave rise to a need for comparative work. We set out to study the incidence and management of trouble in two dispersal prisons over similar periods of time in relation to constants and variables in regimes, routines and social relationships. The main study was conducted over successive five month periods at Long Lartin and Albany prisons (see chapter 3 for a discussion of the choice of these two prisons).

We brought to bear the same strategies as at Wakefield, but in more systematic and detailed ways. These had three main components. First, in each prison we spent several hundred hours in informal familiarization, observation and talk with staff and prisoners. This was a lengthy process, largely because research of this kind requires establishing a position within the institution which is as far as possible acceptable to all parties, albeit remaining alert to the conditional nature of such acceptance. The process of familiarization thus sought to achieve:

1. trust—to the extent that people accepted sufficiently our guarantees of confidentiality and good faith;
2. credibility—in becoming sufficiently knowledgeable for people to think it worthwhile speaking to us, such that they felt we understood (to some significant degree) what we were seeing and hearing, and that we were taking note of their viewpoints.
3. access—to all relevant departments, people, and information.

One governor likened this process to watching a game of draughts. This metaphor is quite vivid: the researcher begins as a rather naive observer, but one who makes presumptions and conjectures about the nature of the game, and aims to become one who is conversant with the game plans of each of the players. How well has the observer learned the rules of the game? Whether he knew it or not this man had enunciated a fundamental theme of interpretive sociology and the philosophy of ordinary language. The researcher is not in any full sense a player, but he or she is a party to the game. If, as Wittgenstein insists, knowing a rule means knowing 'how to go on' we might of course remain forever excluded from full knowledge. We might nevertheless hope to learn 'what is going on', in the same sense that a really knowledgeable spectator can know about cricket without her/himself ever learning how to bat or bowl.

Secondly, we conducted 'general' and 'specific' interviews, as detailed in chapter 3. Thirdly and finally, we gathered statistical information about aspects of population, regime, and indices of control problems. Thus, for example, populations may be broken down by age, offence, sentence, security category, ethnicity. Meanwhile, indices of control problems include: recorded incidents, alarm bells, the use of administrative segregation, transfer of prisoners (for example under CI 10/74), Governors' adjudications and awards, and so forth.

Among the particular contributions which this research seeks to make are the following. First it tries to move beyond the simple description of prison regimes to develop a systematic analysis of the prevalence of particular 'control problems' and conflictual situations in two very different prisons. Secondly, this in turn informs theoretical understanding of the prison as a social institution and the conditions which tend to produce stability or instability within it. Thirdly, it constructs these analyses on the basis of thorough and grounded attention to the viewpoints of both prisoners and staff in the context of their everyday activity and social relationships.

Research as Activity and Experience: the Researcher's Role

The researcher's role in prison is inherently problematic. This has been noted many times. Sykes (1958: 135–6), Cressey (1962: 1–12), King and Elliott (1977: 33), Cohen and Taylor (1972; 1977), McDermott and King (1988) and Fleisher (1989) are among the important sources on the varying ways in which this is so. In this paper we can add only a few notes on the researcher's role as we have experienced it, and as it has structured our activity.

As we have already suggested the researcher, at least one coming into a particular prison setting for the first time, sets out with few natural advantages. He looks naive, 'green', uncomfortable, out of place.[4]

He has no uniform, no keys, no proper job or activity which (at least at first), prisoners and staff are likely to recognize as such.[5] He can expect to be routinely misidentified as one or other of the things he resembles which might have some reason to be there—a psychologist, a psychiatrist, a probation officer, a trainee staff member, a reporter, a member of the inspec-

---

[4] We will use the masculine form from now on simply because we are all male and we are discussing our own experience. However, much of the best recent first-hand research in British prisons has in fact been done largely or wholly by women. We include here work by Pat Carlen, Kathleen McDermott, Elaine Genders and Elaine Player, and Alison Liebling. Gelsthorpe and Morris (1988) set out a number of advantages relating to the reception of and insights gained by women researchers in men's as well as women's prisons. There are also problems, however. These include the anxieties, protectiveness, and occasional hostility of staff. Prisoners too are predominantly conservative, masculine men who may express some aspects of their feelings in some areas to women (face-threatening anxieties, family problems?) but not necessarily others (masturbation, homosexuality, use of violence?). Most of the interesting questions in the gender politics of prison research seem as yet to be unresolved, and it seems likely that research by both men and women, separately and together, will continue to be necessary.

[5] We took a principled decision not to carry keys despite being repeatedly offered them. The obvious disadvantages of not having keys are considerable as is the ambiguity of a position in which one has no keys and yet is frequently unescorted. Yet these problems are trivial compared to the benefits in solving the problem of misidentification by prisoners and differentiating ourselves in their eyes from any employee of the prison. This is quite apart from the number of conversations and contacts initiated while waiting at gates with prisoners or moving through them with staff. We did admittedly get extremely cold on winter nights in both Wakefield and Albany. Fleisher (1989) carried keys and was deservedly taken to task for it by prisoners.

torate, a new governor, a CID man, a man come to fix the television. If he is alone, and unrecognized, he can expect to be challenged by staff.

As a stranger and interloper he should expect to invite some suspicion and curiosity. How, after all, did he come to be there? He must have, people *correctly* infer, friends or contacts in high places. He must be 'reporting back' to somebody. He is in a private place, a place where people live and work, take showers, go to the toilet, try to have personal conversations, read letters from home, try to get some peace and quiet. His very presence is potentially intrusive and impolite—a reminder to prisoners and staff that they do not own their environment and that they can have people foisted on them whom they did not ask for. The researcher is in a doubly tricky position. He is an ignorant spy.

On the other hand our implicit connection with 'the powers that be' was by no means wholly disadvantageous. Certainly it was important for people, especially prisoners, to know that we were not directly employed Home Office staff, but that we worked for a university and were jealous of our academic independence. Yet we were also told many times that we were worth talking to in part because our report might find its way onto the relevant desks, and because the cachet of our university meant that it might not be entirely ignorable. It was important to some of our 'subjects' that we were not simply satisfying our own scholarly curiosity but that we also hoped to exert some small influence on penal policy, or at least that we offered a channel that might let their perspective find a hearing. Such institutional connections are thus deeply double edged. To deny them is not simply to be untrustworthy but potentially something worse, namely to have no position or purpose and hence assume a low status in prisoners' scale of evaluations as a 'chancer', a 'wanker', a 'plonker'—in short a fool. And only a fool, they reasoned, would do as we did, spending months on end hanging around in prisons, living away from home, unless they were being well paid (though this was always hugely overestimated) and with some definite purpose in view.

It may be that the best one can hope for as a researcher is to move, over the course of time, from being a grudgingly tolerated fool to a fairly welcome one. In each of the three prisons we studied we gradually became a 'feature'. As time went by these two men in civilian clothes walking around, talking to people, occasionally disappearing with them for hours on end, became a familiar sight.[6] Thus, our identity gradually changed and

[6] The two in question being Will Hay and Richard Sparks, with Tony Bottoms as overall director of the project making less frequent visits to the research 'sites' where necessary, especially at the beginning and end of our periods there. As the remarks reported here imply, Will and Richard were indeed almost always together whilst on the job, including for the great majority of the interviews. This was for several reasons. It boosted our confidence. It reassured staff as to our physical safety. It enabled us to take turns at leading interviews when we got tired or when the person

we would be greeted not with 'Look out, the spies are here', as at first, but rather as 'Pinky and Perky' or 'Bill and Ben' or 'the Dynamic Duo' or just 'not you two again!'.

There are a number of distinct staging posts in the development of an acceptable researcher role, but they do not take place automatically. They require effort and thought. However, it may be possible to formalize them, provisionally, as a series of injunctions, of which the following is an incomplete list:

1. Put in the time. Time is a basic structuring dimension of prison life for both the prisoners and the staff. Everyone is 'doing time'. Prison officers often describe their careers in these terms, and explain both their practical wisdom and world-weariness by reference to how many years they 'have in'. Furthermore, time is marked out in particular ways both in terms of the long duration of a career or a sentence but also in the division of daily time by routines, shifts and events. Researchers need to understand these features of time and their activities must in a sense mirror its 'flow'. Moreover, both prisoners and staff have a certain regard for those who are prepared to 'put in' the hours and the days, and who know the pattern of the routine from early unlock to evening bang up, who know the geography of the prison, its folklore and leading personalities. Conversely, to work a nine to five day is to be defined as a 'civilian' and hence axiomatically as one who does not know what prison is all about.

2. Chat to people and learn their language. Prison talk is marked by the use of jargon and argot. If the researcher is not familiar with these vocabularies in use he cannot claim to understand what is being said. The researcher must show willing in being instructed in this language. Moreover, being prepared to sit and chat, to be seen to listen and take note of what is said, are fundamentally important activities. Certainly, it is the case that progress in research depends on subsequently beginning to formalize and focus the kind of 'talk' one undertakes (cf. Cohen and Taylor, 1977). But this can only be done on the basis of informed under-

we were talking to seemed happier addresssing themselves more to one of us than the other. It meant that one of us could generally listen whilst the other interacted, and it meant that we could discuss our impressions immediately and on the basis of the same information. Working as a pair does also have the advantage that where necessary we could literally be in two places at once. This was most helpful, e.g., during association periods when it would be very difficult for one person to form an adequate impression of the different activities and interactions taking place throughout the quite large and labyrinthine space of a prison wing. The 'binocular vision' that follows from having two people present is useful in constructing a sense of the topography of that social space. We would not presume to prescribe any such procedure for others, but it rapidly became our preferred and most comfortable way of working; and it contributes to our strongly held boast that the whole research was a joint enterprise, in execution as well as in writing.

standings and on terms which are agreeable to the various parties. The researcher must have at least some awareness of the locally variable factors involved in talking about what might seem at first sight to be 'standard' issues. For example, amongst staff, their feelings and commitments about their jobs and tasks may vary in relation to aspects of the institutional history of a particular prison and be defined partly in opposition or contrast to their perceptions of other prisons. Similarly, prisoners' perceptions of their position and treatment also have regard to customary expectations and felt entitlements in their own and other prisons. Such considerations are always in play in shaping the relationship between researcher and researched. Does the researcher see the researched in the role of 'informant' or 'expert witness' or 'storyteller' or merely as 'subject'? And how in turn are researchers and the drift and manner of the questioning to be considered?

3. Ask and answer questions. The development of a research process is thus a sequence of stages in 'learning how to ask' (Briggs, 1986). It seems to us to be both practically and morally inescapable that the entitlement to ask certain kinds of questions (which may be personal, painful, taxing, incriminating) cannot be taken for granted. An interview is voluntarily undertaken, on the basis of undertakings given. This is not just a question of the privilege or confidentiality of the interview, nor even of discretion in the subsequent uses made of 'data', though these are all imperative. It also means a certain manner of approaching people and asking them for their time and co-operation. It means agreeing the terms of the interview in advance. It means answering the questions which people may have of you about your identity, purposes and affiliations before assuming the right to ask questions of them. It means not foreclosing the acceptability of the answers they may want to give. It may mean in certain cases that a formal interview will not be possible whilst an informal conversation is quite acceptable. It certainly means, we want to argue, that any kind of covert or devious research stratagem is untenable: it is difficult to defend in principle and it will almost inevitably be found out and challenged.[7] This is especially true where the researcher needs similar kinds of co-operation from both staff and prisoners, not only the hammer but also the anvil. Only under conditions of the most stringent candour are prisoners and staff likely to recognize the researcher's capacity to speak to other parties

[7] In this regard none of the terms which Burgess uses to summarize postures often adopted by field researchers quite captures our own position. We were not 'going native'; nor were we 'undercover agents'; neither were we in a consistent position of 'advocate research' (Burgess, 1984: 20). True 'participant observation' in prisons is rare, though many have fancied themselves in those clothes. In our view non-participant observation (or 'friendly stranger') roles are considerably more defensible. One does not set out to participate, even if one must be mindful of the ways in which one cannot avoid doing so.

without prejudice and to acknowledge the researcher's prerogative of interpreting the results. Meanwhile, this also imposes on the researcher the need
to admit some kind of reciprocity and to give something back. The interview may represent a number of different things for the interviewee. It may
mean a simple break in routine, a chance to get off work for a while, to
introduce a little novelty into a tedious pattern of life. It may mean an
opportunity to unburden himself, to vindicate his actions, to sound off
without repercussions, to have his opinions taken note of, to alleviate his
loneliness, to reflect on his position. It may simply provide a vicarious contact with the outside world. It may also mean an opportunity to ask for
information or advice about prospects of parole or promotion or any number of other anxieties. The researcher must make plain the limits of his
knowledge, entitlements and roles. He cannot become an intermediary. He
cannot trespass upon the terrain of probation officers or psychologists. He
must avoid becoming embroiled in controversy or dispute. He must ask to
be excused any such demand. Neither, however, can he simply disengage at
the end of the interview and scurry to the gate.

In each of the above reflections we have tried to draw out the connections
between the intellectual, practical, and personal demands of doing prison
research. Doing research means developing elements of practical as well as
discursive expertise, some of which may become virtually habitual. Just as
prison officers may demonstrate interpersonal skills of the most subtle and
nuanced kind and yet have difficulty articulating what it is they do, so for
the researcher an effort of reflection is necessary in connecting what he did
and what he thought he was doing. Doing research in prison is, willy-nilly,
'being there' as a physical and social presence, not an inert camera or 'fly
on the wall'. It means standing in certain places, having conversations, taking jokes, approaching particular people in certain ways, inquiring, asking,
answering, waiting at gates, keeping appointments. There is no sharp distinction between its 'method' and its etiquette.

It also follows that the research process is inherently fallible and subject
to contingencies. In that it is conducted in and through talk, and is never
more than a particular purposive form of social interaction, there is no
foolproof way of assuring its outcomes. A researcher can, for example, easily alienate staff by seeming to place himself in an exposed or dangerous
position, by allowing himself to be surrounded by a knot of curious prisoners or by disappearing from sight round corners. Equally it is irritating to
prisoners if he is not at ease walking, talking and sitting amongst them.
Similarly the researcher cannot know in advance all the dynamics of the
relationships in the midst of which he finds himself. It is, after all, his task
to find out about them. He is thus always at risk of being seen as too close
to one group or another—to be too friendly with the 'nonces' for the liking
of 'gangsters', too attentive or inattentive to one ethnic group, to be

thought of by prisoners as 'pissing in the same pot' as the staff, to be too pally with the Governor for the liking of the POA. In a situation marked by plural conflicts of interest and personality there is no insurance policy against making mistakes or giving offence. An inherent part of the task of defining the researcher's role is that of becoming, however temporarily and peripherally, a kind of member of the 'prison community' and hence establishing a set of practices and proprieties and learning to live with the resulting anxieties.

Perhaps the most anxious of all the facets of the researchers' role is leaving, taking one's farewells, and travelling the geographical and social distance back to one's own normality. Then, under conditions of the calm and safety of a university office, one has to begin to write, to analyse and impose some kind of fixity and communicability on diffuse and open-ended material. But that is another story, one that is only now reaching its tardy conclusion.

Conclusions

In this postscript we have outlined a number of intellectual and practical issues arising from one programme of research in prison. We have tried to present the conduct of this research as a sequence of decision stages beginning with the identification of a particular 'problem' and proceeding via the division of the problem into a series of questions, through the formulation of a research 'project', and ending with its actual execution. In so doing we have tried to differentiate between the 'map' of the field (the formalization of research agendas) and the 'territory' in which the activity of researching takes place. The aim of a research report is to integrate these planes in an intelligible and defensible way.

The research reported here can lay claim to some measure of success, at least in having gained the co-operation of staff and prisoners and in generating a rich and comparatively well—focused corpus of data. It may turn out even now that, however 'adequate' our text, it will retain an 'unfinished' and insufficient character. This may indeed be inescapable. It may also prove, as Becker insists, that a 'good' report in the applied social sciences 'will make somebody angry' (1967), though making people angry is not a sufficient criterion of goodness. These things remain to be demonstrated.

One of the primary tasks within a revived enterprise of prison studies will be to provide people living and working within the prisons with opportunities to reflect upon their own positions, purposes, and commitments in a shared and constructive activity of research, evaluation, and discussion. This may indeed sound a somewhat starry-eyed (if not impossibly bland) way of conceiving of research in a setting so peculiar, so fraught, and so often bloodily conflictual as a long-term prison. It courts the possibility of seeming to minimize the asymmetries of power and conflicts of interest that provide the institution's very basis. Moreover, where it is not overtly partisan but rather attempts some more bilateral engagement *verstehen* research may find itself accused of lacking critical edge, of having been assimilated, even of legitimating the very institutions it sets out to examine. Since our first day in the prisons, now so long ago, we have never been entirely free of the unease that our position there engendered. One reason for appending this discussion to our text is to allow those ambivalences which we regard as *inherent* in the practice of prison research to surface explicitly. Quite often we toyed with the idea of conveying the ironies and contradictions that we observed in ways other than a conventional research report or book. In our hotel rooms we dreamed up scenarios for film scripts. In the end we simply concluded that uncertainty and ambiguity must just be lived with, thought about and incorporated reflexively into what one writes. No novelist or dramatist would feel themselves constrained to settle every question, or to suggest that a position that is socially uncomfortable is one from which one cannot write. Yet there are styles of sociological writing which still strive for Olympian detachment and impersonality. There are others also which seem to compel a more one-dimensional kind of side taking, and to resolve the tension between involvement and detachment decisively in favour of one party, regarded as the underdog. The defence of our position (which is not the same as its resolution) lies in our underlying conceptions of, and commitments to, (1) a *dialogical* understanding of the practice of research and (2) a certain view of the critical tasks of social science.

Our model here must in part remain the early Mathiesen. One of the beauties (not too strong a word) of *The Defences of the Weak* is its precise awareness that in a 'disrupted society' the language of underdogs and overdogs breaks down to the point of uselessness. Even though it is a plain fact that staff are vested with power over prisoners and that this power is exercised, no-one experiences themselves as powerful. No one believes that they can grasp onto power and bend it to their will. Even Foucault's sophisticated notion of the dispersed, 'capillary' nature of power will not serve: what it lacks is a sense of pathos.

It follows that the sociologist concerned with imprisonment can never rest entirely content with a singular role, whether as neutral rapporteur, or as advocate, or as adviser to policy makers. Even so, not to advocate or advise may still be an inexcusable abstention. It is partly for this reason that our work since embarking on this project has fallen into two distinct phases. In the first we produced our report to the Home Office, as well as a variety of memoranda, position papers, conference contributions, talks to practitioners and so on. Then, secondly, we embarked on a process of theoretical development and refinement. Thus, our earlier writings were somewhat less encumbered by theory than this one, and were more overtly interventionist in tone. They were not, it is true, entirely 'managerial'; they did not confine themselves solely to 'programme evaluation'; and they may have given rise to some puzzlement and dissatisfaction in some of their more administratively-minded readers. Moreover it was in the process of writing them that we formed and developed our current views. We immodestly attach an example of our work in this vein as a second Appendix. What it implicitly says is that we too have served our time. We do not disavow anything we have written, but ultimately it is not towards a view of the researcher as 'consultant' that our theoretical and methodological preferences eventually lead.

One way through the tensions between the demands of policy relevance and those of theoretical innovation and new interpretation is suggested by Bryant (1991). In Bryant's view one does not necessarily 'make sociology apply' in the most effective way by reining in its ambitions, adopting an 'instrumentalist' relation to its subject matter and offering incremental improvements to strategies and problems already formulated by policy makers. To the contrary there may be strong institutional reasons (of the kind that sociologists ought to be able to analyse) why such inputs or recommendations are rarely taken up. Indeed, Bryant cites Weiss in arguing that research may more successfully influence policy makers by offering changes of perspective rather than 'specific, immediately implementable findings' (Weiss, 1980: 264). Bryant also finds support for such a 'dialogical' view in Giddens's theory of structuration. Giddens rejects the view of social science as 'revelation' of transparent and unalterable truth. Rather, the 'double hermeneutic' which characterizes social science's relation to the world provides that 'the concepts, theories and findings provided by sociology "spiral in and out" of social life' (Giddens, 1987: 32). Social scientific concepts can be appropriated by their subjects, whether on the level of criticism of false belief, alteration of self-understanding, or opening out onto glimpses of possible worlds. In Giddens's terms (1984: 340):

social beliefs, unlike those to do with nature, are constitutive of what it is they are about. From this it follows that criticism of false belief is a *practical intervention* in society, a political phenomenon in a broad sense of that term.

For such reasons the 'application' of social research is better thought about in terms of persuasion, communication between distinct cultural contexts and conceptual innovation rather than in prescriptive or 'policy science' terms (Giddens, 1987: 47–8; Bryant, 1991: 194–5). In Giddens's view it is only such a conception which connects at all intelligently to the 'institutional reflexivity' so characteristic of contemporary institutions.

Finally, these considerations bear upon the *critical* nature of social science research on imprisonment. In Giddens's view social research is inherently bound up with social critique. If the 'double hermeneutic' means that social scientific ideas can be absorbed back into the discourse and practice of social actors they also reconstitute and alter that field of practice (1989: 289). In Giddens's view such reflexivity connects with critique because 'innovations in social science create windows on possible worlds for lay social actors' (ibid.). To the extent that one opens up the question of alternative possibility then stances of moral evaluation, counter-factual thinking and normative reflection are all part of what practising social scientists do (ibid.: 290–1). This is in part what we have attempted to do by placing the question of legitimacy (in both its descriptive and normative senses) close to the core of our concerns in this book. It is through the use of such concepts, we believe, that social research can clarify discussion of what it is and is not possible or desirable for prisons to be like, and indeed the extent to which they must exist at all. The 'positive' or constructive aspects of such notions suggest the outlines of agendas for penal change. But the limits on legitimacy are also crucial. They expose problems and contradictions of imprisonment that seem inherent (and which have led abolitionist thinkers such as Mathiesen to see the prison as in some sort an impossible institution). We have tried to act somewhat in the manner of messengers and translators, bearing news of what it means to live within certain forms of institutional control to those who do not know or inhabit them. We have endeavoured to render something of the human intelligibility of the positions and actions of prisoners and staff and to explore some features of the predicaments in which they are each enmeshed. We are persuaded that only close institutional analysis of contemporary prisons can enable us to guess at what the prisons of the future may be like, and which of them we can avoid building.

Appendix B
Lord Justice Woolf's Inquiry into Prison Disturbances: Evidence submitted by the Authors

I. Introduction

1. We are grateful for the invitation to submit evidence to the Inquiry.

2. We have no first-hand knowledge of the events leading up to the serious disturbance at H.M. Prison, Manchester. Our evidence therefore relates only to the second part of the Inquiry, on 'the more general issues as to the causes of disturbances of this sort, and the steps which should be taken to seek to avoid them in the future'.

3. Our main qualifications for submitting evidence to the Inquiry are twofold:

(i) We were members of a research team from the Institute of Criminology, University of Cambridge, commissioned by the Home Office to carry out a qualitative sociological research project on 'the nature of control problems among long-term prisoners and their emergence, including a study of the circumstances in which prisoners are transferred from normal location'. The main part of this study was conducted in Albany and Long Lartin Prisoners, and the research report was submitted to the Home Office early in 1990.

(ii) Professor Bottoms was a member of the Home Office Research and Advisory Group on the Long-Term Prison System (1984–90). This Group was set up as 'a source of advice on the research needs arising from the report of the Control Review Committee' [which had reported in 1984 on control problems in dispersal prisons], and 'to advice on the planning, co-ordination and evaluation of the proposed long-term prisoner units' for control-problem prisoners.

4. We are attaching to this evidence four documents, namely:

Paper A. *Control Problems and the Long-Term Prisoner* by Will Hay and Richard Sparks, in collaboration with Anthony Bottoms.

This is the Institute of Criminology's final report on the research project noted above.

Paper B. 'Situational and Social Approaches to the Prevention of Disorder in Long-Term Prisons', by Anthony Bottoms, Will Hay and Richard Sparks. This is a theoretical paper arising out of the Albany/Long Lartin research, and is to be published in the Philadelphia-based *Prison Journal* later this year.

Paper C. 'The Control of Long-Term Prisoners in England: Beyond the Control Review Committee Report' by Anthony Bottoms. This is the text of a paper delivered at the University of Hull conference on 'Special Units for Difficult Prisoners', April 1990.

Paper D. 'The Aims of Imprisonment' by Anthony Bottoms. This paper was published in 1990 by the University of Edinburgh Centre for Theology and Public Issues in a booklet entitled *Justice, Guilt and Forgiveness in the Penal System*, edited by David Garland. It is less directly concerned with order in prisons than are the other three papers, but does contain some discussion of issues which are, in our view, relevant to problems of order (see further below).

5. In preparing this note of evidence, we have seen little purpose in rehearsing at length issues already discussed fully in the above four papers. We have, rather, confined ourselves to some key issues arising out of our previous work. We have chosen to concentrate our remarks upon three of the topics selected by the Inquiry for the public seminars to be held in the autumn of 1990: namely—

    (i) justice within prisons;
    (ii) the need for active regimes, and how to achieve them;
    (iii) the tactical management of prisons and the prison population.

II. Justice within Prisons

6. We strongly concur with the Inquiry's decision to pay special attention to the issue of justice in prisons. In our experience, perceived injustice is a factor especially likely to lead to discontent among prisoners, though such discontent will not necessarily erupt into disorder (for example, it will not usually do so where the inmates believe themselves to be in a powerless situation: see the discussion of the Vulnerable Prisoner Unit at Albany in chapter 6 of *Paper A*).

7. We hope that the Inquiry will interpret the term 'justice in prisons' in a broad way, and not narrowly so as to include only, for example, formal disciplinary procedures. The term certainly needs to include at least the following:

   (i) the use of administrative control measures such as Rule 43 GOAD, and transfer under CI 10/1974;

   (ii) the adequacy or otherwise of the accountability structures in the prison system; and

   (iii) the adequacy or otherwise of grievance procedures.

8. But even the above are all *formal* matters, and in our view the term 'justice in prisons' should be construed even more widely, to embrace general issues of fairness in the day-to-day running of regimes (see the tradition in political philosophy of treating 'fairness' as a central features of the concept of justice: Rawls (1971)). The research work of the Norwegian sociologist Thomas Mathiesen (1965) made an important contribution to prison studies by emphasising:

   (i) that prisoners often perceive themselves to be in a very dependent position vis-à-vis staff;

   (ii) that staff have much discretionary power over the minutiae of the daily life of prisoners, and that such (apparently trivial) matters can acquire tremendous significance in the eyes of the prisoners;

   (iii) that prisoners often engage in 'censorious' behaviour (blaming staff and/or the system) concerning matters of perceived unfairness.

9. It can be strongly argued that, on moral grounds, we should as a society be concerned about unfairness in prison regimes, even if this does not lead to disorder, since:

'Justice is the first virtue of social institutions, as truth is of systems of thought . . . laws and institutions no matter how efficient and well-arranged must be reformed or abolished if they are unjust' (Rawls 1971, p. 3).

These remarks are certainly apposite in respect of, for example, the general question of race relations in prison (see Genders and Player 1989).

10. For the purposes of the Inquiry, however, it is appropriate to note that unfairness (and perceived unfairness) can lead through 'censoriousness' into disorder. Two central reasons for this are:

   (i) Because *routines*—the stuff of everyday life—can be shown on theoretical grounds to be central to both psychic security and the reproduction of day-to-day order (Giddens 1984: for an elaboration see *Paper B*), and thus perceived unfairness in day-to-day regime delivery can be of great importance to the individual, and can easily lead to unforeseen social consequences (including disorder);

   (ii) Because, in the old cliche, most prisons run on the consent of the inmates—or, to put the matter more sociologically, they require a degree of legitimation to function smoothly on a day-to-day basis.

Perceived unfairness in regime delivery is particularly likely to lead to a loss of legitimacy (see *Papers A and B*).

11. Of course, perceived unfairness is not always actual unfairness; and in any case, it is not easy to specify in the abstract what constitutes a fair regime. We will not pursue such matters here: they are more appropriately taken up by others with greater practical experience of prisons. We would, however, urge the Inquiry to place the issues of fairness and justice high on its conceptual agenda. A strong case can be made to the effect that recent official formulations concerning the aims and tasks of the prison service have severely underestimated the importance of this point (see *Paper D*, though the point is arguably understated there also).

12. A specific (and formal) dimension of justice in prisons concerns the administrative control mechanisms of Rule 43 GOAD and transfer under CI 10/1974. The usual justification offered for such mechanisms is straightforwardly utilitarian; but they can be easily criticised on grounds of justice, and regularly are so criticised by prisoners. In chapter 9 of *Paper A* we suggested keeping the mechanisms (because of their usefulness to the maintenance of control in the prison system), but injecting greater elements of procedural fairness into their use; and we would urge the Inquiry to consider adopting a similar policy approach.

III. The Need for Active Regimes and How to Achieve Them

13. We are more ambivalent about this topic, as formulated by the Inquiry, than about the topic of 'justice in prisons'. We concur with the general sentiment that regimes need to be more active, especially in local prisons (see *Paper D*), and like most other observers of the prison scene we were shocked by King and McDermott's (1989) demonstration of declining regime delivery despite increased staffing. But we think there is some danger that 'an active regime' will come to be seen as a panacea for prisons in general and disorder in prisons in particular. It is therefore worth noting that, for example:

(i) In King and McDermott's research study, dispersal prisons had more active regimes than most other kinds of prison (both in 1970–72 and in 1986–87), yet dispersal prisons were by some distance the main site for prison disorders during the period 1970–85 (see the report of the Control Review Committee: Home Office 1984, Annex D).

(ii) Barlinnie Special Unit has in some ways a very inactive regime, but seems to be successful in avoiding disorder (see Cooke 1989; see also the discussion in *Paper B*).

14. In more general terms, it is worth making a number of points about the relationship between regimes and potential disorder:

(i) There is an understandable tendency to believe that potential disorder requires various kinds of special administrative structure to
forestall it. The Control Review Committee (C.R.C.) in some
ways exemplifies this tendency. After a number of years' reflection on the relevant issues, and in the light of the Albany/Long
Lartin research, Professor Bottoms reached the view that the
C.R.C. had placed too much emphasis on structural issues, and
too little on the day-to-day reproduction of order in the wings
and workshops of dispersal prisons themselves (see Paper C).
Both topics are important, but they have to be considered
together in the closest possible conjunction.

(ii) It is important that 'activity' should not be overstated by comparison with other features of regimes which might be relevant to
potential disorder. These certainly include, in our view, the extent
to which the regime delivers respect, care and hope to its inmates
(see *Paper D*); and the orientation of prison staff on two dimensions, namely, closeness/distance of staff–inmate relations, and
consistency/flexibility in the staff's enforcement of rules (see
Paper A, pp. 100–1).

(iii) Even when considering regime activities themselves, it is very
important to talk to prisoners about their perception of such
activities, and not simply to assume that all activities will be
appreciated. While prisons clearly cannot be expected to offer
every activity demanded by inmates, nor always to refrain from
requiring prisoners to carry out activities which they dislike, nevertheless an interest in issues of legitimation (see above) necessarily requires an element of serious consultation with prisoners
about activities. Our experience in long-term prisons would suggest, for example, that full delivery of gym and education activities are likely to be significantly more important to prisoners than
increasing the number of hours per week worked in the workshops.

15. A further matter which we would wish to bring to the attention of the
Inquiry concerns the use of what might be called 'social' as against 'situational' (opportunity-reducing) approaches to the task of reducing disorder
in prisons: a matter which we came to see as of special importance following our detailed study of Albany and Long Lartin Prisons. As fully discussed in *Paper A*, though these two prisons had some features in common,
the former tended to rely more strongly on opportunity-restriction, and the
latter on the creation of a particular kind of 'social climate', as a way of
reducing disorder. Neither prison came out of the research comparison as a
clear 'winner' or 'loser'. As may be seen from the statistics presented in the
Appendix, Albany, the more restrictive and less popular prison, had a

higher rate of disciplinary offences and recorded 'control problem' incidents; but Long Lartin's relaxed ethos, much valued by most of its prisoners, produced some greater opportunities for disorder, resulting in a higher rate of genuine (as well as false) alarm calls, and more 'hidden' incidents leading to prisoners receiving head injuries. Full details of this rather complex comparison may be found in *Paper A*.

16. As a result of this empirical work, we were led to consider systematically, and in a theoretical way, the advantages and disadvantages of 'social' and 'situational' measures for preventing disorder in prisons (see *Paper B*). At the end of this work, we felt able to offer a number of conclusions:

(i) Some measure of 'social' crime prevention in prisons is essential, and this fact in itself of *legitimation*, and hence to the daily routines of the prison, the level of services and privileges offered, etc. Both *absolute* and *relative* aspects of routines and service delivery are likely to be important in this respect.

(ii) Social crime prevention has its inevitable costs, notably in increased opportunities.

(iii) It is therefore worth looking carefully at situational methods of opportunity-reduction which may reduce disorder, within a framework committed to a 'social' crime prevention approach. In doing so, one must remember that prisoners react subjectively to all such measures.

(iv) There are advantages, therefore, in employing (wherever possible) less personally restrictive rather than more personally restrictive situational measures, since the former will threaten legitimation less than the latter.

17. We commend these concepts to the Inquiry as a useful organising framework for thinking about disorder in the prison, though, as we said at the end of *Paper B*, their application in any particular prison setting requires a thorough understanding of the specific features of that setting.

IV. The Tactical Management of Prisons and the Prison Population

18. Under this heading, we shall confine ourselves to a few remarks about the management of sex offenders and other vulnerable prisoners.

19. We have noted suggestions in some quarters that sex offenders might be freely mixed with other prisoners within an 'open' regime, and other prisoners taught/encouraged to modify their attitudes and behaviour towards them. Long Lartin attempted, in some ways, an approach of this kind. It was not wholly successful. Some sex offenders were genuinely fearful, and disliked this 'open' regime (with its greater opportunity for assault) more than other regimes; others were prepared to take the risk

(because of the other benefits of the regime) but were under no illusions that the risks were real. 'Straight' (non-sex offender) prisoners expressed particular revulsion that they should have to share their *living space* with sex offenders.

20. The Albany Vulnerable Prisoner Unit offered a different solution: the vulnerable prisoners were strictly segregated from the main part of the prison. Their living conditions were quite good and spacious, certainly by comparison with alternative possibilities under Rule 43 OP, such as the segregation unit at Wandsworth. But both they, and the staff, were aware of their vulnerability and powerlessness; and this situation was shown in the research to tend to produce a degree of 'heavy policing' by staff, and staff carelessness on issues such as race relations, which would not have been attempted with a less vulnerable prisoner group. There seem, there-fore, to be a number of potential problems with the 'isolation unit' solu-tion, even though, by isolation, the vulnerable prisoners avoid the risk of assaults by prisoners from 'the mainstream'.

21. Although we have not researched it, we are impressed with the think-ing behind the vulnerable prisoner wing at Littlehey Prison. This wing keeps vulnerable prisoners together in a residential unit, but encourages them as soon as possible to go to work in the ordinary prison workshops, alongside non-vulnerable prisoners from other wings. On theoretical grounds, this seems to combine a number of promising features, reminis-cent of the *environmental management* strategies recommended by situa-tional crime prevention theorists (see Clarke 1983). Residential quarters for the 'mainstream' and 'vulnerable' groups are kept separate, and this is important because living units are the site of maximum potential tension between the two groups (see para. 19). Vulnerable prisoners are, however, encouraged to go out to work in ordinary workshops and to participate in other regime activities: here they are less likely to be at risk. This strategy seems likely to reduce the general sense of vulnerability and lack of self-confidence among sex offenders; and this in turn may discourage the staff in their living units from adopting the kind of response found among some of the staff in the Albany V.P.U. We repeat that these latter remarks are not based on direct research evidence, and in any case are derived from a unit in a Category C prison, so we would not wish to place too much weight on this particular example. But given the deep hatred of many non-sex-offender prisoners for sex offenders, we would certainly be sceptical about arguments to the effect that such prisoners can easily be persuaded to live peaceably alongside sex offenders; in view of this, and our own findings at Long Lartin and Albany, a creative environmental management approach seems on theoretical grounds to be the most promising one, though such a view would certainly need to be tested by empirical research in the future.

V. Conclusion

22. The theoretical approach to social studies which we favour (based on Giddens's (1984) structuration theory: see *Paper B*) argues that no general theories of social change are possible. For similar theoretical reasons, we are inclined to the view that no general theories of prison disorder are possible; nor is it possible to predict with certainty which disorders will escalate into major disturbances and which remain as minor incidents.

23. However, though complete predictability is (given the nature of the human condition) not available, it does not follow that sensible general steps aimed at the prevention of disorders in prisons can not be taken. In this brief note we have tried to indicate some creative general ways of thinking about prevention, though we would be the first to recognise that our ideas would require considerable practical elaboration if one were interested in putting them into operation.

24. We would be glad to develop the remarks in this note if that would be of interest to the Inquiry.

References

Clarke, R. V. G. (1983) 'Situational Crime Prevention: its Theoretical Basis and Practical Scope', in M. Tonry and N. Morris (Eds.) *Crime and Justice: an Annual Review of Research*, vol. 4, pp. 225–6.

Cooke, D. J. (1989) 'Containing violent prisoners: an analysis of the Barlinnie Special Unit', *British Journal of Criminology*, 29, 129–43.

Genders, E. and Player, E. (1989) *Race Relations in Prisons*, Oxford: Clarendon Press.

Giddens, A. (1984) *The Constitution of Society*, Cambridge: Policy Press.

King, R. D. and McDermott, K. (1989) 'British Prisons 1970–87: the ever deepening crisis', *British Journal of Criminology*, 29, pp. 107–28.

Mathiesen, T. (1965) *The Defences of the Weak*, London: Tavistock Publications.

Rawls, J. (1971) *A Theory of Justice*, London: Oxford University Press.

Bibliography

Adams, R. (1992) *Prison Riots in Britain and the USA*, London: Macmillan.

Adler, M. and Longhurst, B. (1989) 'Towards a new sociology of imprisonment: prison discourse to-day', Paper presented to British Criminology Conference, Bristol, July 1989.

Adler, M. and Longhurst, B. (1994) *Discourse, Power and Justice*, London: Routledge.

Advisory Council on the Penal System (1968) *The Regime for Prisoners in Conditions of Maximum Security* (Radzinowicz Report), London: HMSO.

Banks, C., Mayhew, P. and Sapsford, R. (1975) *Absconding from Open Prisons*, London: HMSO.

Barak-Glantz, I. L. (1981) 'Towards a conceptual schema of prison management styles', *The Prison Journal*, 61: 2.

Beck, U. (1992) *Risk Society*, London: Sage.

Becker, H. (1967) 'Whose side are we on?', *Social Problems*, 14, 3.

Beetham, D. (1991) *The Legitimation of Power*, London: Macmillan.

Bettelheim, B. (1960) *The Informed Heart*, Glencoe, Illinois: The Free Press.

Bottomley, A. K. (1994) 'Long-term prisoners' in E. Player and M. Jenkins (eds.) *Prisons After Woolf*, London: Routledge.

Bottomley, A. K. and Hay, W. (eds.) (1991) *Special Units for Difficult Prisoners*, University of Hull.

Bottomley, A. K., Jepson, N., Elliott, K. and Coid, J. (1994) *Managing Difficult Prisoners: the Lincoln and Hull Special Units*, London: HMSO.

Bottomley, A. K., Liebling, A., and Sparks, R. (1994) *The Barlinnie Special Unit and Shotts Unit*, Edinburgh: Scottish Prison Service.

Bottoms, A. E. (1977) 'Reflections on the renaissance of dangerousness', *Howard Journal of Criminal Justice*, 16: 70–96.

Bottoms, A. E. (1991) 'The control of long-term prisoners in England: beyond the Control Review Committee Report', in A. K. Bottomley and W. Hay (eds.) *Special Units for Difficult Prisoners*, University of Hull.

Bottoms, A. E. (1992) 'Violence and disorder in long-term prisons: the influence of institutional environments', *Criminal Behaviour and Mental Health*, 2: 126–36.

Bottoms, A. E. (1993) 'Recent criminological and social theory', in D. P. Farrington, R. J. Sampson, and P-O. Wikstrom (eds.) *Integrating Individual and Ecological Aspects of Crime*, Stockholm: BRA report 1993: 1.

Bottoms, A. E. (1995) 'The philosophy and politics of punishment and sentencing', in C. Clarkson and R. Morgan (eds.) *The Politics of Sentencing Reform*, Oxford University Press.

Bottoms, A. E., Hay, W., and Sparks, R. (1990) 'Situational and social approaches to the prevention of disorder in long-term prisons', *The Prison Journal*, LXX: 83–95.

Bottoms, A. E. and Light, R. (eds.) (1987) *Problems of Long-Term Imprisonment*, Aldershot: Gower.

Bottoms, A. E. and Wiles, P. (1994) 'Crime and insecurity in the city', paper presented to the International Society of Criminology's International Course, University of Leuven, 1994.

Bourdieu, P. (1993) *Sociology in Question*, London: Sage.

Bowker, L. H. (1977) *Prison Subcultures*, Lexington: D. C. Heath and Co.

Boyle, J. (1984) *The Pain of Confinement*, London: Pan.

Briggs, C. (1986) *Learning How to Ask*, Cambridge University Press.

Bryant, C. (1991) 'The dialogical model of applied sociology' in C. Bryant and D. Jary (eds.) *Giddens' Theory of Structuration: A Critical Appreciation*, London: Routledge.

Bryant, C. and Jary, D. (1991) *Giddens' Theory of Structuration: A Critical Appreciation*, London: Routledge.

Burgess, R. (1984) *In the Field*, London: Unwin Hyman.

Caird, R. (1974) *A Good and Useful Life*, London: Hart-Davis, MacGibbon.

Canter, D. (1987) 'Implications for "New Generation" prisons of existing psychological research into prison design and use' in A. E. Bottoms and R. Light (eds.) *Problems of Long-Term Imprisonment*, Aldershot: Gower.

Canter, D. and Ambrose, I. (1980) 'Prison Design and Use Study: Final Report', Guildford: University of Surrey (mimeo).

Carlen, P. (1983) *Women's Imprisonment*, London: Routledge and Kegan Paul.

Carlen, P. (1986) 'Psychiatry in prisons', in P. Miller and N. Rose (eds.) *The Power of Psychiatry*, Cambridge: Polity Press.

Carroll, L. (1974) *Hacks, Blacks and Cons*, Lexington: D. C. Heath and Company.

Christie, N. (1968) 'Changes in penal values' in *Scandinavian Studies in Criminology vol. 2*, Oslo: Universitetsforlaget.

Christie, N. (1980) *Limits to Pain*, Oxford: Martin Robertson.

Christie, N. (1989) Address to the conference on 'The meaning of Imprisonment', Lincoln, July 1989.

Clarke, J., Cochrane, A. and McLaughlin, E. (1994) (eds) *Managing Social Policy*, London: Sage.

Clarke, R. and Martin, D. (1971) *Absconding from Approved Schools*, London: HMSO.

Clarke, R. and Mayhew, P. (1980) *Designing Out Crime*, London: HMSO.

Clemmer, D. (1940) *The Prison Community*, New York: Holt, Rinehart and Winston.

Cohen, A. K. (1976) 'Prison violence: a sociological perspective', in A. K.

Cohen, G. F. Cole, and R. G. Bailey (eds.) *Prison Violence*, Lexington, Mass.: D. C. Heath and Co.

Cohen, S. (1985) *Visions of Social Control*, Cambridge: Polity Press.

Cohen, S. (1988) *Against Criminology*, Oxford: Transaction Books.

Cohen, S. and Taylor, L. (1977) 'Talking about prison blues' in C. Bell and H. Newby (eds.) *Doing Sociological Research*, London: George Allen and Unwin.

Cohen, S. and Taylor, L. (1981) *Psychological Survival*, Harmondsworth: Penguin (2nd. edition).

Cooke, D. J. (1989) 'Containing Violent Prisoners: an analysis of the Barlinnie Special Unit', *British Journal of Criminology*, 29,2: 129–43.

Cooke, D. J. (1991) 'Violence in prisons: the influence of regime factors', *Howard Journal*, 30, 2: 95–107.

Cornish, D. and Clarke, R. (1975) *Residential Treatment and its Effects on Delinquency*, London: HMSO.

Cousins. M. and Hussain, A. (1984) *Michel Foucault*, London: Macmillan.

Cressey, D. (1961) (ed.) *The Prison: Studies in Institutional Organization and Change*, New York: Holt, Rinehart and Winston.

Davies, W. (1982) 'Violence in Prisons', in M. P. Feldman (ed.) *Developments in the Study of Criminal Behaviour* (*vol 2*), New York and Chichester: John Wiley and Sons.

Davis, M. (1995) 'Hell factories in the field', *The Nation*, 20 February 1995.

DiIulio, J. (1987) *Governing Prisons*, New York: The Free Press.

Dobash, R. E., Dobash, R. P., and Gutteridge, S. (1986) *The Imprisonment of Women*, Oxford: Blackwell.

Douglas, M. (1986) *Risk*, London: Routledge.

Douglas, M. (1992) *Risk and Blame: Essays in Cultural Theory*, London: Routledge.

Dreyfus, H. and Rabinow, P. (1982) *Michel Foucault: Beyond Structuralism and Hermeneutics*, University of Chicago Press.

Dunbar, I. (1970) 'Long Lartin: the development of a concept', *Prison Service Journal*, April.

Dunbar, I. (1985) *A Sense of Direction*, London: H.M. Prison Service.

Evans, R. (1982) *The Fabrication of Virtue: English Prison Architecture, 1750–1840*, Cambridge University Press.

Feeley, M. (1979) *The Process is the Punishment*, New York: Russell Sage.

Feeley, S. and Simon, J. (1992) 'The new penology: notes on the emerging strategy of corrections and its implications', *Criminology*, 30, 4: 449–74.

Field, S. (1989) 'Review of Bottoms and Light (1987)' in *Journal of Law and Society*, 16, 2.

Finkelstein, E. (1993) *Prison Culture: an Inside View*, Aldershot: Avebury.

Fitzgerald, M. (1977) *Prisoners in Revolt*, Harmondsworth: Penguin.

Fitzgerald, M. (1987) 'The telephone rings: long-term imprisonment' in

A. E. Bottoms and R. Light (eds.) *Problems of Long-Term Imprisonment*, Aldershot: Gower.

Fleisher, M. (1989) *Warehousing Violence*, London and Beverly Hills: Sage.

Foucault, M. (1979a) *Discipline and Punish*, London: Penguin.

Foucault, M. (1979b) 'On Governmentality', *Ideology and Consciousness*, no. 6: 5–21.

Foucault, M. (1982) 'The subject and power' in H. Dreyfus and P. Rabinow *Michel Foucault: Beyond Structuralism and Hermeneutics*, University of Chicago Press.

Foucault, M. (1984) *The Foucault Reader* (P. Rabinow ed.), London: Penguin.

Garfinkel, H. (1967) *Studies in Ethnomethodology*, Englewood Cliffs, New Jersey: Prentice-Hall Inc.

Garland, D. (1985) *Punishment and Welfare*, Aldershot: Gower.

Garland, D. (1990) *Punishment and Modern Society*, Oxford University Press.

Garland, D. (1992) 'Criminological knowledge and its relation to power', *British Journal of Criminology*, 32, 4: 403–22.

Gearty, C. (1991) 'The prisons and the courts' in J. Muncie and R. Sparks (eds.) *Imprisonment: European Perspectives*, Hemel Hempstead: Harvester Wheatsheaf.

Gelathorpe, L. and Morris, A. (1988) 'Feminism and criminology in Britain' in P. Rock (ed.) *A History of British Criminology*, Oxford University Press.

Genders, E. and Player, E. (1989) *Race Relations in Prisons* Oxford: Clarendon Press.

Genders, E. and Player, E. (1995) *Grendon: a Study of a Therapeutic Prison*, Oxford University Press.

Giallombardo, R. (1966) *Society of Women*, New York: Wiley.

Giddens, A. (1976) *New Rules of Sociological Method*, London: Hutchinson.

Giddens, A. (1977) *Studies in Social and Political Theory*, London: Hutchinson.

Giddens, A. (1982) *Profiles and Critiques in Social Theory*, London: Macmillan.

Giddens, A. (1984) *The Constitution of Society*, Cambridge: Polity Press.

Giddens, A. (1987) *Social Theory and Modern Sociology*, Cambridge: Polity Press.

Giddens, A. (1989) 'A reply to my critics' in D. Held and J. B. Thompson (eds.) *Social Theory of Modern Societies: Anthony Giddens and His Critics*, Cambridge University Press.

Giddens, A. (1990) *The Consequences of Modernity*, Cambridge: Polity Press.

Giddens, A. (1991) 'Structuration theory: past, present and future' in C. Bryant and D. Jary (eds.) *Giddens' Theory of Structuration: a Critical Appreciation*, London: Routledge.

Glaser, B. and Strauss, A. (1967) *The Discovery of Grounded Theory*, Chicago: Aldine.

Glaser, D. (1964) *The Effectiveness of a Prison and Parole System*, New York: Bobbs-Merrill.

Goffman, E. (1959) *The Presentation of Self in Everyday Life*, New York: Doubleday.

Goffman, E. (1961) 'On the characteristics of total institutions' in D. Cressey (ed.) *The Prison: Studies in Institutional Organization and Change*, New York: Holt, Rinehart and Winston.

Goffman, E. (1968) *Asylums*, Harmondsworth: Penguin.

Gomersall, J. (1991) 'Monsters, beasts and animals', *Prison Service Journal*, Winter 1990/91.

Gordon, P. (1980) *Power/Knowledge*, Sussex: Harvester Press.

Gostin, L. and Staunton, M. (1985) 'The case for prison standards' in M. Maguire, J. Vagg and R. Morgan (eds.) *Accountability and Prisons*, London: Tavistock.

Gottfredson, M. R. and Hirschi, T. (1990) *A General Theory of Crime*, Stanford: Stanford University Press.

Gottfredson, S. and Gottfredson, D. (1993)The long-term predictive utility of the base expectancy score', *Howard Journal of Criminal Justice*, 32, 4: 276–90.

Gregory, D. (1989) 'Presences and absences: time–space relations and structuration theory' in D. Held and J. B. Thompson (eds.) *Social Theory of Modern Societies*, Cambridge University Press.

Gregson, N. (1989) 'On the (ir)relevance of structuration theory to empirical research', in D. Held and J. B. Thompson (eds.) *Social Theory of Modern Societies: Anthony Giddens and His Critics*, Cambridge University Press.

Gunn, J., Maden, T., and Swinton, M. (1991) *Mentally Disordered Offenders*, London: HMSO.

Haines, K. (1989) *After-Care Services for Released Prisoners: A Review of the Literature*, unpublished research report by the Cambridge Institute of Criminology to the Home Office.

Harding, C., Hines, B., Ireland, R., and Rawlings, P. (1985) *Imprisonment in England and Wales: a Concise History*, London: Croom Helm.

Harvey, D. (1989) *The Condition of Postmodernity*, Oxford: Basil Blackwell.

Hay, W. and Sparks, R. (1991a) 'What is a prison officer?', *Prison Service Journal*, 83: 2–7.

Hay, W. and Sparks, R. (1991b) 'Maintaining order in the English dispersal system' in A. K. Bottomley and W. Hay (eds.) *Special Units for Difficult Prisoners*, University of Hull.

Hay, W. and Sparks, R. (1992) 'Vulnerable prisoners: risk in long-term prisons', in A. K. Bottomley, A. J. Fowles, and R. Reiner (eds.) *Criminal Justice: Theory and Practice*, London: British Society of Criminology.

Hay, W., Sparks, R., and Bottoms, A. (1990) *Control Problems and the Long-Term Prisoner*, Unpublished report submitted to the Home Office Research and Planning Unit by the University of Cambridge Institute of Criminology.

Heffernan, E. (1972) *Making it in Prison*, New York: Wiley.

Held, D. and Thompson, J. (1989) (eds.) *Social Theory of Modern Societies: Anthony Giddens and His Critics*, Cambridge University Press.

Hennessey, Sir J. (1986) *A Review of the Segregation of Prisoners Under Rule 43*, London: HMSO.

HM Chief Inspector of Prisons (1987) *Report of an Inquiry by Her Majesty's Chief Inspector of Prisons for England and Wales into the disturbances in prison service establishments in England between 29 April–2 May, 1986*, London: HMSO.

HM Chief Inspector of Prisons (1992) *Report of an Inspection of HM Prison Long Lartin*, London: HMSO.

HM Chief Inspector of Prisons (1993) *Report of an Inspection of HM Prison Albany*, London: HMSO.

HM Chief Inspector of Prisons (1994) *Report of an Inquiry by Her Majesty's Chief Inspector of Prisons for England and Wales into the Disturbance at HM Prison Wymott on 6 September 1993*, London: HMSO.

Home Office (1959) *Penal Practice in a Changing Society*, Cmnd. 645, London: HMSO.

Home Office (1966) *Committee of Enquiry into Prison Escapes and Security* (Mountbatten Report), London: HMSO.

Home Office (1973) 'Report of the Working Party on Dispersal and Control' (Cox Report), unpublished.

Home Office (1977) *Report of an Inquiry by the Chief Inspector of the Prison Service into the Cause and Circumstances of the Events at HM Prison, Hull* (Fowler Report) London: HMSO.

Home Office (1979) *Committee of Inquiry into the United Kingdom Prison Services* (May Committee), London: HMSO.

Home Office (1982) *Home Office statement on the background, circumstances and action subsequently taken relative to the disturbance in 'D' wing at HM Prison Wormwood Scrubs on 31 August 1979; together with the Report of an Inquiry by the Regional Director of the South East Region of the Prison Department*, London: HMSO.

Home Office (1984) *Managing the Long-Term Prison System: The Report of the Control Review Committee*, London: HMSO.

Home Office (1985a) *Report of the Committee on the Prison Disciplinary System* (2 vols) (Prior Committee), London: HMSO.

Home Office (1985b) *New Directions in Prison Design*, London: HMSO.

Home Office (1987) *Special Units for Long-Term Prisoners: A Report by the Research Advisory Group on the Long-Term Prison System*, London: HMSO.

Home Office (1988) *Prison Statistics for England and Wales, 1987*, London: HMSO.

Home Office (1989) *Management of Vulnerable Prisoners Working Group Report*, HM Prison Service internal document.

Home Office (1990) *Crime, Justice and Protecting the Public Cm 965*, London: HMSO.

Home Office (1993) *Digest 2: Information on the Criminal justice System in England and Wales*, London: Home Office Research and Statistics Department.

Hope, T. (1994) 'Community crime prevention' in M. Tonry and D. Farrington (eds.) *Preventing Crime: Crime and Justice 19*, University of Chicago Press.

Ignatieff, M. (1978) *A Just Measure of Pain*, London: Penguin.

Irwin, J. (1970) *The Felon*, Englewood Cliffs, New Jersey: Prentice-Hall Inc.

Irwin, J. (1980) *Prisons in Turmoil*, Chicago: Little Brown.

Irwin, J. and Cressey, D. (1962) 'Thieves, convicts and the inmate culture', *Social Problems*, vol. 10.

Jacobs, J. (1977) *Stateville: the Penitentiary in Mass Society*, Chicago: Chicago University Press.

Jacobs, J. (1983) *New Perspectives on Prisons and Imprisonment*, Ithaca: Cornell University Press.

Jefferson, T. (1990) *The Case Against Paramilitary Policing*, Buckingham: Open University Press.

Jefferson, T. (1993) 'Pondering paramilitarism: a question of standpoints?', *British Journal of Criminology*, 33: 374–81.

Jenkins, M. (1987) 'Control problems in dispersals' in A. E. Bottoms and R. Light (eds.) *Problems of Long-Term Imprisonment*, Aldershot: Gower.

Jepson, N. and Elliot, K. (1985) *Shared Working Between Prison and Probation Officers*, London: Home Office.

Jones, K. and Fowles, A. (1984) *Ideas on Institutions*, London: Routledge and Kegan Paul.

Kalinich, D. (1980) *Power, Stability and Contraband: The Inmate Economy*, Prospect Heights, Illinois: Waveland Press Inc.

Kamenka, E. and Tay, A. (1975) 'Beyond bourgeois individualism: the contemporary crisis in law and ideology' in E. Kamenka and R. Neale (eds.) *Feudalism, Capitalism and Beyond*, London: Edward Arnold.

King, R. D. (1985) 'Control in Prisons' in M. Maguire, J. Vagg and R. Morgan (eds.) *Accountability and Prisons*, London: Tavistock.

King, R. D. (1987) 'New generation prisons, the building programme, and the future of the dispersal policy', in A. E. Bottoms and R. Light (eds.) *Problems of Long-Term Imprisonment*, Aldershot: Gower.

King, R. D. (1990) 'Evidence submitted to Lord Justice Woolf's Inquiry into Prison Disturbances', (unpublished ms.).

King, R. D. (1991) 'Maximum security confinement in Britain and the USA: a comparison between Gartree and Oak Park Heights', *British Journal of Criminology*, 31, 3.

King, R. D. (1994) 'Order, disorder and regimes in the prison services of England and Wales and Scotland', in E. Player and M. Jenkins (eds.) *Prisons After Woolf*, London: Routledge.

King, R. D. and Elliott, K. (1977) *Albany: Birth of a Prison, End of an Era*, London: Routledge and Kegan Paul.

King, R. D. and McDermott, K. (1989) 'British Prisons, 1970–1987: the ever-deepening crisis', *British Journal of Criminology*, 29: 107–28.

King, R. D. and McDermott, K. (1990) ' "My geranium is subversive": some notes on the management of trouble in prisons', *British Journal of Sociology*, 41: 445–71.

King, R. D. and McDermott, K. (1995) *The State of Our Prisons*, Oxford University Press.

King, R. D. and Morgan, R. (1980) *The Future of the Prison System*, Farnborough: Gower.

Klapp, O. (1956) 'Heroes, villains and fools as agents of social control', *American Sociological Review*, 19, 1: 56–62.

Lash, S. and Urry, J. (1987) *The End of Organized Capitalism*, Cambridge: Polity Press.

Lash, S. and Urry, J. (1994) *Economies of Signs and Space*, London: Sage.

Layder, D. (1993) *New Strategies in Social Research*, Cambridge: Polity Press.

Liebling, A. (1992) *Suicides in Prison*, London: Routledge.

Liebling, A. and Bosworth, M. (1995) *Incentives in Prison Regimes: a Review of the Literature*, London: HM Prison Service.

Lind, E. A. and Tyler, T. (1988) *The Social Psychology of Procedural Justice*, New York: Plenum.

Livingstone, S. (1994) 'The changing face of prison discipline' in E. Player and M. Jenkins (eds.) *Prisons After Woolf*, London: Routledge.

Livingstone, S. and Owen, T. (1993) *Prison Law*, Oxford University Press.

Logan, C. (1990) *Private Prisons: Cons and Pros*, Oxford University Press.

Lucas, J. R. (1980) *On Justice*, Oxford University Press.

Lygo, R. (1991) *Management of the Prison Service*, London: HMSO.

McDermott, K. and King, R. D. (1988) 'Mind games: where the action is in prisons', *British Journal of Criminology*, 28, 3: 357–77.

McEwan, A. (1986) 'A comparison between the population of HMP Frankland and HMP Albany', (unpublished ms.).

McLaughlin, E. and Muncie, J. (1994) 'Managing the criminal justice system' in J. Clarke, A. Cochrane and E. McLaughlin (eds.) *Managing Social Policy*, London: Sage.

McVicar, J. (1974) *McVicar by Himself*, London: Hutchinson.

Maguire, M., Vagg, J., and Morgan, R., eds.(1985) *Accountability and Prisons*, London: Tavistock.

Manderaka-Sheppard, A. (1986) *The Dynamics of Aggression in Women's Prisons*, London: Gower.

Marquart, J. and Roebuck, J. (1985) 'Prison guards and "snitches": deviance within a total institution' *British Journal of Criminology* 25, 3.

Marsh, A., Dobbs, J., Mark, J., and White, A. (1985) *Staff Attitudes in the Prison Service* London: HMSO.

Mathiesen, T. (1965) *The Defences of the Weak*, London: Tavistock.

Mathiesen, T. (1971) *Across the Boundaries of Organizations*, Berkeley: The Glendessary Press.

Mathiesen, T. (1974) *The Politics of Abolition*, Oxford: Martin Robertson.

Moore, W. J. (1994) 'Locked in', *The National Journal*, 30 July: 1784–8.

Morgan, R. (1994) 'Inspecting prisons—the view from Strasbourg', *British Journal of Criminology*, 34, 1: 144–59.

Morris, T. and Morris, P. (1963) *Pentonville*, London: Routledge and Kegan Paul.

Mott, J. (1985) *Adult Prisons and Prisoners in England and Wales, 1970–1982*, (Home Office Research Studies no. 84), London: HMSO.

Neale, K. (1991) 'The European Prison Rules' in J. Muncie and R. Sparks (eds.) *Imprisonment: European Perspectives*, Hemel Hempstead: Harvester Wheatsheaf.

New York State Special Commission on Attica (1972) *Attica*, New York: Bantam Books.

O'Kane, R. (1993) 'Against legitimacy', *Political Studies*, XLI, 3: 471–87.

PA Consultants (1989) *Organisation of the Prison Service Above establishment Level—Executive Summary of Report*, London: PA Consultants.

Pahl, R. (1977) 'Playing the rationality game: the sociologist as a hired expert', in C. Bell and H. Newby (eds.) *Doing Sociological Research*, London: George Allen and Unwin.

Peters, A. (1986) 'Main currents in criminal law theory', in J. van Dijk et al. (eds.) *Criminal Law in Action*, Arnhem: Gouda Quint.

Pilling, J. (1988) 'A View from the Director of Personnel and Finance', *Prison Service Journal*, No. 71:3–4.

Piven, F. F. and Cloward, R. (1977) *Poor People's Movements*, New York: Vintage Books.

Pollitt, C. (1993) *Managerialism and the Public Services* (2nd. edition), Oxford: Blackwell Publishers.

PROP (1990) 'Evidence submitted to Lord Justice Woolf's Inquiry' (unpublished ms.).

Pugh, D. S. (1990) *Organization Theory*, London: Penguin (3rd edition).

Quinn, P. (1985) 'Prison Management and Prison Discipline: a case study of change' in M. Maguire, J. Vagg, and R. Morgan (eds.) *Accountability and Prisons*, London: Tavistock.

Rabinow, P. (1984) 'Introduction' in *The Foucault Reader* (P. Rabinow ed.), London: Penguin.

Radzinowicz, L. and Hood, R. (1986) *The Emergence of Penal Policy*, Oxford University Press.

Reiner, R. (1988) 'British criminology and the state', in P. Rock (ed.) *A History of British Criminology*, Oxford University Press.

Richardson, G. (1985) 'The case for prisoners' rights' in M. Maguire, J. Vagg and R. Morgan (eds.) *Accountability and Prisons*, London: Tavistock.

Richardson, G. (1993) *Law, Process and Custody: Prisoners and Patients*, London: Weidenfeld and Nicolson.

Richardson, G. (1994) 'From rights to expectations' in E. Player and M. Jenkins (eds.) *Prisons After Woolf*, London: Routledge.

Rosenbaum, D. P. (1988) 'Community crime prevention: a review and synthesis of the literature.' *Justice Quarterly* 5, 323–95.

Ryan, M. (1992) 'The Woolf report: on the treadmill of prison reform?', *Political Quarterly*, 53, 1: 50–6.

Ryan, M. and Ward, T. (1989) *Privatization and the Penal System*, Milton Keynes: Open University Press.

Sampson, A. (1994) 'The future for sex offenders in prison', in E. Player and M. Jenkins (eds.) *Prisons After Woolf*, London: Routledge.

Scarman, Lord (1981) *The Brixton Disorders April 10–12, 1981: Report of an Enquiry*, London: HMSO.

Scottish Prison Service (1990) *Opportunity and Responsibility*, Edinburgh: Scottish Prison Service.

Scottish Prison Service (1992) *The Scottish Prison Survey*, Edinburgh: Scottish Prison Service.

Scraton, P., Sim, J., and Skidmore, P. (1991) *Prisons Under Protest*, Buckingham: Open University Press.

Sheath, M. (1990) Confrontative work with sex offenders: legitimised nonce-bashing? *Probation Journal* 37, 4: 159–62.

Sherman, L. W., Gartin, P. R., and Buerger, M. E. (1989) 'Hotspots of predatory crime: routine activities and the criminology of place', *Criminology*, 27, 27–55.

Shichor, D. (1995) *Punishment for Profit*, London: Sage.

Shils, E. (1975) *Center and Periphery: Essays in Macrosociology*, University of Chicago Press.

Sim, J. (1990) *Medical Power in Prisons*, Buckingham: Open University Press.

Sim, J. (1992) ' "When you ain't got nothing you got nothing to lose": the Peterhead rebellion, the state and the case for prison abolition', in A. K. Bottomley, A. J. Fowles and R. Reiner (eds.) *Criminal Justice: Theory and Practice*, London: British Society of Criminology.

Sim, J. (1994) 'Reforming the penal wasteland: a critical reading of the Woolf report' in E. Player and M. Jenkins (eds.) *Prisons After Woolf*, London: Routledge.

Simon, J. (1988) 'The ideological effects of actuarial practices', *Law and Society Review*, 22: 772–800.

Smart, B. (1985) *Michel Foucault*, London: Tavistock.

Sparks, J. R. (1994a) 'Can prisons be legitimate?', *British Journal of Criminology*, 34: 14–28.

Sparks, J. R. (1994b) 'The Barlinnie Special Unit as prison and escape', *Prison Service Journal*, no. 95: 2–6.

Sparks, J. R. (1995) 'Penal "austerity": the doctrine of less eligibility reborn?', in R. Matthews and P. Francis (eds.) *Prisons 2000*, London: Macmillan.

Sparks, J. R. and Bottoms, A. E. (1995) 'Legitimacy and order in prisons', *British Journal of Sociology* 46, 1: 45–62.

Street, D., Vintner, R. D. and Perrow, C. (1966) *Organization for Treatment*, New York: The Free Press.

Sykes, G. (1958) *The Society of Captives* Princeton NJ: Princeton University Press.

Sykes, G. and Messinger, S. (1960) 'The inmate social system', in L. Radzinowicz and M. Wolfgang (eds.) *Crime and Justice* vol. III, New York: Basic Books.

Thomas, C. and Petersen, D. (1977) *Prison Organization and Inmate Subculture*, Indianapolis: Bobbs-Merrill.

Thomas, J. E. (1972) *The English Prison Officer Since 1850*, London: Routledge and Kegan Paul.

Thomas, J. E. (1994) 'Woolf and prison staff: still looking for good gaolers' in E. Player and M. Jenkins (eds.) *Prisons After Woolf*, London: Routledge.

Thomas, J. E. and Pooley, R. (1980) *The Exploding Prison*, London: Junction Books.

Thompson, E. P. (1968) *The Making of the English Working Class*, Harmondsworth: Penguin.

Thompson, J. B. (1989) 'The theory of structuration', in D. Held and J. B. Thompson (eds.) *Social Theory of Modern Societies*, Cambridge University Press.

Toch, H. (1992) *Living in Prison*, Washington DC: American Psychological Association.

Train, C. (1985) 'Management accountability in the Prison Service' in M. Maguire, J. Vagg, and R. Morgan (eds.) *Accountability and Prisons*, London: Tavistock.

Twining, W. and Miers, D. (1982) *How to do Things with Rules* (2nd. edition), London: Weidenfeld and Nicolson.

Tyler, T. R. (1990) *Why People Obey the Law*, New Haven: Yale University Press.

United States Department of Justice (1994) 'Prisoners in 1993' *Bureau of Justice Statistics Bulletin*, Washington DC: Department of Justice.

Urry, J. (1991) 'Time and space in Giddens's social theory' in C. G. A. Bryant and D. Jary (eds.) *Giddens's Theory of Structuration: A Critical Appreciation*, London: Routledge.

Vantour, J. (1991) 'Canadian experience: the special handling unit', in A. K. Bottomley and W. Hay (eds.) *Special Units for Difficult Prisoners*, University of Hull.

Waddington, P. A. J. (1993) 'The case against paramilitary policing considered', *British Journal of Criminology*, 33: 353–70.

Walmsley, R. (1989) *Special Security Units*, London: HMSO.

Walmsley, R. (1991) 'Assessing the effects of special units in England' in A. K. Bottomley and W. T. Hay (eds.) *Special Units for Difficult Prisoners*, University of Hull.

Walmsley, R., Howard, L. and White, S. (1992) *The National Prison Survey 1991: Main Findings*, London: HMSO.

Ward, D. (1987) 'Control strategies for problem prisoners in American prison systems' in A. E. Bottoms and R. Light (eds.) *Problems of Long-Term Imprisonment*, Aldershot: Gower.

Ward, D. and Schoen, K. (1981) *Confinement in Maximum Custody*, Lexington: D. C. Heath and Company.

Windlesham, Lord (1993) *Responses to Crime, volume 2: Penal Policy in the Making*, Oxford University Press.

Williams, M. and Longley, D. (1987) 'Identifying control problem prisoners in dispersal prisons', in A. E. Bottoms and R. Light (eds.) *Problems of Long-Term Imprisonment*, Aldershot: Gower.

Williams, R. (1976) *Keywords*, London: Fontana.

Willis, A. (1989) 'Review of Bottoms and Light (1987)', *British Journal of Criminology*, 29: 199–200.

Woodcock, J. (1994) *Report of the Enquiry into the Escape of Six Prisoners from the Special Security Unit at Whitemoor Prison, Cambridgeshire, on Friday 9th September 1994 Cm 2741*, London: HMSO.

Woolf, Lord Justice (1991) *Prison Disturbances, April 1990*, London: HMSO.

Wrong, D. (1994) *The Problem of Order*, Glencoe, Illinois: The Free Press.

Young, P. (1987) 'The concept of social control and its relevance to the prisons debate' in A. E. Bottoms and R. Light (eds.) *Problems of Long-Term Imprisonment*, Aldershot: Gower.

Zamble, E. and Porporino, F. J. (1988) *Coping, Behaviour and Adaptation in Prison Inmates*, New York: Springer-Verlag.

Zimring, F. and Hawkins, G. (1994) 'The growth of imprisonment in California', *British Journal of Criminology*, 34, 1: 83–95.

Index